I0813765
ENTRY
SERV. R.
HALL
STUDY
BATH #2
GUEST RM.
LIVING RM.
ENTR. HALL
MRS. DRESS
MAST. BATH
GALLERY
MR'S DRESS
TERRACE
MASTER BED RM.
SUN DECK
FLOOR PLAN
RESIDENCE MR. & MRS. RICHARD C. ADAMS
9425 EL DORADO LANE - LA MESA - CALIF.
LEOPOLD FISCHER
ARCHITECT

Exiled in L.A.

Exiled in L.A.

The Untold Story of Leopold Fischer's Domestic Architecture

Volker M. Welter

Getty Research Institute Los Angeles

To Renate & Maoz Azaryahu, Tel Aviv

Contents

Notes to the Reader

The houses and homes referred to in this book are not open for viewing by the public; please respect the privacy of residents and owners. Houses designed by Leopold Fischer and fellow German-speaking émigré architects are identified by the names of the original clients and city, town, or district; address details are given only when absolutely necessary for the scholarly arguments.

Leopold Fischer was born in Silesia, Austria-Hungary, which has been part of Poland since the end of World War I. As Fischer was a native German speaker, German place names are used for locations in Silesia, and today's Polish place names are added in parentheses at their first occurrence in each chapter. Émigré architects and designers who anglicized or otherwise adjusted in exile their first and/or last name are referred to by the amended names; the original names and intermediate name changes are recorded in table 2.1.

Throughout the book, the terms *immigrant architect(s)* and *émigré architect(s)* refer solely to German-speaking architects (regardless of their national background) who migrated to California during the first half of the twentieth century. Any arguments made using these terms do not suggest that those arguments also apply to immigrant and émigré architects of other national or ethnic backgrounds.

Unless noted otherwise, all translations from the German are by the author.

At least as known by early February 2025, the wildfires that swept through Pacific Palisades and Altadena in January 2025 destroyed the following houses and neighborhoods that are referenced, discussed, or illustrated in this book:

- Gregory Ain, Park Planned Homes (1947–48), Altadena, California (twenty-one of twenty-eight houses are destroyed);
- Fredric R. Frankel, Frankel house (1948), Altadena, California;
- Harwell Hamilton Harris, Pauline Lowe house (1934), Altadena, California; and
- Rolf Sklarek, Meier house (1941), Pacific Palisades, California.

Best way to live in California is to be from somewheres [*sic*] else.

—Cormac McCarthy, *No Country for Old Men*

Los Angeles forgets mostly those who don't belong here and never belonged here.

—Kevin Vennemann, *Sunset Boulevard: Vom Filmen, Bauen und Sterben in Los Angeles*

I was sitting among refugees.
All of them had taught themselves not to let their sorrow show . . .
but rather to come to terms with their nostalgia alone,
within their own four walls.

—Christa Wolf, *City of Angels; or, The Overcoat of Dr. Freud*

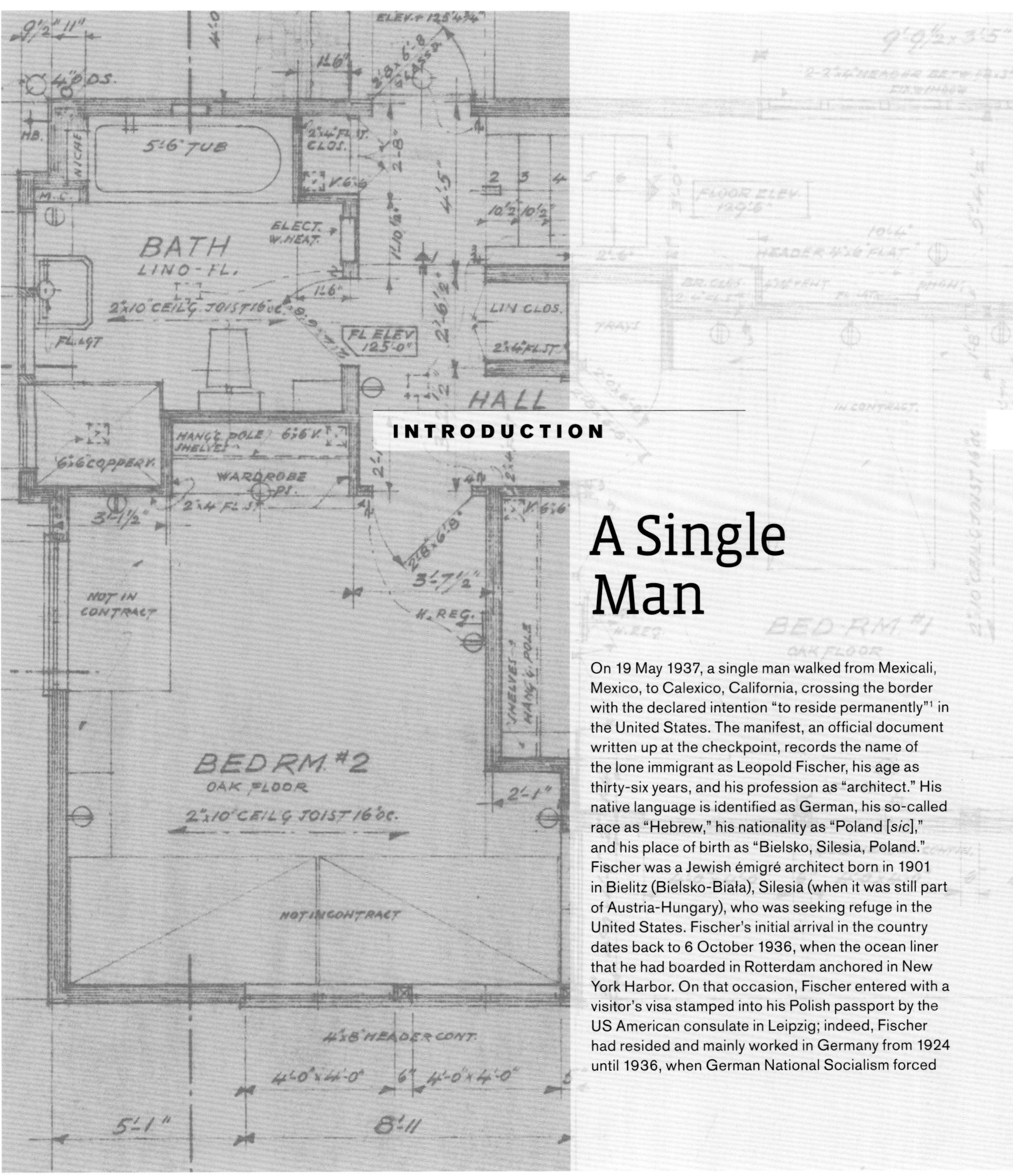

INTRODUCTION

A Single Man

On 19 May 1937, a single man walked from Mexicali, Mexico, to Calexico, California, crossing the border with the declared intention "to reside permanently"[1] in the United States. The manifest, an official document written up at the checkpoint, records the name of the lone immigrant as Leopold Fischer, his age as thirty-six years, and his profession as "architect." His native language is identified as German, his so-called race as "Hebrew," his nationality as "Poland [*sic*]," and his place of birth as "Bielsko, Silesia, Poland." Fischer was a Jewish émigré architect born in 1901 in Bielitz (Bielsko-Biała), Silesia (when it was still part of Austria-Hungary), who was seeking refuge in the United States. Fischer's initial arrival in the country dates back to 6 October 1936, when the ocean liner that he had boarded in Rotterdam anchored in New York Harbor. On that occasion, Fischer entered with a visitor's visa stamped into his Polish passport by the US American consulate in Leipzig; indeed, Fischer had resided and mainly worked in Germany from 1924 until 1936, when German National Socialism forced him into exile. From New York, Fischer traveled by train to his destination, Los Angeles. The trip from there to Mexico served the purpose of obtaining an official United States immigration visa, the first step toward citizenship.

Salka Viertel, the Austrian-Jewish actress and later Hollywood screenwriter who had lived in Santa Monica since 1928, explains in her memoirs how such a trip to Mexico had worked when she, her husband, Berthold Viertel, and their sons applied for immigration visas early in 1932.[2]

> Our Visitors' Visas had expired and we had to apply for an Immigration Quota: Berthold . . . for an Austrian number . . . and I for a Polish. After much red tape and hundreds of dollars spent on cables and lawyers, we finally had the necessary documents assembled, and took off . . . for Ensenada in Baja California. . . . It was late when we arrived . . . we were the only guests in the hotel. . . . We went to the American Consulate and the Consul told us that it would take a few days, perhaps a week, until our various quota numbers arrived. Finally, our quota numbers arrived and we could leave. We presented our passports to a disgruntled immigration officer and were admitted to the United States.[3]

Like Salka Viertel, Fischer reentered the United States under the Polish immigration quota. But Fischer's trip to Mexico was probably less pleasant than the one the Viertels spent on the Pacific coast in the comfort of a former casino turned into a hotel. Fischer stayed somewhere in Mexicali, an inland town just to the south of the border, from 17 to 19 May 1937, carrying with him the sum of $300 ($6,573 in 2024 money),[4] almost a third more than the average sum immigrants had on them in 1937.[5]

Unlike the Viertels, Fischer traveled to and waited in Mexicali on his own. Indeed, upon readmission into the United States on his new immigration visa, Fischer responded "None" when asked for the "Name and address of nearest relative or friend in country whence alien came." Factually, this response was correct because Fischer most likely did not know anyone in Mexicali. Equally correct, however, was Fischer's earlier reply to a similar question upon arriving in New York in October 1936, when he stated that a sister (he had three) lived in Berlin.[6] Perhaps Fischer was simply being truthful about not knowing anyone in Mexico in 1937, or perhaps he feared a different answer would cause harm to his sister in National Socialist Germany. Whatever the case, once uttered, the claim of being without family, relatives, and friends, which also suggests being without a past and a history, reverberated throughout Fischer's life.

• • •

This undertone of a lost past echoes today throughout California architectural history, which does not know much, if anything, about Leopold Fischer (1901–75), a surprising reality considering that Fischer's architectural education in Vienna paralleled that of fellow Austrians Rudolph Schindler and Richard Neutra. Those towering figures in California architectural history studied with Adolf Loos, the Austrian protomodernist, before World War I; after the war, Fischer followed in their footsteps, making him the third Loos student to practice in Los Angeles. But this was still in the future. The mid-1920s saw Fischer briefly employed in the Dessau office of Walter Gropius, the founder of the Bauhaus, who left Nazi Germany for the United Kingdom in 1934 and went to the United States in 1937. By 1926, at just twenty-five years old, Fischer was the chief architect of a regional housing cooperative that built social housing estates in Dessau and elsewhere in the state of Sachsen-Anhalt.[7] Until the early 1930s, Fischer planned approximately thirty-two hundred housing units, of which he supervised the erection of about four hundred houses, primarily semidetached or terraced.[8]

Irrespective of this background, employment, and early experience in social housing (one of the most influential design achievements of Weimar Germany architectural modernism), Fischer's architectural oeuvre did not register in architectural history for decades. In the case of Austrian history of architecture, Fischer's anonymity is perhaps most easily understood because the architect seems not to have worked in his native country beyond his brief employment by Loos. After World War II, Fischer's German social housing legacy was located inside the communist German Democratic Republic (GDR), where it did not generate much historical inquiry. In the reunited Germany, Fischer's oeuvre was pulled back from oblivion when, in the early 1990s, Dr. Irene Below and her students researched the Dessau region for an exhibition on life in Weimar Republic social housing estates.[9]

Despite this impeccable background in the European modernist movement in architecture of the 1920s and 1930s, Fischer and his exile oeuvre in the Los Angeles region have found no attention in California architectural history, especially that of domestic architecture—a field that for decades has studied and even celebrated German-speaking modernist architects who migrated to California in the early twentieth century. Rudolph Schindler and Richard Neutra are often considered the harbingers, if not the most influential creators, of modernism in California architecture; and Eric Mendelsohn's California works have repeatedly interested historians ever since the last period of his exile took him to California, a time that began (via the United Kingdom and Palestine) with an exhibition of his works at the Museum of Modern Art in New York at the end of 1941.[10] More recently, scholarly publications in English and German have explored the lives and works of such architects in California—to where they had moved during the 1910s and 1920s or fled as refugees after 1933—as, in alphabetical order, Fritz Block and his business partner Ernst Hochfeld, Julius Ralph Davidson, Paul Theodore Frankl, Oskar Gerson, Victor Gruen, Maria Kipp, Paul László, Jock Peters, and Kem Weber.[11] To this one has to add the names of several then (and still today) little-known, often Jewish designers who fled the Nazi occupations of Austria and settled in California. These designers, including Arthur Grünberger, Frederick Reichl, and Liane (Juliana) Zimbler, are documented in the extensive catalog *Visionäre & Vetriebene: Österreichische Spuren in der modernen amerikanischen Architektur* (Visionaries & the expelled: Austrian traces in modern American architecture), which accompanied an exhibition on Austrian and Austrian-Hungarian architects working and living abroad.[12]

No such interest has been extended to Fischer and his designs in California, even though almost all of his buildings are extant. The list of works produced in exile encompasses thirty-nine entries, of which twenty-six are confirmed as having been built; these buildings are still standing except for one that was demolished and four others whose fate is currently unknown. From 1938 onward, commissions for individually designed domestic architecture were the staple of Fischer's California work, supplemented after World War II by anonymous domestic designs like apartment buildings and a small suburban neighborhood with standardized types of houses. A brief collaboration in 1959 with the inventor and designer Walter S. White Jr., who practiced in the Coachella Valley east of Los Angeles, added some business premises and more private homes to Fischer's portfolio. Once in exile, Fischer never again designed social housing (known in the United States as public housing). Nor is his exile oeuvre, while modern, easily classifiable as *modernist* architecture, whether such architecture is defined by the principles of the Bauhaus or those of the International Style exhibition shown at the Museum of Modern Art in New York in 1932.

The trajectory of Fischer's domestic designs begins in Weimar Germany, continues in California before World War II with a version of Frank Lloyd Wright–influenced domestic architecture, moves after the war to domestic projects that comment on contemporary houses by Richard Neutra and midcentury modernists, from there to suburban standardized dwellings in the early 1950s and sprawling ranch houses in the later 1950s, and, finally, to a small all-glass pavilion in the 1960s. As a historian, one might be inclined to detect in this path an evolution or some form of development of an architectural oeuvre, an approach for which the German language has coined the term *Werkbiographie,* the depiction of an individual professional life based on studying and analyzing the works of an architect. In her study of the exile of the German-Jewish modernist architect Adolf Rading (a contemporary and acquaintance of Fischer's), Regina Göckede discusses whether this concept of "a body of architectural works"—the typical methodological means that architectural history has used to assess the meaning, relevance, and importance of an architect's oeuvre, including ordering buildings and designs throughout an architect's life according to rubrics like periods, areas, and types of buildings—is suitable for architectural exile studies. When applied to exiled architects, this means creates a "major difficulty," for it "implies genealogy [*Genese*], coherency, continuity, and linearity,"[13] concepts that grant little room for life-changing events and thus can acknowledge only indirectly the possibly traumatic break of an enforced exile.

In Fischer's case, such an undertaking is made even more complex due to the unknown whereabouts of the architect's professional and private papers, which, even after extensive searches, have never been located. The lack of drawings, sketches, lists of works, correspondence with clients, photographs, and comparable documents makes it nearly impossible to learn about Fischer's designs and buildings, not to mention their conception, development, and history. Similarly, no letters, diaries, calendars, photographs, or personal and other belongings are extant to help derive knowledge or even an impression of Fischer's life as an architect and private person. Turning to Leopold Fischer's exile in California, the dearth of private and professional documents echoes the loudest. Any thoughts, fears, and despair that Fischer may have felt, any expectations and hopes that he may have harbored when fleeing Germany, upon arriving in the United States, and while living in California for the rest of his life remain a sealed-off territory unless new archival sources one day come to light. In short, a historian cannot read Fischer's life from the inside out, to paraphrase a much-beloved tenet of modernist architecture.

The one notable exception is the archive of Fischer's buildings within the urban fabric of the metropolitan region of Los Angeles. Spanning every decade (except the 1970s) of Fischer's time in Southern California, the still-existing buildings are the main witnesses to Fischer's work and life there. Once in exile, Fischer picked up his first architectural design projects as early as 1938, which indicates his unbroken will to architecture, to paraphrase Friedrich Nietzsche's *Will to Power.* His first projects must have posed questions to him about the ongoing relevance of architectural works created and professional experiences made in the country from which he had just fled. Was his pre-exile oeuvre still relevant? Could it be made applicable to the new surroundings, and to what degree? Also, essential to working as an architect in exile were questions about what one had to learn about one's new surroundings and its architectural culture. To ask comparable questions as a historian means to begin to contextualize Fischer's exile oeuvre and to differentiate between the works of Fischer and of other contemporary German-speaking architects practicing in California. They may have all arrived during the early decades of the twentieth century, but that similarity fades when one asks after the specific moments and circumstances of the individual arrivals.

At first sight, the broad trajectory of Fischer's California architecture suggests a pattern of gradually blending more and more into new surroundings. That said, in all of Fischer's domestic designs during his exile, references to his Central European architectural background remain a constant feature, even if detectable to different degrees of subtlety. Their continuous presence recalls how another Central European, Alexander von Humboldt, thought already in the mid-nineteenth century about travelers and explorers coming to terms with living for long periods—in Humboldt's case, ultimately for a limited time—in surroundings they had never been to before. In "Reflections on the Enjoyment Presented to Us by Nature," Humboldt explains that upon arrival in a distant country, one tends to see and perceive things and phenomena in the new surroundings that *appear* similar, if not identical, to home. At the same time, the apparent similarities are overlaid and eventually dominated by clearly perceivable new, different things and phenomena. Humboldt stresses that this parallel perception of the familiar and unfamiliar helps to comprehend the new while leaving one grounded in the old, a process of becoming familiarized "by degrees, and almost imperceptibly...with a new home and a new climate." Humboldt concludes that "man habituates himself to that which surrounds him" while continuing to perceive traces of the familiar from the past in the new home, which helps to keep from "breaking the links of association that bind him to the home of his childhood."[14] As described, the process is open-ended and repeats whenever and wherever one faces new surroundings, or perhaps each time an émigré architect like Fischer tackled a new design commission in exile.

Indeed, as an analogy, this parallel perception of the familiar and the unfamiliar in order to make a home in the latter can help the historian comprehend Fischer's exile oeuvre. Each of Fischer's architectural commissions becomes an opportunity to tease out what is "unfamiliar," which means "Californian" or "American," in the designs and the buildings, and what is "familiar," understood as references to Fischer's past works. Whether this mimics how Fischer approached his commissions and designs remains arguable and, in the absence of his professional papers, can perhaps never be decided with any degree of certainty. Whether it allows one to develop an understanding of what *life* in exile meant to Fischer personally is also arguable, for without primary sources about his exile experiences available, how can the historian confidently distinguish between reasonable assumptions, wishful thinking, and mere speculations when pondering a life lived in exile? Yet, Humboldt's reflections on living in a foreign place do make it possible to contextualize Fischer's California oeuvre without first pressing it, and thereby also its architect, into the molds of preconceived expectations of what an emigrant to California (who happened to be a German-speaking modern or modernist architect) was supposed to design and contribute to California architecture.

• • •

The goals of this book are then twofold. The first is to compile an account of Fischer's California exile architecture: What did he design and build, and for whom, where, and when? The answers are an architectural-historical end in themselves. They also constitute a means—a single case study—to a second goal, which expands on the aforementioned issue of Fischer's exile designs recalling aspects of his pre-exile oeuvre. In addition to Humboldt's juxtaposition of the unfamiliar and the familiar, my approach to this issue is to some extent guided by Katherine C. Grier's readings on Victorian parlors, their interior designs, and the objects within their space, which continuously oscillated between expressing what Grier calls "Culture" and "Comfort." These shorthand terms signal an "interest in being cosmopolitan" on the one hand and "the complex of ideas we now call *domesticity*" on the other.[15] By way of analogy, the study at hand analyzes Fischer's architectural designs in exile as oscillating between a comparable pairing, which in his case are California as the new surroundings in which Fischer set out to design homes for his clients, and his cosmopolitan Central European professional life that easily and repeatedly had crossed borders. (In addition to Austria and Germany, Fischer claimed to have also worked in Czechoslovakia, France, and Switzerland. He also designed an apartment building in his hometown in Poland.)[16]

Accordingly, selected examples of Fischer's California domestic designs are analyzed in light of his professional life in exile and his professional pre-exile work; the degree to which either was more critical for a particular project became evident as I repeatedly visited buildings and sites, studied sets of blueprints that some owners preserved, considered comparative buildings and designs by fellow émigré architects and other California architects, and discussed Fischer with fellow architectural historians. Perhaps this multifaceted, if not fuzzy, approach mimicked how Fischer may have felt in exile, suspended between two (if not more) worlds. It certainly helped clarify time and again a related question that also informs this study: Is California architectural history—or, more precisely, can it be—at ease with an oeuvre like Fischer's?

This in turn leads to yet another question: How can an architect with a professional education that follows that of Schindler and Neutra have been absent from California's history of domestic architecture, a field that has always been interested in exploring the oeuvres and impacts on California architecture of German-speaking modern architects who migrated to the state? This question is timely, for if architectural history wants to diversify its subject matter, then it should be of interest to inquire why and how the field conceives and writes architectural history in ways that leave large numbers of buildings, their designers (be they architects, builders, or other), and of course their users and owners unconsidered. The case study of Fischer in California answers these endeavors regarding German-speaking émigré architects practicing in California who were forced into exile by National Socialism.

Chapter 1, "A Man without History?," offers a thematic, chronologically arranged overview of Fischer's European pre-exile life and works, including the first-ever accounts of Fischer's early life in Austrian Silesia and of his architecture studies at the Technische Hochschule Vienna before he joined the Bauschule of Adolf Loos. Loos was also Fischer's first employer. The section on Fischer in Germany from 1924 to 1936 focuses on selected social housing estates designed by Fischer, the professional arguments Walter Gropius instigated with his young colleague, and the domestic architectural designs for individual clients to which Fischer turned after his social housing work had ended.

Chapter 2, "Immigrant Architects or Émigré Architects: An Excursus," revolves around methodological issues arising from the observation that many German-speaking architects forced into exile by National Socialism are persistently absent from California architectural history. The chapter looks at the discipline through shifting methodologies in exile studies. Overall, these studies have long abandoned focusing on the potential gains émigrés brought to their host countries in favor of contextual approaches that center on the everyday exile experiences and the give-and-take between émigrés and their host countries. However, this more fine-grained understanding of exile has not yet made inroads into California architectural history, where heroic accounts of German-speaking architects bringing architectural modernism to California continue to thrive.

As an alternative to stereotyping German-speaking architects in California in this way, I propose a distinction between German-speaking *immigrant architects* (who migrated to California for various reasons before 1933) and *émigré architects* (who, like Fischer, were *forced* to flee by the Nazis). A brief survey of selected German-speaking architects and designers arriving in California between the 1910s and 1940s proves this distinction to be an essential factor in determining the diverging careers of these architects, their possible impacts on the state's architecture, and the resonance they have accordingly found in California architectural history. The survey also introduces as a peer group of Fischer's a small number of émigré architects arriving in California around the same time, for similar reasons, and of approximately the same age as Fischer. Selected works in exile of this peer group serve in the subsequent chapters as a suitable framework to contextualize Fischer's designs in exile.

Chapter 3, "Mapping Leopold Fischer in Los Angeles," is the first-ever account of Fischer's life and work in exile in Los Angeles and Southern California. It is a thematic and chronological overview that follows the trajectory of Fischer's architectural career by tracing, for example, his places of residence in Los Angeles, his social circles, and his contacts and friends among architect colleagues including his fellow émigré peers. This chapter also offers an overview of Fischer's buildings and clients. Interwoven are accounts of Fischer's acquaintanceship with a California musician mother and musician daughter who helped the architect escape Nazi Germany in 1936; Fischer's first contact in Los Angeles with Arnold Schönberg, who introduced Fischer to Frank Lloyd Wright; and, as a result of this welcome gesture, Fischer's time with Wright in Taliesin in 1937.

Chapter 4, "Around 1941, Around 1951," centers on two of Fischer's major commissions. In 1941, Fischer completed the Kohlmeier house in South Pasadena and, in 1951, the Slechta house in View Park. That these two homes were designed a decade apart is a historical coincidence; that they were separated by World War II goes to the heart of the differences between émigré architects and immigrant architects. The critical analysis and discussion of the two houses by Fischer within the context of the domestic architecture that immigrant architects and émigré architects built "around 1941" and "around 1951" illustrate in an exemplary manner two comparative criteria that contributed crucially to the diverging careers of the two groups of architects in California and, accordingly, to their subsequent inclusion in the history of architecture. The first criterion concerns the differences between deliberately innovative early designs in California by many immigrant architects and early designs by most émigré architects that tended to blend in with the existing built environment. The second criterion concerns the length and scope of a career in California before the United States entered World War II, which for émigré architects meant only a few short years with barely more than one or two architectural commissions. After World War II, émigré architects like Fischer could not return to a prewar career again as many immigrant architects could; instead, they had to start their career in exile for a second time.

Chapter 5, "Into the Suburbs," zooms in on Verdugo Village, a small suburban neighborhood in the Mount Washington area of greater Los Angeles for which Fischer designed standardized types of houses from 1953 onward. Once built out, the neighborhood was to comprise approximately fifty private dwellings; at least twelve were built according to Fischer's designs. That Fischer received commissions for suburban homes in this neighborhood indicates that he was aware of and integrated into the contemporary architectural scene of the Los Angeles area.

Conceptually, Fischer approached Verdugo Village by developing a typology of standardized dwellings that harked back to his social housing schemes in Weimar Germany, and he looked forward to possible follow-up commissions for comparable suburban developments. That never happened, leaving Verdugo Village as the sole neighborhood that subtly inscribes traces of Weimar Republic social housing into the suburban fabric of metropolitan Los Angeles. At the same time, Verdugo Village exemplifies Fischer's most Californian houses, not least as he perfected a commonly used floor plan that also populated many of Southern California's suburbs.

The book's conclusion wraps up the account of Fischer's life in exile by discussing his last built project, a small glass room in the back of an inconspicuous Long Beach home. The project evokes faint echoes of the Bauhaus on the Pacific combined with deft architectural comments by Fischer on the follies of much of midcentury California modernism. Most notable among the latter was, indeed still *is,* the focus on innovation as *the* characteristic of California modern architecture, which segues into the final summary that discusses whether Fischer was, architecturally speaking, at home in exile and whether or how California architectural history can ever be at ease with an oeuvre like Fischer's.

Notes

Epigraphs (p. viii): Cormac McCarthy, *No Country for Old Men* (New York: Alfred. A. Knopf, 2005), 233; Kevin Vennemann, *Sunset Boulevard: Vom Filmen, Bauen und Sterben in Los Angeles* (Berlin: Suhrkamp, 2012), 16; and Christa Wolf, *City of Angels; or, The Overcoat of Dr. Freud* [2010], trans. Damion Searls (New York: Farrar, Straus and Giroux, 2013), 74.

1 Unless otherwise noted, all data and facts concerning Fischer's immigration into the United States in 1937 were taken from "Manifest Port of: Calexico Calif. Date: 5-19-37 Serial No 498"

(line 1 recto). (The National Archives and Records Administration; Washington, DC; Manifests of Alien Arrivals at Calexico, California, March 1907–December 1952; NAI: 2843448; Record Group Title: Records of the Immigration and Naturalization Service, 1787–2004; Record Group Number: 85; Microfilm Roll Number: 10; ancestry.com, subscription required.)

2 Date taken from Salomea Sara Viertel, "Declaration of Intention No. 63594, District Court of the United States at Los Angeles, 1 September 1933" (The National Archives in Washington, DC; Washington, DC; [Roll 222] Petitions for Naturalization 60627-61057; 9/8/38–10/7/38; Record Group Title: Records of District Courts of the United States, 1685–2009; Record Group Number: 21; ancestry.com, subscription required).

3 Salka Viertel, *The Kindness of Strangers* (1969; New York: New York Review Books, 2019), 168–69.

4 "Calculate the Value of $300 in 1937: What Is 300 Dollars in 1937 Adjusted for Inflation? Convert $300 from 1937 Dollars to 2024 Dollars," *DollarTimes,* https://www.dollartimes.com/inflation/inflation.php?amount=300&year=1937.

5 Harold Fields, *The Refugee in the United States* (New York: Oxford University Press, 1938), 22.

6 "Leopold Fischer," line 18, list 2, SS *Volendam* passengers sailing from Rotterdam, 26 September 1936, arriving at Port of New York, NY, 6 October 1936, in *List or Manifest of Alien Passengers for the United States Immigration Officer at Port of Arrival,* p. 155 (The National Archives in Washington, DC; Washington, DC, USA; Passenger and Crew Lists of Vessels Arriving at New York, New York, 1897–1957; Microfilm Serial or NAID: T715; RG Title: Records of the Immigration and Naturalization Service, 1787–2004; RG: 85; ancestry.com, subscription required).

7 David H. Haney, *When Modern Was Green: Life and Work of Landscape Architect Leberecht Migge* (London: Routledge, 2010), 165.

8 Counts range from "over 300" to 474. See Bauhaus Dessau e.V., ed., *Leopold Fischer: Architekt der Moderne* (Dessau-Roßlau: Funk Verlag Bernhard Hein e.K., n.d. [2007]), 18, 26, 105–13.

9 Irene Below and Babette Scurrell, eds., *es gab nicht nur das bauhaus: wohnen und haushalten in dessauer siedlungen der 20er jahre* (Dessau: Stiftung Bauhaus Dessau, 1994); see the bibliography for additional publications on Fischer by Dr. Below.

10 See, for example, Hans R. Morgenthaler, "'It Will Be Hard for Us to Find a Home': Projects in the United States 1941–1953," in *Eric Mendelsohn: Architect 1887–1953,* ed. Regina Stephan (New York: Monacelli, 1999), 242–61; and Museum of Modern Art, New York, *Architecture of Eric Mendelsohn, 1914–1940,* 26 November 1941–4 January 1942, https://www.moma.org/calendar/exhibitions/2092. Before he came to the United States, Mendelsohn initially fled Germany for the United Kingdom and then moved to Palestine.

11 Roland Jaeger, *Block & Hochfeld: Die Architekten des Deutschland Hauses; Bauten und Projekte in Hamburg 1921–1938, Exil in Los Angeles* (Berlin: Gebr. Mann, 1996); Roland Jaeger, *Photo-Eye Fritz Block: New Photography, Modern Color Slides* (Zurich: Scheidegger & Spiess, 2018); Lilian Pfaff, *J. R. Davidson: A European Contribution to California Modernism* (Basel: Birkhäuser, 2019); Christopher Long, *Paul T. Frankl and Modern American Design* (New Haven: Yale University Press, 2007); Wolfgang Voigt, *Hans und Oskar Gerson: Hanseatische Moderne; Bauten in Hamburg und im kalifornischen Exil 1907 bis 1957* (Hamburg: Dölling und Galitz, 2000); M. Jeffrey Hardwick, *Mall Maker: Victor Gruen, Architect of an American Dream* (Philadelphia: University of Pennsylvania Press, 2004); Alex Wall, *Victor Gruen: From Urban Shop to New City* (Barcelona: Actar-D, 2005); Marlyn Musicant, "Maria Kipp: Autobiography of a Hand Weaver," *Studies in the Decorative Arts* 8, no. 1 (2000): 92–107; Anne Lawrence, "Feminist Design Methodology: Considering the Case of Maria Kipp" (master's thesis, University of North Texas, 2003); Monica Penick, "Paul László and the Atomic Future," in *Émigré Cultures in Design and Architecture,* ed. Alison J. Clarke and Elana Shapira (London: Bloomsbury Academic, 2017), 91–104; Christopher Long, *Jock Peters, Architecture and Design: The Varieties of Modernism* (New York: Bauer and Dean, 2021); and Christopher Long, *Kem Weber: Designer and Architect* (New Haven: Yale University Press, 2014).

12 Matthias Boeckl, ed., *Visionäre & Vertriebene: Österreichische Spuren in der modernen amerikanischen Architektur* (Berlin: Ernst & Sohn, 1995).

13 Regina Göckede, *Adolf Rading (1888–1957): Exodus des Neuen Bauens und Überschreitungen des Exils* (Berlin: Gebr. Mann, 2005), 50.

14 Alexander von Humboldt, "Reflections on the Enjoyment Presented to Us by Nature" [1845], trans. E. C. Otté, in *German Essays on Science in the 19th Century,* ed. Wolfgang Schirmacher (New York: Continuum, 1996), 3.

15 Katherine C. Grier, "The Decline of the Memory Palace: The Parlor after 1890," in *American Home Life, 1880–1930: A Social History of Spaces and Services,* ed. Jessica H. Foy and Thomas J. Schlereth (Knoxville: University of Tennessee Press, 1992), 51–63; the quotations are from pages 53 and 54 (emphasis in original). See also Katherine C. Grier, *Culture & Comfort: People, Parlors, and Upholstery, 1850–1930* (Amherst: University of Massachusetts Press, 1988).

16 On Fischer's places of employment, see "Leopold Fischer," license file, California Architects Board. For more on the apartment building in Poland, see this volume, "List of Selected Architectural Works."

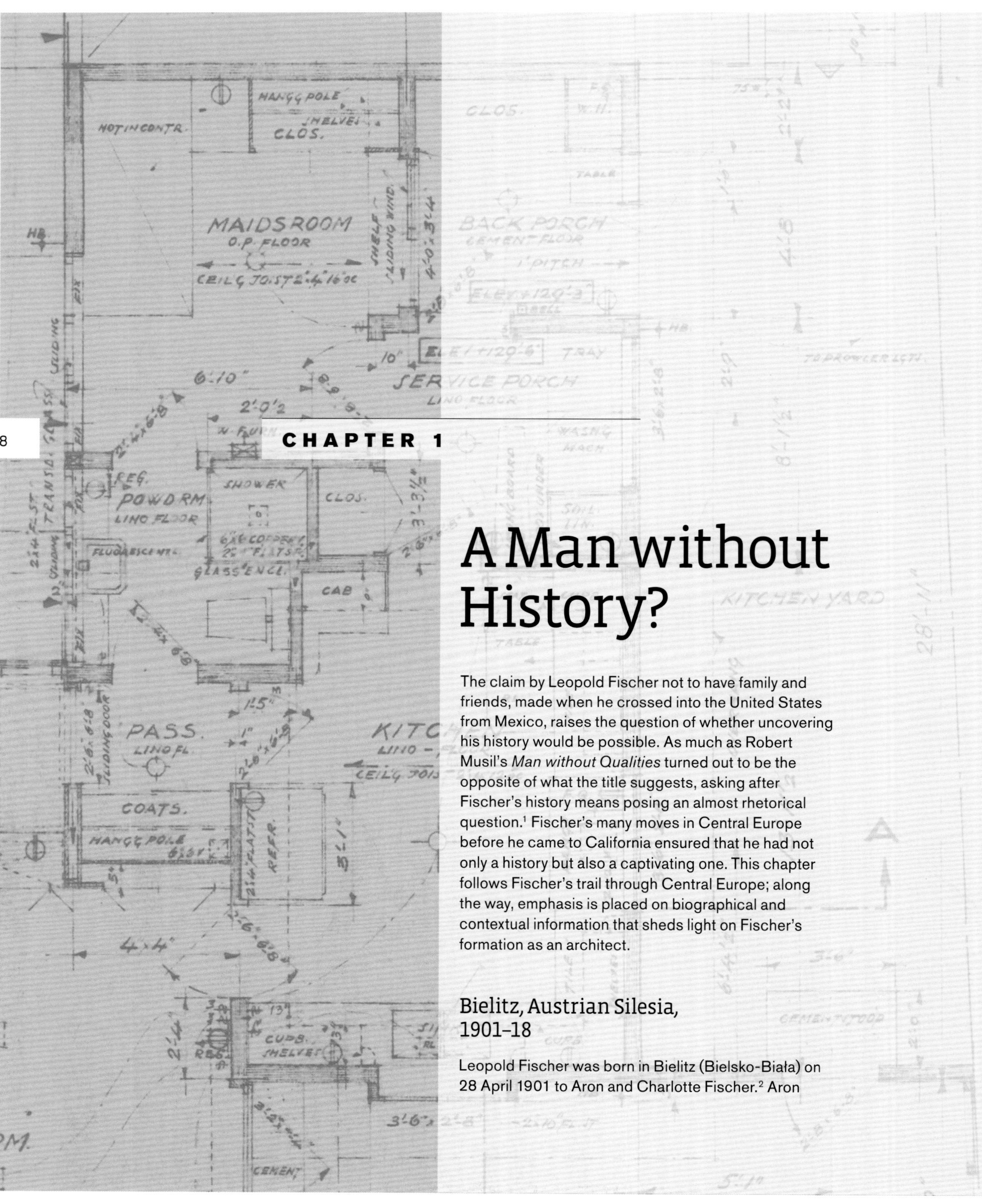

CHAPTER 1

A Man without History?

The claim by Leopold Fischer not to have family and friends, made when he crossed into the United States from Mexico, raises the question of whether uncovering his history would be possible. As much as Robert Musil's *Man without Qualities* turned out to be the opposite of what the title suggests, asking after Fischer's history means posing an almost rhetorical question.[1] Fischer's many moves in Central Europe before he came to California ensured that he had not only a history but also a captivating one. This chapter follows Fischer's trail through Central Europe; along the way, emphasis is placed on biographical and contextual information that sheds light on Fischer's formation as an architect.

Bielitz, Austrian Silesia, 1901–18

Leopold Fischer was born in Bielitz (Bielsko-Biała) on 28 April 1901 to Aron and Charlotte Fischer.[2] Aron

Fischer (1859–1922) was born in Ujsoły, a mountain village south of Bielitz where his parents, Hirsch and Fradl Fischer, lived. Because Bielitz was a German-speaking enclave within Poland, Aron was also called Adolph or Adolf. Leopold's mother, Charlotte Rosa Wurzel (1869–1934), was born in Krakau (Kraków). She was the daughter of Israel and Minna Wurzel, originally from Auschwitz (Oświęcim), halfway between Krakau and Bielitz.[3] Aron and Charlotte married in Bielitz on 10 April 1900. Leopold was their first child and only son, followed by three daughters, Frida, Olga, and Martha (fig. 1.1). Aron Fischer was a timber and lumber merchant in Bielitz. In 1901, he and his wife resided at Ringplatz 19 (Rynek 19); Leopold Fischer was born in the house in the central town square. The Fischers rented their private accommodations but owned Gartengasse 3 (Inwalidów 3), where their lumberyard was. In 1917, during World War I, the property was sold, whether due to economic hardship or another cause is unknown.

Because of their passing in 1922 and 1934, respectively, Fischer's father and mother were spared the worst after the Germans attacked Poland on 1 September 1939, thereby launching World War II and the Holocaust. Fischer's exile meant that he also escaped the Holocaust; by comparison, the fates under National Socialism of his three sisters were very different. Little to nothing is known about Frida Fischer (born in 1902), the oldest sister, with one notable exception. The passenger information that the shipping company was obliged to furnish upon arrival of its ocean liner in New York on 6 October 1936 records as a relative of Leopold Fischer a Ms. F[rida] Fischer living on Königsweg 23 (renamed Wundtstraße in 1936) in Berlin.[4] The street address denoted the Liebfrauen Ober-Lyzeum, a Catholic girls' school, boarding school, and kindergarten run by nuns of the order Schwestern unserer Lieben Frau (Sisters of Our Lady).[5] Until the school was forcefully dissolved by the Nazi regime in 1941, the nuns hid Jewish children and adults in the residential building of the boarding school.[6] Presumably, any Jews thus hidden in 1941 would have been deported to concentration camps if caught. According

1.1. Leopold Fischer with his parents and sisters, ca. 1910–11.

From left to right: Leopold Fischer (age 9 or 10), Olga Fischer, Charlotte Rosa Fischer (née Wurzel), Frida Fischer, and Aron Fischer.

to Fischer family lore, however, Frida Fischer had converted to Catholicism and lived in a Catholic convent near Tschenstochau (Częstochowa), Poland, though it is unclear whether the residence in the convent refers to the time before or after the Holocaust.[7]

Olga Fischer (1904–2002) and Martha Fischer (1911–92) both survived the Holocaust by escaping to the territory of the Soviet Union when the Germans attacked Poland on 1 September 1939. They returned to Bielitz after the war[8] and later emigrated to Eretz Israel. Olga Fischer married Leo Fink (1886–1942), a middle-school teacher in Bielitz. They fled Poland with their mutual child Laura (or Lora) Fink (1927–2012) and with two children from Leo Fink's first marriage. Leo Fink starved to death in Samarkand, Uzbek Soviet Socialist Republic, and Laura Fink was rescued as one of the Tehran Children. This was a group of one thousand Jewish children that the Iranian emperor, Shah Mohammed Reza Pahlavi, permitted to travel from Central Asia to Tehran. Subsequently, the Jewish Agency for Palestine and international Jewish and Zionist organizations secured permission for the children to immigrate to Palestine. The children arrived in Palestine in February 1943 after a journey by boat from Iran to what is today Pakistan, then around the Arabian Peninsula and through the Red Sea to Suez, Egypt.[9]

Martha Fischer married Emil Zollmann, and it was for Emil Zollmann and Stefanie (or Stefanja) Schmalzbach (born 1903),[10] a sister of Mr. Zollmann, that Leopold Fischer designed an apartment building in Bielsko in 1936. Indeed, Fischer signed the drawings for the building on 8 September 1936, which indicates that he visited his family in Bielsko shortly before he boarded the ocean liner to New York later in the month (fig. 1.2).[11]

1.2. Leopold Fischer in Bielitz (Bielsko-Biała), 1930s, possibly September 1936, when he visited family in Bielsko shortly before immigrating to the United States later that month.

• • •

At the time of Fischer's birth, Bielitz was part of Austrian Silesia; it became Polish with the end of World War I and, since 1939, has been one-half of the double city of Bielitz-Biala, two cities that face each other across the Bialka (Biała) river.[12] By the eighteenth century, Bielitz had developed into a center for the production and trade of woolen cloth; other industries, often construction-related, such as timber production and trade, grew markedly during the nineteenth century.[13] Jewish life in Bielitz traces back to at least the mid-seventeenth century, when Jews were employed in the financial and other service of the local and regional nobility.[14] By the turn of the nineteenth century, a growing community of Jewish businesspeople and industrialists lived in and around the city.[15]

From the late nineteenth century onward, Bielitz rapidly expanded,[16] which enticed many Viennese architects and town planners—such as Otto Wagner's students Max Fabiani (1865–1962), Leopold Bauer (1872–1938), and Hans Mayr (1877–1918)—to work there.[17] Other Viennese architects who worked in Bielitz had roots in the area. For example, Alexander Neumann (1861–1947) and Ernst Lindner (1870–1965), who had studied architecture under the Jewish professor Carl König (1841–1915) at the Technische Hochschule Vienna (TH Vienna), were sons of Jewish industrialists from Bielitz.[18]

After World War I, members of Fischer's generation took their turn to leave Bielitz for architectural studies. Besides Fischer, Egon Riss and Munio Gitai Weinraub were two modernist architects from Bielitz and nearby. Born in the same year as Fischer but in Lipnik (Lipník), east of Bielitz, Egon Riss (1901–64), the son of a Jewish merchant in Bielitz, studied at the TH Vienna from 1919 to 1920. Riss's designs from before 1938 (when he was forced into exile to England and Scotland) have been called the works "of one of the most innovative architects from the years between the wars."[19] Munio Gitai

Weinraub (1909–70), who had grown up in Bielitz,[20] picked the Bauhaus in Dessau when deciding where to study architecture.[21] His choice illustrates that knowledge about contemporary avant-garde architecture had reached deep into the provinces of the former Austro-Hungarian Empire. How could young men like Riss, Fischer, and Weinraub learn about architectural modernism while living in Bielitz? Architectural historians point to at least three possible paths.

First, at that time, Bielitz and Biala looked to Vienna when it came to art, fashion, architecture, and interior design. In 1907, the Biala-born art historian Josef Strzygowski (1862–1941) remarked that in his hometown, "art is not rooted locally, but aspires to keep up with the latest fashion in Vienna, the centre of the empire. Anybody who wants to be completely sure of this commissions his house from a Vienna architect, and even more likely orders his furniture in Vienna."[22]

Second, Bielitz was home to a large construction company owned by Carl Korn (1852–1906), a Jewish *Baumeister* (master builder), and his son, Friedrich Korn (1890–1931).[23] The Korn company had expanded into Vienna, where it erected modernist buildings including the Wittgenstein house (1926–28), a collaborative effort of the philosopher Ludwig Wittgenstein and the architects Paul Engelmann (1891–1965) and Jacques Groag (1892–1962), two students of Adolf Loos.[24] As the son of a Bielitz lumber merchant who most likely did business with the Korn company, Fischer may have also learned about modern architecture in Vienna, perhaps even about Loos, from, say, the younger Korn, who was not that much older. Indeed, in 1936, when Fischer designed the apartment building in Bielsko for his sister's husband, Emil Zollmann, and Zollmann's sister, Stefanie, the Korn company subsequently built Fischer's design.[25]

Finally, modernist architects occasionally worked in the larger region around Bielitz. For example, Eric Mendelsohn executed various projects in the region in the early 1920s, including the Seidenhaus Weichmann (1922–23), a silk store in Gleiwitz (Gliwice).[26] In short, budding architects had opportunities to see modernist architecture near their hometown—however, Vienna was *the* place to be to study architecture.

Vienna, Austria, 1918–24

The sparse literature about Fischer usually singles out that he was a student of Adolf Loos. That Fischer attended Loos's Bauschule is documented, but "the Bauschule...was more of an informal discussion circle"[27] than a degree-issuing architecture school with a formalized plan of studies. Other students of Loos—for example, Richard Neutra and Ernst L. Freud before World War I—had enrolled at the TH Vienna while concurrently attending the Bauschule. Fischer followed that established pattern when he enrolled at the TH Vienna in the winter semester of 1918/19[28] after he had completed schooling at Bielitz's k.k. Staats-Oberrealschule with the Realmatura, the formal qualification necessary to attend higher-education institutions.[29]

Architectural studies at the TH Vienna typically lasted nine semesters or five years and comprised architectural subjects, drawing, technical and mathematical classes, and natural-scientific courses.[30] Students completed their studies with two general exams, the first at the end of a two-year-long phase of studies and the second after at least three more semesters.[31] Contemporaries and later historians have variously characterized architecture studies at the TH Vienna as traditional, conservative, and even reactionary, not least because of a focus on historical styles.[32] A strong emphasis on the functionality of architectural designs nevertheless underpinned this narrow-appearing conception of architecture. Accordingly, when emerging modernism prioritized the functionality of buildings in the early twentieth century, the impact of the TH Vienna students on Viennese and Austrian architecture was consequential.[33] Credit for this belongs to Carl König, who had been teaching at the school since 1865. König was the first Jewish professor of architecture at the TH Vienna, and his presence also attracted many Jewish students to the school.[34]

Fischer was enrolled at the TH Vienna for seven semesters, from the winter semester of 1918 to the winter semester of 1921, but he never officially completed his studies. In the summer semester of 1922, he lost his official status as a student because of unpaid fees.[35] During the first phase of his studies, Fischer attended most of the prescribed courses but never took all individual exams and could not sit the first general exam. Subsequently, university regulations allowed him to enroll in classes of the second phase but not to take exams, including the second general one. Instead, Fischer pragmatically focused on acquiring technical and natural-scientific knowledge in, for example, mathematics, construction, chemistry, and geology, as well as on perfecting his skills in drawing and drafting. The death of his father in January 1922 was most likely the cause for his inability to pay the fees for the summer semester of 1922. Yet, Fischer's studies at the TH Vienna had effectively ended the previous academic year (1920–21), as he already attended Adolf Loos's Bauschule.

With Adolf Loos, October 1919 to October 1924

When Loos opened his Bauschule in the fall of 1912, he expected students attending his private school to have prior architectural knowledge.[36] Studying at the Bauschule would take three years, with Loos offering instruction in art and architectural history, interior design and outfitting (*technischer Ausbau*), and materials in the form of lectures, seminars, discussion groups, city walks, and (planned) international study tours.[37]

The goals were to teach students about the primacy of the functionality and use of a building versus mere facade designs; the importance of the history of architecture for a much-needed reevaluation of traditions versus re-creating historical styles; and, finally, the economical use of materials for both financial prudence and aesthetic effects.[38] Most important, however, was an emphasis on architectural practice, an end to which Loos employed students in his office to work on his design commissions.[39]

After its closure during World War I, the Bauschule reopened in the fall of 1919,[40] almost a year after Fischer had enrolled at the TH Vienna. Loos's prewar students are reasonably well documented: among them were Rudolph Schindler and Richard Neutra, both of whom later rose to fame in Southern California; Ernst Freud, the architect son of Sigmund Freud,[41] whose career in Berlin was cut short when he and his family fled to the United Kingdom in 1933; and Felix Augenfeld, who fled the Nazis for the safety of New York. The students of the postwar period, however, "are neither all known by their names nor can accurately be accounted for by the years of their studies," a lacuna that started to be filled by Peter Plaisier's publication on the students of Loos.[42] Regardless, when Fischer worked during a formative period of his life with Loos, the young architect's personality impressed itself on others as that of "a loveable and talented human being of unbelievable modesty" (fig. 1.3).[43]

According to Fischer's later recollections, he joined the Bauschule in October 1919.[44] Robert Hlawatsch, a fellow Loos student, confirmed that he and Fischer attended the Bauschule during the academic years of 1920–21 and 1921–22, two years in which Heinrich Kulka, another Loos student, and Fischer "were already working in the office of Loos . . . even though they kept quiet about it."[45] The 1920–21 academic year was also the last one during which Fischer took exams at the TH Vienna; presumably, studying with and working for Loos occupied most of his time.

1.3. Leopold Fischer in attendance at Adolf Loos's sixtieth birthday, Společenský Club, Prague, 10 December 1930.

Loos is seated in the center (seventh from the left) and Fischer is standing immediately behind him.

In the aftermath of the war, housing for the working and middle classes was one of the most pressing issues, and Loos was deeply involved in this effort. In 1921, he became the chief architect of the municipal office in charge of developing plans for *Siedlungen* (housing estates).[46] Loos's interest in the housing question spilled over into the Bauschule. In fact, the topic of the 1920–21 academic year was Siedlungen, with students working in the municipal *Siedlungsamt* (office for housing estates) and Loos organizing a student competition for a housing estate.[47] One of the "open-minded idealists" drawn to the "invaluable pioneering work"[48] of housing estates was Leopold Fischer, who decorated the interior of the first completed home in Lainzer Tiergarten, an estate Loos designed in 1921 for war invalids.[49]

Fischer would have also learned from Loos about the United States, where the latter had lived from 1893 to 1896, years in which Loos acquired a lasting veneration of the country, its architecture, and its way of life that was consequential for his subsequent work as an architect, cultural critic, and teacher in Europe. The American way of life became Loos's "school of independence,"[50] and, once back in Vienna, Loos rarely missed talking to his students, including students like

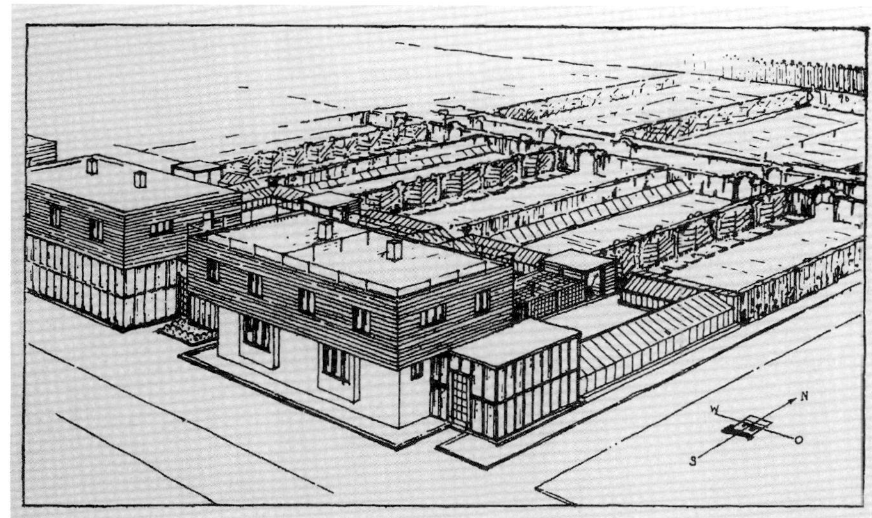

1.4. Leopold Fischer (US American, 1901–75, b. Austria-Hungary) and Leberecht Migge (German, 1881–1935).

Drawing of two-story semidetached model houses.

From *Heim und Scholle* [Home and soil] exhibition, Braunschweig, Germany, June to July 1925.

From Leberecht Migge, *Deutsche Binnen-Kolonisation: Sachgrundlagen des Siedlungswesens* (Berlin-Friedenau: Deutscher Kommunal-Verlag, 1926), 65.

Schindler and Neutra,[51] "about his life in America for the benefit and moral uplift of many."[52] Loos admired Americans' welcoming openness to foreigners and their pragmatic attitude toward life, as well as the solidarity among the urban working classes and immigrant communities centering on the American dream of improving oneself. He was captivated by life in small cities, towns, and the outskirts of big cities, which architecturally meant a preference for detached houses on individual plots of land.

When Loos worked in Vienna on his design of a gigantic Doric column for the Chicago Tribune Tower competition in 1922, Fischer was a member of the team.[53] Loos and Fischer collaborated again when designing the Spanner country house in Gumpoldskirchen, Austria, in 1923. Yet, in the summer of 1924, a disagreement with the City of Vienna about housing politics led to Loos's departure for Paris, leaving Fischer responsible for supervising the completion of the construction of the country house, the first detached house Fischer was ever involved with.[54]

Germany, 1924–36

In Vienna, Fischer met the landscape and garden architect Leberecht Migge (1881–1935) through Adolf Loos. Migge was an important, colorful figure in the post–World War I housing movement who lived in Worpswede, an artist colony near the city of Bremen in northern Germany. By 1925, Migge was working for the Anhaltischen Siedlerverband, a housing cooperative in Dessau, which, as will be seen, led to Fischer becoming involved with the cooperative. Eventually Fischer became its chief architect.

The cooperation between Fischer and Migge began in October 1924[55] with two projects: an extension of Migge's house Sonnenhof in Worpswede, and designs for settler houses and gardens for the *Heim und Scholle* exhibition that was held in Braunschweig from 7 June to 8 July 1925 (fig. 1.4).[56] The names of the two projects reference sun, home, and soil and illustrate the range of both men's thoughts about social housing estates. Right after the war, Migge promoted gardening one's own piece of land for self-sufficiency to combat the housing crisis, unemployment, and hunger.[57] On a regional and even national scale, Migge's ideas were part of the contemporary call for *Binnenkolonisation,* domestic or interior (to a nation) colonization that would result in housing estates and neighborhoods for the working classes and war veterans. On a smaller domestic scale, Migge envisioned the house and garden as the center of an autarkic life of the family. Members of this basic social unit would sustain themselves by working their garden and land. Politically, Migge's vision appealed to housing reformers and architects, like Loos and Fischer, who were attracted to the concepts of garden city and garden suburb as the path for reforming both the housing situation and modern metropolitan life.

WITH WALTER GROPIUS, AUGUST TO DECEMBER 1925

The history of modern architecture knows about Dessau primarily because of the Bauhaus's move from Weimar in the state of Thuringia to Dessau in Anhalt, where the art school reopened in April 1925. Dessau and Anhalt had a history of social-democratic, progressive policies, especially in combating the housing crisis before and after World War I.[58] As part of the move, the city wanted the Bauhaus to contribute to the municipal social housing program an estate on the southern edge of Dessau, the future Dessau-Törten neighborhood.[59] Because the Bauhaus was still without an architecture department, Walter Gropius secured the commission for his private office and employed Leopold Fischer to work on the plans for the Törten estate. Precise details of Fischer's stint in the office remain unclear, though according to a curriculum vitae Fischer compiled in 1946 in California, he worked for Gropius for four months between August and December 1925.[60] On 5 June 1926, Gropius's wife, Ise Gropius, noted in her diary that Fischer, who "had worked for a while in Gropius's office," was fired because of "far too little capabilities."[61] As it turned out, the lack of capabilities more likely afflicted the office of Gropius (if not Gropius himself) than Fischer.[62]

Contemporaries already noted the broad similarities between the Törten estate and Loos's patent from 1921 for "a house with only one wall" that had been applied to the construction, for example, of the Heuberg estate in Vienna.[63] This similarity was Fischer's contribution to the Törten scheme. Loos's patent proposed housing in the form of rows of attached two-story homes separated by load-bearing walls that cut across the depth of each row. Consequently, the ceiling beams carrying the upper level ran from one load-bearing wall to the next, making the street and garden facades non-load-bearing infill walls. When in 1929 *Wasmuths Monatshefte* published a photograph of Fischer's Knarrberg estate in Dessau-Ziebigk (fig. 1.5), the magazine drew a comparison to the Törten estate that was not flattering for Gropius.[64] The earliest Törten houses, the Sietö Type 1 house, were marred by a significant construction flaw: their stairs to the upper level ran perpendicular, not parallel, to the span of the ceiling beams. This led to a need for additional, costly structural supports, thus making unfeasible any efficient use of the capacity of the load-bearing beams and walls. The error may have contributed to cracks in the facades of the row houses.[65] Fischer knew well Loos's patent for erecting social housing using the most efficient structural methods that were at the same time most cost effective, and he would have realized the possible consequences of wrongly oriented staircases.[66] But he was no longer in the Gropius office when the direction of the stairs was decided.[67]

Fischer's firing did not endear either man to the other and led to a festering animosity between the older and younger modernist architects. *Wasmuths Monatshefte* had reported that Fischer's Siedlung was sometimes identified inaccurately as a "Bauhaus-Siedlung"—in retrospect a compliment for Fischer, considering the art school's international fame, and also, indirectly, for the Bauhaus, not least as this housing estate by Fischer is nowadays celebrated as an early example of ecological architecture.[68] Yet, Gropius rallied allies to take up the "fight against imitators and the ignorant" and charged Fischer's client for the Knarrberg estate with falling for a "fashionable flattening out" of both roofs and architectural concepts; to make things even worse, all was done "in close vicinity to the Bauhaus." Gropius concluded by exclaiming, "Yes to the rational garden designs by Migge; No to formalistic flat roofs by Fischer."[69] Fischer's immediate response, if any, is unknown to us, though the Bauhaus, excepting Gropius, thought highly of Fischer. Once Gropius had left the school in 1928, the incoming director, the architect Hannes Meyer, tried to recruit Fischer for the newly established architecture department.[70]

Ultimately, Gropius's argument with Fischer evolved around competing social housing concepts,

1.5. Leopold Fischer (US American, 1901–75, b. Austria-Hungary) and Leberecht Migge (German, 1881–1935).

Knarrberg estate (1926–28), Dessau–Ziebigk, Germany, 1928 or earlier, aerial photograph.

1.6. Leopold Fischer (US American, 1901–75, b. Austria-Hungary).

Two-story semidetached houses, Knarrberg estate (1926–28), Dessau–Ziebigk, Germany, 1929 or earlier.

Street view.

1.7. Leopold Fischer (US American, 1901–75, b. Austria-Hungary).

Semidetached houses, Knarrberg estate (1926–28), Dessau–Ziebigk, Germany, 1929 or earlier.

Partial view of rear garden, showing winter garden (glass-enclosed veranda), upper-level balcony, stables for small livestock, espaliers (free-standing and against walls), and fruit and vegetable gardens to the left.

which Gropius envisioned as mass housing achievable through a technocratic, rational application of technology and Fischer saw as the basis of a life rooted in land ownership. For Gropius, Törten was an experiment in rationalizing and industrializing large building sites to allow speedy and affordable construction with standardized components (pre)fabricated on-site. In contrast, Fischer followed Migge and Loos; for the three of them, social housing equaled homes arranged in garden city–like Siedlungen that included individual gardens to cultivate, thereby putting the owner on a path to an autarkic way of life.

In 1924, Loos left his municipal job in Vienna because of a comparable argument over competing visions of social housing. Then Loos's and Migge's ideas were cast aside when the city and Viennese architects fell for the strong visual symbolism of huge *Wohnhöfe,* communal housing blocks with hundreds or more rental apartments that organized the inhabitants' lives around collective facilities.[71] Gardens attached to individual homes as part of an autarkic life were not part of these grand schemes. Yet, when in 1926 Fischer was hired by a regional housing cooperative, he was able to develop in close vicinity to the Bauhaus more fully his (and Migge's and Loos's) vision for social housing.

SOCIAL HOUSING ARCHITECT IN DESSAU AND BEYOND, 1925/26–31

The earliest social housing projects on which Fischer worked in the eastern parts of Germany were probably arranged through Migge. Beginning in 1925, Fischer signed off on drawings for houses for an estate in Coswig (a town close to Dresden) for the Anhaltischer Siedlerverband.[72] This regional housing cooperative planned and financed housing estates in the state of Anhalt. In February 1926, the first of Fischer's thirty-eight semidetached houses was completed for an estate in Kleinkühnau, a neighborhood in Dessau.[73]

The Knarrberg estate was the first large-scale project that Fischer worked on in cooperation with Migge. Upon its completion in 1928, the project comprised just over 180 homes, most of them as semidetached, two-story buildings, with each half offering a two-story home (fig. 1.6).[74] The estate realized in an exemplary manner Migge's concept of gardens for self-sufficient living, which Fischer complemented with semidetached houses placed along the eastern and western perimeters of the four oblong blocks that constituted the neighborhood. Long, narrow gardens—one for each home—occupied the land between the rows of buildings. The layout and functionality of dwellings and gardens dovetailed tightly with the annual cycle of gardening activities. Winter gardens, chicken coops, espaliers trained against masonry walls storing the heat of the sun, yards for plant and animal husbandry, and so on were all expressive of the symbiosis between organic life (including the lives of the occupants), architecture, and nature that Fischer and Migge sought to achieve (fig. 1.7). This symbiosis included such details as the occupants' excrement, which was to be harvested with a compost toilet Migge had invented.[75] At least in theory, together the cubic, flat-roofed buildings (some with projecting oriel windows) and the gardens served the socioeconomic

1.8. Leopold Fischer (US American, 1901–75, b. Austria-Hungary).

Friedrichshöhe estate, also called Zickzackhausen (1928–30), Bernburg, Germany, 1929 or earlier.

mission of enabling the working classes to acquire home and ground to achieve a self-sufficient life.[76]

Fischer and the Anhaltischer Siedlerverband planned and realized social housing estates all over the former Duchy of Anhalt. Most notable among Fischer's other designs is the Friedrichshöhe estate (1928–30) in the city of Bernburg (fig. 1.8).[77] The estate's nickname is Zickzackhausen, which plays on the zigzagging of the sawtooth pattern in which the terraced houses were arranged to maximize sunlight inside the homes. The estate was planned to encompass 2,800 buildings, but only ninety were realized.[78] Then, after Gropius departed from the Bauhaus in 1928, Fischer was commissioned by the Anhaltischer Siedlerverband to complete the estate in Dessau-Törten with thirty two-story houses; the elegant rhythm of his semidetached houses with narrow gaps between them contrasts with the rigid aesthetic of Gropius's rows of partially prefabricated buildings.[79] In 1931, the bankruptcy of the Anhaltischer Siedlerverband ended rather abruptly Fischer's career as a social housing architect.

SELF-EMPLOYED DOMESTIC ARCHITECT, 1931–36

Fischer also occasionally designed detached houses and, once laid off by the housing cooperative, relied exclusively on commissions for private homes. As noted, Fischer's first domestic project in Germany was the remodel of Leberecht Migge's Sonnenhof between 1924 and 1925 to accommodate the growing Migge family; the bourgeois, comfortable urban life that Migge's wife, Andrea Migge, expected even in a rural artist colony; and Mr. Migge's vision of self-reliant living off the land.[80] During the 1920s, Fischer designed three more detached homes for individual clients: the Liebig villa in Dessau (1927–28); the Theis house (1929), which was located within the Knarrberg estate; and the Krause house in Oranienbaum (ca. 1929–30). Another five detached homes were part of the Knarrberg estate, where they prominently marked street corners along some of the estate's borders. From the 1930s, an additional seven domestic projects are known to us thanks to the research of Dr. Irene Below. Two buildings are located in Westfalen: the Tittel house (1931) in Bielefeld and the Steinborn house (1933) in nearby Werther. In the same year, 1933, Fischer also planned the Hummel house in Stuttgart. In 1935, he designed the Vogt house and the Mutzenbecher house, two homes on a suburban street developed in Berlin-Wannsee that year. Finally, there are the Dobert house in Dresden (after ca. 1930) and the Kunkat house (date unknown) in Kronach, Upper Franconia, Germany.[81] This small oeuvre of domestic designs sheds some light on characteristics of Fischer's architecture beyond social housing and on the social circles in which Fischer moved during the 1930s.

1.9. Leopold Fischer (US American, 1901–75, b. Austria-Hungary) and his fiancée, Gerda Vogt (German, 1905–2002), in Dresden, where they met.

Undated photograph.

Networks of Clients, Friends, and Acquaintances

Fischer's clients for these detached houses came from the upper-middle classes, or bourgeoisie as they are usually called in European parlance; some may have identified with the *Bildungsbürgertum* (the educated bourgeoisie) and others as reform-minded, even if not avant-garde artists. Paul Hummel was a salesperson; Hedwig Liebig a milliner and dressmaker; Rudolf Steinborn a medical doctor; Emil Theis a portrait photographer; and Dr. Paul Tittel a college teacher and collector of modern art. Klara Vogt, a widow, was a manufacturer of cosmetic products. Her neighbor Franz Mutzenbecher was an artist, as was Margarete Dobert.[82] This group circumscribes a social class and also Fischer's circle of friends and acquaintances, some of whom I discuss in greater detail below.

Upon losing his employment in Dessau, Fischer relocated to Dresden, where he was in contact with Dobert, a sculptor; and Peter August Böckstiegel (1889–1951), a painter and sculptor. In Dresden, Fischer also met his future fiancée, Gerda Vogt (1905–2002), the daughter of Klara Vogt (fig. 1.9).[83] Dobert, Böckstiegel, and Vogt were linked with Dresden's contemporary world of modern art and culture. Dobert studied in the later 1920s at the Wegschule, an art school that the artist Edmund Kestings had established in Dresden.[84] Since a pre–World War I stint as a student at the Königliche Akademie der bildenden Künste (Royal Academy of Fine Arts)[85] in Dresden, Böckstiegel was a member of Dresden's expressionist circle and a friend of many younger artists such as Conrad Felixmüller.[86] Gerda Vogt studied at the Mary Wigman-Schule in Dresden; Wigman was one of the creators of *Ausdruckstanz* (modern dance).[87]

Coincidentally, Böckstiegel and Vogt each had roots in Westphalia: Vogt came from Bielefeld, and Böckstiegel was born in a village just north of that city. These regional roots may explain why Fischer received the commissions for the houses in Bielefeld and Werther, two locations in Westphalia. Further cementing the connection between members of Fischer's circle, Westphalia, and Fischer is the fact that Böckstiegel contributed a large relief that hung above the fireplace in the Werther home of Dr. Steinborn.[88]

Finally, Klara Vogt commissioned one of Fischer's houses in Berlin-Wannsee, and again, one finds links with modern art and culture, in this case specifically physical culture (*Körperkultur*), women as entrepreneurs, and modernist architecture. Klara Vogt owned the Fischer-designed home[89] and cohabited it with Margarete Meeths, who ran a school for gymnastics in Berlin. In 1929, the women together founded a manufacturing company for cosmetic products with the brand name Smell, a rather unfortunate translation of the German word *Duft* (scent). From then on, the two women, their joint business (Smell Kosmetische Präparate), and Meeths's school for gymnastics were listed in Berlin directories at Cicerostraße 56a in Berlin-Wilmersdorf.[90] This address was part of the Wohnhausgrundstücksverwertungs Aktiengesellschaft, or, for short, WOGA, complex that Eric Mendelsohn had planned and built between 1925 and 1931 at Lehniner Platz just off Kurfürstendamm. Fronting the boulevard were the Universum Cinema (today the Schaubühne) and a *Rauchtheater* (smoking theater), appropriately named, as its ventilation and fire safety features allowed Berliners to indulge safely in their beloved habit of smoking everywhere and at any time. Cicerostraße stretches south from behind the cinema, and along the street Mendelsohn had designed a five-story apartment complex in which Vogt and Meeths had rented accommodations.

Among the neighbors of Vogt and Meeths in Fintelmannstraße were the painter Franz Mutzenbecher and his wife, Clara Mutzenbecher. It is possible that the Mutzenbechers became Fischer's clients for a house because the painter and Fischer had each collaborated at times with Bruno Taut, then one of Berlin's best-known modernist social housing architects. Mutzenbecher frequently contributed mural paintings and artworks to the interiors of buildings designed by Taut and other modernist architects. Taut and Fischer, in turn, had collaborated on the Ratskiefern estate in Coswig, near Dessau, between 1925 and 1927. Perhaps Mutzenbecher and Fischer met thanks to this Taut connection.[91]

Private Detached Homes

Fischer's designs for these detached houses are best comprehended by looking at the plans, spaces, and rooms rather than elaborating on outward architectural appearances. Externally, the designs vary between modern (most commonly) and more traditional (occasionally). The Liebig villa (fig. 1.10) and the Krause, Theis, Tittel (fig. 1.11), and Steinborn houses are modernist in form; their volumes are cast into cubes that are two or three stories tall, sometimes with projecting or receding smaller cubic volumes that create additional spaces and rooms, indoors and out. They all possess flat roofs, a modern feature that attracted special interest. When in 1932 Dr. Steinborn pondered plans for a new house, Böckstiegel, in a letter to his wife, Hanna Böckstiegel, praised Fischer as an architect who had "built truly beautiful houses with a flat roof,"[92] singling out this one detail as not contradicting beauty while underlining the impression of modernity that it signaled.

The use in Böckstiegel's letter of the Low German, regional word *platt* for flat instead of the common *flach* recalls the local roots of the artist; Böckstiegel did not see any contradiction between modernist buildings and, for example, the vernacular, rural surroundings of a small town like Werther. Fischer (and his teacher, Adolf Loos) would have agreed: Loos especially emphasized that modern architecture is rooted in traditions derived from vernacular architecture. That the Vogt and Mutzenbecher homes in Berlin and some of the semi-detached houses on the Dessau-Kleinkühnau estate (1926–28) feature pitched roofs and other traditional

1.10. Leopold Fischer (US American, 1901–75, b. Austria-Hungary).

Liebig villa (1927–28), Dessau, Germany, shortly after completion, n.d.

View of east facade.

1.11. Leopold Fischer (US American, 1901–75, b. Austria-Hungary).

Tittel house (1931), Bielefeld, Germany, ca. early 1970s.

Garden facade.

details does not contradict the modernity of the architecture of Fischer; rather, this illustrates Fischer's roots in a strand of modern architecture that did not seek a radical break with the past and history.[93]

Internally, the arrangement of the floor plans and the spaces provided evolve around the needs and aspirations of the clients and illustrate the wished-for solidity of a middle-class, if not bourgeois, life. Most of Fischer's two-story buildings group private spaces such as bedrooms in one area (for example, on the upper levels); and public ones, like living rooms, on lower, easier-to-access floors. In some houses, workspaces intersect with this basic division. Steinborn's house included his medical office comprising rooms for waiting and consultations. The Theis house was extended with a large photography studio on the first floor, accessible from an outside stair and connected to the upper-level living room through pocket doors. In the middle-class, detached houses on the Knarrberg estate, an "Arbeits-Zimmer" (workroom) is provided without specifying whether this is for domestic or professional work. The plans for the lower two levels of the Liebig villa are organized around the owner's dressmaking business, which required a sewing room, a fitting room, and an office for Ms. Liebig. These examples illustrate that the houses were homes but also often part of the economic foundation of the occupants' lives.

The life envisioned in the homes becomes tangible when considering, for instance, the locations of the kitchens. Usually, these kitchens are spatially separated from the dining areas; sometimes the former are even located on a different floor, which suggests that the inhabitants relied on a maid or domestic staff to prepare and serve meals. Accordingly, dedicated bedrooms or, as in the Liebig villa, even a small apartment had to be provided for the staff. In the Steinborn and Tittel houses, the kitchen and dining areas are on separate levels and linked by dedicated staircases. In the Liebig villa, a modern lift brings meals to the dining room, and in the Tittel house, the stairs even extend to the second upper level, where this staff staircase ends beside the owners' bathroom.[94] Even the plans of the detached middle-class houses on the Knarrberg estate show a comparable separation of kitchen and dining areas; apparently, the estate aimed at an autarkic life for both working *and* middle classes without challenging social conventions and class differences.

While Fischer's modernist-appearing homes thus contain established elements of bourgeois domestic architecture, these are not delivered in conventional plans. Instead, Fischer provides differences in floor levels and heights of individual rooms, evoking Adolf Loos's *Raumplan,* a design concept that Heinrich Kulka, a student of Loos at the same time as Fischer, summarized once as follows:

> Thinking freely in space, the planning of spaces resting at different heights and that are not joined to any regular system of the horizontal layering of floors, the composing of connected spaces into a harmonic and inseparable whole and a spatially economic entity. Depending on their purpose and importance, the spaces not only had varying sizes but also varying heights.[95]

Adopting the Raumplan resulted in internal spaces that, in the case of Fischer's Steinborn house, offered visual "interaction, outlooks, and interesting transitions between rooms."[96] These interrelationships focus on the interior and are centered around the inhabitants of the houses. The outside is not ignored but exactingly drawn close to the interior by such spatial means as winter gardens and roof terraces; nature is selectively allowed alongside, even onto (if not into), the architecture in the form of plantings in beds and pots and creepers growing up facades.

In short, Fischer's domestic designs for detached private homes adopt Loos's dictum that a house should be like a case for a precious piece of jewelry: it had to be plain so that nothing would distract from the sparkle of the things inside.[97] Indeed, the house had to be inconspicuous to be modern, which meant attracting the least attention.[98] The plainness on the outside was more than a means to create contrast; it expressed the architect and client's responsibility toward the public realm, the public space that is framed by buildings including private houses whose facades are therefore constituent elements of this realm.

Going into Exile

The precise date of Leopold Fischer's departure from Germany was recorded in a letter from Peter August Böckstiegel to Hanna Böckstiegel on 28 September 1936: "I paid a brief visit to Fischer who will depart tonight to be tomorrow night at the ship in Rotterdam."[99] A letter from a week earlier described Fischer's intentions in more detail: "Next Thursday Fischer will go for two months to California, America, some ladies invited him over there, [he] wants to try his luck."[100]

In 1936, the year Fischer left Nazi Germany, the legal situation of especially Jews and other "non-Aryans"

1.12. **Leopold Fischer and his fiancée, Gerda Vogt, in September 1936, the day before Fischer embarked from Rotterdam into exile in California.**

deteriorated even faster than during 1933, when the first discriminatory laws were issued that, for example, banned Jews from holding positions in a government office and affiliated administrations. In September 1935, the infamous Nuremberg Laws created a legal-seeming basis for the racist policies of the regime and, in hindsight, a first step toward the Holocaust. One of these laws, the Reich Citizenship Law, which reserved citizenship (*Reichsbürgerschaft*) exclusively for "Aryans" and denigrated "non-Aryans" to mere state subjects (*Staatsangehörige*), did not immediately affect Fischer as a Polish citizen. Yet, the Law for the Protection of German Blood and German Honor forbade marriage and all sexual relations between "Aryans" and "non-Aryans" and declared Fischer's engagement with Gerda Vogt, who was not of Jewish descent, illegal.[101] It is not known how Fischer and Vogt came to terms with this discriminatory law, but any possible thoughts about a future marriage and life in Germany were rendered void.

Fischer sailed on the SS *Volendam* that left Rotterdam on 26 September 1936 and arrived in New York on 6 October.[102] Over half of the passengers—including Fischer—traveled as "first cabin" passengers, not necessarily because they were wealthy but because the class guaranteed faster disembarkation and processing by immigration officers.[103] Fischer had booked a round trip at a Leipzig travel agency (with a return date of 21 November 1936) via New York to Los Angeles that included the train journey to and accommodation at the final destination. He arrived in New York with $100 cash—twice as much as legally required—and was the only passenger who named the Los Angeles office of American Express as his contact at his final destination. These arrangements suggest that Fischer prepared for the journey most likely with the help of his California hosts and, probably, with their financial support.

Gerda Vogt had accompanied her fiancé to Rotterdam, where the couple said farewell by taking a final photograph with the camera's self-timer. As it happens, this is the last-ever photograph showing them together. Vogt's wretched face speaks of pain and parting, and Fischer looks sternly, even somewhat defiantly, toward the camera and into the unknown future (fig. 1.12). Little did Fischer know then that the expected two months abroad would turn into a lifetime, much of which he dedicated to rebuilding his life and career as an émigré architect in California.

Notes

1 Robert Musil, *The Man without Qualities,* trans. Eithne Wilkins and Ernst Kaiser, 3 vols. (London: Secker & Warburg, 1953–61). The main protagonist, Ulrich, did have qualities, but constant self-reflection liberated him from all of them, a precondition for the sought-after self-realization. See Judith Burckhardt, *"Der Mann ohne Eigenschaften" von Robert Musil, oder das Wagnis der Selbstverwirklichung* (Bern: Francke, 1973).

2 The biographical and geographical information on the Fischer family in Bielitz was kindly supplied by Mag. Piotr Kenig from the Muzeum Historyczne w Bielsku-Białej (Historical Museum Bielsko-Biala). Mag. Piotr Kenig, emails to the author, 26 and 28 August and 2 September 2020.

3 In some documents, Charlotte Rosa Wurzel is called Cäcilie; the reason is not known.

4 "Leopold Fischer," line 18, list 2, SS *Volendam* passengers sailing from Rotterdam, 26 September 1936, arriving at Port of New York, NY, 6 October 1936, in *List or Manifest of Alien Passengers for the United States Immigration Officer at Port of Arrival,* 155 (The National Archives in Washington, DC; Washington, DC, USA; Passenger and Crew Lists of Vessels Arriving at New York, New York, 1897–1957; Microfilm Serial or NAID: T715; RG Title: Records of the Immigration and Naturalization Service, 1787–2004; RG: 85; ancestry.com, subscription required).

5 *Berliner Adreßbuch 1936*: *Unter Benutzung amtlicher Quellen,* vol. 3, pt. 4 (Berlin: Scherl, [1936]), 1078.

6 Heinrich-Wilhelm Wörmann, *Widerstand in Charlottenburg* (Berlin: Gedenkstätte Deutscher Widerstand, 1991), 181. The building was severely damaged in a bomb attack in 1944; see Katholische Schule Liebfrauen Gymnasium, Berlin, "Chronik der Katholischen Schule Liebfrauen," https://www.ksliebfrauen.de/Schulchronik.html.

7 Video conference and email communications of the author with Dr. Esther Cohen, Arnat Ornstein, and Yael Cohen Weitz, Israel, June 2024. Unless noted otherwise, all details about the lives of Fischer's three sisters were kindly provided by their relatives. I wish to thank especially Dr. Esther Cohen and Arnat Ornstein for generously sharing information about their families; and Professor Maoz Azaryahu, University of Haifa, for establishing the crucial, initial contact with Mrs. Ornstein.

8 "Olga Fink," Wykaz ocalałych Żydow polskich (List of surviving Polish Jews) (United States Holocaust Memorial Museum; Washington, DC, USA; Wykaz ocalałych Żydow polskich [Sygn.307]; Record Group Number: RG-15.057M; File Name: RG-15.057M_0053_RG-15.057M.0053.00000550; ancestry.com, subscription required). The same entry also mentions Olga Fink's sister Marta Follman (i.e., Martha Zollmann).

9 "Testimony of Lora (Fink) Noy, born in Bielsko, Poland, 1927, regarding her experiences in Lwow, labor camp in the Soviet Union, Siberia, Samarkand and aliya to Eretz Israel, 1943, as part of the Tehran Children," *Yad Vashem,* video (in Hebrew), https://collections.yadvashem.org/he/documents/7535944. The video is also available on YouTube: https://youtu.be/AB8ETW87rXc?. See also "Tehran Children," United States

Holocaust Memorial Museum, Washington, DC, https://encyclopedia.ushmm.org/content/en/article/tehran-children; and Mikhal Dekel, *In the East: How My Father and a Quarter Million Polish Jews Survived the Holocaust* (New York: W. W. Norton, 2021).

10 "Stefania Schmalzbach," *Yad Vashem,* https://collections.yadvashem.org/en/names, search "all collections" for "Stefanie Schmalzbach."

11 For details about this apartment building, see this volume, "List of Selected Architectural Works."

12 For the year of the merger of the two cities, see Gerd-Ulrich Piesch, "Zum Jugendstil in Bielitz: Zwei Bauten des Wiener Architekten Hans Mayr," *Oberschlesisches Jahrbuch* 12 (1996): 77.

13 Walter Kuhn, *Geschichte der deutschen Sprachinsel Bielitz (Schlesien)* (Würzburg: Holzner, 1981), 336.

14 Kuhn, *Geschichte der deutschen Sprachinsel Bielitz,* 233.

15 Kuhn, *Geschichte der deutschen Sprachinsel Bielitz,* 343.

16 Ursula Prokop, *Zum jüdischen Erbe in der Wiener Architektur: Der Beitrag jüdischer ArchitektInnen* [sic] *am Wiener Baugeschehen 1868–1938* (Vienna: Böhlau, 2016), 76.

17 All examples cited from Piesch, "Zum Jugendstil in Bielitz," 77–79. For more on Mayr, see also Jutta Brandstetter, "Hans Mayr," *Architektenlexikon Wien 1770–1945,* ed. Architekturzentrum Wien, http://www.architektenlexikon.at/de/390.htm.

18 On the importance of König for architectural education in Vienna before World War I, see Christopher Long, "An Alternative Path to Modernism: Carl König and the Architectural Education at the Vienna Technische Hochschule, 1890–1913," *Journal of Architectural Education* 55, no. 1 (September 2001): 21–30. On Neumann, see Jutta Brandstetter, "Alexander Neumann," *Architektenlexikon Wien 1770–1945,* ed. Architekturzentrum Wien, http://www.architektenlexikon.at/de/425.htm. See also Prokop, *Zum jüdischen Erbe in der Wiener Architektur,* 70. On Lindner, see Prokop, *Zum jüdischen Erbe in der Wiener Architektur,* 76–80; and Piesch, "Zum Jugendstil in Bielitz," 78. See also Ursula Prokop, "Ernst Lindner," *Architektenlexikon Wien 1770–1945,* ed. Architekturzentrum Wien, http://www.architektenlexikon.at/de/1343.htm.

19 Prokop, *Zum jüdischen Erbe in der Wiener Architektur,* 183–87. See also Petra Schumann, "Egon Riss," *Architektenlexikon Wien 1770–1945,* ed. Architekturzentrum Wien, http://www.architektenlexikon.at; and "Egon Riss," *Dictionary of Scottish Architects 1660–1980,* http://www.scottisharchitects.org.uk.

20 Weinraub was born in Szumlany, Austrian Galicia (Shumlyany, Ukraine).

21 Richard Ingersoll, *Munio Gitai Weinraub: Bauhaus Architect in Eretz Israel* (Milan: Electa, 1994), 24.

22 Josef Strzygowski, *Die bildende Kunst der Gegenwart: Ein Büchlein für Jedermann* (Leipzig: Quelle und Meyer, 1907), 61, quoted from Piesch, "Zum Jugendstil in Bielitz," 78.

23 Prokop, *Zum jüdischen Erbe in der Wiener Architektur,* 118n153, 136, and 136n181.

24 Paul Wijdeveld, *Ludwig Wittgenstein: Architect* (1993; Amsterdam: Pepin, 2000); Inge Scheidl, "Paul Engelmann," *Architektenlexikon Wien 1770–1945,* ed. Architekturzentrum Wien, http://www.architektenlexikon.at/de/108.htm; and Ursula Prokop, "Jacques Groag," *Architektenlexikon Wien 1770–1945,* ed. Architekturzentrum Wien, http://www.architektenlexikon.at/de/182.htm.

25 For details about this apartment building, see this volume, "List of Selected Architectural Works."

26 Prokop, *Zum jüdischen Erbe in der Wiener Architektur,* 184. See also Kathleen James, "Zwischen Expressionismus und Neuer Sachlichkeit: Das Seidenhaus Weichmann in Gleiwitz," *Oberschlesisches Jahrbuch* 10 (1994): 153–62.

27 Prokop, *Zum jüdischen Erbe in der Wiener Architektur,* 133.

28 Hauptkatalog der ordentlichen Hörer für das Studienjahr 1918/19, Matr. Nr. 180 (Leopold Fischer), Technische Universität Wien Archiv (TUWA) (hereafter Hauptkatalog 1918/19 [Leopold Fischer]).

29 Mag. Piotr Kenig, email to the author, 9 September 2020.

30 See the matriculation record of Fischer, Hauptkatalog 1918/19 (Leopold Fischer); and also Long, "An Alternative Path to Modernism," esp. 23.

31 Long, "An Alternative Path to Modernism," esp. 22.

32 Iris Meder, "Offene Welten: Die Wiener Schule im Einfamilienhausbau 1910–1938" (PhD diss., Institut für Kunstgeschichte der Universität Stuttgart, 2004), 22–29; and Prokop, *Zum jüdischen Erbe in der Wiener Architektur,* 44–51. For contemporary characterizations as reactionary, see Long, "An Alternative Path to Modernism," esp. 21.

33 Long, "An Alternative Path to Modernism," esp. 25–28.

34 Meder, "Offene Welten," 2–29; and Prokop, *Zum jüdischen Erbe in der Wiener Architektur,* 49–50.

35 The detailed information about Fischer's course of studies at the TH Vienna derives from Hauptkatalog 1918/19 (Leopold Fischer).

36 Burkhardt Rukschcio and Roland Schachel, *Adolf Loos: Leben und Werk* (Salzburg: Residenz, 1982), 171.

37 Rukschcio and Schachel, *Adolf Loos,* 168–71, 186–90.

38 Dietrich Worbs, "Die Loos-Schule," *Bauforum* 16, no. 98 (1983): 27.

39 Worbs, "Die Loos-Schule," 27–28.

40 Rukschcio and Schachel, *Adolf Loos,* 239.

41 Volker M. Welter, *Ernst L. Freud, Architect: The Case of the Modern Bourgeois Home* (Oxford: Berghahn, 2012).

42 Rukschcio and Schachel, *Adolf Loos, Architect,* 239; and Peter Plaisier, *De leerlingen van Adolf Loos* (Delft: Delftse Universitaire Pers, 1987).

43 Elsie Altmann-Loos, *Adolf Loos, der Mensch* (Vienna: Herold, 1968), 85. While Fischer was remembered, Altmann-Loos calls him Heinrich Fischer, an error she corrected in a subsequent edition of her memoirs. See Elsie Altmann-Loos, *Mein Leben mit Adolf Loos* (Vienna: Amalthea, 1984), 122.

44 "Leopold Fischer," license file, California Architects Board.

45 Robert Hlawatsch, "Erinnerungen an Adolf Loos und an die Loos-Schule," *Bauwelt* 72, no. 42 (1981): 1893.

46 The German words *Siedlung* and *Siedler* translate as settlement and settler, respectively, two words that evoke images of colonialist settling of foreign lands, especially in the American and Anglo-Saxon context. These connotations also exist in German-speaking countries. However, the words as used by the housing movement after World War I denote the demand to be able to settle on a piece of land—for example, on the fringes of cities such as Vienna in order to make a living from working the land. The use of the German words in this book indicates this specific meaning.

47 Rukschcio and Schachel, *Adolf Loos,* 251.

48 Rukschcio and Schachel, *Adolf Loos,* 251.

49 Altmann-Loos, *Adolf Loos* (1968), 103–5. See also Rukschcio and Schachel, *Adolf Loos,* 536–39.

50 Rukschcio and Schachel, *Adolf Loos,* 27. Unless noted otherwise, all information on Loos's time in the United States is from Rukschcio and Schachel, *Adolf Loos,* 21–32.

51 For example, see Richard Neutra, *Life and Shape* (1962; Los Angeles: Atara, 2009), 162–76; and Rukschcio and Schachel, *Adolf Loos,* 30–31.

52 Rukschcio and Schachel, *Adolf Loos,* 22.

53 Altmann-Loos, *Adolf Loos,* 127. See also Rukschcio and Schachel, *Adolf Loos,* 273–77.

54 Rukschcio and Schachel, *Adolf Loos,* 292–93, 582–83.

55 The start date is taken from "Leopold Fischer," license file, California Architects Board.

56 David H. Haney, *When Modern Was Green: Life and Work of Landscape Architect Leberecht Migge* (London: Routledge, 2010), 161–64. For Fischer's exhibits, see Irene Below, "Leopold Fischer—der Architekt von 'Zickzackhausen,'" in *Bernburger Heimatblätter 2001,* ed. Kulturbund Bernburg e.V. (Bernburg: Salzland Druck, 2001), 13.

57 Haney, *When Modern Was Green,* 86–154.

58 On Dessau and Anhalt's progressive policies, see Walter Scheiffele, *Bauhaus Junkers Sozialdemokratie: Ein Kraftfeld der Moderne* (Berlin: Form + Zweck, 2003).

59 On the history of the estate, see, for example, Scheiffele, *Bauhaus Junkers Sozialdemokratie,* 130–59.

60 "Leopold Fischer," license file, California Architects Board.

61 Ise Gropius, diary entry, 5 June 1926, typed copy, p. 136, Bauhaus Archiv Berlin, here cited from Irene Below, "Das Leben von Leopold Fischer," in *Leopold Fischer: Architekt der Moderne,* ed. Bauhaus Dessau e.V. (Dessau-Roßlau: Funk Verlag Bernhard Hein e.K., n.d. [ca. 2007]), 18. I have been unable to verify whether the dates for his time in the Gropius office as given by Fischer are correct or a later period based on Ise Gropius's diary entry. According to Below, Fischer started with Gropius at the "end of April 1926," which would mean approximately five weeks of employment if one applies the 5 June date of Ise Gropius's entry about Fischer's dismissal; Irene Below, "Der unbekannte Architekt und die andere Moderne: Leopold Fischer in Dessau," in *Mythos Bauhaus,* ed. Anja Baumhoff and Magdalene Droste (Berlin: Reimer, 2009), 251. Below gives no source, but Scheiffele points out that the City of Dessau held first discussions with Gropius about planning the Dessau Törten estate in April 1925 and that the city council awarded the contract for planning and building the estate late in June 1926. Scheiffele, *Bauhaus Junkers Sozialdemokratie,* 130 and 132. This sequence of events supports Fischer's recollections of the dates of his time with Gropius because the latter's office will have produced an initial masterplan and design for the estate to convince the city to award the contract.

62 Fischer's buildings were by no means flawless. Early in 1933 he agreed to contribute to the repair costs for some houses erected to his designs in Dessau and Bernburg. See Below, "Leopold Fischer—der Architekt von 'Zickzackhausen,'" 15.

63 Hans Josef Zechlin, "Siedlungen von Adolf Loos und Leopold Fischer," *Wasmuths Monatshefte für Baukunst* 13, no. 2 (1929): 70–78.

64 The estate is differently named in various sources. I adopted the name "Knarrberg estate," used in Ute Bednarz et al., eds., *Sachsen Anhalt II Regierungsbezirke Dessau und Halle* (Munich: Deutscher Kunstverlag, 1999), a volume in the series Dehio Handbuch der deutschen Kunstdenkmäler, a semiofficial inventory of noteworthy and listed buildings in Germany.

65 Zechlin, "Siedlungen von Adolf Loos und Leopold Fischer," 76. Zechlin's remarks referred to the houses of types SIETÖ I–1926 and SIETÖ I.2–1927; see Andreas Schwarting, *Die Siedlung Dessau-Törten 1926–1931* (Leipzig: Spector, 2012), 24–35.

66 On this debate, see also Below, who posits, convincingly, that Fischer injected ideas from Loos and Migge into the early planning of the Törten estate, whereas Rudolf Lückmann downplays this influence in an apparent attempt to defend Gropius against possible charges of plagiarism. Below, "Der unbekannte Architekt"; and Rudolf Lückmann, "Walter Gropius ./. Leopold Fischer—Ungleiche Rivalen um die Gartenstädte der Moderne," in *Zukunftsfähige Perspektiven in der Landschaftsarchitektur für Gartenstädte,* ed. Nicole Uhrig (Wiesbaden: Springer Fachmedien, 2020), 85–112.

67 Tina Hausdörfer, "Dessau-Ziebigk—Selbstversorgersiedlung am Knarrberg 1926," in *Das "Land in der Mitte" Architektur, Denkmals—und Wohnungsbauprojekte der Moderne,* ed. Christiane Wolf (Weimar: Bauhaus-Universität Universitätsverlag, 2004), 107.

68 Zechlin, "Siedlungen von Adolf Loos und Leopold Fischer," 70.

69 Walter Gropius to Carl Fieger, 1928, here cited from Juliane Vierich, *Die Villa Liebig: Denkmalpflege der Moderne,* diploma thesis (Köthen: Edition der Hochschule Anhalt, 2006), 28.

70 Below, "Das Leben von Leopold Fischer," 19.

71 For a history of Viennese social housing, see Eve Blau, *The Architecture of Red Vienna, 1919–1934* (Cambridge, MA: MIT Press, 1999).

72 Wolfgang Paul, "Siedlungen in Zerbst, Köthen und Coswig sowie solitäre Bauten in Dessau und Oranienbaum," in Bauhaus Dessau e.V., *Leopold Fischer,* 96.

73 Paul, "Siedlungen," 100; and Lückmann, "Walter Gropius ./. Leopold Fischer," 94.

74 The count of how many houses were erected varies slightly from 182 to 184, the number of types from four to five. See, for example, Wolfgang Paul and Juliane Vierich, "Die Lage der Bauten Fischers im heutigen Sachsen-Anhalt," in Bauhaus Dessau e.V., *Leopold Fischer,* 106; and Schwarting, *Die Siedlung Dessau-Törten,* 97.

75 Apparently, the compost toilets and graywater recycling were abandoned early on for reasons of functionality, hygiene, and general comfort. Fritz Becker, "Aus den Erinnerungen eines Erstbewohners," in Bauhaus Dessau e.V., *Leopold Fischer,* 49–50.

76 This goal was rarely met. In 1928, along the three main streets of the Knarrberg estate in Dessau-Ziebigk, working-class families occupied four out of thirty-five houses on one street, three out of eighty-two houses on the second, and six out of fifty-one on the third. The other houses were occupied by salaried clerks (*Angestellte*) and the self-employed. Hausdörfer, "Dessau-Ziebigk," 113.

77 The estate is differently named in various sources. I adopted the name "Friedrichshöhe estate" used in Bednarz et al., *Sachsen Anhalt II;* see note 64 above.

78 Paul and Vierich, "Die Lage der Bauten Fischers," 108.

79 Wolfgang Paul, "Leopold Fischers Bauten und Siedlungen im ehemaligen Anhalt," in Bauhaus Dessau e.V., *Leopold Fischer,* 26.

80 Haney, *When Modern Was Green,* 131. Kathrin Kleibl, Heinrich-Vogeler-Museum, Barkenhoff-Stiftung Worpswede, Germany, kindly supplied information on Andrea Migge (née Stindt, 1879–1956).

81 For the names, locations, and dates of the houses, I wish to thank Dr. Irene Below. For individual references to these houses, see Dr. Below's writings on Fischer, listed in this volume's bibliography.

82 On Liebig, see Vierich, *Die Villa Liebig,* 29; on Theis, see Below, "Das Leben von Leopold Fischer," 21; on Steinborn and Tittel, see David Riedel, *Dunkle Jahre, voller Farben: Der Künstler Peter August Böckstiegel 1933–1945,* exh. cat. (Werther: Museum Peter August Böckstiegel, 2020), 73; on Vogt, see *Berliner Handels-Register* 67 (Berlin: Ullstein, 1931), 998; and on Mutzenbecher, see *Amtliches Fernsprechbuch für Berlin und Umgegend April 1936* (Berlin: Reichspostdirektion, 1936), 807.

83 Below, "Das Leben von Leopold Fischer," 20.

84 Katja Wedhorn, *Licht und Schatten: Neue Gestaltungsweisen der Fotografie von 1920 bis 1960 und der Beitrag Edmund Kestings* (Marburg: Tectum, 2021), 153n480.

85 Today the Hochschule für bildende Künste Dresden.

86 David Riedel, *Peter August Böckstiegel: The Expression of His Roots* (Munich: Klinkhardt & Biermann, 2021), 60.

87 On Wigman, see, for example, Susan A. Manning, *Ecstasy and the Demon: Feminism and Nationalism in the Dances of Mary Wigman* (Berkeley: University of California Press, 1993).

88 Riedel, *Dunkle Jahre, voller Farben,* 73–80.

89 *Berliner Adressbuch 1936,* vol. 1 (Berlin: August Scherl Deutsche Adressbuch-Gesellschaft, n.d. [1936]), 2834.

90 *Berliner Handels-Register,* vol. 67 (Berlin: Ullstein Verlag, 1931), 998; and, for example, *Berliner Adreßbuch 1932,* vol. 3 (Berlin: August Scherl Deutsche Adressbuch-Gesellschaft, n.d. [1932]), 1322. Today, house number 56a does not exist and it is unclear to which part of Mendelsohn's buildings the house number referred to. From 1936 onward, city and telephone directories list both women and the cosmetic company at Fintelmannstraße 5; an entry for the school of gymnastics can no longer be found. See *Amtliches Fernsprechbuch für Berlin und Umgegend April 1936* (Berlin: Reichspostdirektion, 1936), 751 (s.v. Meeths), 1126 (s.v. Smell), and 1239 (s.v. Klara Vogt). This directory was based on listings from 6 January 1936, suggesting that the Vogt house was built during 1935.

91 Paul and Vierich, "Die Lage der Bauten Fischers," 111.

92 Peter August Böckstiegel to Hanna Böckstiegel, 13 September 1932, Legat der Peter-August-Böckstiegel-Stiftung, Kreisarchiv Gütersloh, Germany, C 01/01-91-17.

93 How much Fischer's design for the two Berlin houses, built in 1935, was also a reaction to the Nazi dictatorship and its reactionary cultural politics would require an analysis of the buildings beyond the scope of this study.

94 It is not clear whether the stair leading to the uppermost level was included when the house was constructed. Bauakte (building file) "Culemann Straße 8," Baueingabeplan Bl. 1 (sheet 1), Bauamt Stadt Bielefeld.

95 Heinrich Kulka, ed., *Adolf Loos: Das Werk des Architekten* (1931; Vienna: Löcker, 1979), 37, quoted in translation from Christopher Long, *The New Space: Movement and Experience in Viennese Modern Architecture* (New Haven: Yale University Press, 2016), 50.

96 David Gropp, "Das Haus des Dr. Steinborn in Werther und sein Architekt Leopold Fischer," *Denkmalpflege in Westfalen-Lippe,* no. 2 (2021): 45.

97 Adolf Loos, "Die Abschaffung der Möbel" [1924], in Adolf Loos, *Trotzdem 1900–1930,* vol. 2 of *Sämtliche Schriften in zwei Bänden,* ed. F. Glück (Vienna: Herold, 1962), 389.

98 Adolf Loos, "Architektur" [1910], in Loos, *Trotzdem 1900–1930,* 312, 313.

99 Peter August Böckstiegel to Hanna Böckstiegel, 28 September 1936, Legat der Peter-August-Böckstiegel-Stiftung, Kreisarchiv Gütersloh, Germany, C 01/01-95-09. Possibly the letter was postmarked a few days after it had been written, as Fischer had departed from Rotterdam on Saturday, 26 September 1936, seen above in note 4.

100 Peter August Böckstiegel to Hanna Böckstiegel, 19 September 1936, Legat der Peter-August-Böckstiegel-Stiftung, Kreisarchiv Gütersloh, Germany, C 01/01-95-06.

101 For a summary of the laws against Jews and other "non-Aryans," see, for example, "'Laws of Persecution—*Reichsgesetzblatt*' Law Summaries—English Translations," Holocaust Claims Processing Office, Department of Financial Services, New York State, https://www.dfs.ny.gov/consumers/holocaust_claims/laws_of_persecution.

102 All information on the journey and arrival of Fischer taken from "Leopold Fischer," line 18, list 2, SS *Volendam* passengers sailing from Rotterdam, 26 September 1936, arriving at Port of New York, NY, 6 October 1936, in *List or Manifest of Alien Passengers for the United States Immigration Officer at Port of Arrival,* 155 (The National Archives in Washington, DC; Washington, DC, USA; Passenger and Crew Lists of Vessels Arriving at New York, New York, 1897–1957; Microfilm Serial or NAID: T715; RG Title: Records of the Immigration and Naturalization Service, 1787-2004; RG: 85; ancestry.com, subscription required), and "Afvaart 'SS Volendam' op 26-09-1936 vanaf haven Rotterdam," Stadsarchief Rotterdam, passenger registers, Archieven van de Holland Amerika Lijn (HAL), 318-04.1020 Register van passagegelden, lijn Rotterdam-New York: 1936, sep.-dec., met vrachtschepen over 1936, 01-09-1936 t/m 31-12-1936, https://hdl.handle.net/21.12133/DEC00734ED764C188CA5F7FA69D7B007; scroll to scan #56 (NL-RtSA_318-04_1020_00056.jpg), the entry for "Fischer, Mr. L[eopold]" is on the fifth line from the top. See also "Mr. L. Fischer in the Rotterdam, Netherlands, Passenger Lists of the Holland-America Line, 1900–1969, Stadsarchief Rotterdam; Rotterdam, Nederland; Archieven van de Holland Amerika Lijn (HAL): Passage A; URL: https://stadsarchief.rotterdam.nl/zoek-en-ontdek; ancestry.com, subscription required.

103 Alexander Granach, *Du mein liebes Stück Heimat: Briefe an Lotte Lieven aus dem Exil,* ed. Angelika Wittlich and Hilde Recher (Augsburg: Ölbaum, 2008), 201.

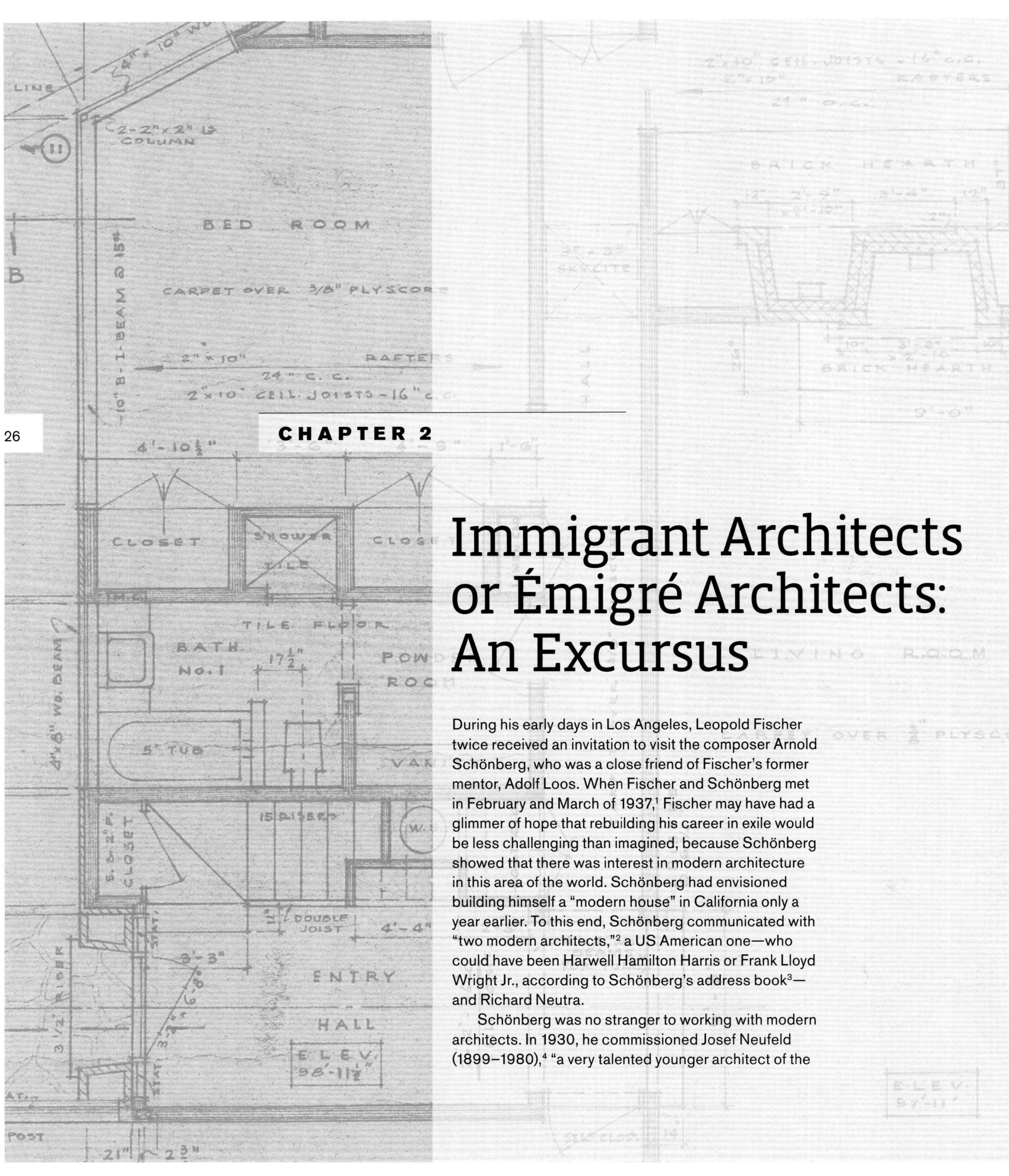

CHAPTER 2

Immigrant Architects or Émigré Architects: An Excursus

During his early days in Los Angeles, Leopold Fischer twice received an invitation to visit the composer Arnold Schönberg, who was a close friend of Fischer's former mentor, Adolf Loos. When Fischer and Schönberg met in February and March of 1937,[1] Fischer may have had a glimmer of hope that rebuilding his career in exile would be less challenging than imagined, because Schönberg showed that there was interest in modern architecture in this area of the world. Schönberg had envisioned building himself a "modern house" in California only a year earlier. To this end, Schönberg communicated with "two modern architects,"[2] a US American one—who could have been Harwell Hamilton Harris or Frank Lloyd Wright Jr., according to Schönberg's address book[3]—and Richard Neutra.

Schönberg was no stranger to working with modern architects. In 1930, he commissioned Josef Neufeld (1899–1980),[4] "a very talented younger architect of the modern movement," to transform into a "little jewel box of the way we live today"[5] an apartment at Nürnberger Platz in Berlin that Schönberg had just occupied. Schönberg was also an exacting potential client. In January 1936, he criticized Neutra for creating "very pretty houses, even if intentionally more doctrinaire than Loos, and not uninfluenced by Bauhaus principles. Nevertheless, he certainly has a Viennese taste and knows what a writer needs." Still, Schönberg also expressed doubts whether Neutra was versed in cladding the interior of rooms in marble (an often-seen feature of Loos's work), indicating the extent to which he envisioned his soon-to-be-built Los Angeles home in Loos-inspired terms.[6]

Eventually, in 1936, Schönberg acquired a Spanish colonial revival–style house.[7] However, if the composer continued harboring dreams about a modern home, Fischer's arrival meant that Los Angeles now had an architect who was closer to Loos in architectural ideas and time than anybody else in California, including Rudolph Schindler and Neutra. Had the composer commissioned a modern home from the recently arrived Fischer, the latter's career in exile might have unfolded differently; indeed, an association with the inventor of modernist twelve-tone music and a prominent Jewish émigré in California would have most likely ensured Fischer a more visible, lasting place in the history of modern architecture in California. But the Schönberg commission was not to be.

This episode circumscribes, in a nutshell, the issues and topics that inform this chapter. The encounters between an internationally well-known composer and an architect little known outside of (and perhaps even within) Dessau, Dresden, Bielefeld, and Berlin in Weimar Germany hint at the importance that was assigned to prominence, inventions, and innovation when émigrés were discussed in contemporary sources. Refugee studies from the late 1930s, for example, claimed that the knowledge and achievements of famous scientists, scholars, and artists were advantageous for the United States; early exile studies after World War II argue in a comparable manner that émigrés constituted a gain for the host country and a loss for the countries of origin.

The hypothetical choice Schönberg had between two foreign-born, modern architects recalls a distinction Erhard Bahr makes between "immigrant modernism" and "exile modernism" when his study *Weimar on the Pacific* turns to modernist architecture in exile in California. Schindler and Neutra represent the earlier version of modernism, which arrived in the state in the 1920s. They were "strictly speaking, immigrants rather than exiles,"[8] and even if still far from the peaks of their fame, both were established modern designers by the late 1930s when Fischer set out to reestablish in Los Angeles his career in exile.

This chapter argues that the continuous focus of California architectural history on the alleged gain—most notably modernist architecture—that German-speaking architects brought to the state in the first half of the twentieth century contributes to Leopold Fischer's invisibility. While California history of architecture tends to emphasize architectural modernism as the common denominator of German-speaking architects who migrated to California during that time, little critical attention is paid to whether someone arrived in California—to paraphrase Bahr—as an *immigrant architect,* which is what I call those who came before the Nazis attained power in 1933, or an *émigré architect,* who, like Fischer, fled the Nazis thereafter. Whether an architect arrived before or after that fateful year deeply impacted that person's career and the subsequent resonances his or her oeuvre found in architectural history.

Émigré Architects in the United States

In 1938, the political scientist Harold Fields published *The Refugee in the United States,* a study that discusses refugees who fled political, religious, and other forms of persecution in Europe and other countries between the end of World War I and 1937.[9] Concerning the twenty-three thousand German immigrants who had arrived in the United States between 1933 and 1937, Fields estimates that thirteen thousand were persecuted refugees.[10] Even when looking at this number as just a statistical quantity, Fields nevertheless emphasizes that the refugees were mainly from the wealthy upper-middle and middle classes and the liberal professions and were well educated at either the Gymnasium (the highest form of schooling in Germany) or a university.[11] A later chapter, "Recent German Refugees," was about those who fled the Nazis. It ends with Fields identifying "famous" émigrés to underline explicitly the gain these refugees would bring to the country. The physicist Albert Einstein, the novelist Thomas Mann, and Hermann Brüning, a former chancellor of the Weimar Republic, formed the apex of German émigrés,[12] followed by "outstanding names"[13] from the arts, sciences, social sciences, and humanities; in short, they were "savants of Germany" who "have been transferred to the United States to make it the richest scholastic country in the world."[14] Schönberg, for example, would be counted in this group. This towering "cultural record" rested on "the achievements of [émigré] manufacturers, middle-class tradesmen and others who have blossomed out in this free atmosphere" of the United States.[15]

Architects appear only once in Fields's study: Walter Gropius, the founder of the Bauhaus art school in Weimar and one of Fischer's employers in Dessau, is named.[16] Yet, a 1947 study of the recent European immigration singles out émigré architects as a positive asset to US American society, claiming they could "perform a useful service in community life," mainly because some states exercised a "broad tolerance of foreign training and experience" when it came to state-specific regulations of the architectural profession.[17] California, however, did not allow émigré architects to bypass the qualifying exam.[18] When the 1947 study identifies individual architects, famous ones feature prominently again, especially Gropius, Ludwig Miës van der Rohe, and Marcel Breuer, all three associated with the Bauhaus; and also Eric Mendelsohn, Martin Wagner, Paul Zucker, and Walter Curt Behrendt. The latter three are today probably best known mainly among experts on Weimar Republic architecture.[19]

• • •

Moving from refugee and émigré studies to the history of architecture in the United States, the triumvirate of Gropius, Miës van der Rohe, and Breuer—and with them, the Bauhaus—cast a deep shadow over the discipline for decades. In the 1960s, William H. Jordy claimed that the trio "most profoundly influenced American developments" because its "impact on American culture may well... have been the most direct legacy of the Bauhaus."[20] In addition to bringing the architects' versions of modernist architecture with them, teaching positions at US American universities also allowed the three to resume their careers successfully.[21] Thus began their assimilation into a new professional life, including studying, for example, "indigenous balloon framing in wood" and "American methods of carpentry and metal framing."[22] All of this amounted to a lasting foundation on which "to put up building after building, to develop an esthetic with the opportunity to work on variations and to explore possibilities."[23] In short, the exile of Gropius, Miës van der Rohe, and Breuer evolved from a state of survival to one of professional success and, ultimately, to a satisfying fulfillment of artistic aspirations that Jordy doubts would have been achievable in Europe and Germany, respectively.

In the later 1990s, scholars of exile and art began to adjust the thrust and details of the established dual focus on the Bauhaus and "famous" émigrés in the United States. The catalog accompanying the exhibition *Exiles + Émigrés: The Flight of European Artists from Hitler* at the Los Angeles County Museum of Art in 1997 no longer viewed the exile of the Bauhaus as equaling a gain for the United States and a corresponding loss for Germany. Instead, it noted that the enforced emigration of *some* Bauhaus members expanded the reach of the school's artistic ideas while other members continued working, even thriving, in Nazi Germany.[24]

This shifting focus on the country of origin was mirrored by a new focus on the country of arrival. Now, the American works of Gropius, Miës van der Rohe, and Breuer are characterized as part of a postwar, newly arising US internationalism in architecture instead of a mere reissue of pre-exile works or even a mere continuation of German architectural modernism in a different country on a different continent.[25]

Eventually, two long-cherished arguments in studies of exile and émigrés from German National Socialism gave way to far more complex considerations of exile as a process of acculturation rather than an equation of gain and loss as the sole variables. This approach finally opened windows through which émigré architects like Leopold Fischer could be seen again. First—and substituting in the following passage the terms in brackets—exile studies stopped asking primarily "whether émigrés continued their previous research [or architectural designs] in their new locations, and to mourn the breakup of scientific schools [or art schools such as the Bauhaus]."[26] In turn, second, the assumption was questioned, if not discarded, that disciplines such as architecture and culture, in general, are static entities "[a]s though the émigrés brought with them finished bits of knowledge, which they then inserted like building-stones into already established cultural constructs elsewhere."[27] Instead of figuring out how a brick culled from an émigré architect's luggage might fit neatly into an edifice in a distant country, "processes and socio-cultural and biographical circumstances"[28] that shaped the émigré's life and work, pre-exile and postexile, moved into the center of interest. These approaches resulted in highly differentiated accounts of émigré architects, as the exhibition *Visionäre & Vertriebene: Österreichische Spuren in der modernen amerikanischen Architektur,* shown in Vienna in 1995, demonstrated in an exemplary manner.[29]

Taking a long view of the architectural relationship of Austria-Hungary (and Austria after 1918) with the United States, which included mutual architectural exchanges and the emigration of Austrian architects well before the German occupation of the country from 1938, the *Visionäre & Vertriebene* project researched numerous émigré architects, including one female designer. The exhibition catalog discusses architects such as Victor Gruen and Paul Theodore Frankl, today well-known names in the history of early and midcentury modern architecture in the United States and California, who are juxtaposed with relatively obscure designers including, for example, Arthur Grünberger (1882–1935), who practiced in San Francisco already from 1923 onward,[30] and Liane (Juliana) Zimbler (1892–1987), an émigré who reached Los Angeles in 1938.[31] These émigré architects are placed into an architectural-historical context that acknowledges the modern architectural scene of the 1920s and 1930s as broad and pluralistic. That context allows, for example, Viennese ideas about comfy bourgeois interiors to exist alongside reductionist, functionalist interiors of, say, Hannes Meyer and the Bauhaus. Then, argues the exhibition catalog, no single version of modern architecture defined modernism in architecture, and today, architectural historians should refrain from retrospectively elevating any one version of architectural modernism to *the* measuring gauge against which all contemporary modern architecture is judged.[32] Similarly, the catalog abstains from trying to define a *singular* gain Austrian émigré architects brought to the United States, as such a step would leave in the shadows of architectural history those émigré architects who pursued other versions of modern architecture.

Leopold Fischer was not included in *Visionäre & Vertriebene,* perhaps an indication of how much his long pre-exile career in Germany contributed to making him invisible in Austria, his country of birth. Regardless, the emphasis the Vienna project placed on contextualizing émigré architects' lives and careers in exile across space and time inspired the present study of Leopold Fischer.

German-Speaking Immigrant Architects and Émigré Architects in California

The historian Harold Kirker documented 117 architects who lived and worked in California during the nineteenth century; twelve were from Germany.[33] The immigration of German and German-speaking architects continued during the next century, as table 2.1 illustrates concerning the period from 1914 to approximately 1948. The selection of immigrant architects and émigré architects was compiled from existing literature and my research; it is neither comprehensive nor representative of all German-speaking architects coming to California during the years flanking National Socialism in Germany and World War II. Still, it allows one to establish patterns concerning the careers of these architects and designers in California. It also allows one to identify a subset of émigré architects as a peer group of Leopold Fischer.

Table 2.1. Selected German-speaking immigrant and émigré architects and designers arriving in California between 1914 and 1948

Arrival in California	Who	Notes
[US: 1914] CA: 1934	Paul Theodore (Theodor) Frankl (1886–1958), Austrian, Jewish father, baptized Catholic	
[US: 1914] CA: late in 1920[1]	Rudolph Michael Schindler (1887–1953), Austrian	Began working for Frank Lloyd Wright in 1917[2]
1914, AUGUST: WORLD WAR I BEGINS		
1914	Kem (Karl Emanuel Martin) Weber (1889–1963),[3] German	On work assignment in San Francisco and stayed there when World War I started
1918, NOVEMBER: WORLD WAR I ENDS		
1922	Kurt Georg Julius Meyer-Radon (1885–1962), German	Brother of Hans Meyer-Radon
	Hans Willy Max Meyer-Radon (1891–1977), German	Draftsman
	Jock (Jacob) Detlef Peters (1889–1934), German	
	Karl Wilhelm Alfred Weidler (1886–1966),[4] German	Architect–artist
1923	Arthur Grünberger (1882–1935),[5] Austrian, Jewish	
[US: 1923] CA: late 1925–early 1926	Richard Josef Neutra (1892–1970), Austrian, Jewish	Immigrated from Germany
1923–24	Julius Ralph Davidson (1889–1977), German, Jewish	
1924	Maria Kipp (1900–1988), German	Textile designer and engineer
1933, JANUARY: HITLER AND THE NAZI REGIME ACCEDE TO POWER IN GERMANY		
1936	Leopold Fischer (1901–75), Austrian, Jewish	Emigrated from Germany
	Paul László (1900–1993), Hungarian, Jewish	Emigrated from Germany
	Rolf Bruno Sklarek (1906–84), German, Jewish	Bauhaus graduate (1931), emigrated from Berlin to Spain in 1933, and via London to California
1937	Herbert Cordier (né Kugelmann, 1915–2002),[6] German, Jewish	Interior designer

The table is ordered by year and alphabetically; spouses and their occupations are omitted.

1 Esther McCoy, *Vienna to Los Angeles: Two Journeys* (Santa Monica: Arts & Architecture Press, 1979), 34.
2 David Gebhard, *Schindler* (San Francisco: William Stout, 1997), 15, 25.
3 Edan Milton Hughes, *Artists in California, 1786–1940* (San Francisco: Hughes, 1989), 594.
4 Hughes, *Artists in California*, 549.
5 "Biographien," in *Visionäre & Vertriebene: Österreichische Spuren in der modernen amerikanischen Architektur*, ed. Matthias Boeckl (Berlin: Ernst & Sohn, 1995), 333.
6 For Herbert Cordier, see "Herbert Kugelmann," *Biografisches Gedenkbuch der Bad Kissinger Juden während der NS Zeit*, n.d., https://www.biografisches-gedenbuch-bk.de/en/database/index.html (search "Database": Kugelmann, Herbert).

Based on their motivation for leaving Central Europe and the time of their arrival, German-speaking architects, designers, and engineers migrating to California and the United States during the early decades of the twentieth century can be divided into three larger groups. For the first group, those who emigrated before World War I, the United States often symbolized architectural modernity, which drew Paul T. Frankl to the United States.[34] The wish to work for Frank Lloyd Wright is what brought Schindler to the United States in March of 1914, though he only began working for Wright in 1917. And Kem Weber decided to stay when World War I broke out in August 1914, while he was temporarily working in San Francisco on a project of the Berlin architect Bruno Paul. The second group is made up of architects who left for California during the economic and societal collapse in Germany and Austria after World War I. For them, economic immigration to the United States was a significant motivation to uproot lives and careers that were often already established in Europe. These two groups of immigrant architects tended to succeed in their profession (to different degrees, of course) despite all the difficulties they may have encountered, at least initially, in the United States.

Table 2.1. Continued

Arrival in California	Who	Notes
1938, MARCH: NAZI GERMANY OCCUPIES AUSTRIA		
1938	Fritz Block (1889–1955), German, Jewish	Partner at Block & Hochfeld, Hamburg
	Ernst Hochfeld (1890–1985), German, Jewish	Partner at Block & Hochfeld, Hamburg
	Oskar Gerson (1886–1966), German, Jewish	Emigrated via UK
	Liane Zimbler (1892–1987),[9] Austrian, Jewish	Architect and interior designer, emigrated via London to US
[US: 1938] CA: 1940	Victor Gruen (né Grünbaum) (1903–80),[7] Austrian, Jewish	Emigrated via Switzerland, France, UK to California
	Ernest Wertheim (1919–2020),[8] German, Jewish	Landscape architect
1939	Ulrich Hermann Plaut (1910–71),[10] German, born Japan, Jewish	Emigrated from Japan via Shanghai to California
	William (Wilhelm) Wolf (1898–1984),[11] Austrian, Jewish	Civil engineer, emigrated to California via Palestine and UK
[US: 1940] CA: ca. 1941	Rudolf Baumfeld (1903–85),[12] Austrian, Jewish, friend of Victor Gruen	Partner of Victor Gruen, in Vienna emigrated via Czech Republic in 1933 and Italy in 1940
1940	Fredric (Friedrich) Rachmiel Frankel (Fränkel) (1909–98),[13] Austrian, Jewish	Imprisoned in Dachau and Buchenwald concentration camps in 1938, escaped to London in 1939
1945, MAY: SURRENDER OF NAZI GERMANY ENDS WORLD WAR II IN EUROPE		
1947	Frederick (Fritz) Reichl (1890–1959),[14] Austrian, Jewish	Exile in Turkey in 1939
1948	Wolf Dieter Ascher (born 1928),[15] German, Jewish	Town planner, exile in Shanghai in 1938, town planner for city of Simi Valley, California, in 1972

7 "Biographien," in Boeckl, *Visionäre & Vertriebene,* 332.
8 Ernest Wertheim with Linda Hamilton, *Chasing Spring* (n.p.: Lulu, 2014), chap. 5.
9 "Biographien," in Boeckl, *Visionäre & Vertriebene,* 349.
10 R. Plaut, son of U. Plaut, email correspondence with the author, 29 July 2021; also Ulrich Plaut Papers, Collection Volker M. Welter.
11 Max Hirschfeld, "Ein Wiener Architekt bei Kaiser," *Der Aufbau–Reconstruction* 9, no. 40 (18 October 1943), Die Westküste section, no. 3, 20, p. 18.
12 "Biographien," in Boeckl, *Visionäre & Vertriebene,* 328.
13 D. Frankel, son of F. Frankel, personal conversation with the author, 17 August 2021.
14 "Biographien," in Boeckl, *Visionäre & Vertriebene,* 340.
15 Wolf Dieter Ascher, *My Three Stories: Shanghai U.S. Air Force City Planner* ([2000]; n.p.: n.p. [2006?]).

The third group comprises émigré architects who were forced to flee when Adolf Hitler and German National Socialism rose to power in early 1933. For them, "departure from Germany [and from Austria from 1938 onward] was a wholly involuntary act" even if "*ex ante* and from the individual's point of view…the decision to emigrate and particularly its timing had large voluntary elements," which, however, diminished rapidly with the Nazi consolidation of power and discriminatory policies.[35] The timing of departure determined one's chances to flee—for example, the architect Fredric Rachmiel Frankel and his wife barely managed to escape from Germany as late as 1939.[36] When it came to reestablishing a career in architecture and cognate designing professions, the age upon arrival in California was a most relevant criterion, as Fields had already pointed to when discussing how refugees between twenty-five and thirty-five or even forty years old encountered greater difficulties in establishing themselves in exile than those under twenty-five years.[37] Émigré architects in their late forties and early fifties had the most challenging time renewing their architectural careers, not to mention fulfilling any dreams of matching their pre-exile successes. Oskar Gerson moved from

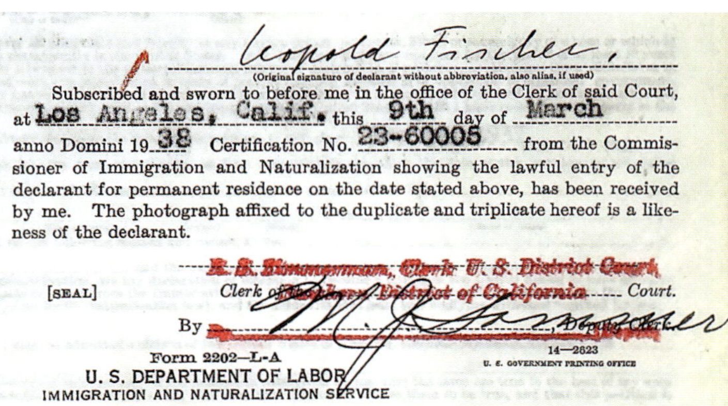

Leopold Fischer

(Original signature of declarant without abbreviation, also alias, if used)

Subscribed and sworn to before me in the office of the Clerk of said Court, at Los Angeles, Calif. this 9th day of March anno Domini 1938 Certification No. 23-60005 from the Commissioner of Immigration and Naturalization showing the lawful entry of the declarant for permanent residence on the date stated above, has been received by me. The photograph affixed to the duplicate and triplicate hereof is a likeness of the declarant.

R. S. Zimmerman, Clerk U. S. District Court,

[SEAL] Clerk of the Southern District of California Court.

By ______ Deputy Clerk.

Form 2202—L—A 14—2823 U. S. GOVERNMENT PRINTING OFFICE

U. S. DEPARTMENT OF LABOR
IMMIGRATION AND NATURALIZATION SERVICE

2.1. Passport-sized photograph and signature of Leopold Fischer from 1938, when he filed for his declaration of intent for citizenship of the United States,

No 123759

Rolf Sklarek

X Rolf Sklarek.

(Original signature of declarant without abbreviation, also alias, if used)

Subscribed and sworn to before me in the form of oath shown above in the office of the Clerk of said Court, at Los Angeles, Cal., this 29 day of June, anno Domini, 1938. Certification 23-62428 from the Commissioner of Immigration and Naturalization showing the lawful entry of the declarant for permanent residence on the date stated above, has been received by me. The photograph affixed to the duplicate and triplicate hereof is a likeness of the declarant.

R. S. Zimmerman, Clerk U. S. District Court,

[SEAL] Clerk of the Southern District of California Court.

By ______ Deputy Clerk.

Form 2202—L—A 14—2823 U. S. GOVERNMENT PRINTING OFFICE

U. S. DEPARTMENT OF LABOR
IMMIGRATION AND NATURALIZATION SERVICE

2.2. Passport-sized photograph and signature of Rolf Sklarek from 1938, when he filed for his declaration of intent for citizenship of the United States.

designing large-scale commercial and business premises in Hamburg to occasional domestic designs in the San Francisco Bay area.[38] Fritz Block turned to architectural photography in the 1940s, and Ernst Hochfeld worked as a set designer for movie studios before he opened a small, private architectural office.[39]

Émigré architects in their thirties and early forties, among them Leopold Fischer (fig. 2.1), set themselves up again as practicing architects and designers, often initially accepting whatever architectural work, projects, and commissions were available but eventually specializing in particular areas of architecture. Professionally, the most successful in this age cohort were Victor Gruen, an Austrian-Jewish architect, and Paul László, a Hungarian-Jewish designer and architect.[40] More interesting in the context of Leopold Fischer, however, are Rolf Sklarek, Ulrich Plaut, and Fredric Frankel, because once in Los Angeles, the professional careers and private lives of these three émigré architects repeatedly overlapped and intertwined with Fischer's.

Rolf Sklarek (1906–84) was born in Berlin (fig. 2.2). From 1926 to 1929, he studied architecture at the Bauhaus in Dessau and worked in Hannes Meyer's office. He graduated in 1931 after interning for several years with architects, among them the Luckhardt brothers and Hugo Häring, prominent modernist architects of the time. Sklarek, who was Jewish, fled Germany in 1933 after a brief arrest by the Gestapo. Until 1935, he worked in Spain, and from 1936 onward, he lived in exile in California.[41] After initially working for the architect John M. Cooper, Sklarek set up his own firm in 1941. Between 1936 and the early to mid-1950s, when he joined the office of Victor Gruen, Sklarek designed at least seven detached houses and some nondomestic projects in the Los Angeles area.

Ulrich Plaut (1910–71), a German Jew, was born in Japan and educated in Munich (fig. 2.3). Upon gradu-

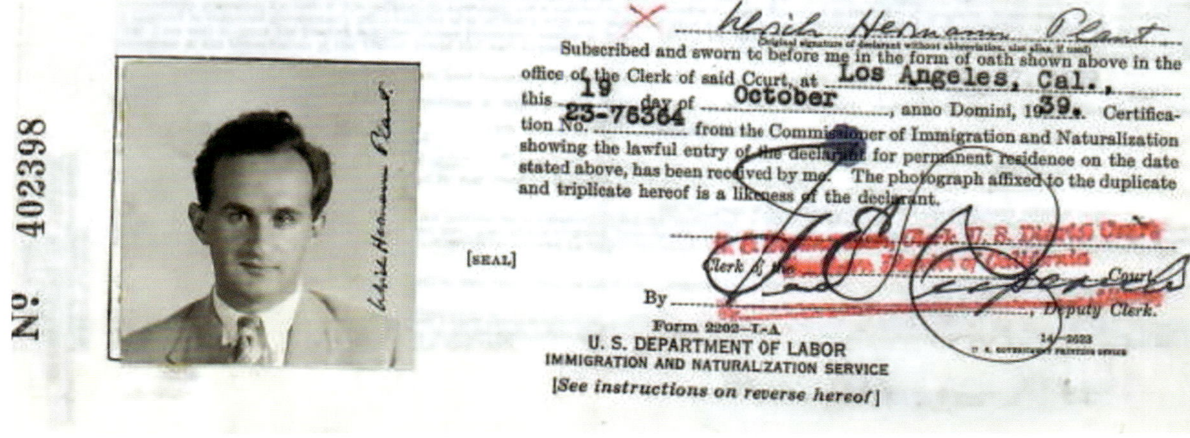

Ulrich Hermann Plaut

(Original signature of declarant without abbreviation, also alias, if used)

Subscribed and sworn to before me in the form of oath shown above in the office of the Clerk of said Court, at Los Angeles, Cal., this 19 day of October, anno Domini, 1939. Certification No. 23-75364 from the Commissioner of Immigration and Naturalization showing the lawful entry of the declarant for permanent residence on the date stated above, has been received by me. The photograph affixed to the duplicate and triplicate hereof is a likeness of the declarant.

[SEAL]

Clerk of the Court.

By, Deputy Clerk.

Form 2202—L-A

U. S. DEPARTMENT OF LABOR

IMMIGRATION AND NATURALIZATION SERVICE

[See instructions on reverse hereof]

No. 402398

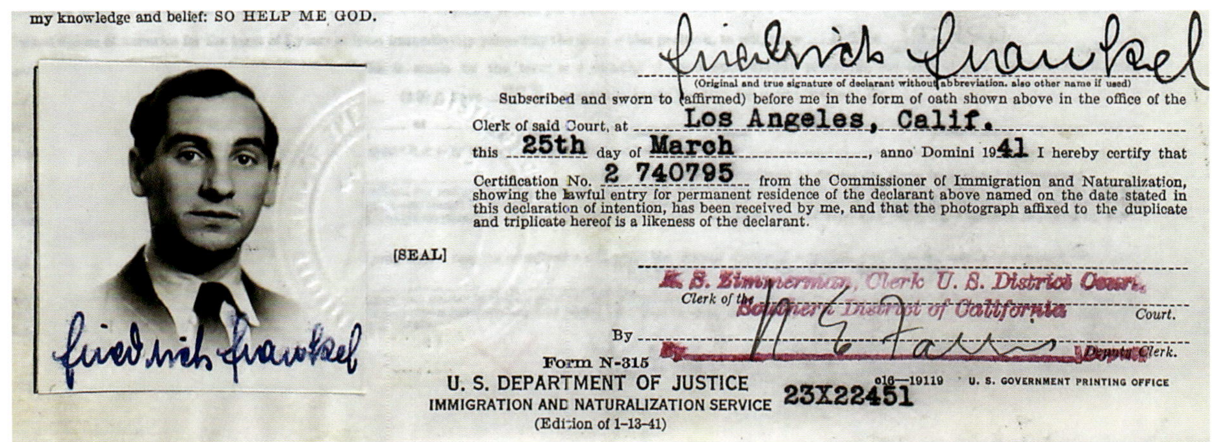

my knowledge and belief: SO HELP ME GOD.

Friedrich Frankel

(Original and true signature of declarant without abbreviation, also other name if used)

Subscribed and sworn to (affirmed) before me in the form of oath shown above in the office of the Clerk of said Court, at Los Angeles, Calif. this 25th day of March, anno Domini 1941 I hereby certify that Certification No. 2 740795 from the Commissioner of Immigration and Naturalization, showing the lawful entry for permanent residence of the declarant above named on the date stated in this declaration of intention, has been received by me, and that the photograph affixed to the duplicate and triplicate hereof is a likeness of the declarant.

[SEAL]

R. S. Zimmerman, Clerk U. S. District Court, Clerk of the Southern District of California Court.

By, Deputy Clerk.

Form N-315

U. S. DEPARTMENT OF JUSTICE

IMMIGRATION AND NATURALIZATION SERVICE

(Edition of 1-13-41)

16—19119 U. S. GOVERNMENT PRINTING OFFICE

23X22451

2.3. Passport-sized photograph and signature of Ulrich Plaut from 1939, when he filed for his declaration of intent for citizenship of the United States.

2.4. Passport-sized photograph and signature of Fredric (Friedrich) Frankel from 1941, when he filed for his declaration of intent for citizenship of the United States.

ating in architecture from the Technische Hochschule Berlin-Charlottenburg in 1934, Plaut immediately went into exile in Shanghai, China. By 1937, he had set up an office in Kobe, Japan. In 1939, Plaut emigrated to California, where he worked until 1942 for the architect Marcus P. Miller, until 1945 as a senior draftsman for a local contractor, and until 1946 for Sklarek. (Plaut and Sklarek had met around 1939.) In 1946, Plaut opened an office in Los Angeles that specialized mainly in designs for commercial and business premises.[42]

Fredric Frankel (1909–98) was born in Vienna, where he also went to school and studied architecture (fig. 2.4).[43] He graduated with a PhD in 1935. In June 1938, Frankel was arrested and imprisoned, initially in the Dachau concentration camp and, from September 1938, in the Buchenwald concentration camp.[44] He managed to flee to London in 1939, where he was briefly associated with the modernist firm Tecton.[45] Early in 1940, Frankel emigrated to New York, and he relocated to California in late 1940, where he met Plaut and was employed for a few months by Neutra. Subsequently, Frankel worked for various Los Angeles firms until in 1945 he entered the office of Marcus P. Miller and took it over in 1949, continuing the firm's focus on shops, shopping centers, and comparable commercial projects.

Sklarek, Plaut, and Frankel form the core of a peer group of émigré architects that also includes Fischer and, at the group's margin, the German-Jewish émigré interior designer Herbert Cordier (né Kugelmann), a onetime Fischer collaborator. Members of this group were born within (or very close to) the first decade of the twentieth century, except for Cordier, who was born in 1915. They arrived in California between 1936 and 1940 and settled in the Los Angeles region, where they only had a few short years to rebuild their careers in exile before the United States entered World War II. Eventually, all returned to careers as independent architects and designers, though for varying lengths of time and with different levels of professional success.

California Architectural History and German-Speaking Architects

Turning to the resonances German-speaking architects arriving in early twentieth-century California found in architectural history, it is clear that immigrant architects are much more present than émigré architects like Leopold Fischer and his peers. Among the latter, Victor Gruen is a notable exception, given that various monographs have been written about him; and the fact that Paul László is rather well known at least in California and among aficionados of modern design is somewhat surprising, as he has not yet been the subject of a monograph.[46] Regardless, the rubrics of immigrant architects and émigré architects are again critical because they intertwine with the gain-loss model that dominated early exile studies and its focus on fame, prominence, and inventions.

Even if exile studies have long turned away from the gain-loss discourse, a version of it continues to thrive in California architectural history. It is, however, a one-sided version of the gain-loss model, as it solely ponders California's gain of architectural modernism while reducing the countries the migrating architects had fled to mere nursing grounds for modernist architectural design skills that came to flourish only in California. The beginnings of Schindler's and Neutra's careers in the state illustrate this narrative well. Both architects erected early on in their residency groundbreaking modernist buildings, the former the Schindler-Chace house (Hollywood, now West Hollywood, 1921–22), and the latter the Lovell Health house (Los Angeles, 1927–29), each a dwelling that may exemplify the transfer of Central European architectural modernism to California. However, in Europe, neither architect had built or designed anything remotely resembling these California houses. What they and other German-speaking immigrant architects "brought" to California was an understanding of modernist architecture as *innovation,* as *inventing* new forms of architecture responding to a natural environment and climate ostensibly favorable to humans living in a then still thinly settled territory that, allegedly, offered little architectural tradition worth considering.

Thus, Schindler, for example, continuously reinvented the architectural forms and shapes of domestic architecture in California.[47] And for Neutra—and many architectural historians after him—California represented the near-perfect tabula rasa, the untouched ground on which modernist architects could build the perfectly designed environment for the perfect society of perfected human beings; after all, another of Neutra's earliest projects in California was "Rush City Reformed" (1929–30), the utopian reorganization of Los Angeles as a rationally ordered rather than haphazardly grown metropolis.[48]

Numerous publications on Neutra and Schindler and also on such immigrant architects and designers as, in alphabetical order, Julius R. Davidson, Paul T. Frankl, Maria Kipp, Jock Peters, and Kem Weber claim in one way or another that these individuals introduced modernism in architecture to California.[49] It suffices to look at one such claim—the avant-garde burden that Jock Peters carried once in California:

> Peters's broader mission of promoting modernism in America faced formidable challenges.... [T]he groundwork for modern architecture and design in Los Angeles had barely been put down.... Only a few modernists were then working in the city.[50]

German architectural history makes comparable claims also for the California oeuvre of selected émigré architects, most notably those with significant pre-exile careers as modern architects such as Block, Hochfeld, Gerson, and László.[51]

Irrespective of how individual architects may have thought about the possible missions of their new professional lives, an architectural history that focuses primarily on architectural modernism by innovation and invention keeps invisible those German-speaking émigré architects like Fischer who, in the early years of their time in California, aimed at finding a place in the architectural scene of metropolitan Los Angeles not by contrasting with the contemporary architecture but by designing modern buildings concurring with and adjusting to it.

The emphasis on what California architecture "gained" is also unsatisfactory from a historiographical point of view. Once upon a time, a heroic avant-garde of modernist architects may have struggled to realize its designs, but modernism in architecture progressed and changed as time went on. This historicization of architectural modernism (which began immediately with the inception of the new architecture), as well as self-criticism by modernist architects of their earliest modernist designs, ensured that during the 1930s, for example, both modernist and modern, contemporary architecture in Germany became more diverse and less "radical" than it had been in the years following World War I.[52] Finding possible traces and echoes of such changes in the California works of the younger generation of, especially, German-speaking émigré architects requires analyzing those architects' designs on their own terms and in their specific contemporary contexts.

And, as Lilian Pfaff points out, "the well-known history" that immigrant architects "brought modern ideas with them" to California ignores "local architects such as Irving Gill, who designed in a pre-modern style that came out of the reduction of Spanish Colonial Style, a totally different origin to that of European Modernism."[53] Prior studies on Gill admitted the architect to the canon of early modernist California architecture primarily through a comparison of his oeuvre with that of Adolf Loos, even arguing that Gill may have known about Loos's works,[54] as if Gill's recognition as a California-grown master architect needed retrospectively the approval of the European master architect who had also taught Schindler and Neutra—and, of course, Fischer.

Modernism in architecture was not only considered California's primary gain but also elevated to the ideal of modern California architecture, around which a hierarchy evolved. Early on, Neutra's architecture set the standard, as illustrated by an episode from the history of Julius R. Davidson's 1941 design for the Thomas Mann house in Pacific Palisades. Once Mann had decided on Davidson, Neutra, who had yearned for the commission, commented, "'Why settle for less—when you can get the best?,'" as if Mann, a connoisseur through and through in literature and life, would have ever considered anything less than perfection. Instead of asking what Davidson had to offer that attracted Mann, scholars have usually explained the choice exclusively in relation to Neutra, even in the literature on Davidson: "Davidson, whose work was always overshadowed by his highly publicized 'friend,' had been the architect that many would-be Neutra clients turned to when rejected by 'the best.'"[55] This Neutra anecdote exemplifies the sway that notions of the "best" brought by modernist immigrant architects to California held over the imagination of architects and clients, a sway that is still exerted today in California architectural history.

In addition, some modern émigré architects are only visible if their names are or can be tied to an acknowledged modernist or otherwise prominent architect. If Ulrich Plaut is known nowadays, it is for his onetime affiliation with Oscar Niemeyer. In 1963, Plaut was the site architect for the Strick house in Santa Monica, Niemeyer's only realized domestic design in the United States.[56] Others, like Leopold Fischer, are barely visible or not visible at all, a fate that Fischer shares with Frankel, Plaut, and Sklarek. The latter, for example, remains virtually unknown despite being the only Bauhaus-trained modern architect who also had a diploma in architecture from the Bauhaus,[57] ever to settle permanently in California, until Herbert Bayer retired to Montecito in the mid-1970s.

In the following chapters, Fischer's life in exile and his California architectural works are contextualized, when appropriate, by drawing on his peer group of fellow émigré architects and on some of their works, as well as on the work of a few older émigré architects like Frederick Reichl (1890–1959) and Liane Zimbler. These comparisons are selective, as researching the exile lives and works of the peer group to the same degree as Fischer's was beyond the scope of this study. My approach foregrounds that émigré architects such as Fischer were "located and locate[d] themselves in multiple contexts, local institutional settings, disciplines, and broader sociocultural groupings."[58] This phrasing comes from Mitchell G. Ash and Alfons Söllner's discussion of how exile studies of émigré scientists, after abandoning the gain-loss discourse, favored contextualizing approaches that overcame a simplistic dualism—for example, "between 'external' and 'internal' factors, or the 'context' and the 'content' of science."[59]

A comparable dualism continues to exist in California architectural history. Early histories of modern architecture in California "were invariably framed around the contributions... of in particular the two Austrian luminaries Rudolf Schindler and Richard Neutra."[60] When other immigrant architects are the subject of scholarly research, Neutra's position shifts from being the focus of inquiry to that of a measuring gauge against which to compare the architectural oeuvres of other immigrant architects, as was noted above with J. R. Davidson and the design of the Mann house. As I illustrate in the subsequent chapters, the dualism between the "luminaries" and the others becomes a hindrance when assessing the exile works of émigré architects on terms adequate to these architects' circumstances. This study does not argue against the importance of the works of the earlier immigrant architects for California architecture, nor does it attempt to dethrone any architect and elevate in a parallel move an architect like Fischer to a historical position equal to that of Neutra and Schindler. Instead, it aims to broaden and diversify whose works are considered in contemporary architectural history.

Ash and Söllner emphasize that modern science was a global undertaking in which émigré scientists often already participated before and after being forced into exile. Accordingly, "the most interesting loci of change and innovation" triggered by exile and immigration "lie above as well as below the disciplinary level."[61] Modernist architecture was also a global discipline discussed if not practiced across the Atlantic and in other parts of the globe as "the International Style."[62] This was the title of a book that coincided with the *Modern Architecture: International Exhibition* with which the Museum of Modern Art in New York aimed to introduce architectural modernism to the United States in 1932.[63] The big patterns of the emergence of global modernist architecture and how it reached California, including the contributions by immigrant architects such as Schindler and Neutra, are well known. Learning about subsequently arriving émigré architects and assessing their architectural historical relevance requires looking first at individual architects, their works, and their lives as examples of change and innovation—and as examples of memories below the level of an entire discipline. It is time to turn to Leopold Fischer.

Notes

1 Arnold Schönberg, private desk diary, 25 February 1937, Arnold Schönberg Center, Vienna, DC13633, https://archive.schoenberg.at/resources/pages/search.php (search: DC13633); and 25 March 1937, Arnold Schönberg Center, Vienna, DC13642, https://archive.schoenberg.at/resources/pages/search.php (search: DC13642).

2 Arnold Schönberg, 5860 Canyon Cove, Los Angeles, to Heinrich Kulka, 24 January 1936, Arnold Schönberg Center, Vienna, ID 2804, https://repo.schoenberg.at/urn:nbn:at:at-asc-BM035314.

3 Arnold Schönberg, undated entry, address section, The Standard Diary 1936, Arnold Schönberg Center, Vienna, DC13596, https://archive.schoenberg.at/resources/pages/search.php (search: DC13596); and entry "Wright Lloyd," record "W" Address files, Arnold Schönberg Center, Vienna, A3869, https://archive.schoenberg.at/resources/pages/search.php (search: A3869).

4 See the correspondence between Schönberg and Neufeld, July–September 1930, Arnold Schönberg Center, Vienna, https://archive.schoenberg.at/letters/letters.php (search with Name [Sender/Receiver] set to "Neufeld, Joseph"). For Neufeld, see Myra Warhaftig, *Sie legten den Grundstein: Leben und Wirken deutschsprachiger jüdischer Architekten in Palästina 1918–1948* (Tübingen: Ernst Wasmuth, 1996), 94–107.

5 Arnold Schönberg, Berlin, to Dr. Curt Sobernheim, Deutsche Bank, Berlin, 4 July 1930, Arnold Schönberg Center, Vienna, ID 1893, https://viewer.schoenberg.at/mirador.php?&id=1893.

6 Arnold Schönberg, 5860 Canyon Cove, Los Angeles, to Heinrich Kulka, 24 January 1936, Arnold Schönberg Center, Vienna, ID 2804, https://repo.schoenberg.at/urn:nbn:at:at-asc-BM035314.

7 Hans Heinz Stuckenschmidt, *Schoenberg: His Life, World and Work,* trans. Humphrey Searle (New York: Schirmer, 1977), 414.

8 Erhard Bahr, *Weimar on the Pacific: German Exile Culture in Los Angeles and the Crisis of Modernism* (Berkeley: University of California Press, 2007), 148.

9 Harold Fields, *The Refugee in the United States* (New York: Oxford University Press, 1938).

10 Fields, *Refugee,* 32–33. As Fields draws on data up to 1937, before Nazi Germany invaded Austria, no section is dedicated to Austrian émigrés.

11 Fields, *Refugee,* 30–31.

12 Fields, *Refugee,* 157.

13 Fields, *Refugee,* 157.

14 Fields, *Refugee,* 159.

15 Fields, *Refugee,* 159.

16 Fields, *Refugee,* 158. Fields also refers to a female student who studied landscape architecture and came to the United States with the help of a "wealthy and aged aunt," but unfortunately, he does not provide either woman's name. Fields, *Refugee,* 161. For more on Gropius and Fischer, see this volume, chap. 1.

17 Maurice R. Davie, *Refugees in America: Report of the Committee for the Study of Recent Immigration from Europe* (New York: Harper & Brothers, 1947), 366.

18 "Refugees and the Professions," *Harvard Law Review* 53, no. 1 (1939): 121–22.

19 Davie, *Refugees in America,* 366–68.

20 William H. Jordy, "The Aftermath of the Bauhaus in America: Gropius, Miës, and Breuer," in *The Intellectual Migration: Europe and America, 1930–1960,* ed. Donald Fleming and Bernard Bailyn (Cambridge, MA: Belknap, 1969), 485.

21 Jordy, "Aftermath," 502.

22 Jordy, "Aftermath," 511.

23 Jordy, "Aftermath," 526.

24 Peter Hahn, "Bauhaus and Exile: Bauhaus Architects and Designers between the Old World and the New," in *Exiles + Émigrés: The Flight of European Artists from Hitler,* ed. Stephanie Barron with Sabine Eckmann, exh. cat. (Los Angeles: Los Angeles County Museum of Art, 1997), 211–23.

25 Kathleen James, "Changing the Agenda: From German Bauhaus Modernism to U.S. Internationalism; Ludwig Miës van der Rohe, Walter Gropius, Marcel Breuer," in Barron and Eckmann, *Exiles + Émigrés,* 235–52.

26 Mitchell G. Ash and Alfons Söllner, "Introduction: Forced Migration and Scientific Change after 1933," in *Forced Migration and Scientific Change: Émigré German-Speaking*

Scientists and Scholars after 1933, ed. Mitchell G. Ash and Alfons Söllner (Cambridge: Cambridge University Press, 1996), 4.

27 Ash and Söllner, "Introduction," 4.

28 Ash and Söllner, "Introduction," 4.

29 Matthias Boeckl, ed., *Visionäre & Vertriebene: Österreichische Spuren in der modernen amerikanischen Architektur* (Berlin: Ernst & Sohn, 1995).

30 "Biographien," in Boeckl, *Visionäre & Vertriebene,* 333.

31 Sabine Plakolm-Forsthuber, "Ein Leben, zwei Karrieren: Die Architektin Liane Zimbler," in Boeckl, *Visionäre & Vertriebene,* 295–309; and "Biographien," in Boeckl, *Visionäre & Vertriebene,* 349.

32 Matthias Boeckl and Otto Kapfinger, "Visionäre & Vertriebene Österreichische Spuren in der modernen amerikanischen Architektur," in Boeckl, *Visionäre & Vertriebene,* 19–20.

33 "Biographical Sources: California Architects in the Nineteenth Century," in Harold Kirker, *California's Architectural Frontier: Style and Tradition in the Nineteenth Century* (Salt Lake City: Gibbs Smith, 1986). On the German architects, see John Apel (203); Henry Geilfuss (207); Charles W. Kenitzer, Henry Kenitzer, Hermann Kohlberg, and Edmund Kollofrath (all on 209); Julius E. Krafft, John P. Krempel, C. J. Kubach, Jacob Lenzen, and Theodore Lenzen (all on 210); August Wackerbarth (215); and Wildrich Winterhalter (216). There are also listed one Polish architect (Harry Blackman [204]), two from Switzerland (William Mooser [211] and James Seadler [214]), and one from the Courland, Russian Empire (today Latvia) (George E. Voelkel [214]), who may have spoken German as their first language.

34 See, for example, Christopher Long, *Paul T. Frankl and Modern American Design* (New Haven: Yale University Press, 2007).

35 Leo Grebler, *German-Jewish Immigrants to the United States during the Hitler Period: Personal Reminiscences and General Observations,* typescript, September 1976, 4. Grebler (1900–1991), a professor of land economics at the University of California, Los Angeles, was a Jewish émigré economist who fled to California from Berlin. He was a year older than Fischer and moved in circles in Berlin that intersected with the Bauhaus and the Mosse publishing family. The latter had commissioned from Eric Mendelsohn the remodel of their company headquarters, a project on which Richard Neutra worked.

36 Ruth E. Wolman, "Fritz Frankel" (interview), *Crossing Over: An Oral History of Refugees from Hitler's Reich* (New York: Twayne, 1996), 77–92; and Ruth E. Wolman, "Gerty Frankel" (interview), *Crossing Over,* 51–76.

37 Fields, *Refugee,* 123.

38 Wolfgang Voigt, *Hans und Oskar Gerson: Hanseatische Moderne* (Hamburg: Dölling und Galitz, 2000). The list of works records twenty designs for detached homes by Oskar Gerson for the period from 1940 to 1957 (118–25).

39 Roland Jaeger, *Photo-Eye Fritz Block: New Photography, Modern Color Slides* (Zurich: Scheidegger & Spiess, 2018); and Roland Jaeger, *Block & Hochfeld: Die Architekten des Deutschland Hauses; Bauten und Projekte in Hamburg 1921–1938, Exil in Los Angeles* (Berlin: Gebr. Mann, 1996).

40 On Gruen, see, for example, M. Jeffrey Hardwick, *Mall Maker: Victor Gruen, Architect of an American Dream* (Philadelphia: University of Pennsylvania Press, 2004); Alex Wall, *Victor Gruen: From Urban Shop to New City* (Barcelona: Actar-D, 2005); and Joseph Malharek, *Free-Market Socialists: European Émigrés Who Made Capitalist Culture in America, 1918–1968* (Budapest: Central European University Press, 2022). On László, see Paul László, *Designing with Spirit: Paul László Interviewed by Marlene L. Laskey* (Los Angeles: Oral History Program, University of California, Los Angeles, 1986), https://archive.org/details/designingwithspi00lasz; and Monica Penick, "Paul László and the Atomic Future," in *Émigré Cultures in Design and Architecture,* ed. Alison J. Clarke and Elana Shapira (London: Bloomsbury Academic, 2017), 91–104.

41 "Rolf Sklarek (1906–1984)," *AIA Historical Directory of American Architects,* American Institute of Architects, https://aiahistoricaldirectory.atlassian.net/wiki/spaces/AHDAA/pages/39682646/ahd1041430; and correspondence of the author with S. Sklarek, a daughter of Rolf Sklarek, July to August 2022. On Sklarek's time in Spain, see Alexander Sepasgosarian, *Mallorca unterm Hakenkreuz 1933–1945* (Göttingen: MatrixMedia, 2017).

42 "Ulrich Plaut," *AIA Historical Directory of American Architects,* American Institute of Architects, https://aiahistoricaldirectory.atlassian.net/wiki/spaces/AHDAA/pages/35315248/ahd1035364; and correspondence of the author with R. Plaut, a son of Ulrich Plaut, July 2022.

43 Unless referenced otherwise in the paragraph, all information on Frankel is from "Fredric R. Frankel," *AIA Historical Directory of American Architects,* American Institute of Architects, https://aiahistoricaldirectory.atlassian.net/wiki/spaces/AHDAA/pages/36939335/ahd1014555; and correspondence of the author with D. Frankel, a son of Fredric Frankel, August 2021. Historical records suggest that Frankel changed his last name from Fränkel to Frankel when he emigrated to the United Kingdom (see note 45 below). At that time, he kept spelling his first name as Friedrich, which he later anglicized to Fredric.

44 "Friedrich Fränkel, born 5 January 1909, Vienna," lines 11–12, page 1.496/GL, "Lists and Registers of German Concentration Camp Inmates, 1946–1958" (The National Archives at College Park; College Park, Maryland; Microfilm: A3355; ARC: 596972; Title: Lists and Registers of German Concentration Camp Inmates, 1946–1958; Record Group: 242; Record Group Title: National Archives Collection of Foreign Records Seized, 1675–1958; ancestry.com, subscription required).

45 "Friedrich Frankel," WW2 Internees (Aliens) Index Card (The National Archives; Kew, London, England; HO 396 WW2 Internees [Aliens] Index Cards 1939–1947; Reference Number: Ho 396/23; ancestry.com, subscription required).

46 For sources on Gruen and László, see note 40 above.

47 See, for example, Judith Sheine, *R. M. Schindler: Works and Projects* (Barcelona: GG, 1998). On the aspect of innovation as a driving force in California modernist architecture, see also Todd Cronan, *Nothing Permanent: Modern Architecture in California* (Minneapolis: University of Minnesota Press, 2023).

48 Barbara Lamprecht, *Richard Neutra, 1892–1970: Survival through Design* (Cologne: Taschen, 2009), 20–21.

49 For the most recent publications, see Lilian Pfaff, *J. R. Davidson: A European Contribution to California Modernism* (Basel: Birkhäuser, 2019); Long, *Paul T. Frankl;* Christopher Long, *Jock Peters, Architecture and Design: The Varieties of Modernism* (New York: Bauer and Dean, 2021); Christopher Long, *Kem Weber: Designer and Architect* (New Haven: Yale University Press, 2014); Marlyn Musicant, "Maria Kipp: Autobiography of a Hand Weaver," *Studies in the Decorative Arts* 8, no. 1 (2000): 92–107; and Anne Lawrence, "Feminist Design Methodology: Considering the Case of Maria Kipp" (master of arts thesis, University of North Texas, 2003).

50 Long, *Jock Peters,* 93.

51 For sources on Block, Hochfeld, and Gerson, see notes 38 and 39 above. On László, see note 40.

52 Franz Schmitz, *Landhäuser in Berlin 1933–1945* (Berlin: Gebr. Mann, 2007), 107–9.

53 Pfaff, *J. R. Davidson,* 9.

54 Thomas S. Hines, *Irving Gill and the Architecture of Reform: A Study in Modernist Architectural Culture* (New York: Monacelli, 2000), 128–33. On the distribution of published images of Loos's architecture as a basis of knowledge about the architect, see also Max Moya, "Who Has Seen Adolf Loos? Images of Adolf Loos's Architecture in the Media 1899–1927" (PhD diss., Akademie der bildenden Künste Wien, 2021).

55 Lilian Pfaff, "J. R. Davidson," in *Thomas Mann's Los Angeles: Stories from Exile 1940–1952,* ed. Nikolai Blaumer and Benno Herz (Los Angeles: Angel City Press, 2022), 187.

56 Kavior Moon, "Strick House," [Santa Monica, California], in *SAH Archipedia,* ed. Gabrielle Esperdy and Karen Kingsley (Charlottesville: University of Virginia Press, 2012), http://sah-archipedia.org/buildings/CA-01-037-0096.

57 Sklarek's Bauhaus diploma is noted in his membership application for the AIA; see "Rolf Sklarek (1906–1984)," membership file, *AIA Historical Directory of American Architects,* https://aiahistoricaldirectory.atlassian.net/wiki/spaces/AHDAA/pages/39682646/ahd1041430; and also in an obituary published in *LA Architect,* May 1984, 10.

58 Ash and Söllner, "Introduction," 12.

59 Ash and Söllner, "Introduction," 12.

60 Iain Boyd Whyte, "Introduction," in *Building Paradise: Exile Architecture in California; Villa Aurora Architecture Symposium 2003,* ed. Mechthild Borries-Knopp (Berlin: Kreis der Freunde und Förderer der Villa Aurora e.V., 2004), 5.

61 Ash and Söllner, "Introduction," 14.

62 Henry-Russell Hitchcock and Philip Johnson, *The International Style: Architecture since 1922* (New York: W. W. Norton, 1932).

63 An exhibition catalog was published as well: *Modern Architecture: International Exhibition,* exh. cat. (New York: Museum of Modern Art, 1932), https://www.moma.org/documents/moma_catalogue_2044_300061855.pdf.

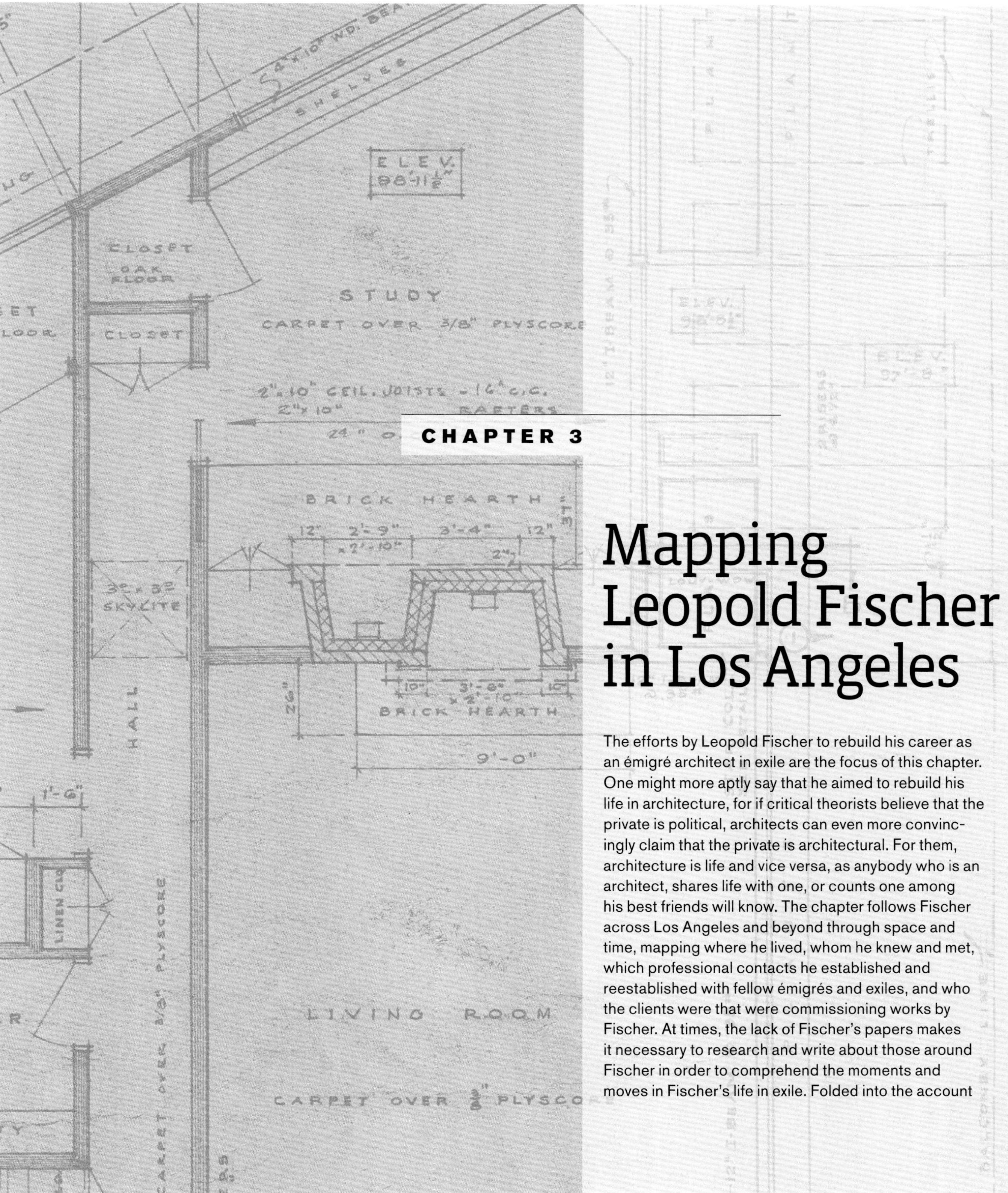

CHAPTER 3

Mapping Leopold Fischer in Los Angeles

The efforts by Leopold Fischer to rebuild his career as an émigré architect in exile are the focus of this chapter. One might more aptly say that he aimed to rebuild his life in architecture, for if critical theorists believe that the private is political, architects can even more convincingly claim that the private is architectural. For them, architecture is life and vice versa, as anybody who is an architect, shares life with one, or counts one among his best friends will know. The chapter follows Fischer across Los Angeles and beyond through space and time, mapping where he lived, whom he knew and met, which professional contacts he established and reestablished with fellow émigrés and exiles, and who the clients were that were commissioning works by Fischer. At times, the lack of Fischer's papers makes it necessary to research and write about those around Fischer in order to comprehend the moments and moves in Fischer's life in exile. Folded into the account

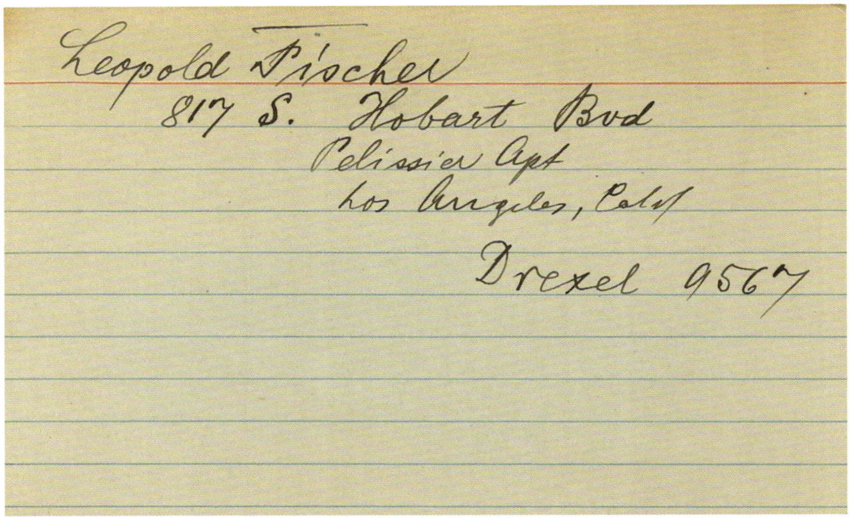

3.1. **Arnold Schönberg (US American, 1874–1951, b. Austria-Hungary).**

Address card with Leopold Fischer's address, ca. 1937.

Vienna, Arnold Schönberg Center.

is an overview of Fischer's architectural oeuvre, at least as far as it has become known to us to date, and of his clients. Moreover, questions are answered about the women who invited Fischer to Los Angeles and thus saved him from becoming a victim of the Holocaust. And the chapter corrects the myth, much repeated in German-language literature on Fischer, that claims the architect sheltered for several years at Taliesin in Wisconsin working with Frank Lloyd Wright.

Leopold Fischer's Homes in Los Angeles and Beyond

Traces of Fischer's early days and weeks in Los Angeles are rare. However, when Fischer was in contact with Arnold Schönberg in early 1937, the composer noted in his address cards that the visitor lived at "817 S. Hobart Bvd, Pelissier [*sic*] Apt, Los Angeles, Calif,"[1] which is the first known address of Fischer in Southern California (fig. 3.1). Compared to his many moves within Europe, especially in Germany, where Fischer often lived temporarily wherever his projects were located, his life settled down once he was in Los Angeles, as documented by the residential and professional addresses compiled in table 3.1.

Geographically, Fischer's private abodes from 1937 to 1940 were to the west of downtown Los Angeles in an area that the *Los Angeles Times* identified as "Wilshire and West" in its contemporary classified pages with rental offerings. In 1937, Fischer rented an apartment at the abovementioned 817 South Hobart Boulevard in the Pellissier apartment building (1926–27), a four-story edifice with forty-six units.[2] Shortly after completion, the mostly studio apartments were advertised for a monthly rent of $55 and up, including

Table 3.1. Residential and professional addresses for Leopold Fischer in the Los Angeles area

When (Earliest and Latest Documented Dates)	**Where**
May 1937–1938	817 South Hobart Boulevard, Pellissier Apartments, Los Angeles
May 1938–1939	672 South Lafayette Park Place, "Granada Buildings," unit R29, Los Angeles
1939–[1940?]	200 South Rampart Boulevard, Los Angeles
April 1940–1950	904 South Lucerne Boulevard, Los Angeles
1952–March 1960	401 Shirley Place, apartment 111, the Gaylida Apartments, Beverly Hills
1955–[1960?]	9507 Santa Monica Boulevard, Beverly Hills (address of Fischer's only known office)
December 1961–1975	125 2nd Street, Seal Beach

Compiled from Historic City and Business & Phone Directories held at the Los Angeles Public Library (https://rescarta.lapl.org/ResCarta-Web/jsp/RcWebBrowse.jsp; "Simple Search," search for Fischer, Leopold); comparable directories, immigration and other records concerning Fischer available via ancestry.com (subscription required); and building permits, blueprints, drawings, and other materials by and about Fischer in archives and privately owned.

3.2. Franklin Harper (US American, 1881–1957).

Granada Buildings (1927), Los Angeles, California, n.d.

Los Angeles, Los Angeles Public Library.

3.3. Architect unknown.

Gaylida Apartments (ca. 1941–42), Beverly Hills, California, 1955.

Los Angeles, USC Libraries.

free parking. Later advertisements stated rents between $35 and $50 per month, with phone services and the building's adjacency to a "complete shopping center" eventually added to the attractions.[3] The brick building was Fischer's first experience with metropolitan apartment buildings in Los Angeles. The edifice was designed by the architect C. W. Powers and followed Powers's usual pattern for this type of accommodation: a facade of moderate architectural interest and decorations (in this case vaguely evoking Spanish colonial architectural details) overlooks the street, and behind this front, a block-like unadorned building stretches into the depth of the lot to accommodate the bulk of the apartments.

The following year, 1938, Fischer's address was 672 South Lafayette Park Place, just south of Lafayette Park.[4] Also called the Granada Buildings (1927), the complex comprises four edifices, each up to four stories tall, grouped around internal open-air courtyards that give access to forty-eight rental units (fig. 3.2).[5] Each unit occupies two stories, combining a shop or studio on the lower level with a "kitchen, living-room, bath and open porch" on the upper level,[6] a spatial arrangement that may have reminded Fischer vaguely of the interior of Le Corbusier's Pavillon de l'Esprit Nouveau (Paris, 1925), where a balcony looks down on the lower level of a double-height living room. Conceptually, the Granada Buildings were the idea of Franklin Harper, a journalist turned architect[7] whose architectural design incorporated "a great variety of playful Spanish Colonial Revival elements—turret, wooden balconies, metal grilles, blue awnings, projecting bays, and round, flat, oval and pointed arches—in scales ranging from tiny to huge."[8]

After a brief interlude at 200 South Rampart Boulevard at an unknown time during 1939, Fischer moved to 904 South Lucerne Boulevard (1922, architect or builder unknown), which was one-half of a single-story duplex building. The move in late 1939 or early 1940 took Fischer farther west into the Wilshire district and a distinctly suburban-appearing neighborhood of single-story houses. The new address signaled a new stability in Fischer's life, as he stayed there for more than a decade.

In 1952, Fischer relocated to the city of Beverly Hills, even farther west, where he rented unit 111 in the Gaylida Apartments at 401 Shirley Place, an elegant neo-Georgian, three-story-tall, twenty-three-unit building (ca. 1941–42, architect unknown),[9] a few streets off Santa Monica Boulevard on the southern edge of central Beverly Hills (fig. 3.3). Fischer now lived in a much wealthier city within the greater Los Angeles area. The location and time of this move coincided with a busy period of architectural commissions for Fischer, who rented an office on nearby Santa Monica Boulevard.[10]

Fischer moved one more time, a rare occasion for which a personal comment survives. By 1960, he was no longer recorded at the Beverly Hills address; by 1961, his office address disappeared from city directories, and by the end of that year, he lived close to the ocean in an apartment in Seal Beach, near Long Beach:

> I spent the entire summer in a small apartment I designed for the owner. Indeed, this is the first time in a long, very long time that I reside again in one of "my own" homes.[11]

While these lines may express disappointment at having never owned a home, they also certainly indicate relief that he resided again in a *modern* apartment of his design. Fischer, by then sixty years old, may have even felt nostalgic about decades earlier when he occasionally lived in his designs, such as in the Liebig villa in Dessau.

• • •

The many moves Fischer made from one apartment to another, especially during his early years in California, familiarized him with a Southern California version of modern, urban life that existed independently of modernism in architecture. In Weimar Germany, modernist architecture was often taken as a necessary precondition of modern urban life (or at least rising together with the latter), as illustrated, for example, in the WOGA complex in Berlin designed by Eric Mendelsohn. There, as discussed in chapter 1, Fischer's Berlin client Klara Vogt had set up the cosmetic company Smell with her business partner Margarete Meeths, who also ran a gymnastic school in the same complex: two independent women going about their businesses within a groundbreaking modernist building in Berlin.

When the Granada Buildings were under construction, contemporary newspaper articles picked up on the work-life spaces as the modern, unusual aspects of the complex. The buildings were "something entirely new in Los Angeles," though with roots in the old world, for "incorporating apartments with shops and studios is said to be similar to the design of specialty shops in Europe."[12] While that is arguable as a general characteristic of modernist architecture in Weimar Germany, Fischer's middle-class domestic architecture did often incorporate spaces where his clients could work at home, and even if the contemporary revival-style architecture of the Granada Buildings may have been alien to Fischer, its middle-class tenants and their businesses were not.

REGISTRATION CARD—(Men born on or after February 17, 1897 and on or before December 31, 1921)
SERIAL NUMBER T 964 | 1. NAME (Print) Leopold — Fischer (First) (Middle) (Last) | ORDER NUMBER T 10773
2. PLACE OF RESIDENCE (Print) 904 So. Lucerne Blvd - Los Angeles - Cal (Number and street) (Town, township, village, or city) (County) (State)
[THE PLACE OF RESIDENCE GIVEN ON THE LINE ABOVE WILL DETERMINE LOCAL BOARD JURISDICTION; LINE 2 OF REGISTRATION CERTIFICATE WILL BE IDENTICAL]
3. MAILING ADDRESS Same
[Mailing address if other than place indicated on line 2. If same insert word same]
4. TELEPHONE G.L. 8441 W.A. 3685 (Exchange) (Number) | 5. AGE IN YEARS 40 DATE OF BIRTH Apr. 28 - 1901 (Mo.) (Day) (Yr.) | 6. PLACE OF BIRTH Bielsko (Town or county) Austria (State or country)
7. NAME AND ADDRESS OF PERSON WHO WILL ALWAYS KNOW YOUR ADDRESS Norma Albers de Garrick – 326 - N. Larchmont
8. EMPLOYER'S NAME AND ADDRESS Architect - self -
9. PLACE OF EMPLOYMENT OR BUSINESS 904 So. Lucerne. Los Angeles - Cal. – (Number and street or R. F. D. number) (Town) (County) (State)
I AFFIRM THAT I HAVE VERIFIED ABOVE ANSWERS AND THAT THEY ARE TRUE.
D. S. S. Form 1 (Revised 1-1-42) (over) ☆ GPO 16—21630-1 Leopold Fischer. (Registrant's signature)

3.4. Leopold Fischer's World War II draft registration card (recto), 4 February 1942.

Among the tenants in 1939 were a number of art- and design-related professionals including an artist, designers of interiors and fashion, a dressmaker, and music teachers. A color photography studio could shoot one's creations, and an ad agency could advertise them in *Styles,* a trade journal published in the complex. Should working in art and design take its toll, a food-making business, two beauticians, and two chiropractors were at hand, and a physician stood by for more severe afflictions.[13] The photographer George Hurrell was one of the early occupants, and the architecture partners Gregory Ain and James Homer Garrott rented a unit in late 1939 or early 1940,[14] approximately the time when Fischer moved out. Ain and Garrott never included their unit number in their correspondence, so we may never know whether they took over unit R29 from Fischer.[15] Regardless, Fischer was the first modern architect residing in the Granada Buildings, which have since "attained an almost mythical quality in the Los Angeles design world as architects, graphic designers and artists have made them their homes."[16] To find out how and why Fischer had ended up in the Granada Buildings, we must knock on the door of the nearby unit R25, where Mae Albers, a voice teacher, worked.

Early Social Circles in Los Angeles

Arnold Schönberg may have been among Fischer's first contacts in Los Angeles, but Schönberg's and Fischer's initial encounters, while of some consequences (as will be seen shortly), did not endure. Schönberg never amended Fischer's details in his address book once Fischer had moved from his first address. Another documented contact from the early exile of Fischer lasted longer and was more consequential. It is also rooted in music—not avant-garde compositions but more traditional European and US American classical music.

When, in early 1942, Fischer registered for possible military service, he identified Norma Albers de Gorricho as the "person who will always know your address" (fig. 3.4).[17] Norma Albers (1914–57) was a California-born pianist who married the Philippine-born tenor Joaquin de Gorricho (1906–88)[18] in 1935. Norma Albers's mother was Mae (originally May) Albers (née Boreham, 1893–1940) a British-born soprano singer and voice teacher married to the violinist August W. Albers (1879–1935), an American with German and English parents.[19]

From the summer of 1925 until early 1932, mother and daughter Albers lived in Europe, mainly in Vienna, where the older woman studied with a voice teacher and the younger at the Vienna Conservatorie (today's University of Music and Performing Arts) (fig. 3.5).[20] Whether the pair followed through with these plans is outside the scope of this book. But I will say at least that one Austrian music critic scathingly described a Vienna performance by Mae Albers as "doing little in the way of fostering international reconciliation through music."[21] Perhaps Mae Albers failed in this rubric, but in 1936, she and her daughter excelled in achieving a standard of international relations that most Germans and Austrians barely came close to—if they ever tried. The Alberses were most likely the women who invited Fischer to California so that he could escape National Socialism. The exact occasion and precise circumstances when the three met remain unclear. But as the two Americans lived for more than half a decade in Vienna, moved around its musical and social circles, and gave concerts in Austria and Germany,[22] their world and Fischer's could have easily intersected because, as an active violin player, Fischer was interested in music and often traveled professionally to Austria, Czechoslovakia, France, and Switzerland.[23]

MAE ALBERS, SINGER, GOING TO VIENNA

Mrs. Mae Boreham Albers, well-known Los Angeles soprano and teacher of voice, will leave shortly for Vienna, Austria, where she will study with Mme. Schlummer, the world-famous vocal instructor. Mme. Schlummer was the teacher of Maria Ivogun, the coloratura soprano who has appeared in this country for the past two seasons with such wonderful success. At the time that Mme. Ivogun appeared as soloist with the Los Angeles Philharmonic Orchestra last winter she met and heard Mrs. Albers sing. It was upon the suggestion of Mme. Ivogun that Mrs. Albers continue her voice work with the famous Vienna teacher. Mrs. Albers plans on remaining abroad for two years, studying with Mme. Schlummer and working up an opera repertoire. She will sail by way of the Panama Canal, going first to Stuttgart, Germany, where she will meet Mme. Schlummer and attend the Stuttgart festival. Norma Albers will accompany her mother and will enter the Vienna Conservatorie.

3.5. "Mae Albers, Singer, Going to Vienna," ***Los Angeles Times,*** **19 July 1925, D10.**

Once Fischer was in California, the three interacted in various ways. As a sitting tenant of the Granada Buildings, Mae Albers most likely helped Fischer to rent a unit there. Early in 1939, Albers left the complex in favor of one unit in a duplex at 904 South Lucerne Boulevard, where she offered voice and speech training from April 1939 onward.[24] By April 1940, when the United States Federal Census was conducted, Fischer was recorded as the householder at the same address, working as an independent architectural draftsman.[25] The same census records Mae Albers and her family lived at a different address,[26] perhaps suggesting that she primarily used the South Lucerne Boulevard location for her music lessons until her death later that year.

The social circles of Mae and Norma Albers overlapped with Fischer's life on other occasions. When Fischer filed his petition for naturalization as a citizen in November 1942, one of his signing witnesses was Albert L. Shriber, an electrical engineer.[27] A few years earlier, in 1938, Shriber had also witnessed the petition for the naturalization of Joaquin de Gorricho, who had married Norma Albers in 1935.[28] Fischer's second witness was Richard Hodges Allen, an interior designer and decorator who taught at schools and offered classes for the University of California Extension program. Allen and Fischer most likely crossed paths at the Granada Buildings, where Allen lived for a few years from 1938 onward.[29]

In short, Fischer arrived in California alone but was not on his own. The contact with Mae and Norma Albers introduced him to a support network that widened and developed once he had moved into the Granada Buildings. This social network was rooted more in music than in architecture, though occasionally, the worlds of music and architecture interacted in a way that significantly helped Fischer to reestablish his architectural career, most prominently when Arnold Schönberg introduced Fischer to Frank Lloyd Wright in March 1937.

Four Months with Frank Lloyd Wright

On 7 January 1947, the German broadsheet newspaper *Die Welt* reported on the delay of a Bauhaus exhibition to be mounted in the Bauhaus building in Dessau. The short article notes that "important members of the Bauhaus are all currently working in the United States." After reporting on Walter Gropius, Ludwig Miës van der Rohe, Ludwig Hilberseimer, László Moholy-Nagy, and Hannes Meyer, the unidentified author writes that "Leopold Fischer is working together with F. H. [*sic*] Wright."[30] The fact that the article counts Fischer among the crucial members of the Bauhaus was a long-overdue public expression of the esteem in which contemporaries held Fischer as a social housing architect in Weimar Germany, especially in Dessau.

The article's reference to Fischer and Frank Lloyd Wright collaborating circumvents in a telling way any acknowledgment of Fischer's enforced exile. The German phrasing for "working together" (*gemeinsam arbeiten*) recalls the deliberate decisions by Rudolph Schindler and Richard Neutra to immigrate to the United States to work with or for Frank Lloyd Wright. That Fischer followed in the footsteps of the two older, well-known modernists is the implied explanation for why he was on the other side of the Atlantic Ocean. Indeed, the article never states that any of the architects named were forced into exile. Still, the remark on Fischer contains a kernel of truth, though as it turns out, Fischer did not work with Wright from 1938 to 1940. These years were originally quoted by Irene Below, from a letter by Fischer's German fiancée; in more recent German-language scholarship, this unconfirmed fact has morphed into a near myth, including speculations, unsupported by any evidence, about which projects Fischer worked on while with Wright.[31]

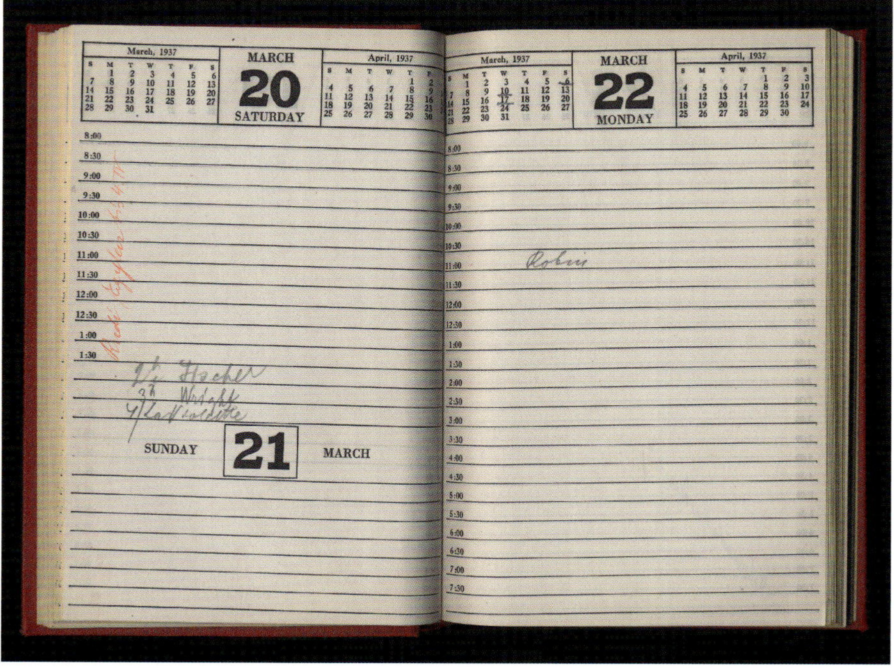

3.6. Arnold Schönberg (US American, 1874–1951, b. Austria-Hungary).

Diary entries noting meetings with [Leopold] Fischer, [Frank Lloyd and, possibly, Lloyd] Wright, and [Wesley] La Violette, Saturday, 20 March 1937.

Vienna, Arnold Schönberg Center.

3.7. Leopold Fischer (US American, 1901–75, b. Austria-Hungary).

Liebig villa (1927–28), Dessau, Germany, during construction, n.d. (ca. 1927–28).

The formwork to cast the central concrete columns with the integrated downpipes as drainage for the roof terrace is clearly visible in the center.

When Schönberg and Fischer met for the second time, on 20 March 1937, Fischer's visit to Schönberg at 2 p.m. was scheduled back-to-back with two more, one by a visitor referred to as "Wright," at 3 p.m., and the other at 4 p.m. by the contemporary US American composer and professor of music Wesley La Violette (1894–1978) (fig. 3.6). A later letter to Wright by La Violette, then based at DePaul University in Chicago, confirms that Wright was at Schönberg's home that day, for La Violette reminded the architect of their meeting at the other composer's residence.[32] Possibly also attending was the architect Frank Lloyd Wright Jr. (commonly called Lloyd Wright to distinguish him from his father), because a corresponding entry in Lloyd Wright's appointment diary references the same date and time together with Schönberg's name.[33] The composer set up this string of appointments to introduce the architects to each other. As it happened, Fischer also met La Violette, and from then on, the two men remained in contact.[34]

After the memorable afternoon at Schönberg's, Fischer corresponded with Frank Lloyd Wright, thanking him on 2 June 1937 for the invitation to visit Taliesin in Wisconsin, which he could now accept as he was finally a legal resident of the United States.[35] Fischer's closing remark references his crossing into the United States from Mexico on 19 May 1937. In response, Wright suggests an arrival date around 20 June and requests that Fischer bring his violin.[36]

Fischer arrived at Taliesin on Wednesday, 23 June 1937, and stayed until October.[37] While a guest of Wright, Fischer, in his own words, "did some detailing for the Johnson factory and residence in Racine, Wis[consin]."[38] The construction of the SC Johnson and Son Administration Building lasted from 1937 to 1939. The interior spaces are famous for their slender, tapering concrete columns, often compared to mushrooms or lily pads because of the circular concrete discs forming their upper endings. Wright's genius apparently led him to the idea of using the hollow core of those columns as a stormwater drain;[39] Fischer had developed a comparable detail on a smaller scale many years earlier when he drained the flat roof of the Liebig villa in Dessau through the hollow cores of some of the structural columns, cast in concrete, that rise through the center of the villa from the lowest floor to the roof (fig. 3.7).[40] In parallel to the office building, Wright worked on the private house for Herbert Fisk Johnson

Jr., the company's president. The house's name, Wingspread, hints at the pinwheel plan upon which the large home is organized. Wingspread would be one of the last Prairie houses Wright would ever design.

While at Taliesin, Fischer may have even found a use for the violin that Wright had requested he bring. Shortly before replying to Fischer, Wright received a letter from La Violette in which the composer accepted Wright's invitation to stay at Taliesin during August. La Violette offered to perform his newly published violin sonata and wondered whether there "would... be a violin player (a good one) on the place?"[41] One of the newspaper columns, which Frank Lloyd Wright and students of the Taliesin fellowship wrote to offer to regional newspapers, indeed recorded that one "evening on one of the terraces" during late August to early September 1937, the Taliesin quartet "played for the first time a quartet by... the Chicago composer who recently visited Taliesin."[42] Whether as a member of the quartet or the audience, Fischer was at Taliesin when the performance occurred. The short period with Wright proved influential for Fischer's attempts to reestablish his architectural career. For example, when applying for an architectural license in California in 1946, Fischer singled out his work for Wright at Taliesin.[43]

Architectural Colleagues and Friends, Old and New

The contact Fischer had with Frank Lloyd Wright early in his exile continued to reverberate through Fischer's professional life. Echoes of Wright's architecture are evident, for example, in Fischer's design of the Kohlmeier house.[44] Equally important is that Fischer occasionally employed the architect James De Long (1921–2013),[45] an apprentice of Frank Lloyd Wright during the late 1940s. In the 1990s, when interviewed by Irene Below, De Long dated to the 1950s his time with Fischer. De Long is known to have kept sets of drawings of projects he worked on for other architects.[46] This habit allowed him to pass on a set of blueprints of the Kohlmeier house to the home's then-owner in approximately the year 2000.[47] The fact that De Long owned these blueprints, which are dated 1941, may indicate that he worked for Fischer even before he studied with Wright.

Fischer also supported other budding architects and designers. In retrospect, the architect Walter S. White Jr. (1917–2002), whose collaboration with Fischer in the late 1950s is well documented, claimed that he was already employed by Fischer sometime between 1937 and 1941,[48] which would make this employment the earliest instance that an aspiring architectural designer in Los Angeles deliberately sought out Fischer's roots in European architectural modernism. Instead of going to college, White pursued his dream career in architecture by apprenticing with various architects for several months at a time. Among these was Rudolph Schindler, for whom White worked for eight months between 1937 and 1938. It is perhaps of little surprise that White was attracted at around the same time by the possibility of working for another modern Austrian architect.

White's acquaintance with Schindler and Fischer brings up the issue of possible contacts between Fischer and fellow Austrian and Loos students Schindler and Neutra. Neither archive of these two pillars of modernist architecture in Southern California seems to contain traces of Fischer. The students of Adolf Loos are sometimes periodized according to their attendance at the Bauschule before World War I, like Neutra and Schindler; or after the war, like Fischer.[49] Perhaps this divide was absolute and precluded contact between the two generations, or perhaps the shared German language was an issue. Dione Neutra, Richard Neutra's wife, stated explicitly that from their arrival in Los Angeles onward, the couple tended to stay away from native German speakers to improve their English and to be American.[50] When émigrés arrived in large numbers in the late 1930s, Dione Neutra retrospectively claimed to have been sympathetic. At the same time, she did not mince her words concerning especially those émigrés who kept reminiscing about their losses rather than rolling up their sleeves for whatever job they could find: "You know, we did not particularly like these immigrants" and, consequently, "we had not too much contact with this whole group."[51] Lastly, Fischer himself may have avoided closer contact with Schindler and Neutra due to architectural disagreements. Schönberg's reservations about Neutra's architecture were cited earlier; Fischer's Slechta house as a statement on, if not a critique of, Neutra's architecture is discussed in chapter 4.

Fischer's contacts and friendships with members of the peer group of émigré architects are much better documented, not least as some contacts within these professional and social networks harked back to Weimar Germany. After World War II, the émigré architect Hannes Meyer corresponded from Mexico with Rolf Sklarek in Los Angeles.[52] Meyer directed the

Bauhaus from 1928 to 1930 but had lived in political exile in Mexico since 1939.[53] With his letter, Meyer wished to renew contacts with former colleagues in preparation for a publication on the Bauhaus. Sklarek reconnected Meyer with Fischer. The three men had known one another since the 1920s. Sklarek and Meyer met when the former was enrolled at the Bauhaus from 1926 until 1931; Sklarek and Fischer when Fischer guided a tour for Bauhaus students through his social housing estate in Dessau-Ziebigk in 1929;[54] and Fischer and Meyer when the latter invited the former to direct the newly founded architecture department of the Bauhaus, as noted in chapter 1.

In a letter, Meyer asked Fischer whether he had photographs of his social housing estates, but Fischer could not help him; apparently, few such items were with Fischer in Los Angeles.[55] The tone of Fischer's reply is puzzling. It was short, focused on the request, and no ink was wasted on personal matters like inquiring about Meyer's fate or conveying details of Fischer's escape to Los Angeles. No ongoing correspondence blossomed from this letter; indeed, it reads more like Fischer did not want contact with Meyer.

Reestablishing contact between Fischer and Sklarek—and establishing it between Fredric Frankel and Ulrich Plaut—was relatively easy, as all moved to Los Angeles once they were in the United States. Fischer and Sklarek only passed through New York, Frankel moved from there as soon as possible, and Plaut immigrated directly to Los Angeles. Initially, the men may not have had professional contacts in the city, though Sklarek and Frankel at least had family connections. Yet, regardless, Los Angeles appealed as "the only place where buildings were a little less traditional," which attracted émigré architects like Frankel, who was "trained in the Bauhaus tradition," as his wife claimed retrospectively.[56] In Los Angeles, they all came to be acquainted through their growing professional and collegial contacts, whether they worked for the same firms or even for one another. Some also shared a fascination with Frank Lloyd Wright's architecture; Frankel, for example, always dreamed of working at Taliesin but was never able to.[57] Indeed, Fischer was the only one who had spent time with Wright and who also knew Wright's son (via Schönberg). It remains unknown whether an interest in Frank Lloyd Wright led Fischer, Frankel, and Plaut to James De Long, himself infatuated with Wrightian designs, or whether De Long could have met the others while maybe working for Fischer on the Kohlmeier house in the early 1940s. In any case, Marilyn De Long recalls that her late husband, Plaut, and Frankel were part of a group of friends and colleagues from work that also included Fischer and other architects.[58]

3.8. Leopold Fischer (US American, 1901–75, b. Austria-Hungary).

Robert Henry Ewing Jr. house (1939–40), Studio City, California, n.d.

On Projects and Clients: An Overview of Fischer's Career in Exile

In the documentation of his entry to the United States by crossing its border with Mexico, Fischer noted his profession as an architect; in his first public city directory entry from 1937, he identified himself as a building contractor.[59] Documented, however, is that Fischer drafted for other architects and, presumably, contractors. The 1940 census notes Fischer as an "architectural draftsman," earning in 1939 a sum of $1,500, or $125 per month, for fifty-two weeks of work. Assuming the monthly rent in 1939 was $40 (as it was in 1940), Fischer could get by without overly pressing money worries but was not living lavishly.[60]

That 1939 income included the fees for the design of the Ewing house in Studio City, Fischer's first design for a detached house in California that marked his return in exile to be a practicing architect (fig. 3.8). The client, Robert Henry Ewing Jr. (1911–89), was a makeup artist at Paramount Studios in Hollywood. In the 1940 census, Ewing claimed to have earned $5,000 in 1939,[61] not quite enough to be invited to the parties of major movie stars for which one had to make that amount weekly,[62] but sufficient to have a home designed by an architect. Chronologically, the Ewing house was preceded in 1938 or 1939 by a mountain cabin for Ralph and Phyllis Kohlmeier. Despite my manifold efforts, the cabin, its design, and its whereabouts remain to be discovered.[63] The cabin and the Ewing house were followed by the Kohlmeier house (South Pasadena) on which Fischer worked from 1940 to 1941. Regardless of the Germanic surname, the clients were born in the United States; indeed, Ralph Kohlmeier was an Angeleno. He studied law at the University of California and was admitted to the bar in 1926, the same year he graduated.[64] Kohlmeier went on to work in a Los Angeles–based attorney and accountant firm, and the couple stayed in their Fischer-designed home until the husband retired around 1970.

After the United States entered World War II late in 1941, Fischer had to register for military service in February 1942. However, he never saw active service either within the United States or abroad.[65] Thanks to his drafting skills and engineering knowledge, Fischer was assigned to Columbia Steel's production facilities in Torrance, south of Los Angeles, from June 1942 to January 1943, where he worked on a planned expansion of the steel mill.[66] Subsequently, until February 1944, Fischer was an assistant engineer at the US Engineering Office in Los Angeles, focusing on military designs and flood control in Southern California. From July 1944 onward, Fischer was the chief of the engineering branch of the San Bernardino Engineer Depot of the US Army Engineers. Fischer also took advantage of the National Engineering, Science, and Management War Training program that offered free college courses to meet the demand for Americans educated in engineering and science during the war.[67] Fischer studied structural design in wood at the California Institute of Technology from July to September 1942 and took two courses in reinforced concrete design at the University of Southern California from February to September 1943.

During the 1940s, Fischer worked on architectural commissions for and with Howard F. Ahmanson (1906–68), the Los Angeles businessman who earned his money in the insurance business and founded the Home Savings Bank. This financial institution was crucially involved in enabling Californians (and other Americans) to realize their longings for suburban single-family homes in the aftermath of World War II.[68] Ahmanson and Fischer knew each other well enough for the former to write a glowing letter of recommendation when the latter applied for his architectural license in 1946. Ahmanson called Fischer "a competent designer" and stated that he "had several occasions to work with him in design and construction of buildings,"[69] presumably in connection with Ahmanson's company providing insurance coverage for the edifices.[70] Fischer's application for an architectural license was successful; he passed the California Architects Registration Board qualifying exams and was issued license number C719 on 10 October 1946.[71] Finally, Fischer could return to full architectural practice.

Right after World War II, Fischer received a commission for the Leroy C. and Carol D. Floyd house (1945–46, demolished) in Santa Monica.[72] Leroy Floyd was a tax accountant and a colleague of Ralph Kohlmeier's at the firm Parker Milliken and Kohlmeier. Surviving photographs show an inconspicuous one-story stuccoed building with hipped roofs, traditional windows, and no visible details hinting at modern or even modernist architecture; the snapshots are taken from too far away to allow any other reasonable comment.

From 1950 to 1951, Fischer worked for Harold Hunt and Agnes K. Johnson (fig. 3.9). Harold Hunt Johnson (1893–1957) was a businessman who made his money in metals. During World War II, he advised the metal division of the war production board; later, he presided over the Los Angeles By-Products Company, a business that the 1950 United States Federal Census describes more pragmatically as "junk processing," certainly a fitting basis for Johnson on which to also run a steel casting company.[73] The Johnson house is in Bel Air, on the western side of Los Angeles. Fischer designed it in cooperation with the émigré interior designer Herbert Cordier (né Kugelmann), who ran an interior design business called Continental House. Apparently, their client wanted to balance his less savory daily dealings with scrap metal and other junk by working with an architect and an interior designer on the private home. *Architectural Digest* included the Johnson house when it published a sampling of interiors by Cordier, marking the only time a Fischer project made it into the pages of this magazine.[74] Sadly, Fischer's name is omitted from the publication; thus, the magazine inadvertently contributed to Fischer's anonymity in California architectural history. Fischer returned to this house in 1960, when he added a partial second story to the building for its new owners, Mr. and Mrs. John N. Mercer. (Regretfully, this study cannot discuss the home, as several attempts to contact the current owner to learn more about the house have remained without reply.)

Fischer never designed houses for clients who shared the émigré and exile experience with him. But in the case of the Adolph and Mary Slechta house in View Park, completed in 1951, the clients were direct descendants of parents who had emigrated from Bohemia to the United States. Adolph Slechta (1904–

3.9. Leopold Fischer (US American, 1901–75, b. Austria-Hungary) and Herbert Cordier (US American, 1915–2002, b. Germany).

Interior of Johnson house (1950–51), Bel Air, Los Angeles, California, showing den with fireplace.

From "Residence of Mr. & Mrs. H. H. Johnson, Bel Air, California," *Architectural Digest* 13, no. 2 (1951), n.p.

92) represents a typical American success story. In the 1930s, he and his wife, Mary, worked middle-class jobs, he as a self-employed accountant and she in a department store. Approximately two decades later, Adolph Slechta was the owner and president of the Great Western Savings & Loan Association and, therefore, an Ahmanson competitor. Slechta had acquired the financial institution, which was founded by members of the Czechoslovakian immigrant community in the United States of the 1920s, in the late 1940s.[75] The Central European, Austrian heritage of the Slechta family (for a time in its history, Bohemia was part of Austria-Hungary) and the origin of Slechta's business in the Czech immigrant community suggest that commissioning Fischer as the architect for the private house may have been a deliberate choice.

Fischer's only known Jewish client was Charles D. Wagner (1899–1969), a US American real estate agent and developer whose parents had immigrated to the United States from the territory in Eastern Europe that historically had been contested between Austria, Germany, Poland, and Russia.[76] In 1952, Fischer designed a two-story apartment building in Beverly Hills for Wagner (fig. 3.10). The building permit references twenty-four rooms for four families, composing four apartments in total, two on each floor, and each 4,700 square feet in area.[77] These apartments were intended for wealthier tenants; apparently, Wagner liked the units so much that he lived in one of them until the 1960s.[78]

In the early 1950s, Fischer returned to designing anonymous domestic architecture when he worked on Verdugo Village in the Mount Washington area of Los Angeles, near Pasadena. A merchant builder had commissioned a subdivision of middle-class and upper-middle-class suburban detached houses that enabled Fischer to draw on his experience with social housing estates in Weimar Germany, even if both kinds of housing aimed at very different social layers of very different societies. Chapter 5 returns to this project in great detail.

3.10. Leopold Fischer (US American, 1901–75, b. Austria-Hungary).

Four-unit apartment building (1952), 349 South Linden Drive, Beverly Hills, California, undated sepia print [ca. 1952].

University of California, Santa Barbara, Architecture and Design Collection.

3.11. Leopold Fischer (US American, 1901–75, b. Austria-Hungary) and Walter S. White Jr. (US American, 1917–2002).

Construction sign for Pearson, Scott & Company and Pearson Mortgage Company building (1959), Indio, California, 1959. Color slide by Walter S. White Jr.

University of California, Santa Barbara, Architecture and Design Collection.

In the later 1950s, Fischer's architectural career changed fundamentally. He produced many more speculative designs and projects: some were never realized, while others were for locations outside of California as he attempted to land commissions. Fischer returned to collaborating with Walter S. White Jr. during this period, but now in reversed roles, as he could help White, who was about to relocate his business and family to Colorado Springs. Fischer continued and completed projects for which White had already been commissioned, and for a while, both of their names appeared on the signage at building sites (fig. 3.11).[79] Their renewed collaboration added entirely new building types to Fischer's exile oeuvre, among them a car dealership made from folded corrugated sheet metal, an idea that White had already used earlier when practicing on his own. Two projects, however, were most likely designed by Fischer. The first one is business premises for Pearson, Scott & Company and Pearson Mortgage Company (Indio, 1959), a wood-framed box with an added wall segment made from square, reconstituted stone blocks (fig. 3.12). On the completed facade, this vertical element is balanced by the dense horizontal lines of a trellis, providing shade to the floor-to-ceiling glass walls farther back.

Fischer also completed the Grover house in Palm Desert in 1961. This project had roots in White's

3.12. Leopold Fischer (US American, 1901–75, b. Austria-Hungary) and Walter S. White Jr. (US American, 1917–2002).

Pearson, Scott & Company and Pearson Mortgage Company building (1959), Indio, California, 1959. Color slide by Walter S. White Jr.

University of California, Santa Barbara, Architecture and Design Collection.

architectural designs but was made over by Fischer, who supervised the construction after White had left the desert. The low-slung single-story home features design characteristics that point to White as the originator, such as a long, curved masonry wall. The wall leads to the main entrance from the adjacent motor court; the latter may have been Fischer's decision as White usually integrated carports much closer to a home instead of separating the parking area in a motor court. Also, Fischer most likely added the outdoor patios at the four corners of the house, each covered by the deep roof overhangs, much deeper than White usually provided for, and wrapped in protective masonry walls.

Toward the end of the 1950s, in the midst of his work with White, Fischer closed his office and moved to Seal Beach. His last known project is a glass room addition transforming a run-of-the-mill suburban tract home in Long Beach; the clients, Ward and Marguerite Youry, had to convince Fischer to come out of retirement to work on this project in 1965.[80] Dr. Ward Youry was a ceramist and founder of the ceramics department at California State University, Long Beach. Subsequent to the glass room, Fischer designed a ceramics studio (unbuilt) to be located in the garden of the Youry house as well as various other additions to the home and garden. The entire project was realized in parts, as is explained in the conclusion to this volume.

• • •

Leopold Fischer's exile oeuvre, the known one at least, is relatively small, which raises the question of how Fischer could make a living. This question can only be satisfactorily answered if and when additional private and professional records by Fischer may one day be found. A different but related question, however, can be asked: On what basis may a smaller oeuvre indicate that an émigré architect succeeded or struggled to resurrect his career? It might be tempting to compare an oeuvre like Fischer's with the works of Richard Neutra, Rudolph Schindler, and Julius R. Davidson, for example, especially when taking into account that they shared a Central European, German-speaking background. The latter three architects had built up substantial lists of works, with Neutra leading the other two regarding the scope and international reach of this oeuvre. Yet, these immigrant architects came to California much earlier and did not face military service or related work assignments shortly after they arrived. Thus, it is far more instructive to focus on Fischer in the context of the narrower peer group of émigré architects, as defined in the preceding chapter. To this end, the following paragraphs look at Fischer and his émigré peer Rolf Sklarek.

Table 3.2 compares Fischer's and Sklarek's early careers in California before and after World War II. Each man completed his first detached house in 1939 and completed his second one in 1941, just before the attack on Pearl Harbor led the United States to enter World War II. During the war, both architects were on war-related work assignments. After the war, the first divergence appeared in the mid-1940s when Sklarek invested in erecting a commercial building that accommodated his office and a rent-paying store. For the second half of the 1940s, Sklarek obtained more commissions for private houses and branched out earlier than Fischer into areas other than domestic architecture, with designs for a music store, a nursery school, and a medical building. Indeed, during this period, a gap exists in Fischer's professional biography; presumably, he worked during some of those years for or with Ahmanson, but to date, details have not come to light.

In addition to the social and professional networks in which both émigré architects moved, Sklarek could rely on familial networks in exile, unlike Fischer. It is true that Fischer found initial support in exile from Mae

Table 3.2. Rolf Sklarek and Leopold Fischer: Early careers in exile, ca. 1938–ca. 1955

ROLF SKLAREK		LEOPOLD FISCHER	
Year	**Building and Location**	**Year**	**Building and Location**
1938–39	Segall house	ca. 1938–39	Kohlmeier mountain cabin
		1939–40	Ewing house
1941	Meier house	1940–41	Kohlmeier house
1945–47	Sklarek office building	1945–46	Floyd house
1945 [or 1948?]	Joseph house		
1946	Ernest R. Lane house		
1948	Hartje house Gateway to Music store		
1949	Sklarek house		
1950	Brentwood nursery school Medical building		
1950–51	Jackson house	1950–51	Johnson house
1951	Sklarek joins office of Victor Gruen	1950–51	Slechta house
		1952	Apartment building, Beverly Hills
		1953–55	Verdugo Village suburban neighborhood (twelve homes designed by Fischer)

All buildings and projects are in the metropolitan Los Angeles area.

3.13. Rolf Sklarek (US American, 1906–84, b. Germany).

Dr. Gabriel and Mrs. Elsie Segall house (1939), Los Angeles, California, demolished 2010.

From "Good Modern Is Livable," *Los Angeles Times Home Magazine*, 19 August 1945, 3.

and Norma Albers, though neither seemed to have ever asked for or had the financial means to commission a design for a home. Moreover, Mae Albers passed away in 1940 and Norma in 1957. Conversely, Sklarek fled to Los Angeles because his mother, a Sigmund Freud–trained psychoanalyst from Berlin, had done the same a few years earlier. By the time Rolf Sklarek arrived, his mother was integrated into the local psychoanalytical community; coming to Los Angeles meant that Sklarek would be close to his mother's social and professional networks, which, in turn, helped him gain commissions early on. Indeed, Sklarek's first independent commission in Los Angeles, on which the architect worked from 1938 to 1939, was a house for a Jewish physician who at some point treated Albert Einstein, a personal friend of the Sklarek family from times in Berlin (fig. 3.13).[81] Thus, Sklarek moved in circles originating in his mother's profession and received commissions from Jewish clients, émigrés or not. In contrast, Fischer relied on clients like Kohlmeier, who acted like patrons but usually commissioned individual projects without follow-up commissions.

Lastly, Sklarek married and started a family in the early 1940s and subsequently built a family home in Pacific Palisades. These life events rooted the architect in the local community, increasing his circle of potential clients, especially when compared to Fischer, who during the 1940s was living as a single man in apartment buildings. In 1951, Fischer married M. Maxine Erhart (1904–54, née Byers), who had divorced her first husband in 1950.[82] This marriage was not blessed by longevity, as Mrs. Fischer passed away in 1954. It also may not have been the happiest liaison, for the deceased's obituary never mentions her second husband. (However, to be fair to Fischer, it also omits husband number one.)[83]

Whether or not Fischer found happiness in his private life in exile, his career is comparable to Sklarek's. The two careers proceeded almost in parallel up to approximately the mid-1940s, when they gradually began to diverge. This divergence was complete when Sklarek joined Victor Gruen's office in 1951 and thus began leaving the world of domestic architecture.[84]

• • •

The clients of the projects and buildings Fischer worked on in California immersed the émigré architect deeply into the state's middle and upper-middle classes. However, no other recognizable focus emerges on, for example, Jewish clients, émigré clients, clients distinctly involved with modern art (as was the case with several of Fischer's German clients), or clients committed to modernist homes or even of a distinct political conviction such as the many left-wing clients for which Gregory Ain became known.[85]

Next to no information is available on how Leopold Fischer met his clients, through which social contacts and networks they got to know him, or vice versa. Most of Fischer's clients were businesspeople involved somehow or other in finance, suggesting that the initial contact with Kohlmeier perhaps led to subsequent commissions. The clients and the kind of domestic architecture they requested indicate that Fischer was well connected in circles whose members wanted to build private homes and had the financial means to do so. Socioeconomically, most clients were of middle-class standing, yet some, such as the Slechtas and Ahmanson, belonged to the upper-middle class.

Robert H. Ewing Jr. and Ward Youry were the only artists among Fischer's California clients, a marked difference from the architect's clients for private houses in Germany. There, Fischer had designed homes that one could often broadly classify as modernist. In contrast, in California, his designs are modern but do not appear modernist or avant-garde. Fischer's California clients liked such architectural modesty. None of them seemed to have held any avant-garde or experimental inclination when it came to the architecture of their homes (or investment, in Charles D. Wagner's case). This characteristic dovetailed well with Fischer's fundamental Loosian understanding of domestic architecture as a public affair, requiring designs that do not focus on contrasting or even challenging their surroundings. The fact that most examples of Fischer's domestic architecture in California still exist and remain surprisingly unchanged speaks well about this approach. The following two chapters turn to selected Fischer buildings in Los Angeles and the city's surroundings.

Notes

1 Arnold Schönberg, address files, USA 1934–1951 A, Arnold Schönberg Center, Vienna, A2120, https://archive.schoenberg.at/resources/pages/search.php (search: A2120); see also Arnold Schönberg, address files, USA 1934–1951 B, Arnold Schönberg Center, Vienna, A3839, https://archive.schoenberg.at/resources/pages/search.php (search: A3839).

2 817 South Hobart Boulevard, Los Angeles, permit no. 28107, 28 September 1926, and Certificate of Occupancy, 25 February 1927 (City of Los Angeles, Dept. of Building and Safety, Search Online Building Records, https://ladbsdoc.lacity.org/ (search: 817 S Hobart Blvd).

3 *Los Angeles Times,* 25 May 1928, A16; and *Los Angeles Times,* 22 September 1940, B5.

4 Granada Shoppes and Studios, 672 South Lafayette Park Place, Los Angeles, National Registry of Historic Places Inventory—Nomination Form, November 20, 1986, in National Archives, *Records of the National Park Service, 1785–2006,* "California SP Granada Shoppes and Studios," https://catalog.archives.gov/id/123859160.

5 David Gebhard and Robert Winter, *A Guide to Architecture in Los Angeles & Southern California* (Salt Lake City: Peregrine Smith, 1982), 200; and Stefanos Polyzoides, Roger Sherwood, and James Tice, *Courtyard Housing in Los Angeles* (New York: Princeton Architectural Press, 1992), 172–77. Commonly the building is dated to 1927; see also "Trio of Major Units to Rise," *Los Angeles Times,* 2 October 1927, E1, except for Polyzoides, Sherwood, and Tice, who date the complex to 1925.

6 "Trio of Major Units to Rise," E1.

7 Los Angeles Conservancy, "The Granada Buildings," n.d., https://www.laconservancy.org/locations/granada-buildings.

8 Charles Moore, Peter Becker, and Regula Campbell, *The City Observed: Los Angeles; A Guide to Its Architecture and Landscapes* (Santa Monica: Hennessey & Ingalls, 1998), 147.

9 401 Shirley Place, Beverly Hills, permit no. 18254, 27 March 1941, Department of Building, City of Beverly Hills, https://cs.beverlyhills.org/cs/?menu=menu1 (search: 401 Shirley Pl).

10 *Beverly Hills City Directory, 1960–61* (Beverly Hills: Chamber of Commerce and Civic Association, 1960), 56.

11 Leopold Fischer to Gerda Vogt, 17 December 1961, Archive Irene Below.

12 "Trio of Major Units to Rise," E1.

13 *Los Angeles City Directory 1939* (Los Angeles: Los Angeles Directory Co., 1939), 109, 379, 546, 711, 812, 1073, 1139, 1204, 1729, 2040, 2063, 2076, 2242, 2290, 2339, 2409, 2427, 2428, 2434, 2438, 2457, 2464, 2466, 2475, 2537, 2538, 2550, 2554, and 2597. Data compiled by searching the online version of the city directory at the Los Angeles Public Library website (https://rescarta.lapl.org) for "S La Fayette Park pl" and then looking for a reference to a rental unit in the Granada Buildings indicated by "R [followed by the number of the unit]."

14 Hurrell: *Los Angeles City Directory 1939,* 1171; and Ain: *Los Angeles City Directory 1941* (Los Angeles: Los Angeles Directory Co., 1941), 109.

15 Email correspondence of the author with Emily Ain, August 2022; Anthony Denzer, August 2022; Edward Dimendberg, November 2022; Anthony Fontenot, November 2022; and Wesley Henderson, December 2022. See also Gregory Ain Papers, Architecture and Design Collection, Art, Design & Architecture Museum, University of California, Santa Barbara; Wesley Howard Henderson, "Two Case Studies of African-American Architects' Careers in Los Angeles, 1890–1945: Paul R. Williams, FAIA and James H. Garrott, AIA" (PhD diss., University of California, Los Angeles, 1992); and Anthony Denzer, *Gregory Ain: The Modern Home as Social Commentary* (New York: Rizzoli, 2008).

16 Polyzoides, Sherwood, and Tice, *Courtyard Housing in Los Angeles,* 175.

17 Leopold Fischer, draft registration card, 14 February 1942 (National Archives in St. Louis; St. Louis, Missouri; WWII Draft Registration Cards for California, 10/16/1940–03/31/1947; Record Group: Records of the Selective Service System, 147; Box: 571; ancestry.com, subscription required).

18 "Harmony Paves Way to Nuptials," *Hollywood Citizen-News,* 22 May 1939, 9.

19 "May B. Albers," 1920 United States Federal Census (Year: *1920;* Census Place: *Huntington Park, Los Angeles, California;* Roll: *T625_119;* Page: *6A;* Enumeration District: *562;* ancestry.com, subscription required).

20 "May Boreham Albers to Make Trip to Vienna," *Los Angeles Evening Express,* 18 July 1925, 7; "Mae Albers, Singer, Going to Vienna," *Los Angeles Times,* 19 July 1925, D10; Elanor Barnes, "'Tone Healing' New Fad Mrs. Albers Is Interested," *Illustrated Daily News* (Los Angeles), 23 February 1932, 26; and W. F. Newman, "Chaperones of Girl Athletes Honored," *Illustrated Daily News* (Los Angeles), 29 July 1932, 13.

21 "Konzerte Musik," *Freiheit!* 3, no. 535 (6 May 1929): 4.

22 Apparently, Mae Albers attended a classical music festival in Stuttgart, Germany, in 1925; "Musicians in Los Angeles," *Los Angeles Times,* 19 July 1925, D10.

23 Leopold Fischer to State Board of Architectural Examiners, Los Angeles, 24 April 1946, "Leopold Fischer," license file, California Architects Board.

24 Advertisement for Music Teachers' Association of California, *Hollywood-Citizens News,* 1 April 1939, 10. Up to February 1939, Albers advertised her Granada Buildings unit as the location for lessons (*Hollywood-Citizens News,* 18 February 1939, 10), dating the move to the new location sometime during February and March 1939. The 1940 city directory lists Mae Albers as householder at 904 S. Lucerne Blvd.; *Los Angeles City Directory 1940* (Los Angeles: Los Angeles Directory Co., 1940), 109.

25 "Leopold Fischer," 1940 United States Federal Census (Year: *1940;* Census Place: *Los Angeles, Los Angeles, California;* Roll: *m-t0627-00402;* Page: *11A;* Enumeration District: *60-320;* United States of America, Bureau of the Census. *Sixteenth Census of the United States, 1940*; ancestry.com, subscription required).

26 "Mae Albers," 1940 United States Federal Census (Year: *1940;* Census Place: *Los Angeles, Los Angeles, California;* Roll: *m-t0627-00396;* Page: *8B;* Enumeration District: *60-1051A;* ancestry.com, subscription required).

27 Leopold Fischer, petition for naturalization, 1942, November 2, no. 102374, District of Los Angeles (National Archives at Riverside; Riverside, California; NAI Number: *594890;* Record Group Title: *Records of District Courts of the United States, 1685–2009;* Record Group Number: *21;* ancestry.com, subscription required).

28 Joaquin de Gorricho, petition for naturalization, 1938, September 2, no. 60579, District of Los Angeles (The National Archives in Washington, DC; Washington, DC; *(Roll 221) Petitions For Naturalization 60204-60627; 8/5/38–9/8/38;* Record Group Title: *Records of District Courts of the United States, 1685–2009;* Record Group Number: *21;* ancestry.com, subscription required).

29 "New Studies Offered for Adults," *Pasadena Post,* 3 October 1930, 5; *Los Angeles City Directory 1939* (Los Angeles: Los Angeles Directory Co., 1939), 119; and "Richard H. Allen," Index to Registers of Voters, Los Angeles City Precinct 991, Los Angeles County California 1942 (California State Library; Sacramento, California; *Great Register of Voters, 1900–1968;* ancestry.com, subscription required).

30 P., "Bauhaus-Schau 1947," *Die Welt: Überparteiliche Zeitung für die Britische Zone,* 7 January 1947. Dr. Achim Reese, Berlin, kindly supplied the bibliographic details.

31 Gerda Vogt to Irene Below, 28 July 1993, referred to in Irene Below, "Das Leben von Leopold Fischer," in *Leopold Fischer: Architekt der Moderne,* ed. Bauhaus Dessau e.V. (Dessau-Roßlau: Funk Verlag Bernhard Hein e.K., n.d. [ca. 2007]), 21; Bernd Polster, *Walter Gropius: Der Architekt seines Ruhms* (Munich: Carl Hanser, 2019), 349; and Rudolf Lückmann, "Walter Gropius ./. Leopold Fischer–Ungleiche Rivalen um die Gartenstädte der Moderne," in *Zukunftsfähige Perspektiven in der Landschaftsarchitektur für Gartenstädte,* ed. Nicole Uhrig (Wiesbaden: Springer Fachmedien, 2020), 135.

32 Wesley La Violette to Frank Lloyd Wright, 3 May 1937, Frank Lloyd Wright Foundation; see also Anthony Alofsin, ed., *Frank Lloyd Wright: An Index to the Taliesin Correspondence* (New York: Garland, 1988), 1:383, FicheID K036C04.

33 Lloyd Wright, appointment calendar 1937, 19 March 1937: "Schoenberg. 3 o'clock Sat. March 20th," Lloyd Wright Papers (Collection 1561), UCLA Library Special Collections, Charles E. Young Research Library, University of California, Los Angeles. I wish to thank Simon Elliott, UCLA, for kindly supplying the date and text of the entry.

34 Wesley La Violette to State Board of Architectural Examiners, Los Angeles, 10 September 1946 ("Leopold Fischer," license file, California Architects Board).

35 Leopold Fischer to Frank Lloyd Wright, 2 June 1937, Frank Lloyd Wright Foundation; see also Alofsin, *Frank Lloyd Wright: An Index,* 1:386, FicheID F025E05.

36 Frank Lloyd Wright to Leopold Fischer, 6 June 1937, Frank Lloyd Wright Foundation; see also Alofsin, *Frank Lloyd Wright: An Index,* 1:386, FicheID F025E06.

37 For the arrival date: Leopold Fischer to secretary of Frank Lloyd Wright, telegram, 21 June 1937, Frank Lloyd Wright Foundation; see also Alofsin, *Frank Lloyd Wright: An Index,* 1:388, FicheID F026A03. For the duration of the stay: Leopold Fischer, "Examination Application for Registration to Practice Architecture in the State of California," section "Experience Record," 24 April 1946 ("Leopold Fischer," license file, California Architects Board).

38 Fischer, "Examination Application."

39 Kelly Minner, "AD Classics: S.C. Johnson and Son Administration Building / Frank Lloyd Wright," *ArchDaily,* 21 November 2010, www.archdaily.com/90519/ad-classics-s-c-johnson-and-son-administration-building-frank-lloyd-wright.

40 Juliane Vierich, *Die Villa Liebig: Denkmalpflege der Moderne,* diploma thesis (Köthen: Edition der Hochschule Anhalt, 2006), 39–40.

41 Wesley La Violette to Frank Lloyd Wright, 3 May 1937, Frank Lloyd Wright Foundation; see also Alofsin, *Frank Lloyd Wright: An Index,* 1:383, FicheID K036C04.

42 "September 5, 1937," in *"At Taliesin": Newspaper Columns by Frank Lloyd Wright and the Taliesin Fellowship, 1934–1937,* ed. Randolph C. Henning (Carbondale: Southern Illinois University Press, 1992), 273. The newspaper column identifies the composer as "Gustav Hoffman, the Chicago composer who recently visited Taliesin." See page 230 of the same book for confirmation that La Violette was for the summer of 1937 musician-in-residence at Taliesin.

43 "Leopold Fischer," license file, California Architects Board.

44 For more on the Kohlmeier house, see this volume, chapter 4.

45 Below, "Das Leben von Leopold Fischer," 22.

46 See "Finding Aid for the James De Long Papers 0000340," Architecture and Design Project Series 5: 1941–1998, Designs by other architects, Architecture and Design Collection, Art, Design & Architecture Museum, University of California, Santa Barbara, www.oac.cdlib.org/findaid/ark:/13030/c8p55szd/entire_text.

47 Email from current owner of the Kohlmeier house to the author, 18 August 2022.

48 On White and Fischer, see Volker M. Welter, *Walter S. White: Inventions in Mid-Century Architecture* (Santa Barbara: University of California, Santa Barbara, 2015), esp. 13–15.

49 Peter Plaisier, *De leerlingen van Adolf Loos* (Delft: Delft Universitaire pers, 1987). A third period and group Plaisier identifies are students of Loos after the Bauschule had officially ceased to exist.

50 Dione Neutra, *To Tell the Truth: Dione Neutra Interviewed by Lawrence Weschler* (Los Angeles: Oral History Program, University of California, Los Angeles, 1983), 124, https://archive.org/details/totelltruthoralh00neut.

51 Neutra, *To Tell the Truth,* 233, 236.

52 Letters from and to Rolf Sklarek, 1946–1947, 164–103–031, Hannes Meyer Nachlass, Deutsches Architekturmuseum, Frankfurt am Main.

53 Klaus Jürgen Winkler, *Der Architekt Hannes Meyer Anschauungen und Werk* (Berlin [DDR]: VEB Verlag für das Bauwesen, 1989), 187–216.

54 For Sklarek and Meyer, see Rolf Sklarek membership file, American Institute of Architects, https://aiahistoricaldirectory.atlassian.net/wiki/spaces/AHDAA/pages/39682646/ahd1041430; and for Sklarek and Fischer, see Rolf Sklarek to State Board of Architectural Examiners, Los Angeles, 21 September 1946, "Leopold Fischer," license file, California Architects Board.

55 Leopold Fischer to Hannes Meyer, 30 December 1947, 164–103–012, Hannes Meyer Nachlass, Deutsches Architekturmuseum, Frankfurt am Main.

56 Ruth E. Wolman, "Gerty Frankel" (interview), in *Crossing Over: An Oral History of Refugees from Hitler's Reich* (New York: Twayne, 1996), 62–63.

57 Conversation of the author with D. Frankel, a son of Fredric Frankel, 17 August 2021.

58 Conversation of the author with Marilyn De Long, 31 July 2022.

59 *Los Angeles City Directory 1939* (Los Angeles: Los Angeles Directory Co., 1939), 711.

60 "Leopold Fischer," 1940 United States Federal Census; see note 25 above.

61 "Robert Henry Ewing Jr.," 1940 United States Federal Census (Year: *1940;* Census Place: *Los Angeles, Los Angeles, California;* Roll: *m-t0627-00394;* Page: *12A;* Enumeration District: *60–97;* ancestry.com, subscription required).

62 Alexander Granach, *Du mein liebes Stück Heimat: Briefe an Lotte Lieven aus dem Exil,* ed. Angelika Wittlich and Hilde Recher (Augsburg: Ölbaum, 2008), 343.

63 Ralph Kohlmeier to California State Board of Architectural Examiners, Los Angeles, 23 September 1946 ("Leopold Fischer," license file, California Architects Board). R. Kohlmeier, Woodland, Calif., to author, n.d. (postmarked 30 December 2022). The Ewing family, Fischer's second California clients, owned a cabin at Malibou Lake Mountain Club, but the Kohlmeier family is not recorded in the club's archives (see Malibou Lake Mountain Club Records, collection no. 0158, Malibu Historical Collection, Special Collections and University Archives, University Libraries, Pepperdine University). Nor could I trace any lots possibly owned by the Kohlmeier family at Lake Arrowhead and Big Bear Lake, two mountain lakes popular at the time with Angelenos who were building weekend cabins.

64 *The American Bar: A Biographical Directory of the Leading Lawyers of the United States and Canada* (Minneapolis: James C. Fifield Co., 1943), 70.

65 "Leopold Fischer," Selective Service Number 10773, Registration Card and Classification Ledger, Selective Service System Records, National Archives and Records Administration, National Archives—Saint Louis, Saint Louis, MO.

66 All information in this paragraph on Fischer's career during World War II is from "Leopold Fischer," license file, California Architects Board.

67 Henry H. Armsby, "ESMWT," *Journal of Higher Education* 15, no. 2 (1944): 86–94.

68 Eric John Abrahamson, *Building Home: Howard F. Ahmanson and the Politics of the American Dream* (Berkeley: University of California Press, 2013).

69 Howard F. Ahmanson to Board of Architectural Examiners, Los Angeles, 14 September 1946, "Leopold Fischer," license file, California Architects Board.

70 Email correspondence of the author with Mr. William Ahmanson, Ahmanson Foundation, August 2022.

71 "Leopold Fischer," license file, California Architects Board.

72 *Demolition Permit Application,* number 05STP0676, 202 21st Place, Santa Monica, 8 November 2004, City of Santa Monica. The house was created before Fischer was licensed as an architect in 1946; accordingly, his name does not appear on the building permit application (*Application for Building Permit,* number B 8415, 5 April 1945, Building Department, City of Santa Monica; https://publicdocs.smgov.net/WebLink/?dbid=0&repo=SMGOV (select "Building Permit Document Archive Search"; enter 202 for street number and set street name to 21ST PL). However, a letter by Kohlmeier records Fischer's authorship; Ralph Kohlmeier to State Board of Architectural Examiners, Los Angeles, 23 September 1946 ("Leopold Fischer," license file, California Architects Board).

73 Obituary of Harold H. Johnson, *Los Angeles Times,* 5 May 1957, 87. "Harold H. Johnson," 1950 United States Federal Census (National Archives at Washington, DC; Washington, DC; *Seventeenth Census of the United States, 1950;* Year: *1950;* Census Place: *Los Angeles, Los Angeles, California;* Roll: *5056;* Page: *16;* Enumeration District: *66-836;* ancestry.com, subscription required).

74 "Residence of Mr. & Mrs. H. H. Johnson, Bel Air, California," *Architectural Digest,* 13, no. 2 (1951): n.p.

75 "History of Great Western," https://web.archive.org/web/19970119201316/http://www.gwf.com/gwhist.html.

76 "Charles D. Wagner," 1930 United States Federal Census (Year: *1930;* Census Place: *Detroit, Wayne, Michigan;* Page: *8B;* Enumeration District: *1082;* FHL microfilm: *2340775;* ancestry.com, subscription required). For the Jewish background of the Wagner family, see the 1910 United States Federal

Census (Year: *1910;* Census Place: *Detroit Ward 3, Wayne, Michigan;* Roll: *T624_681;* Page: *8A;* Enumeration District: *0319;* FHL microfilm: *1374694;* ancestry.com, subscription required).

77 349 South Linden Drive, permit no. 26948, 12 May 1952, Department of Buildings, City of Beverly Hills, https://cs.beverlyhills.org/cs/?menu=menu1 (search: 349 S Linden Dr).

78 See entry "349 South Linden Drive Beverly Hills" for the years 1956 and 1960 in the *Los Angeles Street Address Directory* (Los Angeles: Pacific Telephone and Telegraph Co., 1956 and 1960).

79 For White's life and work, see Welter, *Walter S. White.*

80 Conversation and email communications of the author with S. Somerville, July 2020.

81 "Good Modern Is Livable," *Los Angeles Times Home Magazine,* 19 August 1945, 3; and personal conversations of the author with S. Sklarek, July to August 2022, and June 2024.

82 For the marriage date: "Leopold Fischer" in *California, U.S., Marriage Index, 1949–1959,* 145 (*California, U.S., Marriage Index, 1949–1959* [database online]; ancestry.com, subscription required). For the date of divorce: "Maxine Erhart," 1950 United States Federal Census (The National Archives in Washington, DC; Washington, DC; *Seventeenth Census of the United States, 1950;* Year: *1950;* Census Place: *Los Angeles, Los Angeles, California;* Roll: *2061;* Page: *76;* Enumeration District: *66-1111;* ancestry.com, subscription required). Irene Below refers to one source according to which Fischer was married to an unidentified wealthy piano player in Los Angeles (Below, "Das Leben von Leopold Fischer," 2). Whether this piano player was Maxine Erhart is unclear. The piano player that we know Fischer knew, Norma Albers, was married from 1935 onward.

83 "Mrs. Maxine B[yers]. Erhart," *Los Angeles Times,* 28 May 1954, part 2, p. 9.

84 "Victor Gruen Associate on BCA Agenda," *Independent Star News,* 7 May 1967, 11.

85 On this aspect of Ain's life and career, see, for example, Denzer, *Gregory Ain;* and Anthony Fontenot, ed., *Notes from Another Los Angeles: Gregory Ain and the Construction of a Social Landscape* (Cambridge, MA: MIT Press, 2022).

CHAPTER 4

Around 1941, Around 1951

In Germany, Leopold Fischer's career ended with designs for detached homes for individual clients. In Southern California, his career began with and was dominated by designs of private houses. The symmetry of commissions across the abyss of exile may suggest a continuity within Fischer's career. However, Fischer turned to bourgeois and middle-class detached houses in Germany mainly after his socially engaged work in mass housing ended with the bankruptcy of the housing cooperative at which he was employed, a sequence of events that raises questions about the importance of Fischer's near-exclusive focus on individual domestic designs in California. Were these detached houses a convenient means or even the *only* means available to earn a living? Or were they signs of a deliberate reorientation toward a specific building type that would allow Fischer to rebuild his architectural career in exile? This chapter argues for the latter position. In the final years of Fischer's stay in Germany, detached private houses signaled the end of his career as a social housing architect. In exile, they signify the attempt to renew a professional life by focusing on domestic architecture for the middle and upper-middle classes—the bourgeoisie, in Central European parlance—a widely accepted and respected design task in Southern California.

At the center of this chapter stand two detached houses by Fischer: the Kohlmeier house in South Pasadena and the Slechta house in View Park. The former is the first major commission in exile Fischer worked on, from 1940 to 1941; its completion just before the United States entered World War II was a significant achievement for an émigré architect who had settled in California only a little more than three years earlier. Then, with the Slechta house's completion in 1951, Fischer could finally design domestic architecture again after the war economy had depressed the market for detached houses well into the conflict's aftermath.

These two homes were separated by a decade that spanned the duration of World War II, which provides a crucial conceptual framework for this chapter. With the United States entering the war, most, if not all, architects' work was impacted, sometimes severely, by the war economy. In retrospect, the Kohlmeier house and contemporary domestic designs by fellow architects appear as built manifestos of domestic architecture from around 1941, frozen in time by historical coincidence. Up to that junction, émigré architects like Fischer and his peer group had—unbeknown to them—only a short window of time to restart their architectural careers in exile. By 1941, they may have designed very few, maybe one or two, detached houses, which affected how they returned to architectural work after World War II. For émigré architects, being able to build again after the war often meant starting their career in exile for the second time. Accordingly, their first postwar domestic design constitutes a second manifesto, illustrating what someone like Fischer envisioned he would finally be able to add to contemporary domestic architecture more than a decade after his initial arrival in Los Angeles. By contrast, the comparable moment for other architects, including immigrant architects, may have meant returning to or at least drawing on prewar careers. I note this difference to direct attention to the difficulties faced by émigré architects like Fischer, not to downplay the efforts, even struggles, of many architects and immigrant architects in the postwar period.

Within this conceptual framework, Fischer's two programmatic buildings are analyzed in the context of selected domestic designs by fellow German-speaking émigré architects and a few others from the periods I call "around 1941" and "around 1951." The sample of detached houses by émigré architects is selective, even if not accidental, as to date, the oeuvres of these architects have received little attention. Still, in addition to contextualizing Fischer's designs, they allow glimpses at the émigré architects' contributions to Southern California domestic architecture.

Modern California: A Paradise of Detached Houses

Detached houses became crucial to developing California after the state joined the United States in 1850, especially during the booster era, which lasted from approximately the mid-1880s to the mid-1920s. During this period, Southern California was widely and aggressively advertised all over the United States as a destination where it was affordable to acquire land to build a home or to purchase a detached house in a newly created suburb.[1]

As early as 1886, California's state engineer envisioned "a region of peaceful homes where light labor would season leisure and add to the enjoyments of life."[2] Almost half a century later, the landscapes and cityscapes of Los Angeles were the subject matter of the German geographer Anton Wagner (1904–2001), who conducted fieldwork in Southern California for six months from August 1932 onward for his dissertation on the urban growth of the metropolis.[3] Wagner's dissertation was published in Germany in 1935, just before Fischer was forced to flee the following year. Coincidentally, Wagner and Fischer are of the same generation, born only three years apart.

Wagner's dissertation begins with repeated and excited references to the "profusion of houses," the "never-ending mass of houses [that] extends across the landscape, as if dropped from a set of giant buildings blocks," and the "immeasurable sea of small houses and large villas" at whose center rose "the multistory buildings of the urban core" (fig. 4.1).[4] Architecture and architects occupy minor, though relevant, roles in Wagner's account of this urban growth. Individual wealthy landowners may have subdivided their (formerly agricultural) landholdings in ways that allowed Los Angeles to grow into "a garden city with widely spaced houses" in the later decades of the nineteenth century.[5] This phenomenon reversed "the meaning of *estate* in and around Los Angeles.... Agricultural properties with houses once treated as unimportant were converted into country estates where agriculture was now regarded as unimportant."[6] Wagner endorsed this appreciation of large estate dwellings such as the "park-like estates and villas designed by the best architects" in Beverly Hills and "the modern villas of millionaires, built in their own parks, [that] grace the slopes of the Santa Monica Mountains."[7]

These detached dwellings set standards for other, usually smaller homes in two ways. First, urban detached houses aspired to be similar to country

4.1. Anton Wagner (German, 1904–2001). Hilltop view east toward Hollywood, Los Angeles, California, 1932–33, gelatin silver print.

San Francisco, California Historical Society.

houses, which resulted in "exclusive residential neighborhoods... [with] homes designed by architects, not standardized dwellings erected by contractors."[8] Second, contractors and developers copied these larger homes as stylistic models by adapting them for much smaller houses, a step that resulted, according to Wagner, in "ugly buildings in bad taste" for "members of the petty bourgeoisie and farmers" who were an "unsophisticated group of inhabitants" from the Midwest and elsewhere in the nation.[9] In Wagner's view, these dwellings did not have the two characteristics that made neighborhoods exemplary: large building lots and generously sized detached homes.[10] Both of these characteristics together resulted in neighborhoods with widely dispersed detached homes, a feature of Los Angeles that contributed to Wagner's fascination with the city that so clearly speaks from the pages of his book.

• • •

How would Leopold Fischer have comprehended the city of Los Angeles? What architecture might have caught his eye when he began exploring the city? One answer is embedded in Edward Dimendberg's critical remark that Anton Wagner "did not acknowledge the extraordinary success of public housing in modernist architectural styles in [German] cities... as precedents from which Los Angeles could learn."[11] If any modernist

4.2. Richard Neutra (US American, 1892–1970, b. Austria-Hungary). Nesbitt house (1941–42), Los Angeles, California, 1941.

View from outside the entrance through the interior toward the garden. Photo by Julius Shulman.

Los Angeles, Getty Research Institute.

Central European émigré architects had been predestined to teach Los Angeles about social housing, it could have been Leopold Fischer, considering that he worked on social housing—called public housing in the United States—with Adolf Loos in Vienna, with Walter Gropius in Dessau, and then on his own. Should Fischer have read Wagner's book, he would have noticed the near-constant praise of architect-designed single-family homes as crucial building blocks of the city, past and present, and the near silence concerning apartment buildings, with no mention of any form of public housing. That observation, together with the visual appearance of the urban fabric of Los Angeles, suggested detached houses as a more promising basis for erecting a new architectural career in exile instead of again pursuing social housing, the professional success of Fischer's pre-exile life.

Moreover, the discussions among Los Angeles architects about domestic designs for detached houses will have sounded familiar to Fischer. His teacher, Loos, considered designing private homes as foundational to the work of the modern architect and taught Fischer about the importance of houses as homes. These ideas grew on Fischer once he was commissioned to design detached houses for individual clients in Germany, and he could fall back on them when asked to create detached dwellings in and around Los Angeles.

Two final points about detached, or freestanding, middle- and upper-middle-class housing in the Los Angeles area must be mentioned. First, as Nicholas Olsberg recently pointed out, the ongoing debate about housing and architecture in California habitually equates "the reinvention of the middle-class home with the rethinking of affordable housing,"[12] a conflation to remember when discussing Fischer, which brings up the second point. Only when adhering to a distinction between middle-class and bourgeois homes on the one side and social or affordable housing on the other can Fischer's detached houses in California be recognized for what they were: attempts to re-create a career in exile by focusing on a type of building that was in considerable demand in greater Los Angeles. They were *not* signifiers of an architect's failure to return in exile to social housing, a past phase of his pre-exile career that had ended even before he was forced to leave Europe.

Around 1941

In the history of the United States, 1941 is remembered because of the Japanese military attack on Pearl Harbor on 7 December, followed by the United States officially entering World War II the next day. In the history of California architecture, 1941 marks the beginning of Richard Neutra's work on the Nesbitt house, which was completed the following year (fig. 4.2). Neutra called the home his "war house" where "life [was] reduced to simplicity,"[13] a phrase with which he referenced both the alleged simple design of the building and the anticipated more modest, even restricted, life that times of war impose. In case the simple life at the Nesbitt house became too strenuous, the home was conveniently located halfway between Riviera Country Club and Brentwood Country Club, where members could enjoy a refined form of the simple life including being tended to by others. Wartime rationing of building materials enforced the use of brick and wood in conjunction with traditional construction methods, yet the floor plan of the Nesbitt home was nothing other than innovative and was not simple at all. It achieved "a new kind of transparency"[14] as interior spaces were pulled apart into separate units (a larger one for a main living area, studio, and bedroom, and a smaller one with an additional bedroom and studio) that were connected by walkways under projecting roofs and pergolas but otherwise open to the surroundings.[15] This expansive distribution of architecturally defined rooms and spaces on the site—without erecting two stand-alone buildings—created, at the same time, numerous possibilities to intertwine architecture and (landscaped) nature. Individual rooms overlook the garden through openable floor-to-ceiling windows; water seeps into interior basins from outdoor ponds; mortar oozes from the joints between the fired bricks; and at the street front, a parapet-height masonry wall creates a zone that intersects inside and outside instead of offering a clearly defined line separating the two realms as a traditional street facade would have achieved.

Esther McCoy identified the home as a turning point in Neutra's career that anticipated his domestic architecture from the later 1940s and beyond;[16] I would add, as argued elsewhere, that the forward-looking design is deeply rooted in Neutra's experience during World War I of nature as a hostile rather than welcoming environment that the architect has to tame.[17] Whether the design was visionary or reflective of past experiences and trauma, the dynamics and fluidity of the interior spaces, the intertwining of indoors and outdoors, and the relationship between architecture and nature made tangible conceptual issues that occupied Neutra around 1941 but that became frozen in time when World War II made private commissions next to impossible.

• • •

During this period, German-speaking émigré architects were designing a very different kind of detached house in the Los Angeles area, as is demonstrated by, for example, Rolf Sklarek's Meier house (Pacific Palisades, 1941) and Lane house (Los Angeles, 1941)—and even the earlier Segall house (see fig. 3.13)—as well as Liane Zimbler's house (Santa Monica, 1941) for the Austrian émigré composer Ernst Toch. Zimbler (1892–1987), an Austrian-Jewish architect, was of Neutra's generation. She fled Vienna in 1938, shortly after passing the qualifying exam to be an architect. Upon arrival in Los Angeles, Zimbler found work with the interior designer Anita Toor and took over the interior design firm after Toor died in 1941.[18] For comparative reasons, this section also includes the Thomas Mann house (Pacific Palisades, 1941), built to plans by the immigrant architect Julius R. Davidson, and the Nürnberg house (Pacific Palisades, 1938), erected by the builder-architect Norris McCauley Knaus (1883–1967) for the German-Jewish émigré journalist Rolf Nürnberg (1903–49).[19]

The houses were commissioned by diverse clients from Fritz Meier, a German immigrant coppersmith, to Thomas Mann, the German Nobel Prize for Literature recipient and an émigré. Their sizes range from four rooms for the Meiers to twenty rooms for the Manns, and the estimated valuations of the edifices, as noted on the building permits, vary from $3,000 (Meier house) to (at least) $20,000 (Mann house). Irrespective

Table 4.1. Select detached houses designed around 1941 by German-speaking émigré architects and other architects

Name of House (alphabetically listed)	Kohlmeier House	Lane House	Mann House	Meier House	Nürnberg House	Toch House
Date of Permit / Year Built	not known / 1941	July 1941/1941	April 1941/1941	September 1941/1941	October 1938 /1938	May 1941/1941
Number of Rooms	8 (drawing)	7	20	4	8	7
Bedrooms / Bathrooms	1/1 + 1/1 (of which 1/1 for maid?)	2 + 2 (of which 1/1 for maid?)	5/3 + 1/1 for maid (drawings)	1/1	5/5	2/2 + 1/1 guest or maid
Construction	• wood frame	• wood frame	• wood frame	• wood frame (blueprint)	• wood frame	• wood frame
Exterior Walls	• wood siding	• stucco	• stucco	• stucco	• stucco	• stucco
Roof: Shape and Materials	• hipped, original materials not known	• hipped, composite	• hipped, composite	• hipped, cedar shingles	• hipped, shingles	• hipped, shingles
Valuation		$7,300	$20,000	$3,000	$10,400	$8,000
Builder		Structon	Ernst M. Schlesinger	Mankin Building and Construction Company	M. S. Jepsen	Mankin Building and Construction Company
Architect	Fischer	Sklarek	Davidson	Sklarek	Knaus	Zimbler

Compiled from publicly accessible sources such as building permits, certificates of occupancy, Los Angeles County Assessor information and the City of Los Angeles Zone Information and Map Access System (ZIMAS), site visits, and, as noted, from privately owned blueprints and drawings.

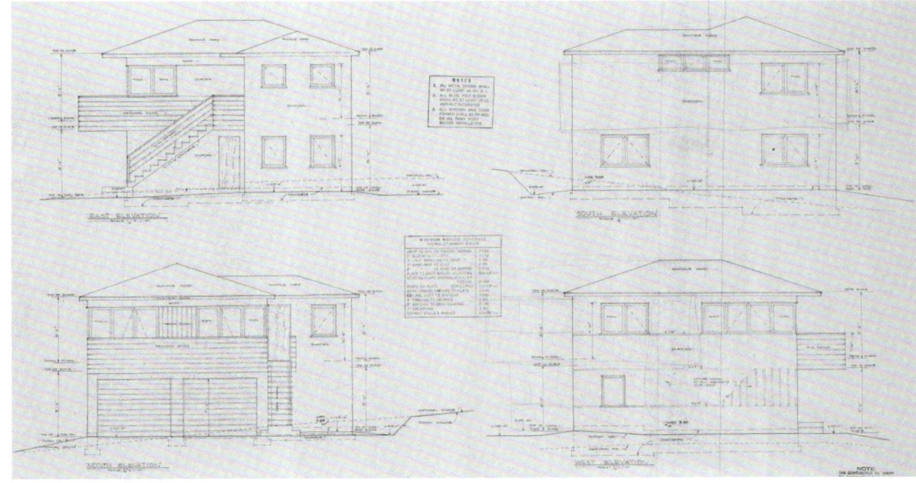

4.3a. Rolf Sklarek (US American, 1906–84, b. Germany).

Meier house (1941), Pacific Palisades, Los Angeles, California.

Elevations, sheet 4, 8 May 1941.

4.3b. Liane (Juliana) Zimbler (US American, 1892–1987, b. Austria-Hungary).

Toch house (1941), Santa Monica, California, ca. 1942.

Street facade. Photo by Julius Shulman.

Blacksburg, Virginia Tech, Special Collections and University Archives.

4.3c. Julius R. Davidson (US American, 1889–1977, b. Germany).

Mann house (1941), Pacific Palisades, Los Angeles, California.

North and south elevations, detail of sheet 3, 28 February 1941.

University of California, Santa Barbara, Architecture and Design Collection.

of quantitative differences, the houses share striking architectural similarities even after accounting for variations (table 4.1). They are usually two stories tall, though some have one-story sections and additions (figs. 4.3a–c). They feature low-hipped roofs with broad overhangs (sometimes combined with roof terraces), and most are covered in stucco without ornament or decoration.

The floor plans are individualized but share crucial characteristics (figs. 4.4a–c). With few exceptions, private rooms are on the upper levels, and living and service spaces are on the lower ones. The floor plans by Davidson, Sklarek, and Zimbler minimize corridor spaces, though Davidson's Mann house did so by the least amount. Zimbler's Toch house substitutes several small halls with multiple doors for corridors so that each room is accessible independently from adjacent ones.[20] All known floor plans maximize usable floor space by offering built-in cupboards and cabinets for storage and even some built-in furniture (though nothing can be said about the Nürnberg house, as plans were not obtainable).

The floor plans do not illustrate an interest by designers and clients in such concepts as an open plan or ideas about dynamic space. For the most part, rooms are separated from each other and assigned distinct functions. All five houses provide professional and occupational workspaces catering to the occupants' needs. The Meier house includes a workshop, the Lane house a den as an office-like space, and the others studies-cum-libraries. The Toch and Mann houses are

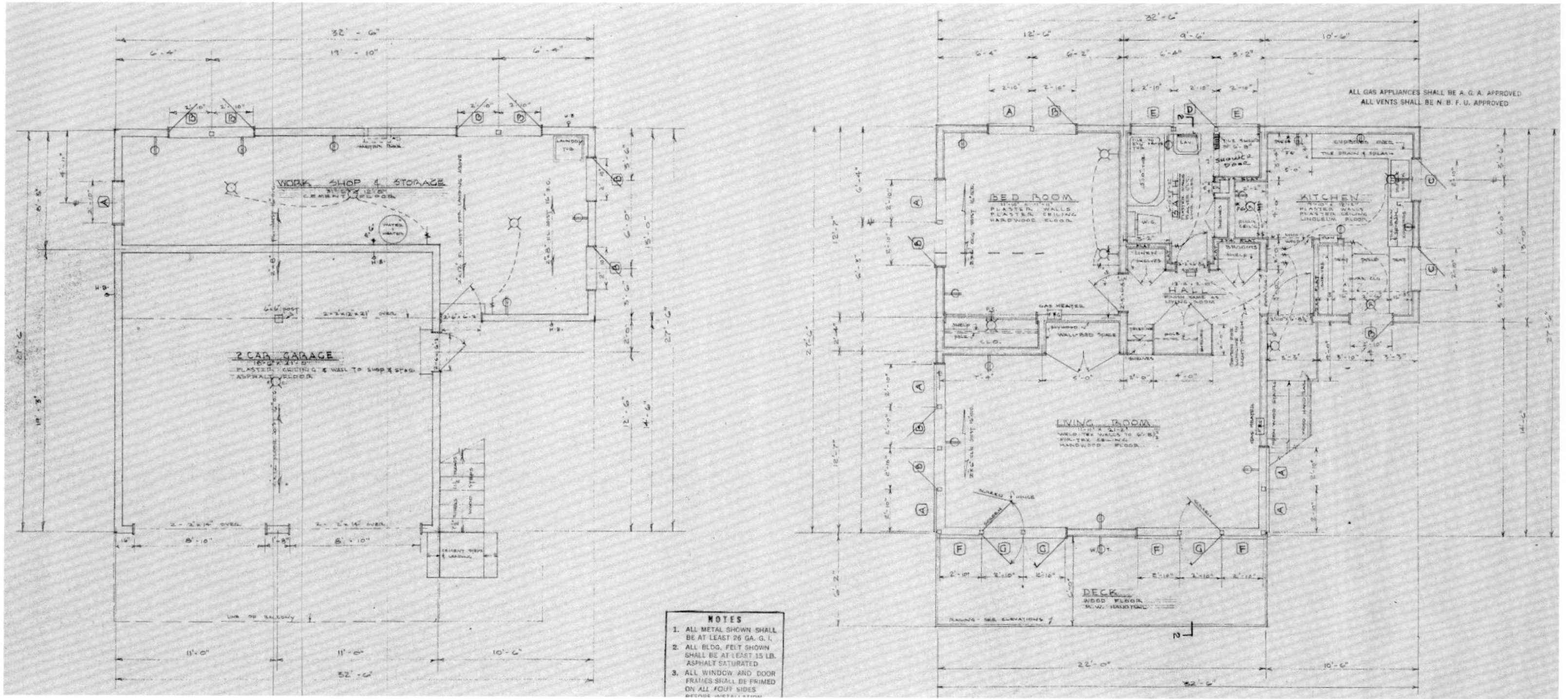

arranged around these study spaces. In the former, a spacious living room doubles as a composition studio, which explains the size and isolated, quiet location on one side of the home, with adjacent rooms acting as sound barriers. In the Mann house, the study is placed in a cubic wing that projects from the main house; indeed, the floor plan's linear sequence "from the profane to the inner sanctum, from the garage on the west to Mann's study on the southeast" culminates in this cube.[21] Mann's study may have been inspired by the one inside the Nürnberg house. When Julius R. Davidson began drafting plans in September of 1940,[22] Mann had just visited Rolf Nürnberg to see the latter's new house. Mann was most impressed, especially by Nürnberg's "complete German library from the best period."[23] Architecturally speaking, the tighter, volumetric massing of the Mann house is the better design, yet the broad similarities between both buildings are intriguing.

Lastly, any intertwining of the indoors with the outdoors is confined to deliberately treating windows and selectively placing traditional outdoor elements such as terraces, patios, and balconies. Windows are usually punched out from the facades where needed. At least one room, often the living room, features either large floor-to-ceiling windows or smaller windows grouped to evoke a horizontal window. The integration

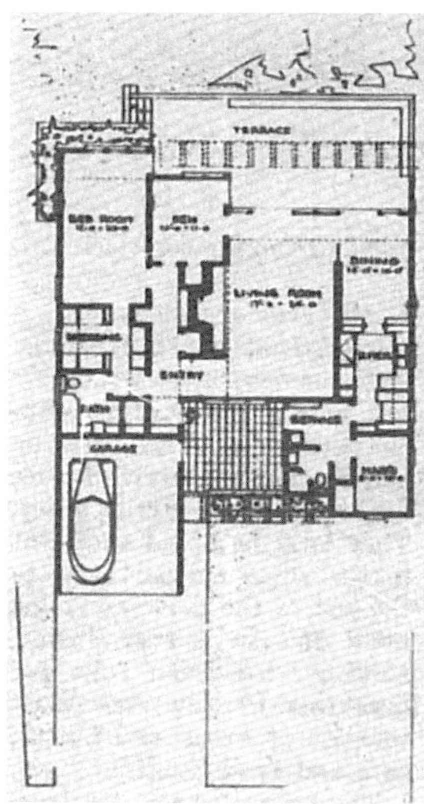

4.4a. Rolf Sklarek (US American, 1906–84, b. Germany).

Meier house (1941), Pacific Palisades, Los Angeles, California.

First- and second-floor plans, sheet 3, 8 May 1941.

4.4b. Rolf Sklarek (US American, 1906–84, b. Germany).

Lane house (1941), Los Angeles, California.

Floor plan for main level, 1941. From "Sleek as a Top Hat," *Los Angeles Times Home Magazine*, 28 April 1946, 3.

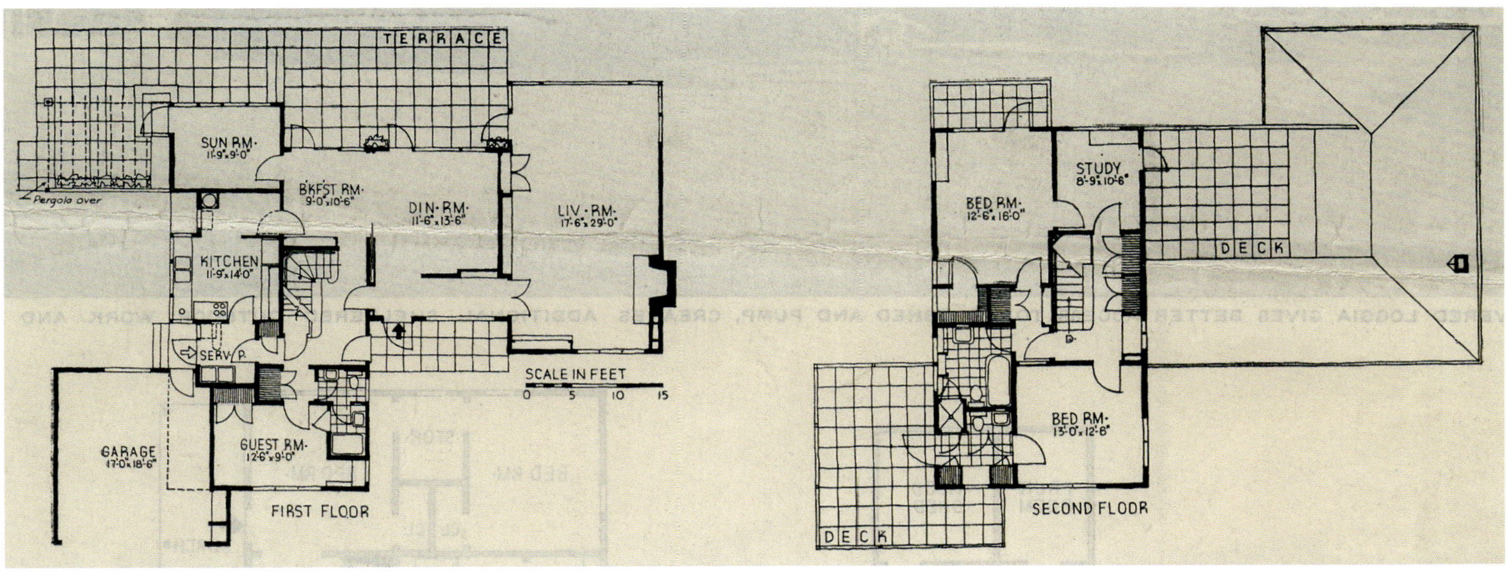

4.4c. Liane (Juliana) Zimbler (US American, 1892–1987, b. Austria-Hungary).

Toch house (1941), Santa Monica, California.

Floor plans for lower and upper levels, 1946 or earlier. From "Suburban House, Santa Monica, Calif.," *Architectural Forum* 84 (May 1946): 85.

Blacksburg, Virginia Tech, Special Collections and University Archives.

of the inside and the outside happens judiciously. Sometimes, every other window of horizontally grouped windows can be opened, as in the Meier house. In the Toch house, an expansive picture window in a living room-cum-composition studio stretches horizontally over an entire wall and pulls around the corners on either end; it grants a panoramic view but no access to the outside. Window walls in living rooms or dining rooms composed of individual floor-to-ceiling windows are another option to link visually to the outside. Usually in these cases, only individual segments allow for ventilation and outdoor access.

The Kohlmeier House in South Pasadena

The Ralph and Phyllis Kohlmeier house (1940–41) was Leopold Fischer's first major commission for a detached house on California soil. The site is on a promontory in the hilly terrain that stretches south from Monterey Road in South Pasadena toward Huntington Drive. A street curves several times around four sides of the irregular seven-sided lot whose other sides abut neighboring lots. The promontory's steep rise on almost every side facing the street prevents comprehensive views of the house when walking or driving up to it but allows at least a glance of one facade, which is crucial for Fischer's design, as is explained below.

The spatial organization of the house combines a composition of distinct geometric volumes with a linear floor plan. The center of the house is a one-story cuboid volume placed centrally atop the promontory (fig. 4.5). Its two long facades are nearly perfectly oriented to the north and south. On the south side, an outdoor terrace parallels the length of the cuboid; it would have offered distant views until the surrounding vegetation grew to its current size. When adding more spaces and rooms on the narrow ends of the cuboid, Fischer took advantage of the steeply sloping grounds. At the east end, a rectangular wing projects north; at its northernmost end, a garage is attached that steps down the slope as a separate geometric body. At the west end, a wing, almost cube-shaped, projects south. It is two stories tall and again placed lower on the slope. Consequently, the upper story lies below the adjacent central cuboid. On its even lower other level, this projecting wing offers storage space that can only be accessed from the outside.

The composition of the house from individual volumes is particularly well articulated in the vertical dimension and through differently shaped roofs. The central cuboid and the upper part of the north wing are on the same level; the former is slightly taller, and both are protected by low-hipped roofs with wide eaves. The near-cubic south wing and the garage at the far end of the north wing are placed farther down the slopes. Both feature flat roofs; the one on the south wing is a terrace. Along the north side of this roof terrace, a slender, narrow cuboid underneath a slightly inclined pent roof extends from the main cuboid; it houses the corridor to access the south cube.

4.5. Leopold Fischer (US American, 1901–75, b. Austria-Hungary).

Ralph and Phyllis Kohlmeier house (1940–41), South Pasadena, California.

Plot plan, October 1940.

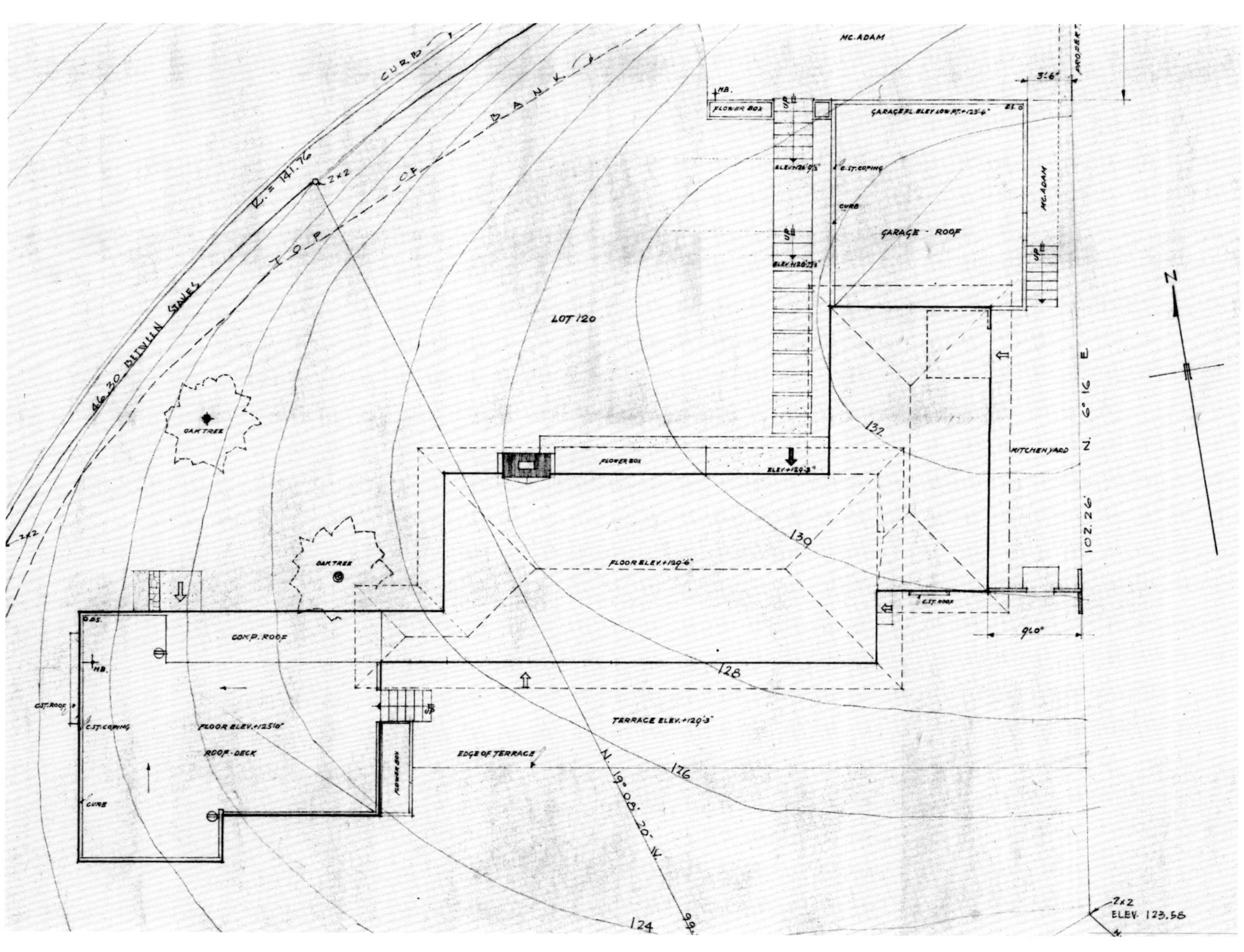

4.6. Leopold Fischer (US American, 1901–75, b. Austria-Hungary).

Ralph and Phyllis Kohlmeier house (1940–41), South Pasadena, California.

Floor plan for main level, October 1940.

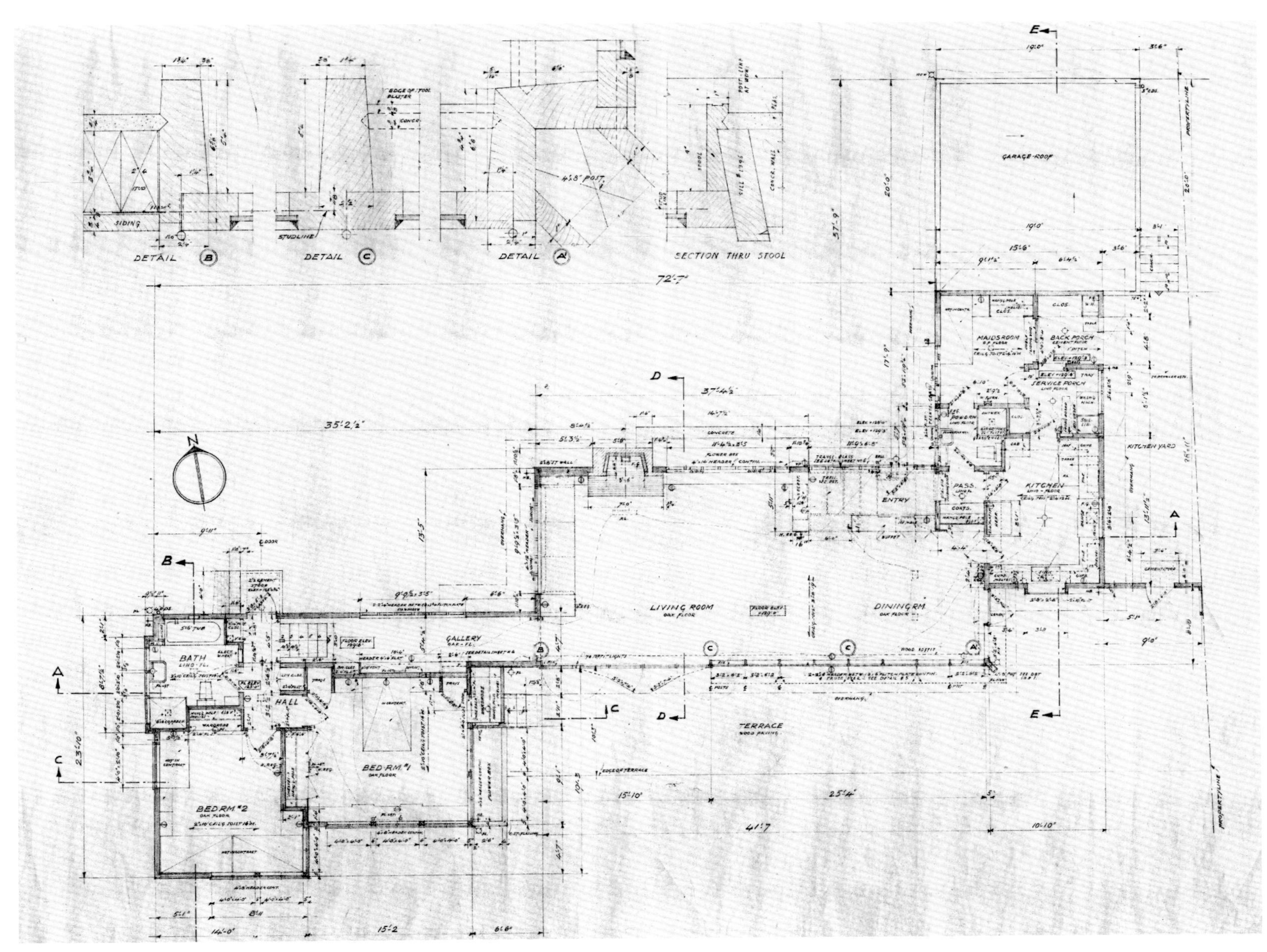

4.7. Leopold Fischer (US American, 1901–75, b. Austria-Hungary).

Ralph and Phyllis Kohlmeier house (1940–41), South Pasadena, California, April 2022.

Interior central cuboid looking toward entrance and dining area.

The internal layout of rooms and spaces reveals the order underpinning this complex arrangement of volumes (fig. 4.6). The central cuboid accommodates the living, dining, and entrance areas of the house. The latter two areas occupy approximately a third of the cuboid and are placed at its east end, from where they connect to service spaces in the north wing. The dining space borders the kitchen, and the entrance area adjoins the service porch and a powder room. The latter doubles up as a bathroom for a maid's room that, together with an adjacent back porch leading to the outside, forms the north end of this wing.

On the other side of the central cuboid, a corridor (which Fischer calls a gallery in his floor plan) extends from the southwest corner of the living room. At its far end, steps go down to the upper level of the two-story near-cubic wing. There, two bedrooms are oriented south, a bathroom looks out west, and a door gives access to a garden to the north. The parents' bedroom, identified as bedroom 1 in the plan, occupies the southeast corner of the cube, with a children's bedroom (bedroom 2) located in the southwest corner; this second bedroom projects farther out, which results in a setback in front of the main bedroom.

In short, the concept of the Kohlmeier house is a linear arrangement of adjacent functional zones and rooms that is overlaid with a strong vertical articulation of the individual volumes, one for each zone. The upright articulation exposes Fischer's skillful use of the house's topographical setting and expresses a hierarchical order of the home's internal spaces and the volumes that accommodate them. The appearance of the entrance area as a small, lower cuboid within the volume of the central cuboid illustrates this order well (fig. 4.7). Two walls separate the small entrance foyer from the adjacent areas. The longer one is a storage wall serving the adjacent dining area. The other accommodates a built-in bureau (*Sekretär*) with a fold-down desk, adding a writing nook to the living area. A lightweight wooden trellis was to cover the entrance area behind those storage walls, which would have furthered the impressions of a room within a room, yet it is unclear whether such a symbolic ceiling was ever realized.

On the exterior, the lively composition of the building is visually unified by horizontal tongue-and-groove wood siding for the facades except for a brick fireplace and chimney on the north facade (fig. 4.8). Limited but repeated window formats add to the repose of the building. Rectangular windows, at times divided into squares, are sometimes arranged as horizontal window bands. The south facade of the central cuboid is a window wall that combines five floor-to-ceiling

4.8. Leopold Fischer (US American, 1901–75, b. Austria-Hungary).

Ralph and Phyllis Kohlmeier house, South Pasadena, California.

Elevations, October 1940.

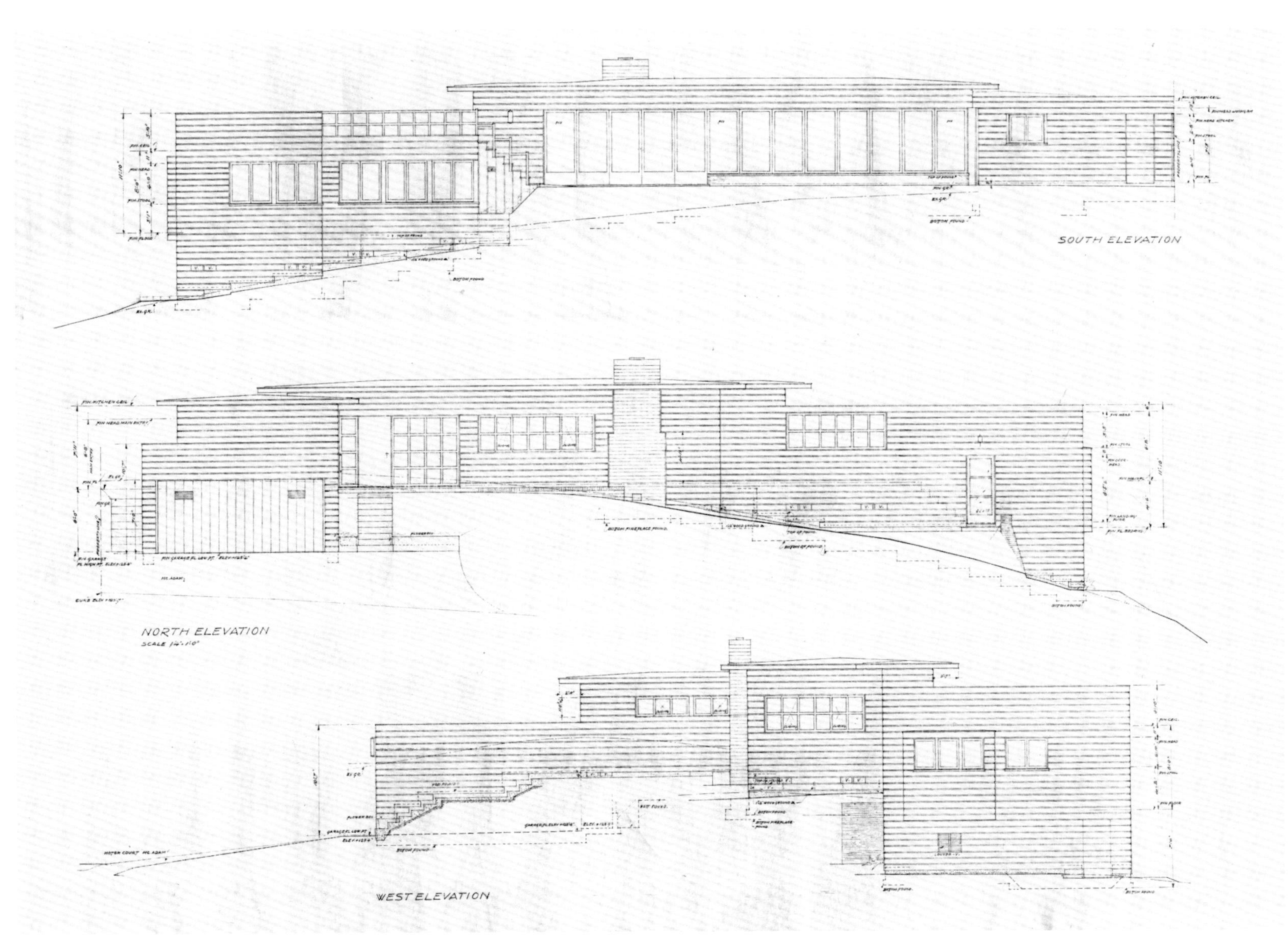

windows on its western end followed by eight shorter ones above a low parapet that stretches to the east. The taller windows include a four-window-wide double door that can be opened in stages. Of the remaining eight shorter windows, the outermost ones are fixed, and the others are openable.

• • •

The design of the Kohlmeier house draws on at least three distinct sources: Frank Lloyd Wright's domestic architecture, Fischer's bourgeois homes in Weimar, Germany, and Adolf Loos's concept of *Raumplan.* At first sight, the building strikes a rather Wrightian tone, which is unsurprising considering that Fischer stayed and worked with Wright at Taliesin in Spring Green, Wisconsin, for a few months in 1937. The overall low-lying and horizontal appearance of the Kohlmeier house may recall Wright's Prairie houses; the wide overhangs of the hipped roofs resemble the eaves at Taliesin, though the projections there are much deeper and the hipped roofs significantly taller than at the Fischer-designed house. The linear arrangement of the internal spaces suggests the broad influences of the American architect, making the house appear almost as a version of Wright's Usonian houses.

Usonian houses were an attempt by Frank Lloyd Wright to design affordable houses for the middle classes that began in earnest in 1936, when the Jacobs house in Madison, Wisconsin, was erected as the first-ever house of this kind. As Madison and Spring Green are not far apart, Fischer may have visited the Jacobs house while he stayed at Taliesin from the end of June to October 1937. Some of the design characteristics of Usonian houses apply to the Kohlmeier house. For example, social spaces are in one wing and private areas in another. Also, in both, a long gallery hallway gives access to the bedrooms; in the floor plan of the Kohlmeier house, Fischer even used the term *gallery* for the corridor leading to the bedrooms, as noted earlier. Other characteristics cannot be found in the Kohlmeier house, such as a concrete-slab foundation, a preference for flat roofs, and a cost-saving carport instead of a garage.[24] The Usonian houses' much richer interior surfaces, including ceiling planes that may vary slightly in height within the same space, and even the occasional use of decorative details such as ornamental bricks or wood carvings, have no equivalents in the Kohlmeier house. And there seem to be no equivalents in Wright's Usonian houses for features of Fischer's Kohlmeier house, of which the maid's room in the latter home is the most apparent difference, hinting at clients from disparate social classes. Fischer's emphasis on the vertical dimension and clear articulation of the separate volumes that make up the house are two more differences. For the likely roots of these two characteristics, it is crucial to look at some of Fischer's designs for detached houses in Germany.

As set out in chapter 1, Fischer's detached houses in Germany were mainly for bourgeois clients. From a formal point of view, Fischer preferred to cast their requirements into self-contained geometric volumes. The two-story Liebig villa (Dessau, 1927–28; see fig. 1.10) was an upright cuboid with smaller volumes either cut out from the main one for a roof terrace or added on for a winter garden. Similarly (before a radical remodel after World War II), the Tittel house (Bielefeld, 1931) was an upright two-story cuboid with an added-on smaller cuboid for a winter garden (see fig. 1.11). Sometimes, these add-ons were barely more than an additional plane placed in front of a facade, as on the south and north sides of the Tittel house (or even earlier in Fischer's design for a demonstration house in Braunschweig in 1925; see fig. 1.4). In the center of the south facade of the Tittel house, a winter garden occupies the add-on cuboid, and the windows on either side are framed by projecting planes created by positioning the brick masonry surrounding the window openings just in front of the brick piers, the major structural components of the two-story house on that side.

Fischer repeats exactly this detail of projecting planes in the facades of the bathroom and the kitchen of the Kohlmeier house, thus leaving visible traces that his German detached houses were on his mind when designing the South Pasadena one. Take, for example, the bathroom that occupies the northwest corner of the two-story cube at the westernmost end of the Kohlmeier house. On the west facade of the cube, Fischer pushes outward the section of the wall behind which the bathroom is located (see fig. 4.6). The projection of nine-and-a-half inches, of which approximately five inches account for the thickness of the wall, barely adds usable space. Instead, it is an aesthetic gesture, for this is the first and only facade that can be fully seen when one drives or walks up to the house (fig. 4.9). Accordingly, it was an excellent opportunity to advertise Fischer's cubic, modernist architecture by visibly demonstrating his skills in designing facades as abstract compositions.

Fischer's preference for enclosed geometric volumes like cubes or cuboids when designing

4.9. Leopold Fischer (US American, 1901–75, b. Austria-Hungary).

Ralph and Phyllis Kohlmeier house (1940–41), South Pasadena, California, 2020.

View of the westernmost facade with the projecting bathroom wall.

detached houses in Germany harks back to Adolf Loos's idea of Raumplan, a method of design in which "depending on their purpose and importance, the spaces not only had varying sizes but also varying heights." Heinrich Kulka, one of Loos's students and the author of an early monograph on Loos, continues explaining, "in this way[,] in the same building envelope, the same foundation, under the same roof, inside the same exterior walls he [Loos] can make more spaces."[25] Raumplan was to counter the notion that domestic architecture meant, in the words of Loos, "the organization of living rooms . . . on a level surface, story by story."[26] Accordingly, Loos conceived edifices like the Rufer house (Vienna, 1922), Moller villa (Vienna, 1926–27), and Müller villa (Prague, 1928–30) as compositions of separate volumetric spaces or rooms, individually dimensioned according to functions and needs, which were then combined in a three-dimensional puzzle within the perimeters of a self-contained larger volume such as an upright cuboid.

Fischer's Kohlmeier house feeds on Loos's Raumplan, as the design is based on the idea that houses should be conceived of rooms and spaces, individually sized in regard to all three dimensions. Fischer, however, translates that foundational idea into a composition that is tightly organized across the site in a legible shape, keeps the individual volumes visible (and experienceable), and avoids any similarity to, for example, the irregularly shaped, expansive country houses of the Arts and Crafts movement or to sprawling ranch houses as they became popular in the mid-twentieth century.

• • •

The indoor-outdoor relationship of the Kohlmeier house transformed Fischer's interest in the intermediate spaces between interior and exterior spaces (as exemplified by his German oeuvre) into the idea of an outdoor room, which was to become influential for most of his California works. To understand that and how the idea of a house as a series of rooms extended for Fischer into the garden requires revisiting Fischer's earliest period in Germany when he collaborated with Leberecht Migge, the landscape architect whom Fischer met through Loos in circa 1924. From 1924 to 1925, Fischer remodeled Migge's home in the artist colony Worpswede near Bremen in northern Germany. For that home, Migge had already created a large garden, including greenhouses.[27] Fischer added "an intimate nook for sitting down, . . . a delightful winter garden for the lady of the house,"[28] and an office space for Migge. The winter garden enlarged an existing living room and connected it with the garden via a wall of floor-to-ceiling, multipane glass doors. Migge called the new room an "intermediate member" (*Zwischenglied*), which he defined as "living spaces that are almost garden, and parts of a garden that are more or less enclosed living spaces."[29] The idea of such interstitial spaces reverberates through Fischer's oeuvre in Weimar Germany and in California.

Subsequently, Migge and Fischer also collaborated on several exhibits for the *Heim und Scholle* exhibition that was held in Braunschweig from June to July 1925.[30] Their main exhibit comprised two two-story, semi-detached houses (*Doppelhäuser*) whose design evolved around interstitial spaces intimately linking house and garden. Here, the overhang of the wood-clad upper story defined spaces around the lower story that, depending on the season, were enclosed with removable glass walls offering temporary greenhouses for growing vegetables and protecting plants during the colder season (see fig. 1.4).

A comparable approach to intertwining indoor and outdoor spaces can be observed at the Kohlmeier house, even if it is unknown whether and, if yes, *how* Fischer laid out any portions of the garden to the south of the home. Indeed, already the south terrace and the central cuboid illuminate in an exemplary manner how Fischer closely interrelated an exterior, intermediate living area with an indoor space while keeping both spatially separated (fig. 4.10). The relation between the inside and the outside is established, for example, by the L-shaped form of the terrace (as drawn in the floor plan) that closely hugs the south-oriented window wall of the interior living-cum-dining area and extends into the recess of the south facade at the kitchen. This relation is functionally expressed by positioning the double door as part of the south window wall immediately opposite the fireplace on the north wall of the living room. Perpendicular to the fireplace, a built-in sofa occupies the west wall of the room. In short, Fischer created a seating area beside the fireplace from which views can go through the double door, closed or opened, across the terrace into the garden.

The spatial separation between the indoor and outdoor realms manifests itself in the south window wall, a hard border that can only selectively be opened without allowing the two adjacent realms to merge or flow into each other. The separation extends to the

4.10. Leopold Fischer (US American, 1901–75, b. Austria-Hungary).

Ralph and Phyllis Kohlmeier house (1940–41), South Pasadena, California, April 2022.

South terrace in front of the central cuboid looking toward the projecting bedroom wing in the background.

4.11. Leopold Fischer (US American, 1901–75, b. Austria-Hungary).

Ralph and Phyllis Kohlmeier house (1940–41), South Pasadena, California, n.d.

Double glass door between the south terrace and living area fully opened with fireplace in background left. Photo by Robert Cleveland.

4.12. Leopold Fischer (US American, 1901–75, b. Austria-Hungary).

Ralph and Phyllis Kohlmeier house (1940–41), South Pasadena, California, April 2022.

Stairs from the south terrace to the roof terrace on top of the bedroom wing.

materials, as the living room floor is oak parkette (covered with rugs), and the terrace is laid with bricks in a square pattern; different floor coverings mark different terrains (fig. 4.11).[31] Whether the trellis covered by canvas fabric offering shade is of Fischer's design is unknown. Regardless, it underlines the terrace as an independent outdoor space that, at the same time, relates to both the indoors and the garden farther south.[32] Significantly, it is here on the outside that the design of the Kohlmeier house takes one of its strongest Loosian turns. Fischer complements the south terrace with a second outdoor space on top of the adjacent two-story cube and connects the two levels with a short, steep stair seen in figure 4.12, thus creating the beginnings of an outdoor Raumplan.[33] That said, once one has climbed onto the roof deck, a sense of disappointment sets in that one cannot continue onto the taller roof of the adjacent cuboid and, from there, onto the central cuboid.

• • •

Where does the Kohlmeier house find its place between Richard Neutra's Nesbitt house and the inconspicuous stucco houses designed by Fischer's émigré peers? The visionary Nesbitt house illustrates Neutra's zest for architectural innovation. This characteristic also expresses the architect's confidence in his position as a modernist figure in Los Angeles whose clients expected unusual houses. By contrast, the houses built around 1941 by émigré architects (and other architects) are more concerned with establishing the professional credentials of their émigré designers and the respectability of the clients if they were émigrés. The plan, appearance, and details of Sklarek's and Zimbler's houses modernized a modern detached home popular at the time. Their reference points were contemporary unadorned detached houses with stucco facades, low-hipped roofs, and even the occasional corner window. One example of these unadorned houses is Knaus's Nürnberg house (scaled up to a wealthy émigré client), and numerous others can be found in the *Los Angeles Times,* demonstrating the popularity of

quired site.

Other deals closed through the McMichael office include the sale of a 13-room two-family dwelling at 633-35 N. Rossmore Ave. to Mrs. Theresa E. Maguire for $9500 and a 10-room dwelling at 6627 Franklin Ave. to Charles A. Bank.

Kenmore Ave. Building Sold

The Cunningham Apartments, four-story, 48-unit building at 610 S. Kenmore Ave., has been bought by G. E. Kinsey from Claude E. Carnes for approximately $125,000. The structure's units recently were redecorated and refurnished.

The purchase was handled for both parties by Clark Hall and A. M. Beaver of the A. M. Beaver Co., brokers.

RECENTLY CONSTRUCTED—Pictured is one of many new dwellings in Culver City. It is at 11017 Barman Ave. Its features include a rather large brick patio opening off living room. Cost of this home was $4500.

Contract Let for Huge Plant

Contract for construction of a $63,000,000 magnesium plant 10 miles easterly of Las Vegas has been awarded to the McNeil Construction Co. of Los Angeles, it was announced as the week was ending.

Construction of the plant, to be largest of the kind in the nation, is being financed by the Defense Plant Corp., and it will be operated by Basic Magnesium, Inc., it was disclosed. The plant is scheduled to be ready for operation Sept. 1, 1942, and will employ about 7500 men.

The exterior of the house is of a modified French style. Colorful gardens enhance the beauty of the design and are centered about a large oak-covered terrace with an outside fireplace which ties into the living room and den chimney.

The plan has been so created that it is possible to go directly to the breakfast room, living room, den, all bedrooms and bath from the entry hall without going through any other room. The living and dining rooms as well as the den and master bedroom have a garden vista.

COMFORT STRESSED

Comfort, spaciousness and a gracious way of living were the ultimate aim of the designer and interior decorator and the pattern of the bedrooms exemplifies the successful execution of this plan, with each a suite in itself,

Turn to Page 2, Column 2

HOME CHARM EXEMPLIFIED—Typical of the scores of beautiful homes built on wide-frontage, shaded sites in scenic Viewpark is above residence on Olympiad Drive near the Olympic Village section. More than $1,025,000 has been expended for home construction in the Viewpark locality this year, the Los Angeles Investment Co. reports.

School Again Opens Contracting Course

Instruction to Qualify for State License

In line with its policy of offering to the public practical and beneficial trade training, the Fremont Evening High School, 7676 S. San Pedro St., is continuing its class in the fundamentals of building contracting and estimating. This is announced as a complete and extensive course in requirements necessary to pass the State contractors' examination. Additionally, the advanced work covers every phase of building contracting, including business administration, legal problems,

OPENING ANNOUNCED—The above attractive two-bedroom-and-den Colonial-type dwelling at 2950 Lorain Road, San Marino, is to be opened today for inspection, it is an-

4.13. Stucco box houses from real-estate article in the *Los Angeles Times,* 14 September 1941, E1.

4.14. South East Housing Architects Associated: Paul R. Williams (US American, 1894–1980), chief architect; Adrian Wilson (US American, 1898–1988); Gordon B. Kaufmann (US American, 1888–1949, b. England); Welton Becket (US American, 1902–69) and Walter Wurdeman (US American, 1903–49); and Richard J. Neutra (US American, 1892–1970, b. Austria-Hungary).

Pueblo del Rio Housing (1941–42), Los Angeles, California, n.d. Photo by Leonard Nadel.

Los Angeles, Housing Authority Collection.

this type of unassuming modern, contemporary home (fig. 4.13). The émigré architects could have even pointed to the visual appearance of early public housing projects in the Los Angeles area—for example, Wyvernwood (1939–42) and Pueblo del Rio (1941–42)—as inspirations (fig. 4.14). Regardless of all differences, "modern" by 1941 meant, to a large degree, a simple, geometric volume, unadorned, most likely rendered in stucco and protected by a low-hipped roof with a wide overhang.

Within the context of these 1941 houses, the Kohlmeier house by Fischer blends in when it comes to details such as hipped roofs, minimal corridor spaces, maximum built-in storage facilities, and generous fenestration. Yet, the house stands out when one considers its internal arrangements, such as rooms conceived as individual volumes arranged linearly and vertically; the complex indoor-outdoor relationship revolving around an interstitial terrace reconfigured as an outdoor room; the evocation of a Raumplan inside and out; and the broadly Wrightian appearance. As a manifesto of the architect's hopes for a new career in exile, the design occupies a halfway position between the Nesbitt house and the contemporary modern houses by Sklarek, Zimbler, Davidson, and Knaus. The Kohlmeier house illustrates Fischer focusing on developing *his* version of a modern detached house suitable for California by merging Loosian-inspired ideas about homes with a fascination for Wrightian designs.

Presumably, Fischer pinned hopes on the Kohlmeier house regarding further commissions for more detached dwellings. Instead, the house became a time capsule of Fischer's architectural aspirations when Japanese military forces attacked Pearl Harbor in Hawaii and the United States subsequently entered World War II. These events put Fischer's newly begun architectural career in exile on hold. Only a decade later, with the Slechta house, was Fischer able to erect a domestic design of architectural qualities comparable to the ones of the Kohlmeier house.

Around 1951

While world history and Southern California architectural history briefly locked steps in 1941, matters after World War II were fuzzier. Some historians claim the launch of the Case Study House program in 1945 as the year when architecture entered the postwar period,[34] while others pin that moment to a different year—1950, for example, when Raphael Soriano conceived some of the most economical and radical modernist architecture that still appeals occasionally to some critics today as a suitable solution to the middle-class housing problems in postwar Los Angeles.[35] New York's Museum of Modern Art favored a time range that stretched from 1945 to the years 1952 and 1953, when "with the mid-century modern architecture has come of age"[36]—or so decreed the publication accompanying the exhibition *Built in USA: Post-War Architecture,* which opened in January 1953.

In contrast, it is often much easier to identify when postwar professional life began for individuals. For Fischer, it was in 1951 when he completed the Slechta house and, consequently, could hope for the second time to return to a career as an independent architect. Other émigré architects expressed a similar awareness that the immediate postwar moment was as crucial for their exile career as the early time in exile that had ended in 1941. Rolf Sklarek, for example, arranged for the *Los Angeles Times* to publish in 1945 and 1946 homes that he had already built in 1938–39 and 1941, thereby hoping to present himself after the war as an established émigré architect with a prewar career.[37] This claim was not unique, but it differed from Neutra's argument for an ongoing continuum between his 1941 design and postwar work when he published, coincidentally in 1951, *Mystery and Realities of the Site.*[38]

The book primarily discusses the Nesbitt house, the Tremaine house (Montecito, 1944–48), and the Kaufmann desert house (Palm Springs, 1946–47), arguing that the three designs were not separated by World War II but constituted instead a coherent development of an unfolding architectural idea whose time finally has come. The designs for the Tremaine and Kaufmann houses build on ideas first experimented with in the Nesbitt house, most notably the dynamic flow of space within the interior of the house and, from there, back and forth between the inside and the outside. These ideas are, however, cast now into materials like concrete and steel instead of brick and executed with perfect finishes such as polished terrazzo and chiseled concrete rather than the rusticity of exposed brick and oozing mortar. The book is Neutra's personal post–World War II manifesto that presents the three homes as buildings "in the wooded foothills," "in the desert," and "in town."[39] They are prototypes of Neutra's environmental architecture suitable for prototypical sites that can "extend the habitable area of the planet into places not yet inhabited and thus unendowed with any tradition of civilized design." Neutra continues:

"There will be many other examples necessary in the jungles of the upper Amazonas [*sic*] or Congo, the Arctic regions, the arid sand wastes of Arabia."[40] Rather than representing made-to-measure responses to three unique California *genii loci,* the reach of the three Neutra designs was intended to be universal.

• • •

Turning to the work of Fischer's peer group of émigré architects, the sample of detached houses from around 1951 is architecturally much more diverse when compared with one another and with their siblings from 1941 (table 4.2; cf. table 4.1). The greater variety suggests that, for émigré architects, establishing their careers for the second time by distinguishing themselves and their work from other architects' designs was by then more critical than establishing credentials in the first instance, as they had aimed for around 1941.

The Frankel house (1948) in Altadena and the Sklarek house (1949) in Pacific Palisades were designed by their architects for their own families. A third example is the Cannon house (1950–51) in Los Angeles for a builder who constructed his house according to plans by the émigré architect Ulrich Plaut. The designs share with one another, and with the examples from 1941, efficient floor plans with distinct private and public areas, now generally separated within single-story homes, except for the two stories of the Cannon house. The interiors are again equipped with multiple built-in storage facilities and furniture and are generously fenestrated. The shapes of roofs are more varied than those in the 1941 examples. Only the Cannon house still sports a hipped roof, whereas the Frankel house and the Sklarek house rely on pent roofs, combined with some flat roofs in the case of Sklarek's design. Gone is the uniform use of stucco for the exterior of the houses in favor of mixing materials such as stucco and wood siding (Frankel house), adding to that mix brick as a third material (Cannon house), and cladding an entire home in redwood (Sklarek house). The most apparent differences between the individual homes from around 1951 and between those homes and the earlier set concern the relationships between the indoors and outdoors. A decade earlier, the indoor-outdoor interconnections were revolutionary in the case of the Nesbitt house and sophisticated in that of the Kohlmeier house but only tentatively developed, if not conventional, in the other examples. Now, each home defined the indoor-outdoor relationship anew and in its own way.

At first sight, Plaut's Cannon house is the more conventional of my three examples, especially regarding the indoor-outdoor relationship. The house is situated on a steeply rising lot that allows placing a garage, storage space, and small maid's apartment on a lower level on the slope (fig. 4.15a; see also fig. 5.17). Because of the lay of the land, the site plan is organized as a sequence of zones, each farther up the hill than the preceding one. The sequence starts with a steep U-shaped driveway leading up to the house, followed by the house and a deep terrace at its back. Next,

Table 4.2. Select detached houses designed around 1951 by German-speaking émigré architects and other architects

Name of House (alphabetically listed)	**Cannon House**	**Frankel House**	**Sklarek House**	**Slechta House**
Date of Permit / Year Built	December 1950/1951	April 1948 (blueprints) /1948	January 1949/1949	not known/1951
Number of Rooms	8	8 (blueprints)	6	12 + 2 in pavilion (blueprints)
Bedrooms / Bathrooms	4/4	4/2 (blueprints)	3/2	2/3
Construction	• wood frame	• steel frame	• wood frame	• wood frame, steel
Exterior Walls	• stucco	• wood siding and stucco	• redwood siding, stucco	• stucco, field stone
Roof: Shape and Materials	• hipped, composite	• pent roof	• pent and flat roofs, composite, gravel	• pent roofs
Valuation	$25,000		$20,000	
Builder	Cannon Construction Company		Samuel [H.?] Kaplan	
Architect	Plaut	Frankel	Sklarek	Fischer

Compiled from publicly accessible sources such as building permits, certificates of occupancy, Los Angeles County Assessor information and the City of Los Angeles Zone Information and Map Access System (ZIMAS), site visits, and, as noted, from privately owned blueprints and drawings.

4.15a. Ulrich Plaut (US American, 1910–71, b. German in Japan), possibly with Leopold Fischer (US American, 1901–75, b. Austria-Hungary).

Cannon house (1950–51), Westwood, Los Angeles, California, n.d.

Detail of street facade. Photo by Douglas M. Simmonds.

4.15b. Ulrich Plaut (US American, 1910–71, b. German in Japan), possibly with Leopold Fischer (US American, 1901–75, b. Austria-Hungary).

Cannon house (1950–51), Westwood, Los Angeles, California, n.d.

Detail of garden facade with eleven-foot roof overhang, indoor fireplace, and chimney block. Photo by Douglas M. Simmonds.

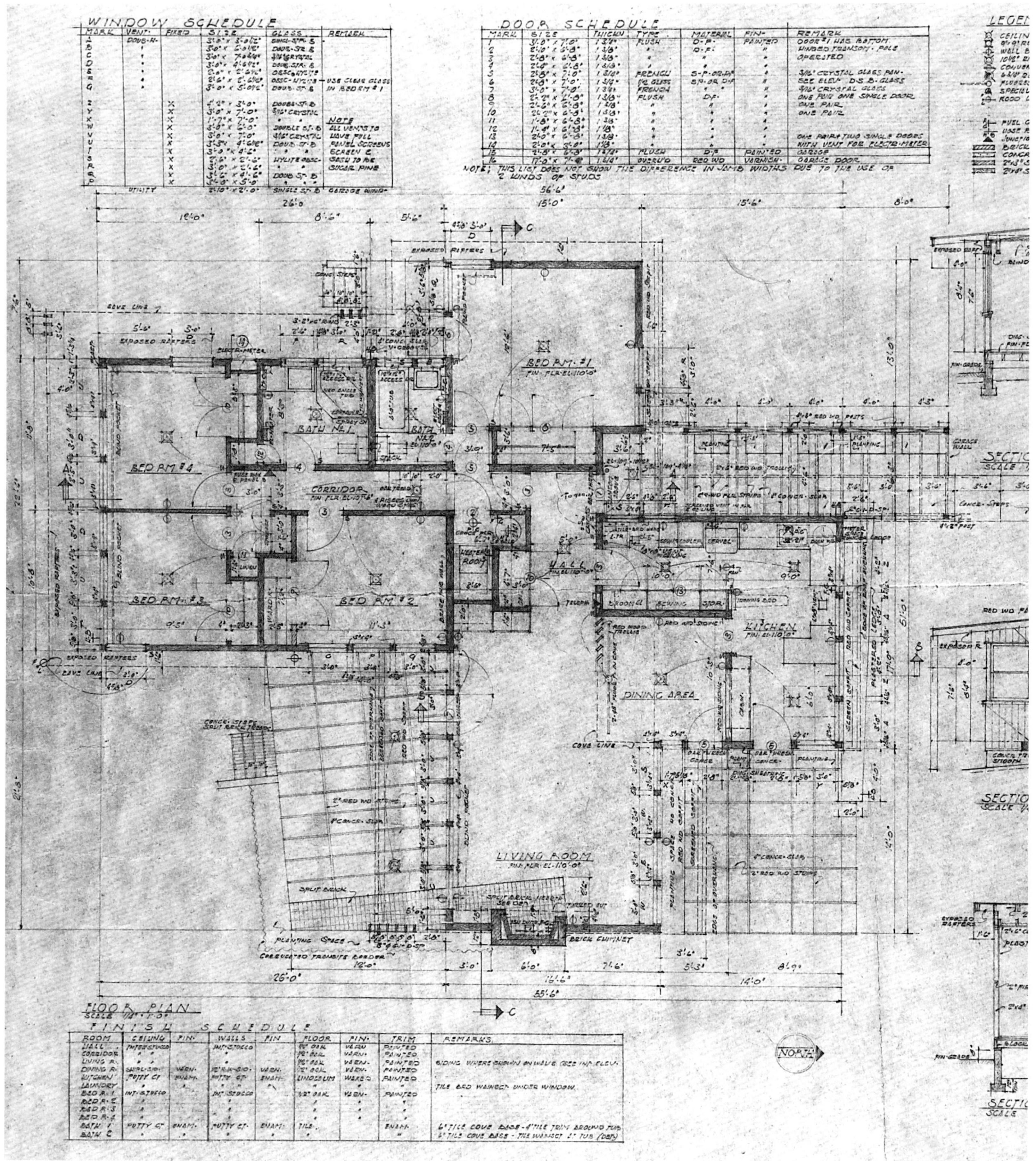

WINDOW SCHEDULE
DOOR SCHEDULE
BED RM. #1
BED RM #4
BATH No 1
CORRIDOR
BED RM. #3
BED RM. #2
HALL
KITCHEN
DINING AREA
LIVING ROOM
BRICK CHIMNEY
FLOOR PLAN
FINISH SCHEDULE
NORTH

4.16. Fredric R. Frankel (US American, 1909–98, b. Austria).

Frankel house (1948), Altadena, California.

Floor plan, 15 April 1948.

"the hillside . . . is terraced for a future swimming pool and badminton court,"[41] neither of which was realized. At the rear of the house, a living-cum-dining room and two bedrooms face the hillside garden with generous windows and sliding glass doors. All four rooms give access to a terrace underneath the hipped roof that projects outward up to eleven feet along the entire facade, creating a strong sense of a protected outdoor room. Indeed, one could say there are two outdoor rooms, as the bedrooms and living-cum-dining room are separated by a large brick fireplace that is part of a massive exposed brick wall at the end of the living room opposite the dining area (fig. 4.15b). This vast mass of masonry protrudes outward well beyond the edge of the roof and upward well above the ridgeline. Looked at from the garden side, the masonry slab cuts deep into the house; visually, it balances the long horizontal lines of the roof. It is also a huge block of thermal mass that is visibly exposed to the living room and the room behind the fireplace. This mass will heat up during days with long sunshine (and of course when a fire blazes in the fireplace) to add warmth to the rooms on either side during the evenings. The warmth is probably welcome, as the rising terrain shades these rooms despite both facing the setting sun. This oversize passive solar feature and a floor plan that anticipates those Fischer developed for the subdivision Verdugo Village raise the possibility that Fischer was involved in the design of this home; chapter 5 discusses both Verdugo Village and Fischer's potential work on the Cannon house.

Compared to the Cannon house, the Frankel house appears rather modest. The slanted pent roofs, facades covered with stucco and wood siding, and windows set in thick wooden frames evoke the impression of a house on an allotment on the edges of Vienna (or even Berlin) that had been added to over time. The building does not offer any visible hint that it is in fact a steel frame construction. Frankel may have encountered this advanced way of building when he worked for Neutra in Los Angeles in 1941, but he decided not to make visible the steel frame inside or outside of his home as contemporary colleagues like Soriano and, soon, some Case Study House architects were beginning to do in the later 1940s.

The Frankel house is located on a sloping lot in Altadena, an unincorporated area in Los Angeles County near the Verdugo Mountains. The compact appearance of the home turns into a rudimentary pinwheel plan when looked at in the drawings (fig. 4.16). The kitchen and main entrance occupy the wing toward the street to the north of the dwelling; to the east, a generous rectangular living-cum-dining room forms a wing with windows on the two long sides and a brick fireplace at the far end. The parents' bedroom constitutes the west wing. Three additional bedrooms (these for the children) and two bathrooms—one accessible only from the parents' bedroom—occupy the south wing. This wing is the longest; it stretches down the slope into the depth of the lot. Just past the first bathroom, a few steps lead down to the second bathroom and the children's bedrooms. Because of the sloping ground, all of these rooms are positioned lower than the rest of the house.

Frankel assigned specific uses and purposes to the four corners created by the pinwheel shape. The northwest corner accommodates a laundry yard, screened from the adjacent main entrance by a fence. The southwest corner offers a private patio for the parents' bedroom, with steps leading down to a narrow garden along the western facade of the south wing. The southeast corner is filled with a raised terrace in front of the living room. Finally, the northeast corner offers a small outdoor eating patio directly accessible from the kitchen and the adjacent indoor dining area. Frankel effectively increases the available space within the house by assigning, if not permanently moving to the outside, some functions to the corners of the pinwheel plan. For example, the large garden to the south of the home offers a fifth outside space or zone that occupies just under half of the entire length of the lot.

The Sklarek house takes a different approach to the indoor-outdoor relationship. Its partially visible wooden post-and-beam structure underneath ever so slightly slanted pent roofs makes a clear, modernist architectural statement (fig. 4.17), as does the floor plan, which can be described either as an *L* with a short stem and a squat leg or as a square with multiple cutouts. Whichever descriptor is selected, those cutouts are crucial, as they create patios and terraces, such as an outdoor living room adjacent to the enclosed living room, a dedicated outdoor eating area opposite the indoor dining room, and a private patio off the parents' bedroom in the southeast corner of the edifice (fig. 4.18). Some outdoor areas are roofed over or shaded with trellises, especially on the large east facade looking out to the garden farther to the east (fig. 4.19). On the southwest corner, a large play yard for the children cuts into the building and extends into the garden facing the road. It is accessible from the children's rooms and overlooked by the kitchen and service area, making it clear that the home—like most midcentury modernist domestic architecture—did

4.17. Rolf Sklarek (US American, 1906–84, b. Germany).

Sklarek house (1949), Pacific Palisades, Los Angeles, California, n.d.

Bird's-eye view.

4.18. Rolf Sklarek (US American, 1906–84, b. Germany).

Sklarek house (1949), Pacific Palisades, Los Angeles, California.

Floor plan, ca. 1948.

From "House by Rolf Sklarek," *Arts & Architecture,* February 1949, 39.

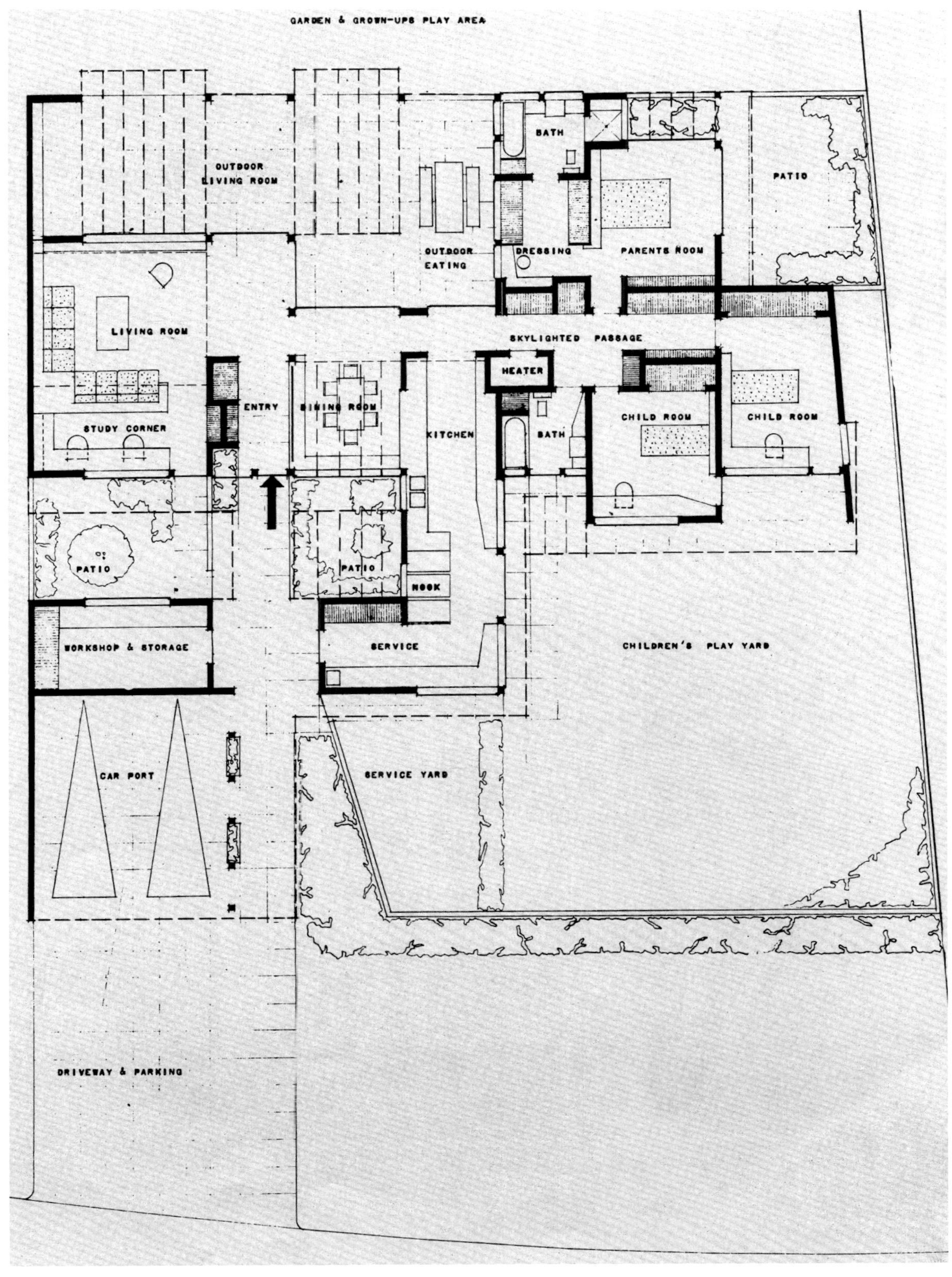

4.19. Rolf Sklarek (US American, 1906–84, b. Germany).

Sklarek house (1949), Pacific Palisades, Los Angeles, California, 1951.

Outdoor eating room. Photo by Julius Shulman.

Los Angeles, Getty Research Institute.

4.20. Rolf Sklarek (US American, 1906–84, b. Germany).

Sklarek house (1949), Pacific Palisades, Los Angeles, California.

Perspective drawing of view from the outdoor eating room into the house, signed "R. Sklarek, del. 4[8?]" in the bottom right corner, ink on paper.

4.21. Leopold Fischer (US American, 1901–75, b. Austria-Hungary).

Adolph and Mary Slechta house (1950–51), View Park, Los Angeles, California.

Entrance facade.

not challenge social conventions as they governed the nuclear family, for example.

Sklarek designed a home that blurs any clear delineation between inside and outside; the design not only obfuscates the border between the two realms but also makes stepping in and out effortless by using floor-to-ceiling sliding glass doors that, when closed, barely obstruct the views through, into, or out from the house, as perspectival drawings illustrate. Figure 4.20 shows a view moving from the outdoor eating area—note the table and bench in the left foreground—through the enclosed living room and dining room toward an outdoor patio (accommodating a banana plant, a signature plant of Sklarek's), beyond which the main entrance faced the street. Only by tracing this view on the floor plan can one truly grasp which parts of the depicted spaces are inside and which are outside; note, for example, the sequence of trellises adjacent to the outdoor eating area, above the indoor dining room, and again above the banana plant. Unless one studies the minor details of the drawing, one can easily miss the fine lines of the window frames for glass-enclosed skylights to be inserted into each opening of the trellis above the interior dining table, the sole visual indicator that the dining space is inside while, for example, the banana plant farther back grows in an atrium-like outdoor space.

The Slechta House in View Park

Leopold Fischer's major post–World War II commission was the Adolph and Mary Slechta house from 1950–51 in View Park, an unincorporated area southwest of downtown Los Angeles. The house shares a curved, high ridge with some of its neighbors at the southwestern edge of View Park, from where the view goes out toward downtown Los Angeles. The gently sloping lot is a trapezoid with a narrow street front at the higher end (to the northwest). The two-story house stands close to the street, taking up the entire width of the lot and dividing it into a narrow strip of landscaping in the front and a large garden in the rear. The footprint of the building is a rectangle with short, oblique sides

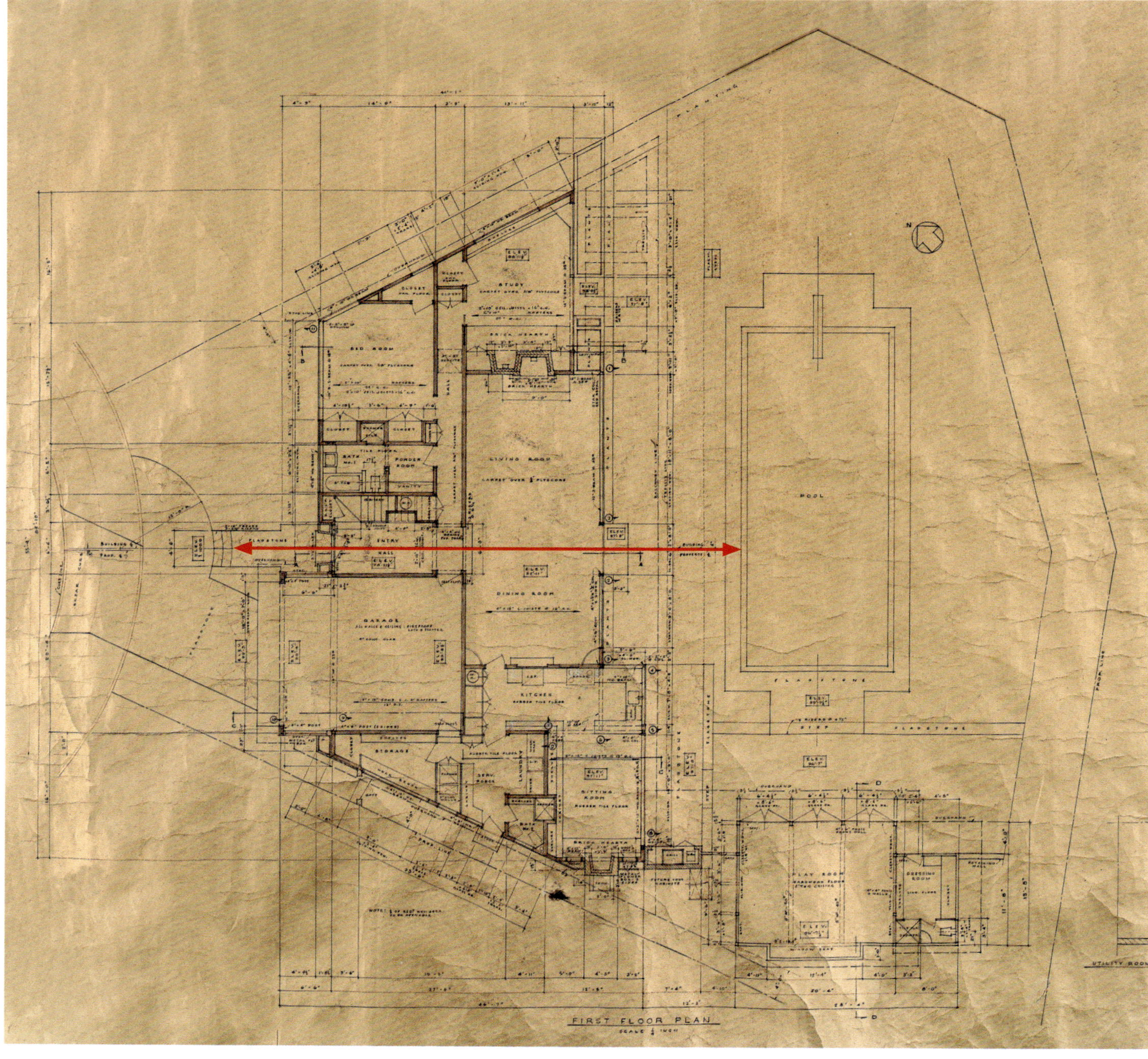

that parallel the northeastern and southwestern property lines. The two levels are strongly articulated in size, materials, and appearance in the vertical dimension. Quarry-faced ashlar masonry, laid in a geometric pattern, clads the facade of the lower story, creating the impression of a broad, substantial foundation for the upper level—not that a strong base was needed, for all it carries is a pavilion, much smaller in size and of little weight, as its stuccoed facade suggests. The deep eaves of a slightly slanted pent roof shade the pavilion on all four sides, while the shallower overhangs of a similar roof on the lower story visibly set apart the two levels (fig. 4.21). In short, the street facade sets an architectural theme—a pavilion on a broad foundation—which is the first of several juxtapositions that bifurcate the design. Additional juxtapositions include the contrast between the street facade and the garden facade; an outdoor room as *the* central space versus the interior rooms; and the isolation of the upstairs pavilion compared to the lower level. Ultimately, these bifurca-

4.22. Leopold Fischer (US American, 1901–75, b. Austria-Hungary).

Adolph and Mary Slechta house (1950–51), View Park, Los Angeles, California.

Floor plan for first floor, January 1950.

Entrance passage and axis are marked in red.

4.23. **Leopold Fischer (US American, 1901–75, b. Austria-Hungary).**

Adolph and Mary Slechta house (1950–51), View Park, Los Angeles, California, May 2022.

Garden facade and outdoor room.

tions are all components of a complex choreography of the indoor-outdoor relationship.

Upon entering the house through the reserved, almost austere front facade, the garden on the other side commands attention. One's gaze goes down a broad entrance passage, across a deep central room two steps below the passage, through a floor-to-ceiling sliding glass door toward a swimming pool (fig. 4.22). Indeed, one can both look down the axis and be drawn to its far end by a bright patch of daylight and reflections from the water in the pool, sparkling in front of lush vegetation rising beyond the pool. Mary Slechta confirms the allure of the garden at the rear of her new home: "With members of our family and our many dear friends, we all enjoyed many happy days there, just being together around the pool, swimming, dancing and just visiting."[42] Clearly, the home was designed for entertaining outdoors, another theme that determined Fischer's design.

In strong contrast with the street front, the rear facade is all about opening up and connecting the interior to an "outdoor room," as I will call from now on the garden, which is the actual center of the home (fig. 4.23). This room is organized into three zones or layers. First, just outside of an expansive floor-to-ceiling glass wall along almost the entire lower story, a deep garden terrace creates an interstitial space between the house and the swimming pool that recalls the terrace at the Kohlmeier house. Steps down to the pool, planters, and low retaining walls define the outer edge of this terrace, whose surface, together with all the architectural landscaping elements, is made from the same honey-colored stone as the street-side ashlar masonry. Second, in the center, the swimming pool

4.24. Leopold Fischer (US American, 1901–75, b. Austria-Hungary).

Adolph and Mary Slechta house (1950–51), View Park, Los Angeles, California, May 2022.

Interior of central cuboid looking northeast to the fireplace. On the right is the recently installed sliding glass wall.

4.25. Leopold Fischer (US American, 1901–75, b. Austria-Hungary).

Adolph and Mary Slechta house (1950–51), View Park, Los Angeles, California, May 2022.

Entrance passage looking toward main entrance door and the stair to the upper level.

surrounded by honey-colored flagstone occupies most of the outdoor room, for which the captivating view of downtown Los Angeles serves as the third zone, providing a background to the southeast. Four distinct "interior elevations" frame the outdoor room. The grandiose view toward downtown is the outdoor room's equivalent to a panorama window. It is followed on the other three sides by, first, the garden facade of the main house, which offers on the upper level a balcony (above the interstitial terrace) as an elevated vantage point to take in the outdoor room; second, a one-story play pavilion opposite the "panorama window"; and third, the dense vegetation behind the pool, though whether Fischer or a landscape architect planned the planting is unknown.[43] Regarding the pavilion, this stand-alone building is connected to the main house via the roof overhang that extends over the interstitial terrace to the pavilion; the latter the Slechtas used for square dancing with friends.[44]

The interior spaces on the lower level of the main house complement the outdoor room as the focus of the home. The lower level is centered on a single cuboid space that accommodates the living and dining areas, an arrangement that again recalls the Kohlmeier house (see fig. 4.6). The kitchen at the southwest end of the cuboid serves the dining area. On its other side, the kitchen gives access to a smaller sitting room with a fireplace at its outer wall. Rubber tiles as the flooring indicate a less formal space to be used by domestic staff or by the inhabitants and guests in conjunction with a built-in barbecue outside of the smaller sitting room. The living area on the opposite side is dominated by a large fireplace with a mantel made from richly veined green serpentine, a semiprecious stone, set in a wall entirely paneled with dark-stained wood (fig. 4.24). On the other side of that wall, a study with another fireplace can be reached from a long corridor branching off the entrance passage just before the latter enters the central cuboid. Along that same corridor, but oriented toward the street, lies a powder room that doubles as the bathroom for an adjacent bedroom.

The pavilion on the upper level accommodates the Slechtas' bedroom. This room constitutes a world on its own that, within the footprint of the plan, is spatially set as far apart from the main floor as possible. And yet, the design of the pavilion's garden facade resonates deeply with that of the lower level. The pavilion can be reached from a stair on the left of the entrance passage, immediately behind the main door into the house (fig. 4.25). A small hall at the upper landing gives access to a storage room (nowadays a bedroom), built-in closet spaces (executed in a much-reduced size compared to the floor plan), and the large bedroom located above the living-room end of the central cuboid (fig. 4.26). A fireplace on the bedroom's northeast wall shares the chimney stack with the two fireplaces below. On the other side of the room, generously sized dressing rooms for the couple—hers larger than his—are separated by a central corridor leading to a bathroom looking out to the southwest (fig. 4.27).

Unlike many midcentury modernist architects, who saw windows simply as sheets of glass to move in order to step outside from enclosed spaces, Fischer went against this fashionable trend (see fig. 4.23). Indeed, he turned the garden facade of the upper-level pavilion into a built lesson about how and why windows are more than and different from those sheets of glass. Views of the outside are granted through a fixed, tripartite floor-to-ceiling window. On one side, an additional corner window looks out toward downtown Los Angeles, and on the other side, a door opens to the balcony stretching along the outside of the pavilion. On the opposite bedroom wall, a clerestory window faces the street (see fig. 4.21). The window allows for cross-ventilation together with the one operable wing of the corner window and a smaller window fitted into the balcony door. How Fischer positioned and sized this multitude of windows and openings to the outside according to their functions became a demonstration of the sheer endless possibilities to capture architecturally an indoor-outdoor relationship. All windows let light into the interior, but only some offer outside views. Others may also ventilate a room—for example, the two dressing rooms. Finally, there is just one narrow door from the bedroom to the balcony. A lookout window is cut into the massive leaf, which, exclamation mark–like, announces that here, and only here, the room may be left to enter the outdoors.

The way Fischer fully develops this example of a contemporary architectural indoor-outdoor relationship is best illustrated in the downstairs living and dining areas of the Slechta house. Even though living and dining share the space of the central cuboid, the floor plan identifies them as the living *room* and dining *room* (see fig. 4.22). They are separated only by the axis leading from the main entrance to the sliding floor-to-ceiling glass door to the outdoor room. This glass door was the sole entrance to the outdoor room from the central cuboid, demonstrating that Fischer's intent was not to merge indoors and outdoors or establish an unimpeded physical flow of space in either direction. Instead, comparable to the Kohlmeier house, Fischer

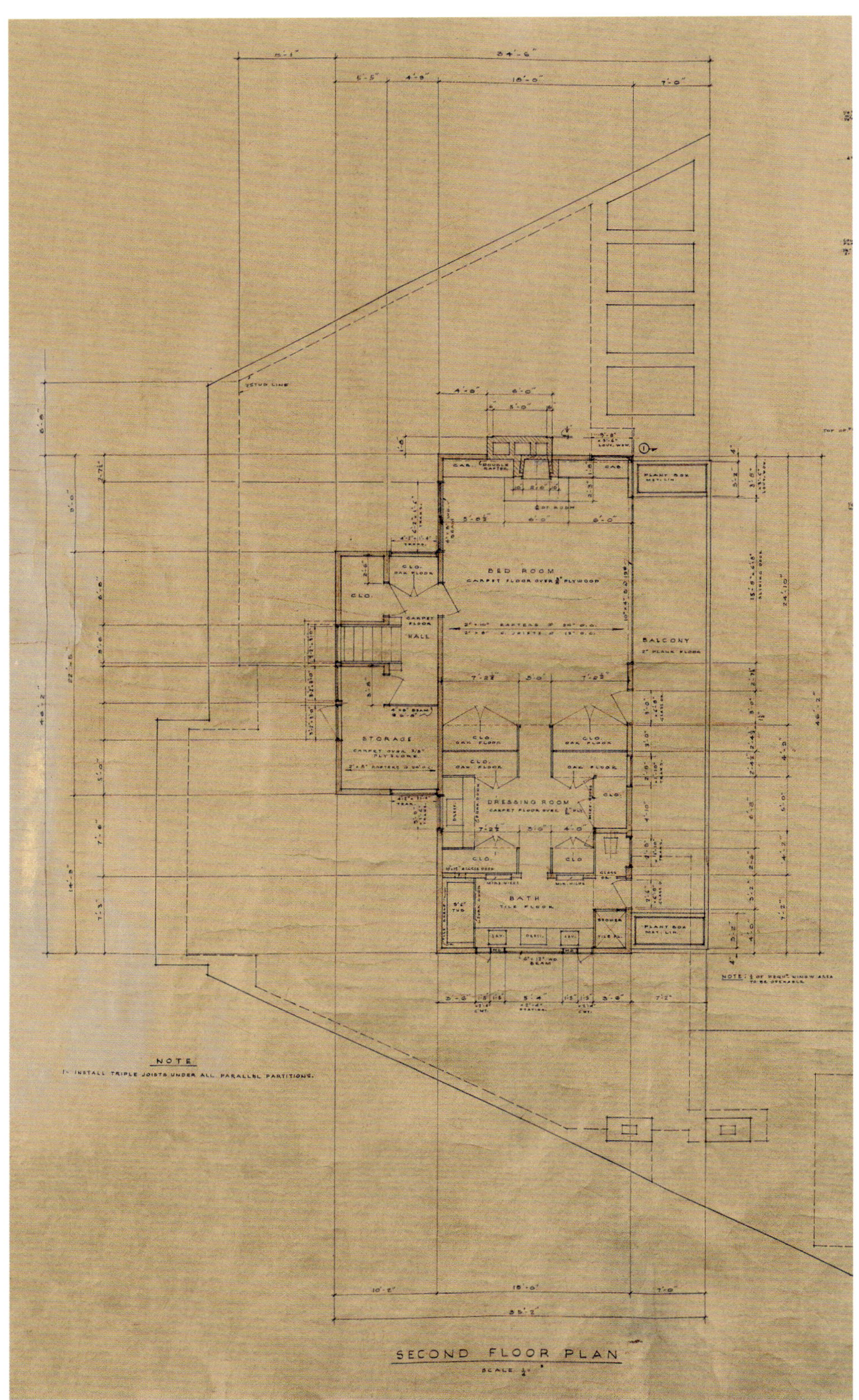

4.26. Leopold Fischer (US American, 1901–75, b. Austria-Hungary).

Adolph and Mary Slechta house (1950–51), View Park, Los Angeles, California.

Floor plan for second floor, January 1950.

4.27. Leopold Fischer (US American, 1901–75, b. Austria-Hungary).

Adolph and Mary Slechta house (1950–51), View Park, Los Angeles, California.

View from bathroom door through dressing room area (hers to the left, his to the right) toward the fireplace on the far wall of the principal bedroom.

defined the volume and expanse of all individual rooms, which included deciding where to enter and exit each one, an essential element of setting the perimeters for each space. Accordingly, the fixed all-glass wall as the cuboid's border with the outdoor room was a crucial element of a layered gradation of rooms from the inside to the interstitial and thence to the outside, and *not* a missed opportunity to connect the inside and the outside. This conclusion is supported by the design of the glass wall of the smaller sitting room next to the kitchen; here, a sliding floor-to-ceiling window fully opens the interior space to the adjacent barbecue area and temporarily creates a continuous indoor-outdoor space.

The opening up of entire walls with the help of foldable, slidable, movable, or lowerable glass panels is rooted in both Central European *and* California architecture. To start with California architecture first (and, for reasons of space, leaving unconsidered the indoor-outdoor relationships of Spanish colonial architecture and later revival styles), excellent early modern examples are Myron Hunt and Elmer Grey's Gillis house (Santa Monica, 1906) and the Gamble house (Pasadena, 1908) by Charles S. Greene and Henry M. Greene. In the former home, an L-shaped corridor—colonnaded and entirely open on one side to the garden—gives access to, and between, social and other spaces on the ground level; in the latter one, various decks and terraces knit together the outdoors with the indoors so that in the end "some 8,000 square feet of indoor floor-space" were complemented with "another 2,000 of covered terraces and sleeping porches."[45] Closer to Fischer's Loosian background are Rudolph Schindler's home on North Kings Road (Schindler-Chace house, Hollywood, now West Hollywood, 1921–22) and his Lovell beach house (Newport Beach, 1922–26). Both houses intricately intertwine interior and exterior spaces, the one for the beach house even vertically between the three levels of the building, thus introducing a version of the Raumplan to Southern California. One can easily imagine Fischer studying on-site the beach house and recognizing that individual features of Schindler's design, such as the entrance passage, were indebted to the Raumplan of the retail spaces inside Adolf Loos's Goldman & Salatsch house (also called the Michaeler house, Vienna, 1909–11).[46] Even closer to Fischer's early years in California is the architect Harwell Hamilton Harris's house on Fellowship Parkway (Los Angeles, 1935), where, in parts of the living room, slidable windows as the sole physical barrier between indoors and outdoors could temporarily be removed and stored during the summer.[47]

Turning to Central European examples, Fischer would also have known, if not seen, the Lange house (Krefeld, 1927–30) and the Tugendhat villa (Brno, 1929–30), where Ludwig Miës van der Rohe installed motorized guillotine windows (*Versenkfenster*) that could be lowered to open selected spaces to the outside. Eric Mendelsohn fitted similar windows into his house in Berlin (1928–30), and Ernst L. Freud, the architect son of Sigmund Freud and a student of Adolf Loos, did so in the Frank country house (Lake Schwielow, near Berlin, 1928–30).[48] The popularity of motorized guillotine windows lasted well into the Third Reich, when architects such as Fritz August Breuhaus and Ernst Petersen installed them in their own houses in Berlin (1934; 1936–37).[49] Not all of these windows, however, gave access to the outside; for example, those in the Tugendhat villa solely granted views of the surroundings, and—when lowered—they opened up the interior spaces to the outside climate.

Likewise rooted in both California architecture and Central European architecture (specifically historical Viennese architecture) as part of the indoor-outdoor relationships of the Slechta house is the pavilion, a motif that also brings us back to Richard Neutra. Well before Fischer started work on the Slechta house, the Tremaine house and the Kaufmann desert house were widely published in national and international architecture magazines, and the fact that Fischer's design shares with Neutra's the feature of a lightweight pavilion on a broad base is a striking similarity. Typologically, these upper-level pavilions were not Neutra's invention but were inspired by contemporary and historical examples. Architecturally, the Tremaine house responded to the earlier von Romberg house (Montecito, 1936–38) that the Santa Barbara architect Lutah Maria Riggs had designed for Max and Emily von Romberg; in 1945, Emily married Burton Tremaine and thus became the sister-in-law of Neutra's clients.[50] When Neutra planned an upper-level bedroom suite for the Tremaines, he drew inspiration from a one-story-and-a-half-tall pavilion, a private studio space for Emily von Romberg that crowned the von Romberg house. A few years earlier, Riggs had already envisioned a comparable woman's room on her own for Marguerite Fischel, a composer, on top of the one-story Ellis and Marguerite Fischel house (Montecito, 1931, not built).[51] Ultimately, the Tremaine pavilion was not realized,[52] but Neutra borrowed the idea in 1946 for the Kaufmann desert house, where an upper-level pavilion was eventually built.

Neutra identified the Central European—in this case Viennese—roots of this motif when, in a drawing from June 1945, he named the upper-level bedroom suite of the Tremaine house a "Gloriette," thereby cross-referencing the pavilion with a type of building that served the leisure and conspicuous consumption of the nobility of European courtly societies.[53] Sometimes also called *Belvedere* (beautiful view) or eye-catcher, a gloriette usually offers impressive views of a nearby palace or over an estate, as exemplified by Austria's most famous gloriette, located on the grounds of Vienna's eighteenth-century Schloss Schönbrunn.[54] As a fellow Austrian and Austrian architect, Fischer would have recognized Neutra's reference to the Schönbrunn gloriette. In short, the Slechta house turns out to be a comment by one Loos student practicing in Los Angeles on two of the most recent detached houses designed by another Loos student in Los Angeles.

• • •

However, neither the formal similarities between the Tremaine, Kaufmann, and Slechta houses nor the shared Viennese and Loosian backgrounds of the two designers can diminish the crucial difference between the careers of an immigrant architect and an émigré architect. By 1951, Neutra had enjoyed almost three decades of career in California. The designs for his two most famous postwar houses had perfected and refined ideas that originated in the Nesbitt house; indeed, the conceptual continuity with the past was as much part of Neutra's postwar designs as was demonstrating a new type of architecturally ordered environment as the appropriate habitat of contemporary humans. In sharp contrast, the Slechta house illustrates Fischer's second attempt to start a career as an independent architect in exile. The design's comments on two recent Neutra houses demonstrate that Fischer was thoroughly versed in the contemporary California debate about domestic architecture. The View Park home's highly complex, choreographed indoor-outdoor relationship indicates Fischer's awareness of the indoor-outdoor relationships as *the* central issue of the architectural debate.

All the houses from around 1951 aimed to integrate the indoors with the outdoors, which raise the importance of carefully looking at the different approaches to how this integration was to be achieved. Neutra's examples formalize ideas first explored with the Nesbitt house into a postwar domestic architecture that closely intertwines inside and outside. Neutra's surname may be an anagram of the word *nature* (as an undergraduate student at UC Santa Barbara once pointed out to me), yet architecture still takes the lead over nature, a basic tenet of the designs for the Tremaine and Kaufmann houses, and one Neutra elevates to a principle for humanity when confronting hostile zones on Earth. By comparison, Plaut (with or without Fischer as codesigner), Frankel, and Sklarek are much more modest concerning the reach of their designs, with all closely focusing on the immediate garden spaces surrounding the homes. The Cannon house takes a sequential approach by layering house and garden across the rising slope. The Frankel house claims areas of the gardens as extension zones of indoor functions; easy access to those exterior areas is given, but the integration creates more functional adjacencies than unity between two different realms. Such unity, however, is the main characteristic of the Sklarek house, which occasionally even obscures—at least momentarily—the clear perception of which realm one is looking at. Accordingly, the designs for the Sklarek house and Neutra's houses integrate dynamic concepts of space.

Unlike these examples, Fischer's Slechta house connects indoors and outdoors in a highly choreographed manner, relying on such compositional means as a view axis, selected access points, and rooms well defined as individual spaces, even if sometimes placed within a single larger volume. These are fascinating architectural means, especially in a modern, even modernist, design. Yet, they raise the question of whether the Slechta house relied on outdated means, especially when compared to the visual lightness of the midcentury modernist Sklarek house, the relaxed functional pragmatism of the Frankel house, and even the radical innovations of Neutra's postwar works.

One must look at the houses from around 1941 and around 1951 together to answer this. The houses from the earlier period, particularly those of the émigré architects and some of their immigrant colleagues, were characterized by architectural uniformity. In contrast, Neutra delivered already at that time a uniquely innovative design with the Nesbitt house. A decade later, the uniformity disappeared in favor of designs visibly differentiating themselves from the others. That does not make all designs exceptionally innovative, especially when measured against Neutra's postwar Tremaine and Kaufmann houses. However, it demonstrates that after World War II, the émigré architects strove to define visibly their individual approaches to contemporary domestic architecture.

Looked at from this angle, the prewar Kohlmeier house and the postwar Slechta house appear consistent in the way Fischer designed them. Fischer did not succumb to the uniformity that characterized around 1941 the works of many émigré architects, nor did he feel a need around 1951 to reinvent or invigorate his approach to domestic architecture by trying to be overly innovative. The Kohlmeier house and the Slechta house are both *representative* designs, the former because Fischer needed to establish himself architecturally in the Los Angeles area with his own version of what a California home should look like. The latter is equally if not even more representative because Fischer was working to establish himself in the Los Angeles area for the second time and to design for a banker, a distinctly upper-middle-class client. In this regard, Frankel's and Sklarek's designs from around 1951 for more average middle-class family homes were more indicative of a building type for which a large and rapidly growing demand existed during the postwar years. Thus, it is unsurprising that Leopold Fischer and other émigré architects turned to suburban housing as the 1950s unfolded.

Notes

1 On the booster era, see, for example, Kevin Starr, *Inventing the Dream: California through the Progressive Era* (New York: Oxford University Press, 1985); Lawrence Culver, *The Frontier of Leisure: Southern California and the Shaping of Modern America* (Oxford: Oxford University Press, 2012); and Paul J. P. Sandul, *California Dreaming: Boosterism, Memory, and Rural Suburbs in the Golden State* (Morgantown: West Virginia University Press, 2014).

2 W. Ham. Hall, *Irrigation Development: History, Customs, Laws, and Administrative Systems Relating to Irrigation, Water-Courses, and Waters in France, Italy, and Spain; The Introductory Part of the Report of the State-Engineer of California on Irrigation and the Irrigation Question* (Sacramento: State Office James J. Ayers, Supt. State Printing, 1886), 6.

3 Anton Wagner, *Los Angeles: Werden, Leben und Gestalt der Zweimillionenstadt in Südkalifornien* (Leipzig: Bibliographisches Institut, 1935). In the following I rely on and cite to the English translation: Anton Wagner, *Los Angeles: The Development, Life, and Structure of the City of Two Million in Southern California,* ed. Edward Dimendberg, trans. Timothy Grundy (Los Angeles: Getty Research Institute, 2022).

4 Wagner, *Los Angeles,* 88, 90.

5 Wagner, *Los Angeles,* 155.

6 Wagner, *Los Angeles,* 161–62 (italics in original).

7 Wagner, *Los Angeles,* 216, 217.

8 Wagner, *Los Angeles,* 251.

9 Wagner, *Los Angeles,* 215.

10 In the chapter "Life and Forms of Appearance of the Contemporary Landscape," Wagner offers a brief evolution of architectural forms of private dwellings and other types of buildings. Yet, he barely moves beyond an evolution of architectural styles when discussing detached homes (Wagner, *Los Angeles,* 248–52).

11 Edward Dimendberg, "Introduction," in Wagner, *Los Angeles,* 25.

12 Nicholas Olsberg, "Common Ground," in *Notes from Another Los Angeles: Gregory Ain and the Construction of a Social Landscape,* ed. Anthony Fontenot (Cambridge, MA: MIT Press, 2022), 88.

13 Richard Neutra, quoted in Barbara Lamprecht, *Richard Neutra 1892–1970: Survival through Design* (Cologne: Taschen, 2009), 51.

14 Esther McCoy, *Richard Neutra* (New York: Braziller, 1960), 16.

15 McCoy, *Richard Neutra,* 16.

16 McCoy, *Richard Neutra,* 13.

17 Volker M. Welter, "From the *Landscape of War* to the Open Order of the Kaufmann House: Richard Neutra and the Experience of the Great War," in *The Good Gardener? Nature, Humanity, and the Garden,* ed. Annette Giesecke and Naomi Jacobs (London: Artifice Books on Architecture, 2014), 216–33.

18 Sabine Plakolm-Forsthuber, "Ein Leben, zwei Karrieren, die Architektin Liane Zimbler," in *Visionäre & Vertriebene: Österreichische Spuren in der modernen amerikanischen Architektur,* ed. Mathias Boeckl (Berlin: Ernst & Sohn, 1995), 303–4.

19 No information about the floor plan was obtainable for the Nürnberg house. Attempts to contact the current owner have remained without response.

20 "Suburban House, Santa Monica, Calif.," *Architectural Forum* 84 (May 1946): 85.

21 Heinrich Wefing, "'We Are at Home where the Desk Stands': Thomas Mann's Residence in Pacific Palisades," in *Building Paradise: Exile Architecture in California; Villa Aurora Architecture Symposium 2003,* ed. Mechthild Borries-Knopp (Berlin: Kreis der Freunde und Förderer der Villa Aurora e.V., 2004), 63.

22 See Wefing, "'We Are at Home where the Desk Stands,'" 57–70; Lilian Pfaff, *J. R. Davidson: A European Contribution to California Modernism* (Basel: Birkhäuser, 2019), 161–74; and Francis Nenik and Sebastian Stumpf, *Seven Palms: Das Thomas-Mann-Haus in Pacific Palisades, Los Angeles* (Leipzig: Spector, 2018), 84–108.

23 Thomas Mann, *Tagebücher 1940–1943,* ed. Peter de Mendelssohn (Frankfurt: S. Fischer, 1982), 2 September 1940, 142. The lack of information about Nürnberg's home allows me only to speculate that the library-cum-study occupied one or more of the projecting bays on the upper level.

24 Alan Hess, "Utopia Promised," in Alan Hess, *Frank Lloyd Wright: The Houses* (New York: Rizzoli, 2005), 226–73. The information discussed in the main text is primarily from pages 230–31.

25 Heinrich Kulka, ed., *Adolf Loos: Das Werk des Architekten* (Vienna: A. Schroll & Co., 1931), 14, quoted in translation from Christopher Long, *The New Space: Movement and Experience in Viennese Modern Architecture* (New Haven: Yale University Press, 2016), 50.

26 Adolf Loos, "Josef Veillich," *Frankfurter Zeitung,* 21 March 1929, quoted in translation from Long, *The New Space,* 48.

27 David H. Haney, *When Modern Was Green: Life and Work of Landscape Architect Leberecht Migge* (London: Routledge, 2010), 131.

28 Rose Lenzner-Migge, "Väterchens Sonnenhof," in *Worpswede und Umzu: Haus und Hof—Land und Leute* [1991], ed. Helmut Böse-Vetter and Hinge Meta-Hülbusch (Marburg: Völker & Ritter, 1998), 66–67.

29 Leberecht Migge, "Der Garten Sonnenhof in Worpswede," *Der Baumeister,* no. 4 (1928): 107, quoted from Jürgen von Reuss, "Leberecht Migge—Spartakus in Grün," in *Leberecht Migge 1881–1935: Gartenkultur des 20. Jahrhundert,* ed. Fachbereich Stadt- und Landschaftsplanung der Gesamthochschule Kassel (Worpswede: Worpsweder Verlag, 1981), 21.

30 Haney, *When Modern Was Green,* 161–64. On Fischer's exhibits, see Irene Below, "Leopold Fischer—der Architekt von 'Zickzackhausen,'" in *Bernburger Heimatblätter 2001,* ed. Kulturbund Bernburg e.V. (Bernburg: Salzland Druck, 2001), 13.

31 The photographer was Robert Cleveland, who noted the job number 334 on the reverse of the image. The finding aids for two Robert Cleveland collections do not reference this job number and, accordingly, the photograph cannot be dated. See finding aid, Robert C. Cleveland Papers (collection no. 1808), Library Special Collections, Charles E. Young Research Library, University of California, Los Angeles; and finding aid, Robert Cleveland Negatives, University of California, Riverside, California Museum of Photography. Fischer's floor plan indicates wood paving for the terrace; whether the bricks were a change made by Fischer is unknown.

32 It is not known whether Fischer was involved in laying out the garden.

33 The double glass doors giving access to the outside from the parents' bedroom (partially visible on the left in figure 4.12) and a set of stone steps going down to the same doors from the south terrace are changes a later owner undertook.

34 For example, Elizabeth A. T. Smith, ed., *Blueprints for Modern Living: History and Legacy of the Case Study Houses,* exh. cat. (Los Angeles: Museum of Contemporary Art, 1989).

35 Kevin Vennemann, *Sunset Boulevard: Vom Filmen, Bauen und Sterben in Los Angeles* (Berlin: Suhrkamp, 2012), 80–81.

36 Philip C. Johnson, "Preface," in *Built in USA: Post-War Architecture,* ed. Henry-Russell Hitchcock and Arthur Drexler, exh. cat. (New York: Museum of Modern Art, 1952), 9.

37 "Good Modern Is Livable," *Los Angeles Times Home Magazine,* 19 August 1945, 3; and "Sleek as a Top Hat," *Los Angeles Times,* 28 April 1946, 3.

38 Richard Neutra, *Richard Neutra on Building: Mystery and Realities of the Site* (Scarsdale, NY: Morgan & Morgan, 1951).

39 Neutra, *Mystery and Realities of the Site,* 19, 33, 44.

40 "Desert House Richard Neutra Architect," *Arts & Architecture* 66, no. 7 (1949): 30.

41 Lee Howard, "Spaciousness a Servant," *Los Angeles Times,* 1 March 1953, H8.

42 Mary Slechta, *My Recollections* (Santa Ana, CA: Friis-Pioneer, 1987), 56.

43 The fact that the sole ladder into the swimming pool is located on the same side as the lush vegetation, indeed the landscaping is so close to the ladder that it can barely be used, may indicate that the planting was not part of Fischer's design.

44 Slechta, *My Recollections,* 56.

45 Reyner Banham, *Los Angeles: The Architecture of Four Ecologies* (London: Allen Lane, 1971), 71.

46 August E. Sarnitz, "Proportion and Beauty—The Lovell Beach House by Rudolph Michael Schindler, Newport Beach, 1922–1926," *Journal of the Society of Architectural Historians* 45, no. 4 (1986): 374–88.

47 Elizabeth Mock, ed., *Built in USA: 1932–1944,* exh. cat. (New York: Museum of Modern Art, 1944), 34–35.

48 Terence Riley and Barry Bergdoll, eds., *Mies in Berlin,* exh. cat. (New York: Museum of Modern Art, 2001), 242–47; Ita Heinze-Greenberg, "'I Often Fear the Envy of the Gods': Success, House, and Home," in *Eric Mendelsohn: Architect, 1887–1953,* ed. Regina Stephan (New York: Monacelli, 1999), 178–79; and Volker M. Welter, *Ernst L. Freud, Architect: The Case of the Modern Bourgeois Home* (Oxford: Berghahn, 2012).

49 On the widespread use of such windows from 1933 onward, see Franz Schmitz, *Landhäuser in Berlin 1933–1945* (Berlin: Gebr. Mann, 2007), 88–92.

50 See Volker M. Welter, *Tremaine Houses: One Family's Patronage of Domestic Architecture in Midcentury America* (Los Angeles: Getty Publications, 2019), chapters 2 and 3, for the dialogue between the designs by Riggs and Neutra.

51 Volker M. Welter, "Lutah Maria Riggs: A Portrait of a Modern Revival-Style Architect," in *The Routledge Companion to Women in Architecture,* ed. Anna Sokolina (New York: Routledge, 2021), 134–35.

52 For the history of the fate of the Tremaine house's upper level, see Welter, *Tremaine Houses,* 79–82.

53 See Welter, *Tremaine Houses,* 80 (fig. 3.15).

54 Another function was to offer a safe space to meet one's mistress, for which the German language coined with its usual blunt directness the word *Lustpavillion.*

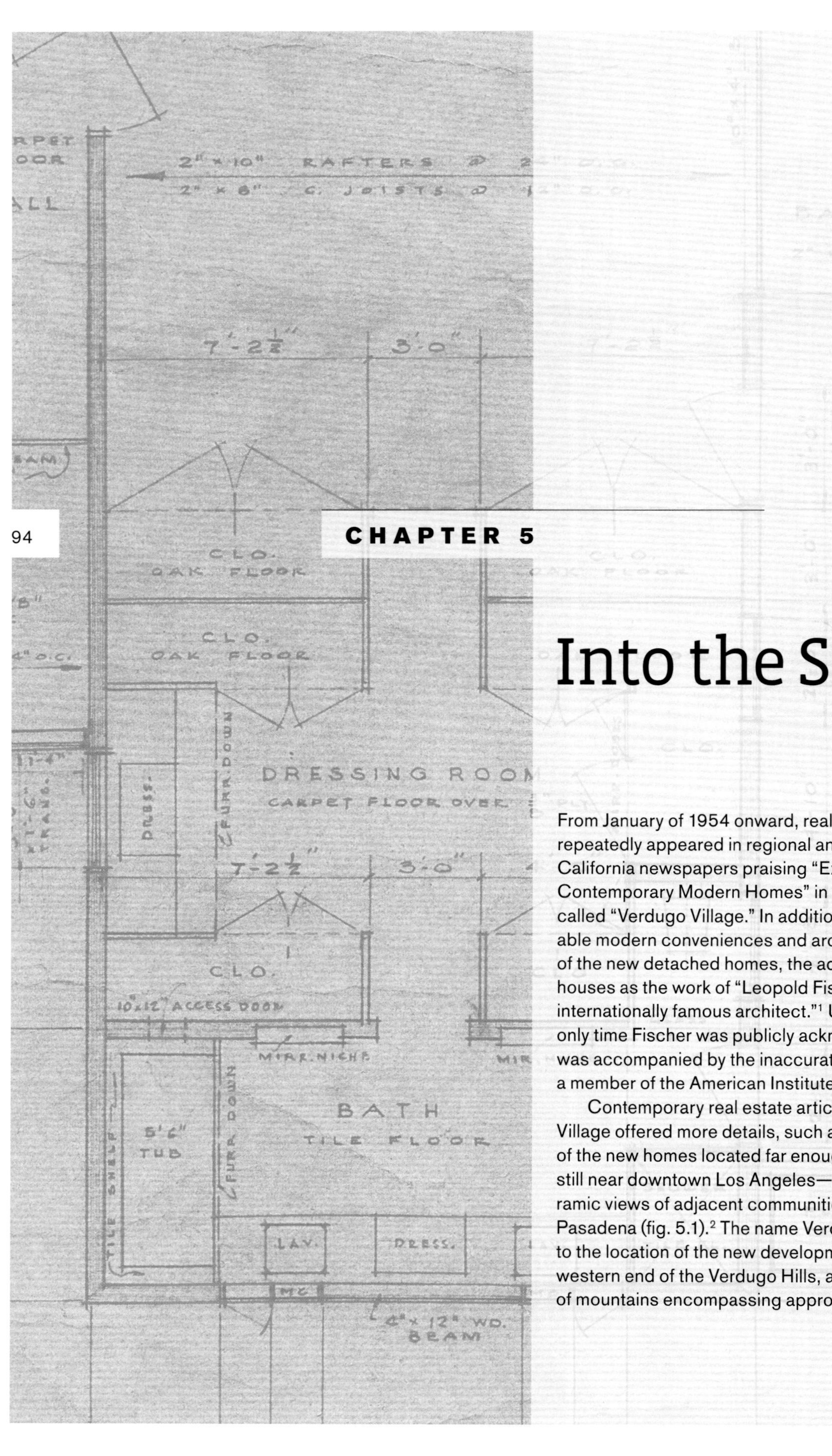

CHAPTER 5

Into the Suburbs

From January of 1954 onward, real estate display ads repeatedly appeared in regional and local Southern California newspapers praising "Exquisitely Designed Contemporary Modern Homes" in a new subdivision called "Verdugo Village." In addition to listing all available modern conveniences and architectural features of the new detached homes, the ads proclaimed the houses as the work of "Leopold Fischer, A.I.A., [an] internationally famous architect."[1] Unfortunately, the only time Fischer was publicly acknowledged as famous was accompanied by the inaccurate claim that he was a member of the American Institute of Architects.

Contemporary real estate articles about Verdugo Village offered more details, such as renderings of some of the new homes located far enough away—though still near downtown Los Angeles—to provide panoramic views of adjacent communities like Glendale and Pasadena (fig. 5.1).[2] The name Verdugo Village referred to the location of the new development at the southwestern end of the Verdugo Hills, a traverse range of mountains encompassing approximately the cities of Burbank in the west, Pasadena in the east, and La Cañada Flintridge in the north. Verdugo Village is east of Highland Park, north of Mount Washington, west of Glassell Park, and south of Eagle Rock. Even if the name never caught on, Verdugo Village refers in this book to the subdivision for which Fischer designed detached houses.[3]

This chapter looks at Fischer's involvement in the suburbanization of the metropolitan Los Angeles region through the lens of Verdugo Village. Studies of suburbs tend to emphasize the scale and speed with which metropolitan regions, such as the one around Los Angeles, were suburbanized after World War II. Accordingly, it may appear counterintuitive to study just one design for a small subdivision within Los Angeles.[4] Yet, for Fischer's career in exile, Verdugo Village marked a critical moment. Up to the early 1950s, individually designed houses had been the staple diet of Fischer's California work; with Verdugo Village, he was asked to envision houses for inhabitants unbeknown to him. Contemporary sources called such projects speculative housing, defined as building "to realize a profit without a particular family in mind."[5] Given their focus on the unknown future occupant, perhaps it is better to call such commissions "anonymous" domestic designs; for example, Fischer's pre-exile social housing estates were mainly of this kind. The attraction of this work was a collaboration between architects, developers, and builders who might be responsible for "50 to 4000 [homes] per year," which resulted in "better-designed developments," the architects receiving fees worth their efforts, and buyers living in "the best house that has so far been available to [them]." *Best* was defined

VERDUGO VILLAGE HOME HAS THREE BEDROOMS AND DEN
. . . panoramic view home in Highland Park priced at $19,000

Verdugo Homes Feature View

Panoramic view homes overlooking Pasadena, Glendale and Hollywood are now available in Verdugo Village, centrally - located development in Highland Park.

Located at Ave. 42, Palmero Drive and Division St., Verdugo Village is within a few minutes driving time from downtown Los Angeles, Pasadena, Eagle Rock, Glendale, Burbank and Hollywood.

Verdugo Village's spacious three-bedroom and den or four-bedroom homes are priced from $19,000.

Each home in the development has a panoramic view of the surrounding area. Many homes overlook the Verdugo Hills, Glendale and Pasadena. Others have a perfect view of Hollywood.

The contemporary modern homes were individually designed for the lots by architect Leopold Fischer.

Features of Verdugo Village homes include wood-burning fireplaces with gas lighters, thermostatically - controlled forced air heating, select oak floors, indoor - outdoor living rooms with covered terraces, huge panoramic view ceiling-to-floor windows, two baths, oversize two-car garages and unusually spacious rooms.

Kitchens are equipped with garbage disposals and exhaust fans. The dining nook has an indoor barbecue.

All sewers and utilities are already installed and paid for.

Verdugo Village's model home, furnished by the David Lewis Co. of Los Angeles, is located at 4360 Palmero Drive, at the corner of Nordica Drive.

For those who prefer to build homes from their own individual plans and with their own contractor, panoramic view lots in Verdugo Village are available from $4000.

Verdugo Village can be reached easily from Pasadena and Los Angeles by this route: Arroyo Seco Freeway to Ave. 52, Ave. 52 to Figueroa, Figueroa to Ave. 50, then right on Ave. 50 to El Paso, west to Division St. and south to Ave. 42 and Palmero Drive.

From Glendale or Hollywood, take Fletcher Drive to Eagle Rock Blvd. to Ave. 40, then east on Ave. 40 to Scandia, north to Ave. 42 and Division Street.

BE AHEAD OF HOT WEATHER

See us NOW for your

GE ROOM AIR CONDITIONER

be ahead too with

Free Installation*

• SAVE MONEY NOW — and a lot of sweltering misery this summer — by ordering your new G-E Room Air Conditioner within the next* 2 weeks! By acting at once you'll get FREE INSTALLATION (*special wiring, if necessary, or use in other than double-hung windows not included.)

As Low As 229[95]

Stop in today and choose your new G-E Room Air Conditioners from the great array of '54 models

E.W. MOORE INC. Refrigeration

AUTHORIZED DEALER GENERAL ELECTRIC APPLIANCES

465 N. Lake Ave., Pasadena

SY. 6-8530

VIEW HOMES

12 MINUTES CAREFUL DRIVING FROM L.A. CIVIC CENTER

3-4 Bedroom or Den Homes
2 Baths, priced from $19,000

LOTS at this most convenient, close-in location — high, dry and level with a magnificent panoramic view — available for purchase . . . for your individual plans from $4000. • Exquisitely designed, contemporary modern homes, of three and four bedrooms or den . . . two baths . . . magnificent panoramic view of Verdugo Hills.

DIRECTIONS

From Hollywood or Glendale — Fletcher Dr. to Eagle Rock Blvd. to Ave. 40, east to Scandia, north to Ave. 42 and Division St. From Los Angeles and Pasadena — Arroyo Seco to Ave. 52, to Figueroa, to Ave. 50 right to El Paso, west to Division St. and south to Ave. 42 and Palmero.

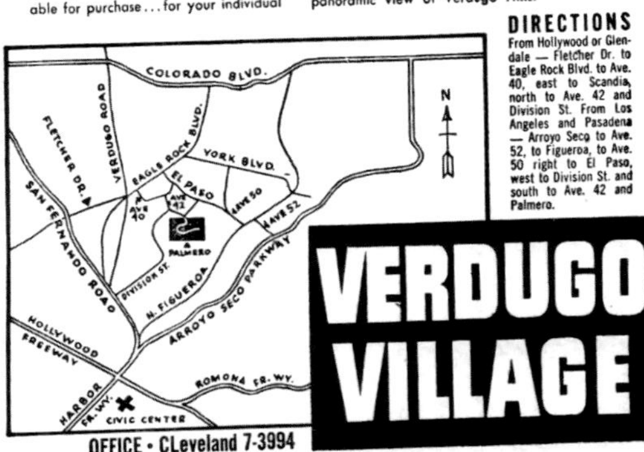

VERDUGO VILLAGE

OFFICE • CLeveland 7-3994

5.1. "Verdugo Homes Feature View," *Pasadena Independent*, 23 May 1954, 18.

as "architect-designed for the average needs of the average family,"[6] which sometimes translated into *ideal* architectural designs, as in the case of Fischer's Verdugo Village. With that subdivision on the drawing board, Fischer might have thought that his exile career had reached a turning point, indeed the point of his return to "anonymous" domestic designs as a mainstay of his professional work.

Et in suburbia ego

Etymologically, suburbs and suburbia are understood to be less ("beneath" or "below" according to the Latin preposition *sub*) than a city, though related to it economically, politically, or geographically, for example. Such etymological subordination does not imply that suburbs were unattractive; rather, the opposite is true. A longing for life close to nature has been a constant feature in the history of Western civilization, as expressed, for example, in classical Greek and Roman depictions of a simpler and thus easier life in the Elysian fields and Arcadia, and in the Judeo-Christian belief that humanity originated in Paradise. Whether rooted in mythology or religion, notions of pastoral life in or at least close to nature developed into powerful recurring motifs in the efforts of the modern urban and architectural reform movements from the nineteenth century onward. The ancient Latin phrase *Et in arcadia ego,* which translates to "And I also in Arcadia," may have once expressed doubts about whether death was truly banned from the afterlife. Yet, to many modern architects and urban planners, the phrase signaled that their professions were destined to create housing and settlements allowing life closer to nature, thus transforming *et in arcadia ego* into *et in suburbia ego.*

How then to define suburbia in regard to Los Angeles, a city that perennially poses the question of whether it is "really a city... once you get past downtown" and that, in reply, is called an "extraordinary landscape"[7] and "a complex entity with a variety of commercial and industrial centers"?[8] Regardless of whether developers, architects, and historians agree on any area being suburban or not, suburban developments and subdivisions are typically anonymous domestic designs. The neighborhoods and houses also often share a particularly close relationship to nature, whether the latter is gardened, landscaped, or left natural.

Accordingly, developments such as Baldwin Hills Village (Los Angeles, 1940–41), the Channel Heights housing project (San Pedro, 1941–43, demolished), the Park Planned Homes (Altadena, 1946–47), and Mar Vista Housing (Los Angeles, 1946–48) would qualify as being in suburban settings or creating suburb-like designed environments. In Baldwin Hills Village, a group of architects led by Robert E. Alexander and Reginald Johnson arranged mostly two-story buildings offering low-cost housing around large courtyards with communal green spaces.[9] At the Channel Heights development, Richard Neutra provided wartime workers with housing in one- or two-story buildings that offered two or four apartments on a site well above but close to the harbor of Los Angeles. The location provided views of the ocean, and the placement of the housing blocks carefully considered the ravines traversing the land.[10] Post–World War II, Gregory Ain conceived Park Planned Homes and Mar Vista Housing as neighborhoods of middle-class, single-story detached homes that, in the earlier scheme, relied on "serial repetition" of identical houses and, in the latter, on creating visual diversity by "mirroring and rotating houses" and varying garages, entrance canopies, and exterior colors. Both schemes offered individual gardens at the rear and a communal "public landscape" in the front that Ain and the landscape architect Garrett Eckbo created by eliminating any markings of boundaries between the individual properties.[11] Whether housing for low-income renters or houses for middle-class buyers, these neighborhoods offered homes designed for anonymous occupants set in attractively landscaped environments.

The trend into the suburbs did not bypass German speakers in the United States, be they visitors, immigrants, or émigrés. Already in the decades around 1900, visitors were fascinated by detached houses and the reduction of density they allowed. In 1876, the geographer Friedrich Ratzel credited single-family and detached houses (*geschlossene Häuser*) with the well-being of their inhabitants and the "filling in" (*Ausfüllung*) of the differences in density of providing houses and housing between city and country.[12] In 1893, Ratzel's colleague Gustav Diercks declared detached houses the "fundamental type of the American home proper."[13] In the mid-1920s, the feminist social reformer Alice Salomon expressed her admiration of the practicality of detached houses, even if she doubted whether the houses meant anything to their inhabitants that came close to the Germanic notion of a house as a home (*Heim*).[14]

Among the émigrés living in California in the 1930s, the theater director Max Reinhardt admired the "vertical grandiosity" of New York. Yet, he decided on Los

Angeles as the ideal location for the vast arts complex that he envisioned building at the end of the decade. The reason was simple: the "rapidly expanding city" of Los Angeles and its surrounding towns "promised to grow into the grandest and most beautiful *horizontal* city on Earth."[15] And early on during his exile in Los Angeles, Theodor Adorno was charmed by the suburban beauty of the landscape north of Santa Monica: "The whole broad locality here is somewhere between city and country.... The houses, all bungalows and never offensive to look at, are spaced far apart."[16]

Émigré architects were equally captivated by notions of a suburban environment, even if it was not always called such, a fascination not necessarily acquired in exile but often imported from pre-exile Central Europe. Modernist architects of the Weimar Republic, for example, looked already in the 1920s to suburbs in the United States as one model of how to modernize housing for the masses; in this context, even a link to Leopold Fischer exists. In 1928, Adolf Rading illustrated a book chapter on the urban form of the loosened-up (*aufgelockerte*) city of the future with Fischer's Knarrberg estate as an example of housing in an open, low-density format, a "loosening up that is accelerated by traffic." In the chapter, titled "Die Typenbildung und ihre städtebaulichen Folgerungen" (The creation of typologies and their urban design conclusions), Rading notes:

> In America, the car as a means of mass transportation has already made possible a quite different pattern of expansion of cities compared to ours and much lower densities in the outer suburbs that are not dependent on the efficiency of a public transport system.[17]

Within a decade, Fischer, Rading, and the architect Fritz Block (the editor of the book that included Rading's essay) were forced to emigrate: Rading, together with his Jewish wife, initially to France, then Palestine, and later the United Kingdom; and Block and Fischer to Los Angeles. In California, with Verdugo Village, at least Fischer worked on a suburban project. He may have even considered this commission as his contribution to the loosening up of the city, which had been out of reach in Berlin and Vienna for so long.

• • •

Once in exile, émigré architects accepted projects in suburbia, ranging from individual houses to entire neighborhoods. An example of the former is the expansive ranch house that Paul László built in the suburban San Fernando Valley in 1939 for the German immigrant movie director Henry (Heinz) Blanke.[18] The Spanish colonial revival–style house featured an open floor plan, built-in modern furniture, and an eclectic decorative scheme. The centerpiece of the latter was a mural of a map with war room–like dimensions depicting Germany with its borders from 1939, surrounded by its immediate neighbors. Germany would soon invade most of these neighbors after the country's attack on Poland on 1 September 1939 started World War II.

Liane Zimbler's professional move into suburbia likewise began with individually designed houses, such as the interior of the Freeman house in the Monte-Mar Vista subdivision (Cheviot Hills, 1952–53, architect B. B. Williams).[19] Around the same time, Zimbler picked up suburban commissions from the real estate agents Lyle and Elizabeth Crinklaw, who lived in San Bernardino and developed tracts on the city's outskirts. Circa 1952, Zimbler designed the couple's new home "from plot plan to wallpaper"[20] on a piece of land at the western edge of the Arrowhead Country Club in the northeast of the city (figs. 5.2a, 5.2b). The 1,600-square-foot, one-story home was not as sprawling as Cliff May's contemporary ranch houses but subscribed to the idea, even ideal, to fill large suburban plots with as large a house as possible.

5.2a. Liane (Juliana) Zimbler (US American, 1892–1987, b. Austria-Hungary).

Lyle and Elizabeth Crinklaw house (ca. 1952–53), San Bernardino, California.

Exterior view.

From Mary Ann Thayer, "Spaciousness Is a State of Mind," *Los Angeles Times Home Magazine,* April 1953, H15.

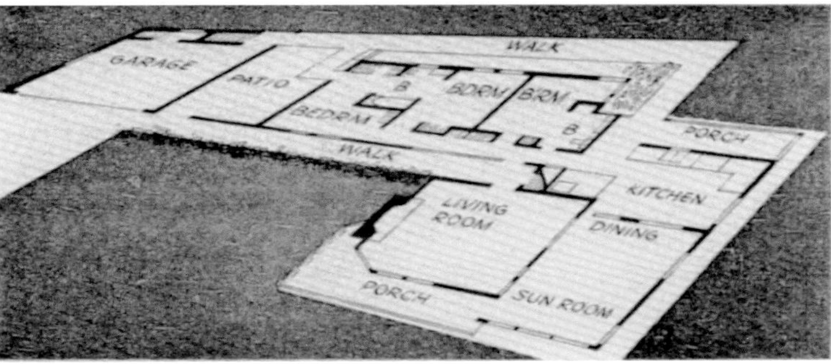

5.2b. Liane (Juliana) Zimbler (US American, 1892–1987, b. Austria-Hungary).

Lyle and Elizabeth Crinklaw house (ca. 1952–53), San Bernardino, California.

Floor plan.

From Mary Ann Thayer, "Spaciousness Is a State of Mind," *Los Angeles Times Home Magazine,* April 1953, H15.

At the same time, the Crinklaws sold lots and new homes to the east of the country club, a one-block development where Zimbler herself also invested in financing and designing homes for sale.[21] Between April and October 1953, newspaper display ads offered houses created by "Designer-Decorator Liane Zimbler of Beverly Hills Los Angeles," bringing metropolitan sophistication to the northeasternmost edge of San Bernardino.[22]

Lastly, the Austrian émigré architect Frederick Reichl became fully immersed in building suburbia once he teamed up with the Canadian immigrant architect Maxwell Starkman (1921–2003); the men had met when working for Richard Neutra. Together, they planned the development of Monterey Hills, which is today part of the city of Monterey Park. The partnership designed standardized floor plans for detached houses to be dressed in various styles. While working in his native Austria, including in Vienna, Reichl had designed housing for workers, an experience that echoed throughout his suburban California designs. The sparse literature on Reichl considers his suburban designs in Southern California under such headings as *villa* and *country house,* rubrics that do not do justice to Reichl's detached California houses and the suburbs they belong to.[23]

Rolf Sklarek, Fredric Frankel, and Ulrich Plaut, the immediate peers of Leopold Fischer, likewise contributed to the rapidly growing suburbia in Southern California, though detached houses were not their primary focus. In the 1950s, Sklarek joined the office of Victor Gruen,[24] who today is occasionally dismissed with little respect as the "megadeveloper... who literally wrote the book on *The Planning of Shopping Centers.*"[25] That said, considering that Gruen grew up in the hustle and bustle of urban life in Vienna's 1. Bezirk, *the* inner-city area of the Austrian capital, his attempt at creating shopping malls as centers of urban life in suburbia is a fascinating response to the experience of exile in Los Angeles. As for Frankel, when in 1949 he took over the office of his employer, the late architect Marcus P. Miller, he inherited many commercial and business clients for which the firm had already designed stores, offices, business premises, and commercial buildings throughout metropolitan Los Angeles and as far as San Bernardino and Bakersfield. Frankel continued this line of architectural work all over Southern California.[26] Finally, Plaut designed commercial buildings across the Los Angeles region for businesses and companies needing production facilities, often close to or even surrounded by suburban subdivisions offering housing for employees working nearby.[27]

Whatever one thinks about mid-twentieth-century suburbia in Southern California today, historically, its development enabled some émigré architects to receive commissions for new buildings. This, in turn, allowed these architects to reestablish their careers in exile during the postwar years after such careers had been cut short first by being forced into exile and then in 1941 by World War II. Suburbia in Southern California may nowadays often be dismissed, if not be despised by critical theorists and historians; exploring suburbia fully as an opportunity for émigré (and immigrant) architects (and clients) awaits further scholarly analysis.[28]

Verdugo Village: A Typology of Detached Homes for Suburbia

The new subdivision of Verdugo Village was advertised as not being part of the city, with the individual lots advertised as offering qualities that distinguished them from their urban counterparts: they provided quiet and seclusion,[29] they impressed with a "panoramic view of the surrounding areas,"[30] and they were "high, dry and level."[31] The last adjective set them apart from those steep elevations that invited enterprising architects and clients to let houses step down a hillside, cantilever them above an incline, or float them in front of the slope by supporting them with spindly posts or stilts rested on point foundations farther downhill.[32] Even calling the subdivision a village suggested a location in the distant countryside, though for the contemporary author and social critic Carey McWilliams, *village* carried far fewer positive overtones. He derided the term for creating a sense of comfort for newcomers to Los Angeles who, as "flatlanders" and "chronic and eternal villagers," allegedly appreciated the repetition of a familiar "village pattern in a metropolitan environment."[33] Perhaps such settlers would have felt dizzy in a village so high above the Los Angeles plain that the views reached as far as Old Baldy Mountain (Mount San Antonio) in the east and Catalina Island in the west.[34] Yet, the elevated position of 800 feet also guaranteed an "almost continuous breeze" and cooler temperatures.[35] One owner of a Fischer-designed home even exclaimed that he found "a new frontier" in Verdugo Village:

> A frontier is supposed to be away out in the hinterlands, on the fringe of a tomorrow that dawn will bring. Miles out beyond the hum and hustle of the roaring city. You don't find

5.3. Detail of a 1956 aerial image of Verdugo Village.

The houses designed by Fischer are marked with red dots.

University of California, Santa Barbara, UC Santa Barbara Library, Geospatial Collection.

all that, in 1955, six miles from Civic Center. . . . But, in Verdugo Village, we did.[36]

Perhaps the writer felt that he was reliving life on an isolated frontier where a new tomorrow was created; regardless, his phrasing definitely recalls the late nineteenth-century historian Frederick J. Turner's depiction of the US American colonial frontier that, on its relentless westward march, had gradually gobbled up allegedly unsettled territories.[37] By linking Turner's thoughts with the speculative houses of Verdugo Village, the writer reimagined the subdivision as a modern-day equivalent to colonial homesteads as outposts of modern civilization amid untamed nature. This kind of perception has been criticized for ignoring the "corporate, bureaucratic and cultural interests" that shaped the settler environments arising along the historical frontier as much as the contemporary suburbanization in the metropolitan region of Los Angeles.[38] However, in the context of Verdugo Village, the quote illustrates that this subdivision was perceived as not just suburban or even rural but also as *close to nature.* Verdugo Village did not physically extend the boundaries of greater Los Angeles by, for example, subdividing areas of the San Fernando Valley or Orange County; instead, it developed a hilltop within Los Angeles that until then was untouched by housing. In short, Verdugo Village was perceived as simultaneously being close to nature and part of Los Angeles. Indeed, Verdugo Village was in such close vicinity to the city that one could conduct business downtown while living high above and thus away from the city.

Historical aerial photographs of the territory where Verdugo Village was about to rise contrast with the idyllic image evoked in the real estate ads and related articles. By 1928, significant portions of a network of streets were in place, especially the imperfect oval of the loop formed by Nordica Drive and Palmero Drive to the southeast of the future Verdugo Village.[39] To the northeast, Oban Drive crept up the hillside, though at that time it ended in a cul-de-sac. By 1940, little had changed except for a path winding along the ridge of the terrain to the west of the loop,[40] indicating the direction of the future continuation of Palmero Drive, as can be seen in an aerial photograph from 1952 that also illustrates the early earthworks approximately at today's street junction between the extended Palmero Drive and Alegre Place branching off to the north.[41] The new stretch of Palmero Drive leads westward from Nordica Drive until, at the westernmost edge of the raised terrain, it turns 180 degrees toward the east and downhill, where eventually a sharp bend directs the street back west until it connects farther downhill with Division Street and West Avenue 42. By 1956, Verdugo Village was fully under development; figure 5.3 shows all the houses that Fischer had designed.

With Palmero Drive as its backbone, Verdugo Village comprises two tracts. Tract no. 18062 encompasses the area from the crossing of Palmero Drive with Nordica Drive to the lots of 4201 and 4202 Palmero Drive (fig. 5.4). From there, the terrain on either side of Palmero Drive to the junction with Division Street farther downhill to the north constitutes tract no. 19490.[42] The former tract was owned by Orb Investment Co. and the latter by Builders Securities Inc.; the two companies were linked through the general contractor and businessman George Elias Brooks (1899–1979), who lived for several years in one of the houses Fischer designed.[43] From 1954 onward, lots were sold in both tracts, but Fischer was only involved with tract no. 18062, the larger of the two, which covered most of the hill's top with its spectacular views. Buyers could purchase a lot and a plan for a Fischer house or just the lot. Whether Fischer supervised the construction of individual houses or supplied only the drawings is unknown.

Tract no. 18062 comprises forty-eight lots along Palmero Drive and the turnaround of Alegre Place; ultimately, Fischer designed homes on twelve of these lots between 1953 and 1955 (see fig. 5.3). Compared to the social housing estates that Fischer designed and built during his years in Dessau, which ranged from one hundred eighty-four units in Dessau-Ziebigk and

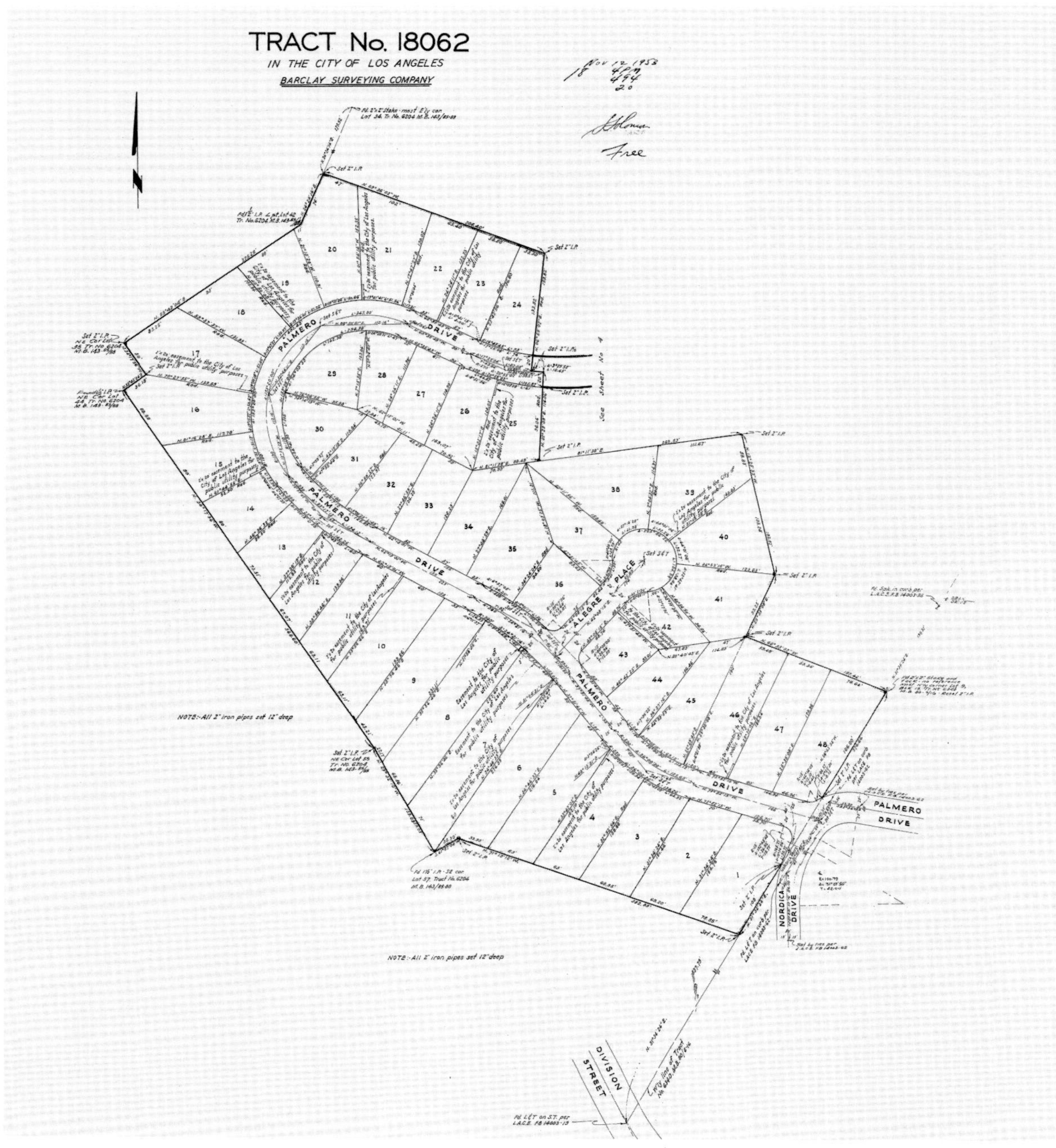

5.4. ***Tract No. 18062 in the City of Los Angeles,*** **sheets 2 (494-20) and 3 (494-21), as recorded 12 November 1953.**

Public Works Los Angeles County.

5.5. Leopold Fischer (US American, 1901–75, b. Austria-Hungary).

Verdugo Village (1953–55), Los Angeles, California.

Typology of houses as reconstructed from outline drawings of each Fischer-designed home documented in City of Los Angeles building permits. Nomenclature for never-built types of houses placed in square brackets.

Reconstruction drawing by Willem Swârt.

ninety units in Bernburg to estates as small as twenty to thirty units, the forty-eight possible homes in the new subdivision were a small- to medium-size commission.[44] Considering Fischer's California career up to 1952, Verdugo Village was a substantial project that could result in more commissions down the line because it was a developer-led subdivision. Fischer was aware of this potential, as he did not design only houses for lots with leveled surfaces for buildings of more or less identical sizes. He went further: he developed standardized variations of a basic type of home, resulting in a typology of detached houses that, in theory, was transferable to any other subdivision.

Fischer was experienced with typological approaches to designing anonymous dwellings thanks to his social housing projects in the Weimar Republic.

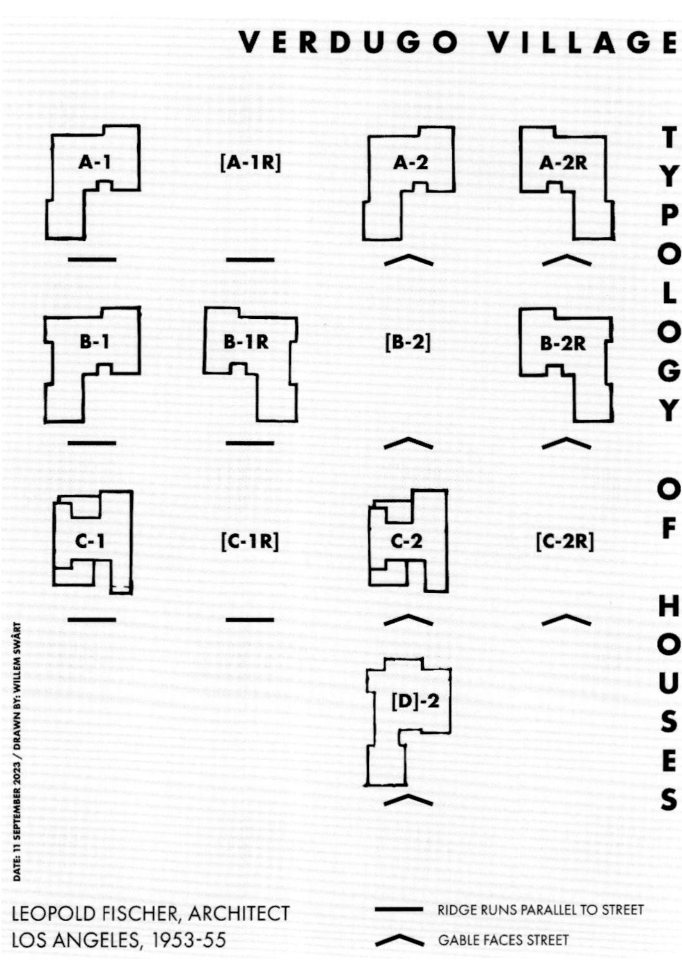

For example, the first terraced houses or row houses that Fischer developed in the office of Walter Gropius for the Siedlung Dessau-Törten were type SIETÖ [*Sie*dlung *Tö*rten] I, which was eventually supplemented with SIETÖ I.2, and other SIETÖ types.[45] The differences between these types relate to features such as construction, materials, and floor plan layout. Gropius and the Bauhaus were fond of approaching housing design through standardization and its (alleged) benefits of efficiency and savings of materials and money. Standardization suggested a rational ordering, even a so-called scientific attitude, toward satisfying a pressing social need.

• • •

The conceptual scope of Fischer's typology of houses for Verdugo Village is illustrated in figure 5.5. It shows the outline drawings and nomenclature identifying the types (A-1, B-2R, C-2, etc.) that are part of the building permits for each house Fischer erected along Palmero Drive. Table 5.1 summarizes the variations between the types that concern the overall size based on the numbers of rooms and whether the dining area is extended or not; the side of the main pitched roof that is oriented toward Palmero Drive, which, in turn, determines the shape of the garage roof; and the location of the garage relative to the main entrance.

The basic division is between Types A and B, with the latter featuring a larger dining area that projects farther out on one side of its location in one of the corners of the main house. This results in a slightly

Table 5.1. Nomenclature of Fischer's typology of detached single-family houses for subdivision of Verdugo Village

	A-1	A-1R	A-2	A-2R	B-1	B-1R	B-2	B-2R	C-1	C-2	[D-1]	[D]-2
Basic one-story house: • 2 bedrooms + den [or 3 bedrooms] • 2 baths • living room • dining area • kitchen • laundry	•	•	•	•					• (layout of plan differs; see pp. 103–4)	• (layout of plan differs; see pp. 103–4)		
The above, plus an extended dining area					•	•	•	•				
Partially two-story building									•	•		•
Roof 1: ridge of main roof parallel to street	•	•			•	•			•			
Roof 2: gable of main roof faces street			•	•			•	•		•		
Garage to left	•		•		•		•					
Garage to right		•		•		•		•				
Garage below									•	•		•
Houses of that type, identified by first owner or occupant	Mendenhall		Gadd, Busby	Randall	Barron	Stiles, Tullar		Brown, Jochheim	Pratt	Fazzi		Brooks

VERDUGO VILLAGE three-bedroom-and-den homes on level lots overlook Glendale and Pasadena, are six miles from Civic Center.

5.6. Perspective rendering of the street view of a Type A-1 or B-1 house.

The larger dining room of Type B-1 would be located at the rear-left corner of the main volume of the house, which is invisible in this presentation drawing.

From "Highland Park District," *The Tidings* (Los Angeles), 9 July 1954, 7.

VERDUGO VILLAGE HOME HAS THREE BEDROOMS AND DEN
. . . panoramic view home in Highland Park priced at $19,000

5.7. Perspective rendering of the street view of a Type A-2 or B-2 house.

The larger dining room of Type B-2 would be located at the rear-left corner of the main volume of the house, which is invisible in this presentation drawing.

From "Verdugo Homes Feature View," *Pasadena Independent*, 23 May 1954, 18.

IN VILLAGE AREA—Shown above is one of the three-bedroom-and-den or four-bedroom homes now available in Verdugo Village, which is situated at Ave. 42, Division St. and Palermo Drive, in Highland Park.

5.8. Three-bedroom plus a den (or four-bedroom) type of house designed by Fischer for Verdugo Village.

From "Verdugo Village Homes Offer Impressive Luxury Appointments," *Los Angeles Daily News*, 4 June 1954, 28.

increased square footage of Type B and a different articulation of one of the long-side facades. The latter begins with the garage's rear wall, recedes in the center, and projects out again at the far corner of the home where the dining area is located (see fig. 5.5, second row from top).

Types A and B are further differentiated by the numbers 1 or 2. Number 1 denotes that the ridgeline of the roof and, accordingly, an eave line run parallel to Palmero Drive (fig. 5.6); number 2 signifies that a gable side faces the street (fig. 5.7). In the first case, the slope of the main roof extends over the garage, visibly making it part of the same building; in the second, the garage appears as a separate volume attached to the house. The letter *R* signifies the garage's location to the *right* of the main entrance, which means mirroring a plan, for example, Type A-1 for A-1R or Type B-2 for B-2R.

Type C is less of a variation of Types A and B and more of a distinct design specifically for lots from approximately the beginning of the 180-degree bend of Palmero Drive to the end of tract no. 18062. Here, the terrain is steeper on both sides of the street and, therefore, individual lots slope, some significantly. For these locations, Fischer elevated the house by slipping the garages underneath the main level and providing outdoor stairs to the living spaces. Type C is an H-shaped building with two parallel wings of different widths and lengths that accommodate the same rooms as Types A and B but in a different layout. The main entrance is in the center of the crossbar of the H shape. The shallower wing to one side accommodates the kitchen, the breakfast area, and a small terrace on top of the garage that looks over the street into the distance. The dining and living areas are in the rear of the deep crossbar between the wings. The wider wing encompasses the bedrooms and a bathroom. Type C maintains the differentiation concerning the street facade; the main roof of Type C-1 faces the street with its ridge and an eave, and Type C-2 with one of the gable sides.

A fourth type of house is a three-bedroom plus a den (or a four-bedroom) home that is only known from an artist's rendering published in newspapers in 1954 (fig. 5.8). Compared to the renderings of the other types, a large window is visible immediately adjacent to the garage, but without a floor plan it is unclear which room was lit by that window. It follows in the corner with the main building, the entrance into the house where all other living and service spaces are located. None of these larger houses were built, and nothing else can be said about them without drawings or blueprints.

Lastly, Fischer designed a four-bedroom house for George Elias Brooks, the owner of Orb Investment Co., at 4259 Palmero Drive. This house is significantly larger, as it occupies one and a half lots. The outline drawing accompanying the building permit shows traces of Fischer's nomenclature, now illegible. It may have originally read "[D]-2," but the lack of further archival sources and additional built examples prevent further analysis of a possible Type D house.

• • •

Already with the basic design of Type A and the four variables of dining area footage, location of the garage, and which side of the roof faced the street (which then also decided the roof of the garage), Fischer could offer eight possible variations for the houses of Types A and B. Type C added at least four more variants, plus an unknown number of variations resulting from the never-built larger home illustrated in figure 5.8 and, perhaps, from a Type D house. Furthermore, depending on the lot that a buyer selected, Fischer provided additional adjustments, such as more doors to the outside and steps leading to lower sections of the garden areas immediately abutting the home. Ignoring individual adjustments, the number of possible standard variations appears relatively large, particularly as Fischer could expect a maximum of forty-eight commissions for detached houses.

Other contemporary developers restricted the number of model types "usually [to] between two and four" and adopted as a rule that "exterior variations were kept to a minimum."[46] These are some of the principles of Eichler Homes, the contemporary merchant builder that tended to develop significantly larger subdivisions with post-and-beam modernist homes that are much celebrated today.[47] All told, however, when compared to variations offered by more prominent commercial developers, Fischer's number of variations is not overly extensive and is rather clever. Larger developers often dressed a series of different floor plans in varying styles, whereas Fischer mainly worked with two floor plans, Type A and Type B (which was a slightly larger version of Type A) plus two possible orientations of the roofs over those plans (Type 1 or 2); the resulting building could then be mirrored to vary the position of the garages. Mirroring and rotating types of houses to achieve variation within an overall unity was not unusual at the time: Gregory Ain's Mar Vista Housing has already been referred to as a scheme that made similar moves, and even earlier Rudolph Schindler's Pueblo Ribera Court (La Jolla, 1923) rotated identical housing units by ninety degrees to each other, ensuring privacy and varying views across the development. Fischer had also mirrored the two units that he combined in the semidetached units in Dessau-Ziebigk, thus setting a precedent for his future work.

But what were Fischer's intentions when conceiving standardized types of homes for a relatively small subdivision? Possible explanations can be found in Fischer's social housing estates in Weimar Germany and in the intended clientele for Verdugo Village. For example, when designing social housing in Dessau, Leopold Fischer developed standardized types of semidetached houses and row (or terraced) houses, according to Irene Below, the author of the only (to date) detailed architectural and social analysis of Fischer's social housing oeuvre in and around Dessau.[48] Fischer's typology for the Knarrberg estate was one reason why Rading illustrated the neighborhood as an exemplary solution for "the creation of typologies and their urban design conclusions," thus the title of his chapter in the aforementioned book edited by Block.[49] The standardized, though variable, types made the Dessau houses suitable to different social layers of the population that urgently needed housing, such as working-class families and low-paid white-collar workers (*Angestellte*).[50] Other intentions in Dessau were to cater to the different needs of future inhabitants, who were unknown to the architect. Comparable reasoning applies to Verdugo Village, which competed with many other subdivisions in and around Los Angeles. The possibility of individualizing one's home with one of the available architectural variations—advertised as the work of an internationally famous architect—increased the curb appeal of the planned development and presumably catered to the sensibilities of the likely buyers. But who *were* these buyers?

The architectural variety of these homes suggests that buyers were members of the middle class—possibly even upper-middle class—and "middle-income working classes,"[51] as can be concluded, for example, from the almost contemporary development of the Levittown Willingboro (1955–59) in New Jersey. There, the developer aimed at buyers from the middle and upper classes by offering homes in different architectural styles priced from $11,500 to $14,500.[52] The higher prices for the homes in Verdugo Village suggest at least comparable clients. The two-bedroom plus a den (or three-bedroom) house of Types A and B were priced at $17,600 in 1954, but by 1955, the figure had fallen to $15,000. The (never-built) four-bedroom (or three-bedroom plus a den) model cost $19,000. These amounts included the lots valued from $3,000 to $4,000 and higher when bought without a Fischer-designed home.[53]

The size of the houses points to the same classes of likely buyers. Types A and B, the smallest of Fischer's typology, were between 1,393 and 1,444 square feet in area, while Fischer's Types C-1 and C-2, with 1,741 square feet and 1,972 square feet, respectively, are close to the 1,852 square feet of the Kohlmeier house (1941) that, however, also included a maid's room.[54] By 1941, that room was already somewhat of an anachronism for an upper-middle-class home; cultural and socioeconomic changes had resulted in fewer and fewer live-in domestic staff from the early twentieth century onward and, accordingly, generally led to smaller middle-class houses.[55] This trend is reflected in the overall sizes of most of the Verdugo Village homes, which were modest, perhaps even small, though certainly not minimum. Terms such as *minimum* and *small* are relative qualifiers conceived during the early twentieth century, often in contrast to the much larger houses erected for the middle classes in earlier decades, as James A. Jacobs pointed out. Definitions of *minimum* were often derived from the minimum property standards defined in the aftermath of the National Housing Act (1934) and those of *small* from efforts of such private organizations as the Architects' Small House Service Bureau (ASHSB). The ASHSB, for example, considered a house "small" when it had up to six rooms and 30,000 cubic feet of volume, which, per Jacobs's calculations, equaled 3,000 to 3,750 square feet.[56]

The housing data compiled in connection with the Mutual Mortgage Insurance Program established by the National Housing Act (1934) allow a more specific contextualization for Fischer's design. This comparison also allows a conclusion about the importance of the subdivision within the trajectory of Fischer's career across the divide of exile. The Verdugo Village homes were eligible for support through the Mutual Mortgage Insurance Program, even though financial details for any specific Fischer-designed home are unknown. The buildings met or exceeded the contemporary minimum property standards set by the Federal Housing Administration for Southern California concerning, for example, the size of the individual lots, the ratio of building size to lot size and dimensions, and the arrangement of spaces and rooms within each house.[57]

The costs of the homes present a more complex picture. Looking at the 1954 administrative regulations for the federal insurance program (the regulations and program were both revised that year), a new, owner-occupied single-family residence may have qualified for insurance of a mortgage of up to $20,000. Assuming the assessed value of a Fischer-designed house was $15,000—the lowest published sales price—the insurance would have covered, in the best-case scenario, a mortgage of up to a tad over $13,000.[58] In the same year, the median property value of a home in California with federal mortgage insurance was $9,641, and houses valued at $15,000 composed only 7.9 percent of all insured properties.[59]

Regarding square footage and the number of rooms, Fischer's houses again stand out from the average of mortgage-insured, new single-family houses. The 1,393 and 1,444 square feet of Types A and B exceeded the nationwide median of 1,157 square feet for homes valued between $15,000 and $15,999, just 3.8 percent of all insured houses. Within that subgroup, the slightly smaller Type A was far more typical than the larger Type B; 33.5 percent of all insured homes comprised "1,200–1,399 square feet" and only 6.8 percent "1,400–1,599 square feet."[60] The six rooms of both types exceeded the average and median numbers of 5.1 and 5.6 rooms, respectively, for all homes in California.[61] Lastly, Fischer's Types A and B were "average" if the den counts as a bedroom, for then they were part of the 75.3 percent of all insured homes in California in 1954 with three bedrooms, making up the vast majority. Without that extra bedroom, the houses were relegated to the second largest group of houses, which came in significantly lower at 11.9 percent.[62]

In summary, Fischer's homes were more expensive and larger by square footage and number of rooms than the average insured, newly built home in 1954. They were intended for families with few children and those capable of paying a premium in exchange for living close to, but high above, downtown Los Angeles. Voter rolls and city directories for Los Angeles support the conclusion drawn, as table 5.2 illustrates (see p. 122). It lists the first adult occupants of the Fischer-designed homes along with their occupations, which range from building contractors, clerks in management positions, and company owners to teachers and sports columnists.

In regard to Fischer's career in exile, Verdugo Village illustrates that by the early 1950s, Fischer had lost neither his interest in standardized houses nor his skills to design them. However, the focus of his designs for anonymous domestic architecture shifted from the working classes in Weimar Germany to the middle and upper-middle classes of Southern California. That Fischer approached the typology of houses for the middle classes with a methodology that he had honed when drafting working-class social housing estates in Weimar Germany recalls Edward Dimendberg's lament, already cited in chapter 4, that Anton Wagner's study of Los Angeles neglected to recommend German social housing programs to the metropolis.[63] Fischer also neglected to recommend these programs, though Verdugo Village inscribed subtle traces of Weimar Republic housing into the urban fabric of Los Angeles.

A *Siedlung* on the Pacific? Echoes of Dessau in Los Angeles

The two floor plans at the center of this section are reconstructions based on a demolition drawing for a remodel of Fischer's Type A-1. The redrawn plans were then checked against exterior and interior photographs of houses of Types A-2, B-1R, and C-2 that the current owners allowed me to take, and they were also cross-checked against other Type A and Type B houses to the extent that those are visible from the street. Additional details came from photographs and videos of homes at the time of purchase that current owners kindly shared. The resulting drawings of the plans of a Type A-1 home (fig. 5.9) and a Type B-2 home (fig. 5.10) illustrate the crucial characteristics of the homes without representing any specific houses on Palmero Drive. The garages of these assumed ideal Fischer-designed homes are located to the left of the main entrance.

Houses of Types A and B are 43 feet wide and 33 feet deep, which ignores recesses and cutouts, and the garages enclose an additional 20 by 20 feet.[64] Accordingly, the main buildings take up almost the entire width of the lots (which are at least 53 feet wide—with most lots around or just over 60 feet, occasionally even up to 75 feet wide), leaving narrow yards on either side of the houses. In front of the buildings, the land is used for a short driveway to the garage and the remaining area is landscaped. The lots are far longer than wide—the shortest is 93 feet long, the longest 169 feet—yet because most lots slope rather deeply or rise steeply at the far end of the graded area on which the houses are centered, only small usable gardens may exist at the rear of the homes, if at all.

The main volume of each home is arranged in three functional zones that stretch from the front of the building toward the rear. The central zone accommodates the living spaces, the zone to the right the private bedrooms, and the one to the left service spaces. The

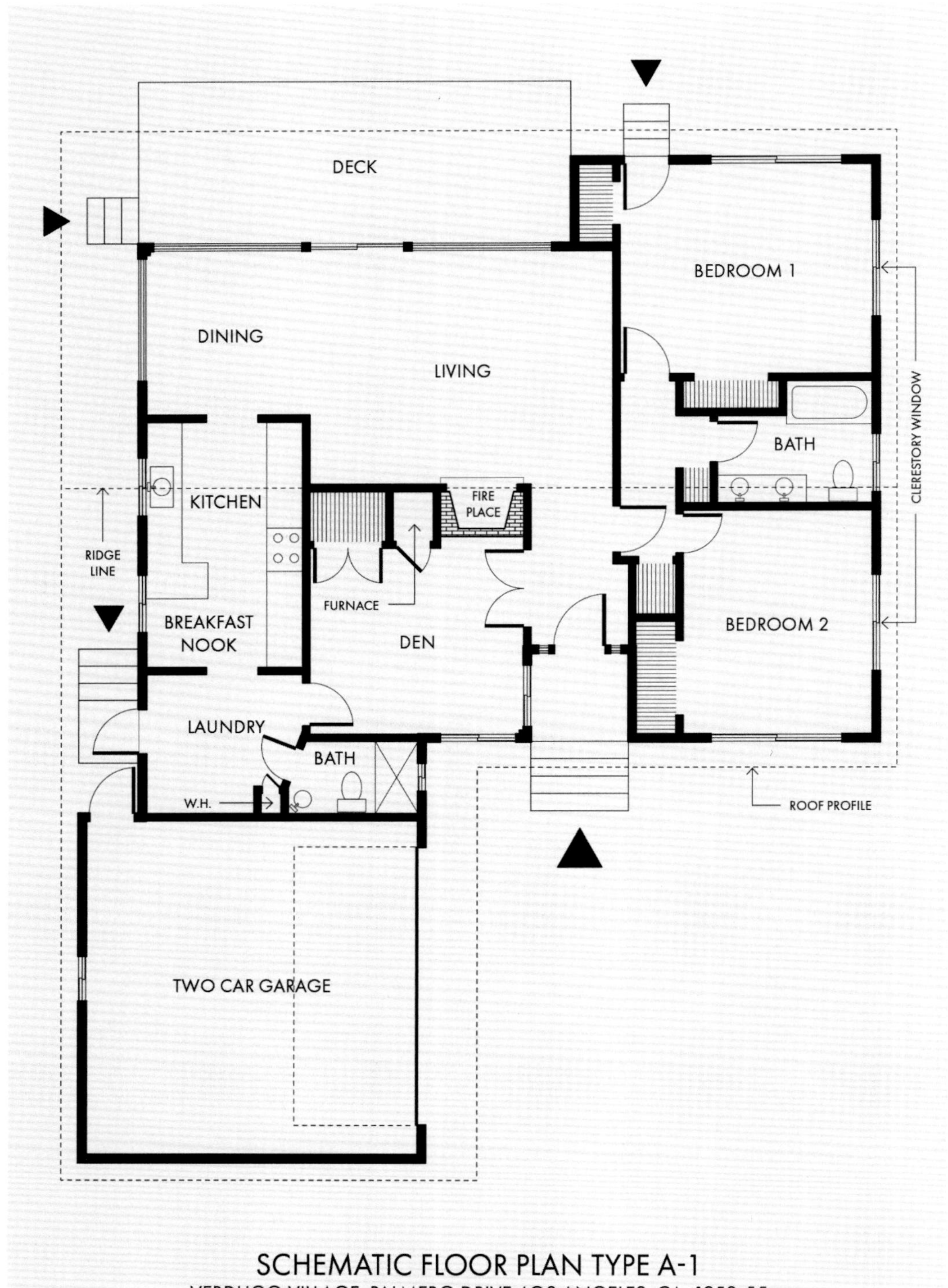

5.9. Leopold Fischer (US American, 1901–75, b. Austria-Hungary).

Schematic Floor Plan Type A-1, Verdugo Village (1953–55), Los Angeles, California.

Reconstruction drawing by Willem Swârt.

5.10. Leopold Fischer (US American, 1901–75, b. Austria-Hungary).

Schematic Floor Plan Type B-2, Verdugo Village (1953–55), Los Angeles, California.

Reconstruction drawing by Willem Swârt.

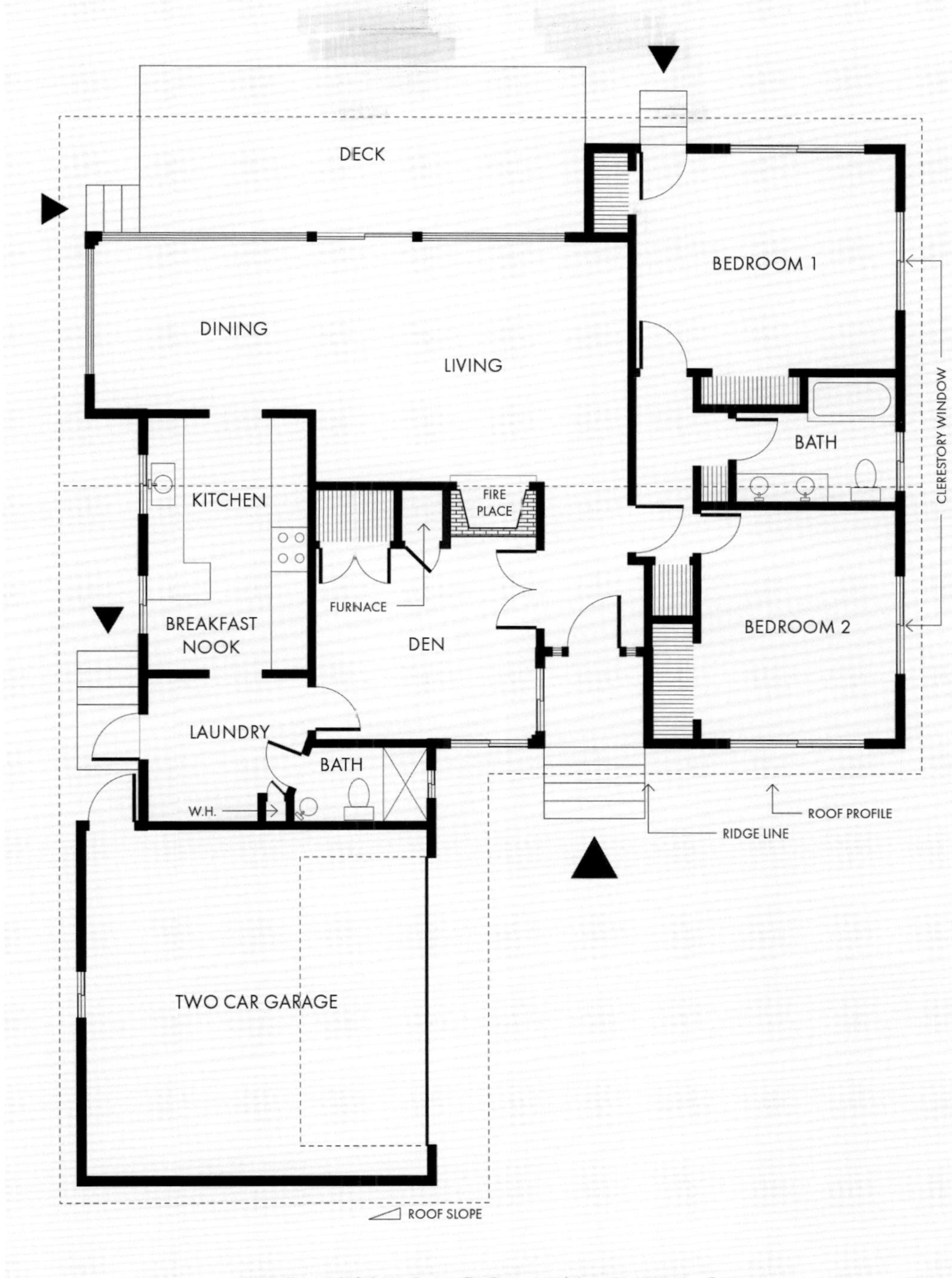

5.11. Leopold Fischer (US American, 1901–75, b. Austria-Hungary).

House Type A-2, Verdugo Village (1953–55), Los Angeles, California, April 2022.

Living-cum-dining room with the window wall in this example pulled around the dining area.

5.12. Leopold Fischer (US American, 1901–75, b. Austria-Hungary).

House Type A-2, Verdugo Village (1953–55), Los Angeles, California, April 2022.

The deck as an outdoor living room.

latter zone includes the garage, which extends that zone beyond the street facade of the main house, thereby creating the L shape of the entire building. The entrance is off-center at the corner of the central zone, where a few steps go up to a small, recessed entrance porch. On the inside, immediately to the left, a double door swings open to a commodious den; ahead lies a short corridor that connects with the living area uninterrupted by a door at its threshold. The living area occupies a rectangular space whose open plan encompasses

5.13. **Leopold Fischer (US American, 1901–75, b. Austria-Hungary).**

House Type A-2, Verdugo Village (1953–55), Los Angeles, California, April 2022.

View from the street.

a dining area at the far end that is square in Type A and rectangular in Type B. Along the entire width of this living-cum-dining room, a floor-to-ceiling window wall grants views of the surroundings, and in some houses, the window wall is pulled around the corner to the side of the dining area (fig. 5.11). Depending on whether the roof is of Type 1 or Type 2, the ceiling of the living-cum-dining room may rise toward the off-center apex of the roof, with the glass wall following the upward incline. Where the living area gives way to the dining area, a single sliding glass door opens up to a deck in front of the window wall; a deep roof overhang covers this outdoor living room (fig. 5.12).

Access to the bedroom zone is from the entrance into another short corridor containing a built-in linen cupboard. One bedroom is placed toward the street, the other toward the rear of the building, and in between is a bathroom with a bathtub. The slightly larger principal bedroom is the one to the rear from which a door and, in some cases, a few steps lead to a small garden area outside the room and adjacent to the deck. The deck in front of the living-cum-dining room looked down to the small garden area outside of the main bedroom but did not initially give access to it via a second set of steps (though today such a set can be found at some houses).

The service zone extends from the dining area to the front of the building. The narrow galley-type kitchen is a separate room, linked to the dining area with an open archway. At its other end, past a small breakfast nook with a window, a door leads to a laundry room from which more doors open to an outside stair onto the narrow yard along that side of the building, to the den adjacent to the main entrance, and to a second bathroom (with a shower). Beyond the latter is the garage, where, after drivers park, they exit through the garage door to enter the home via the main door. A secondary exit for the garage is through a rear door leading again to the narrow yard on the side of the house and from there into the home through the laundry room.

The exteriors of the houses are plain and unadorned; metal-framed windows sit flush with walls covered in stucco and are protected by roof overhangs. Vertical wooden cladding replaces the stucco in select areas such as the garages, usually clad in wooden boards, enhancing the impression of an additional building added to the main house. Sometimes, cladding can be seen just above the main entrance, and occasionally, an entire street facade was covered with vertical wooden boards; this later variation no longer exists because of renovations. Vertical cladding is also often used for the facades of the dining area, which consequently can appear from the outside as a small wooden cabin slipped underneath the roof of an adjacent, larger stuccoed home. In the case of houses with Type 2 roofs, a recessed porch visually emphasizes the main entrance, and as the porch rises to the full height of the facade, it grants glimpses of the wooden skeletons of the homes (fig. 5.13). At the apex, immediately to the right of the recess, the ridge beam prominently projects from underneath a deep roof overhang. Rafters and wooden boards as sheathing on top of them rise visibly across the recess toward the ridge beam. A little under halfway down, a beam spans the recess horizontally at its outer edges, almost like a lintel with no door below it. For houses with Type 1 roofs, the entrance porch is an upright rectangular recess in the stucco facade; in these cases, the two outer beams spanning the depth of the garages are pulled forward so that they rest visibly on posts in front of the garage. Occasionally, Fischer added versions of wooden trellises—for example, a series of slender posts holding up the roof overhang of the facade of the garage toward the street or a few posts rising in front of the bedroom window looking out the same direction.

• • •

Even if generally smaller than the Kohlmeier house and the Slechta house, the houses of Verdugo Village share features with both, especially with the 1941 house. The arrangement of the floor plan into functional zones is reminiscent of the Kohlmeier house, except that in Verdugo Village, the three zones are more condensed, whereas in the South Pasadena home they were drawn out linearly and were vertically differentiated by taking advantage of the slopes of the elevated building site. Regardless of whether they were designed for specific individuals or for anonymous buyers, the functional zones of Fischer's designs for private homes in California occupy distinct areas adjacent to one another while spatially being clearly defined and separated. The exceptions are the living and dining areas, which share the same continuous space and volume in the houses for the new subdivision and the two larger, individually designed ones. Moreover, in all examples, an all-glass wall overlooks an outdoor room (terrace or deck). Among the fixed glass panels, one usually finds just *a single* glass door to the outside, a feature the smaller homes share with their larger predecessors.

Irrespective of all differences (such as size), the conceptual similarities between the Verdugo Village homes and the Kohlmeier house are particularly interesting, as they point to different sources upon which Fischer drew specific to each commission. The Kohlmeier house illustrates Fischer's familiarity with Frank Lloyd Wright's Usonian houses as affordable, standardized middle-class US American houses, more upper-middle class in the case of the Kohlmeier couple. By contrast, when, in conjunction with the commission for Verdugo Village, the possibility arose to perhaps contribute to meeting the demand for housing in Southern California—which during World War II had been left unsatisfied—Fischer resorted to his pre-exile experience with standardized typologies of anonymous domestic architecture as one source of his designs.

Up to this juncture, the floor plans for Type A and Type B houses in Verdugo Village have been analyzed functionally. However, considering them formally, they compose a central square that accommodates the main house and most service spaces. Two rectangles are added to two sides of the square, the bedroom wing on one end and the garage with a small portion of the service spaces on the other, resulting in a slightly asymmetrical, almost perfect ninety-degree-angle footprint. In Southern California architectural history, designing domestic architecture based on such an angle recalls the How house (Los Angeles, 1925) by Rudolph Schindler. This building refined this type of plan with its near-planar symmetry across a diagonal axis through the main square at the angle's center.[65] In contrast, Fischer borrowed from his earlier social housing estates not to ideally order abstract geometries but to practically arrange tight spaces by enclosing them into the least wasteful volume. Looking at Fischer's social housing estates in Germany from this perspective, an almost direct line can be drawn from the semidetached houses of the Knarrberg estate in Dessau-Ziebigk to the houses for Verdugo Village.

The aerial view of the Knarrberg social housing estate that is shown in figure 1.5 illustrates the rigid lineup of the mainly semidetached houses along newly built streets in the middle of formerly agricultural land; these kinds of settlements were part of a suburbanization process that took place on the edges of cities where such housing projects were often located. The standard building type was a semidetached, two-story house that accommodated two private homes, one in either half. At the rear, each home was assigned a private garden, which was supposed to help produce, if not completely supply, each family's foodstuffs.

The differences between the Knarrberg estate and Verdugo Village are apparent—such differences include, for example, a straight geometric urban order versus houses along a curvilinear street; semidetached houses organized over two levels versus detached homes with all spaces on one level; extensively used gardens assigned to each home versus outdoor decks that grant views of a distant landscape or cityscape feature; and a *Siedlung* officially for the working

5.14. Leopold Fischer (US American, 1901–75, b. Austria-Hungary).

Type 1 home, Knarrberg estate (1926–28), Dessau-Ziebigk, Germany.

Floor plan, 1928 or earlier.

Illustrated is the left home of two semidetached homes sharing one building and identical, but mirrored, floor plans. The left side (here: lower half) of the drawing illustrates the lower level (*Erdgeschoss*) and the right side (here: upper half) illustrates the upper level (*Obergeschoss*) of the same home. (The image is turned 90 degrees counterclockwise to make the basic L shape visible.)

From Fritz Block, ed., *Probleme des Bauens: Der Wohnbau* (Potsdam: Müller & Kiepenheuer, 1928), 81.

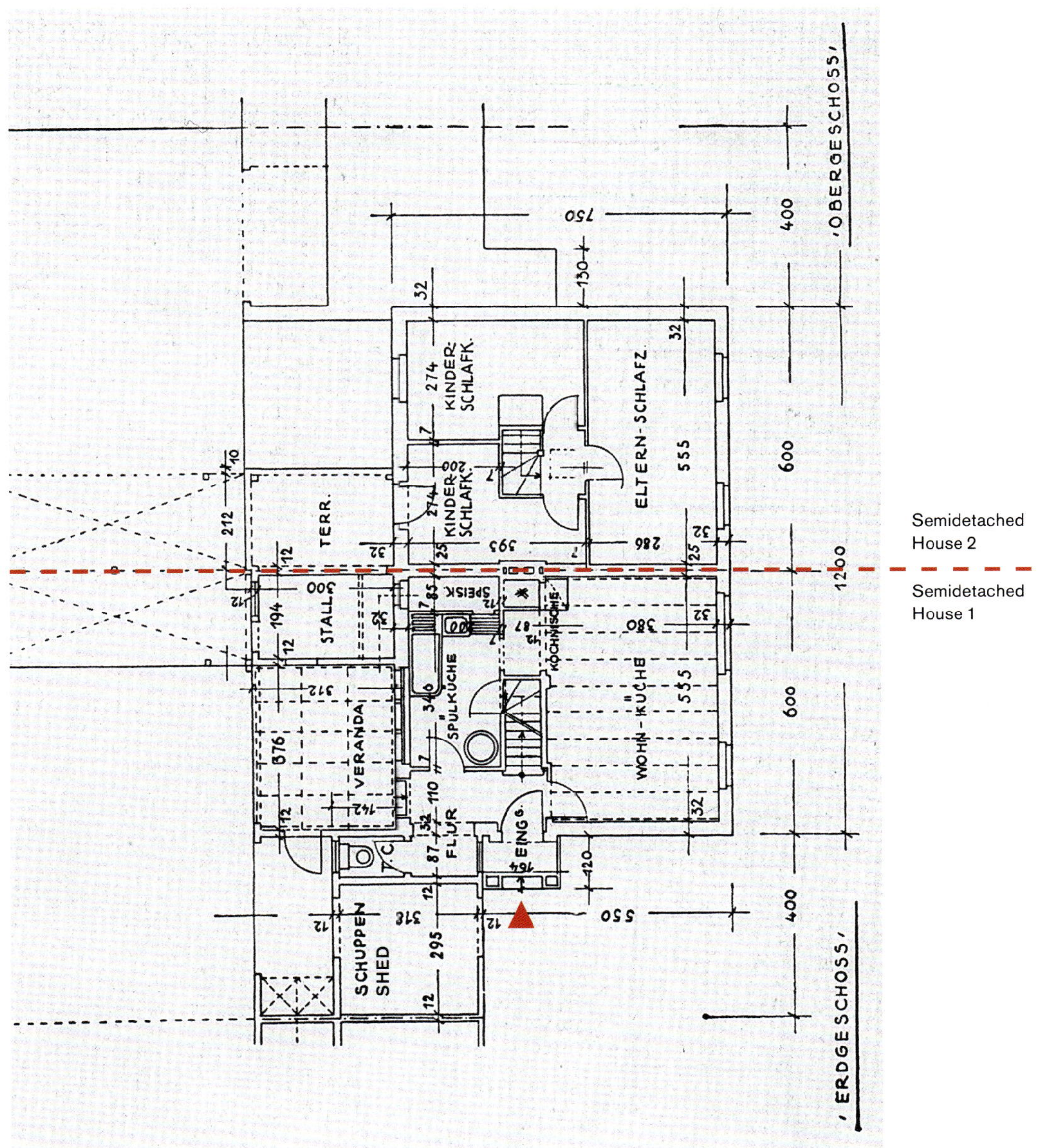

classes (though as noted in chapter 1, that was more an ideal than reality) versus a subdivis on or neighborhood for the middle and upper-middle classes.

The similarities are less visible but more consequential. Zooming in on just one of the two semidetached homes on the Knarrberg estate in Dessau-Ziebigk, the basic footprint is an L-shaped or a ninety-degree angle with the two parts of the *L* having different dimensions (fig. 5.14). The entrance into the home is in the inner corner of the angle. To the left, Fischer placed a shed (*Schuppen*)—which, at the time of completion, was already intended to accommodate a possible automobile[66]—with a door to the garden at its rear and, from there, to the veranda. The space of the actual angle is filled with service spaces such as the main entrance, a corridor, scullery (*Spülküche*), kitchen, and stair to the upstairs. Added on to the exterior are transitionary spaces like a glass-enclosed veranda or winter garden, a small stable, and a terrace that leads to the garden. This overall layout of the semidetached homes in an L shape is broadly comparable to the arrangements of the Type A and B houses in Verdugo Village, with the significant difference being that planning one-story standardized homes for Los Angeles required placing the bedrooms on the same floor as all other spaces. Fischer resolved this by substituting the bedrooms for the living rooms, which were moved beyond the service spaces (see figs. 5.9, 5.10).

Other details from the houses of the Knarrberg estate have been transposed to California without much adjustment. For example, in the Dessau houses, the toilet serving the home is accessed from the corridor on the lower level, but the space it occupies is carved out from the shed. Switching back to the floor plans in Verdugo Village, the second, smaller bathroom adjacent to the laundry room occupies a comparable spot at the border between the volume of the main house and the garage. In the plan, the bathroom appears to be part of the former volume. Yet, on the outside, the bathroom window appears as an element of the garage's elevation, unmistakably so because it is cut to the right and slightly higher than the garage door into the garage's facade, thereby signaling that the bathroom is part of the volume of the garage rather than that of the main house (see fig. 5.13).

A third, though less immediately visible, similarity arises from the relationships Fischer established in Dessau-Ziebigk between the living room and such service spaces as the kitchen and the scullery. These arrangements were the decisive difference between the two semidetached floor plans, Type 1 and Type 2, that Fischer had designed in 1926 for Dessau-Ziebigk. In the following, I focus on Type 1, which was the more innovative design (see fig. 5.14).[67] On the lower level of these Type 1 houses, a *Wohnküche* (a living room-cum-kitchen) is the most significant room that occupies all the space to the right of the entrance. In addition, among the service spaces on the inner side of the angle of the L shape is a generously sized Spülküche, for cleaning dishes, doing laundry, and allowing the inhabitants a weekly hot sitz bath. Between the Spülküche and the Wohnküche, one stair, accessible from the corridor, leads down to a partial basement, and another, this one accessible from the scullery, to the upper level. Beyond those stairs, a *Kochnische* (cooking niche) is placed between the Spülküche and Wohnküche; it is accessible from both adjacent rooms. Employing a foldable door, the cooking niche "could be closed after use so that an ordinary living room remains," instead of the combination of kitchen and living room, as Fischer explains in a contemporary journal. He continues:

> this foldable door can also be opened in a manner that divides the living area [of the Wohnküche] into a dining room and a living room proper. Accordingly, the *gute Stube* [parlor or best room] becomes superfluous.[68]

To design a kitchen large enough to double up as a living room for a family—or, to look at it the other way around, to conceive a living room that can also be used for cooking and uniting a family for a meal—is a legacy of Adolf Loos, who usually preferred a Wohnküche for social as much as for economic reasons in his social housing designs.

Such ideas echo in Fischer's placement of dining areas and living areas within the same larger room, as in the Kohlmeier and Slechta houses and those of Verdugo Village. That the kitchens in the California homes are spatially more clearly separated from the living-cum-dining space than in Fischer's prewar housing is due to the differences in the social classes of clients and inhabitants, respectively. The Kohlmeiers and the Slechtas relied, at least temporarily, on domestic staff working the kitchen. In the standardized types of houses for Verdugo Village, Fischer adjusted the spatial relationship between the living room, dining room, and kitchen to the contemporary likings of homebuyers and their likely social aspirations that would value a separate dining room. (As it happens, too many spatial experiments in this area may have jeopardized the sale of the houses.) Still, some aspects of his pre-exile social housing designs were clearly on Fischer's mind when he worked on Verdugo Village while in exile. Fischer not only thought about but also applied his experience with social housing in Weimar Germany to his designs of detached homes for the middle and upper-middle classes. Though conceived for a specific subdivision, the typology of single-family houses that Fischer created was his contribution to the contemporary architectural debate about detached houses—potentially to be producible in large numbers—for subdivisions and suburbs alike. The following section discusses the contributions of Fischer's standardized plans to that debate.

Perfecting the Average Suburban Home

Regardless of the whispers about Leopold Fischer's social housing in Weimar Germany that fill the nooks and crannies of the homes in Verdugo Village, ultimately, the homes' floor plans are typical for California and

American domestic architecture from at least the 1930s to the 1950s and, indeed, beyond. The houses may not have targeted the masses of homebuyers in the Los Angeles region, but they are still representative of the mass of contemporary speculative housing. Historians of housing point out that all over the United States, suburban houses of the 1920s and 1930s offered a three-room arrangement that comprised "generally ... a single multipurpose living room and a dining room ... with a modern and efficient kitchen." This typical arrangement of a two-story, pitched-roof house with bedrooms and a bathroom upstairs remained the popular model for the middle classes and well-paid working-class families until at least the early 1950s.[69] The rapidly growing housing market of the West Coast complemented the two-story type of house with "Western 'ranch houses' ... characterized by their single-storey [*sic*], basement-less, flat-roof configuration."[70] Crucial in this development was not so much the change of the shape of the roof or the omission of a basement[71] but the change from two stories to one, a consequence of the taller buildings being "excessive in both size and cost" when looked at through the lens of the Federal Housing Authority.[72] According to Dianne Harris, the "common configuration" of the resulting one-story homes "included two bedrooms, one bathroom, a living room, and a kitchen that might include a small area for dining"[73] or for breakfast. This layout raises two challenges for the architect. The first one concerned how and where to locate, relative to existing ground-level rooms of such houses, the bedrooms and bathrooms that used to be upstairs; Fischer also had to address this challenge when transforming the plan of a semidetached two-story unit from Dessau-Ziebigk into a single-story house in Verdugo Village. The second issue was where to place new types of rooms, such as a family room, that became popular during the 1950s.[74]

Accordingly, the Verdugo Village floor plans are once more of interest, with the focus shifting back to the three functional zones (living spaces, private bedrooms and bathrooms, and service spaces like a kitchen and, possibly, a garage) that characterize Fischer's designs. This type of three-zoned plan was not specific to or even invented by Fischer but was widely used in contemporary domestic architecture.[75] Figures 5.15a–d illustrate the floor plans of California houses published in 1935 and 1936, when Fischer arrived in exile in the state. Irrespective of differences in their overall shape, the depicted houses share a similar (even identical, for three of them) organization that establishes three functional zones. The living quarters occupy the center of the houses, close to the main entrance, with a bedroom zone (including a bathroom) on one side and a service zone on the other. The fourth, slightly divergent plan illustrates a variation that still revolves around organizing the functional zones within the home. Externally, the appearances of the houses totally differ, ranging from an Andalusian revival design by the architect Walter G. Byrne to a modernist home titled "Brick Up to Date," which for its designer, Richard Neutra, was an unusual composition of chunky masses made from brick; a modernist stucco box by Gregory Ain; and plenty of wood siding under a hipped roof with deep overhangs by Harwell Hamilton Harris.[76]

From the late 1930s onward, demonstration houses publicly advertised the three-zoned plan (figs. 5.16a–d). At the end of 1938, Homewood house opened in the Brentwood-Westwood area of Los Angeles. It was a sprawling one-story, ten-room building planned by the architect George C. Anderson for upper-middle-class buyers.[77] The significantly smaller Dual Duty Home by Henry S. Churchill was exhibited as the Town of Tomorrow Home No. 1 at the New York World's Fair in 1939 and addressed a broader audience.[78] It shared with the architect Sumner Spaulding's House in the Sun (which opened to the public in North Hollywood in January 1940)[79] that different rooms and spaces like the garage were deliberately intended for multiple purposes. In 1950, the three-zoned plan debuted at the Museum of Modern Art in New York when a model home by Gregory Ain was exhibited.[80] With 1,450 square feet and estimated costs between $15,000 and $19,500, the house comes close to Fischer's designs for Verdugo Village, at least by the numbers. Compared to Spaulding's design, Ain's is compact in overall volume and form, perhaps even too tight, as Ain felt obliged to create an "illusion of spaciousness" with sliding walls.[81]

Ain's designs frequently employed the three-zoned plan for individually designed homes like the Edwards house (Los Angeles, 1936–37) and the Blumstein house (Los Angeles, 1946) and for mass housing schemes like the Low-Cost Community Housing project (South Gate, 1940, unbuilt) and the Mar Vista Housing project (Los Angeles, 1946–48), where at least one house type adopted the plan. As noted, we do not know whether Ain and Fischer knew each other from their tenancies at the Granada Buildings in downtown Los Angeles. That both resorted at times to the three-zoned plan for their anonymous housing designs adds another instance of their work mirroring each other, even

114

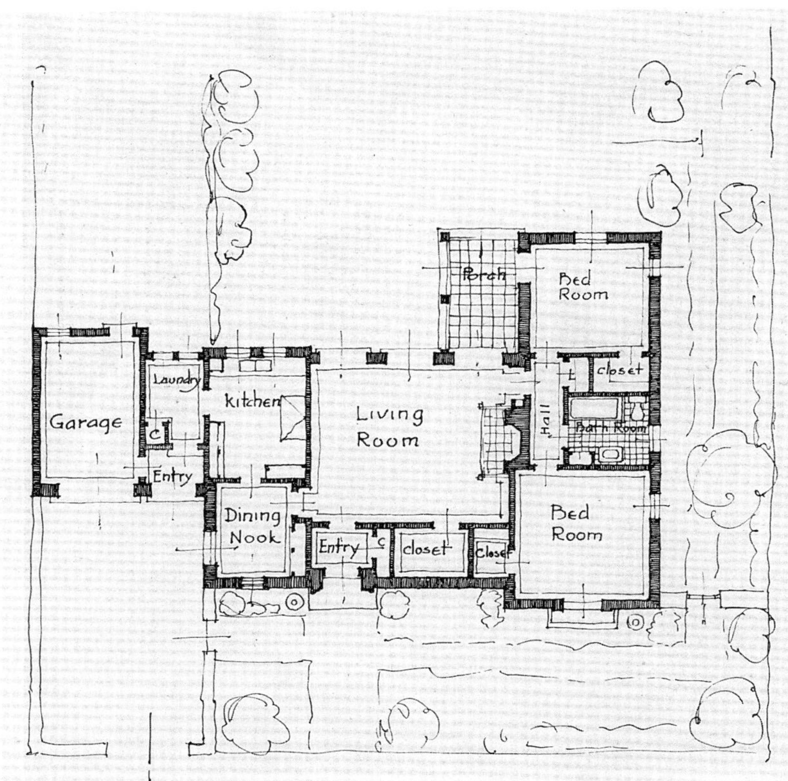

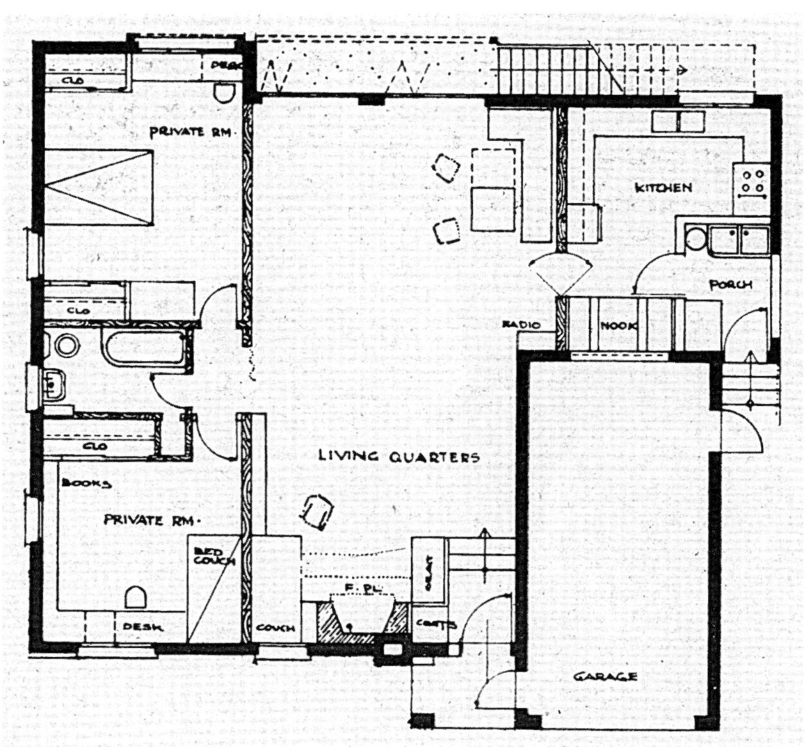

5.15a. Walter G. Byrne (US American, 1891–1949).

Untitled design for an Andalusian revival–style home, floor plan, 1935 or earlier.

From Margaret Atchley, ed., *California Homes and Gardens* (Los Angeles: n.p., 1935), n.p.

5.15b. Richard Neutra (US American, 1892–1970, b. Austria-Hungary).

"Brick Up to Date" floor plan, 1935 or earlier.

From Margaret Atchley, ed., *California Homes and Gardens* (Los Angeles: n.p., 1935), n.p.

5.15c. Gregory Ain (US American, 1908–88).

Charles H. Edwards house (1936), Los Angeles, California.

Floor plan, n.d.

University of California, Santa Barbara, Architecture and Design Collection.

5.15d. Harwell Hamilton Harris (US American, 1903–90).

Pauline Lowe house (1934), Altadena, California.

Floor plan, 1936 or earlier.

From Architectural Forum, ed., *The Book of Small Houses* (New York: Simon and Schuster, 1936), 99.

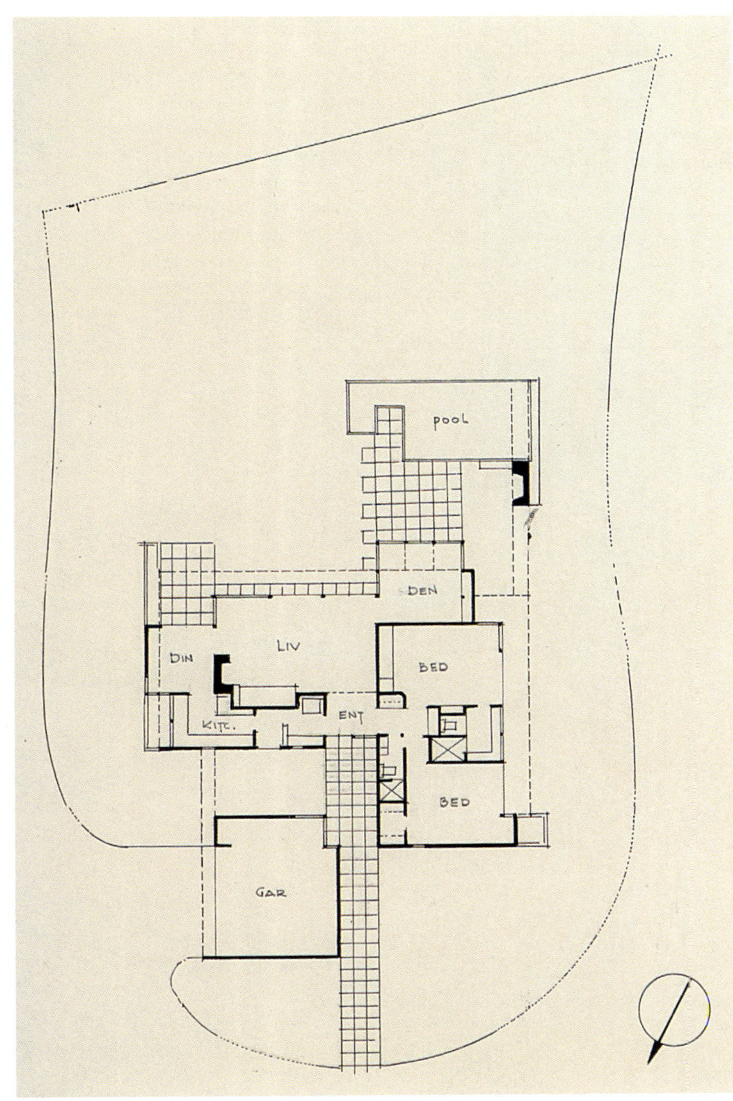

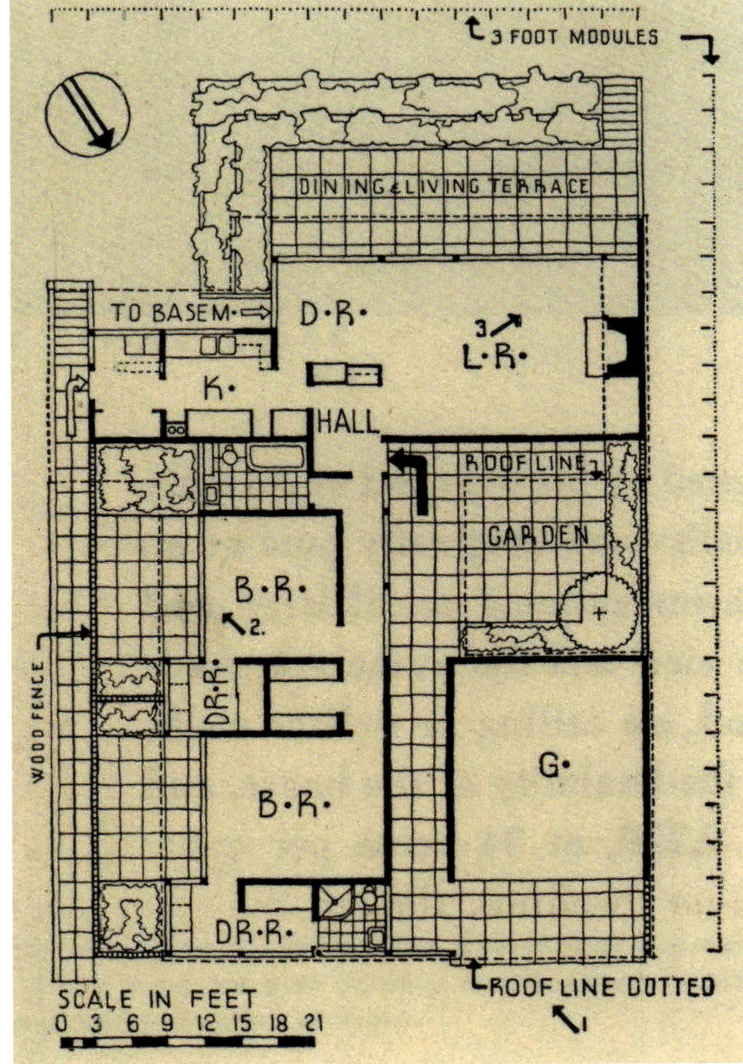

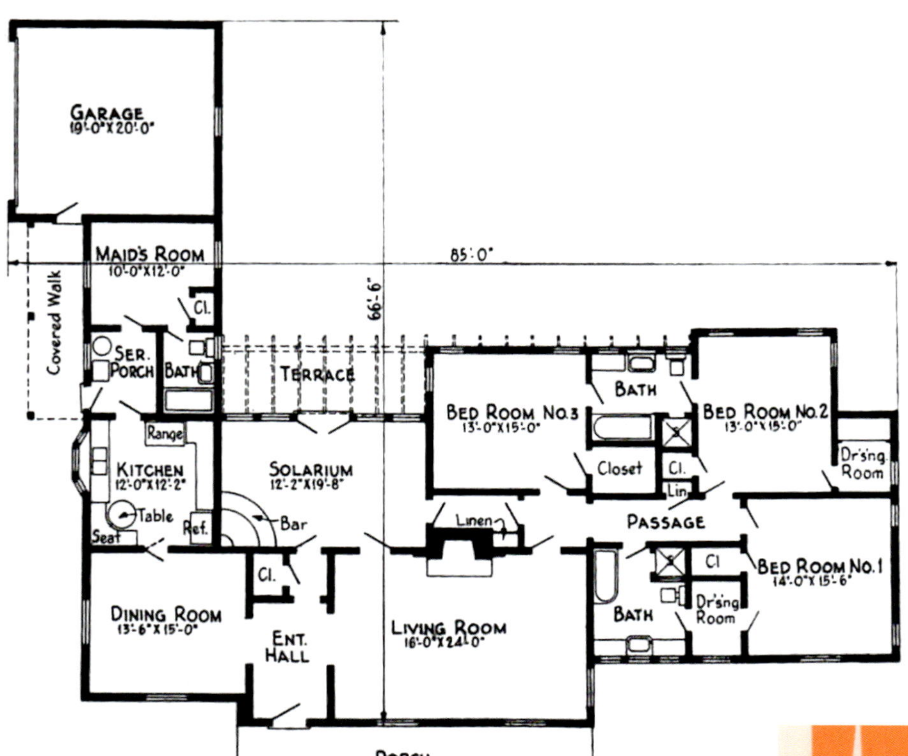

5.16a. George C. Anderson (US American, 1901–75).

Homewood house (1938), Beverly Hills, California. Floor plan, 1941 or earlier.

From *Security Homes: Suggestions for Planning, Building, Financing* (Chicago: Simmons-Boardman, n.d. [1941]), 28.

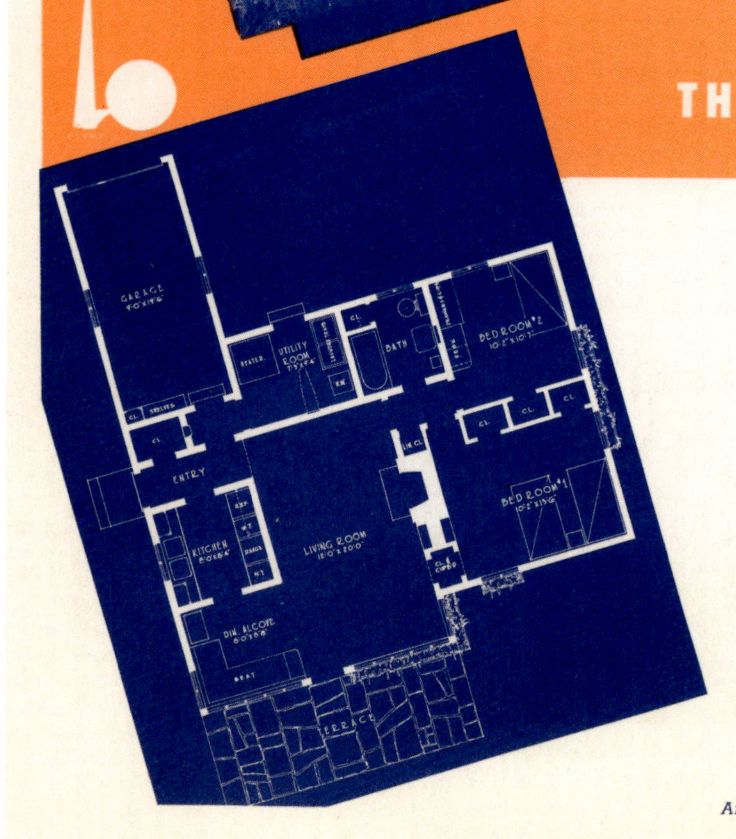

5.16b. Henry S. Churchill (US American, 1893–1962).

Dual Duty Home, exhibited as Town of Tomorrow Home No. 1 (1939), New York World's Fair.

Floor plan, 1939 or earlier.

From New York World's Fair, *The Town of Tomorrow: House No. 1—No. 1: The Dual Duty House* (New York: Burland, [1939]).

5.16c. Sumner Spaulding (US American, 1892–1952).

House in the Sun (1940), North Hollywood, Los Angeles, California.

Floor plan, 1941 or earlier.

From *Security Homes: Suggestions for Planning, Building, Financing* (Chicago: Simmons-Boardman, n.d. [1941]), 73.

5.16d. Gregory Ain (US American, 1908–88).

Floor plan for model home, 1950.

New York, Museum of Modern Art.

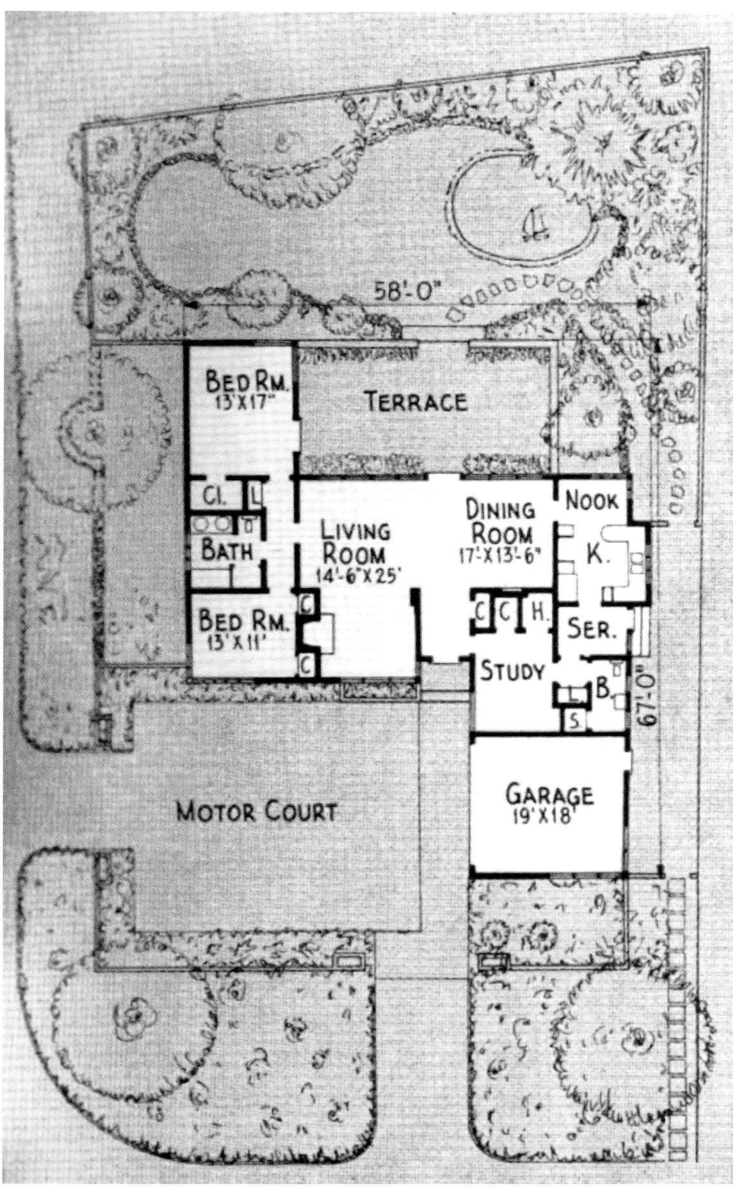

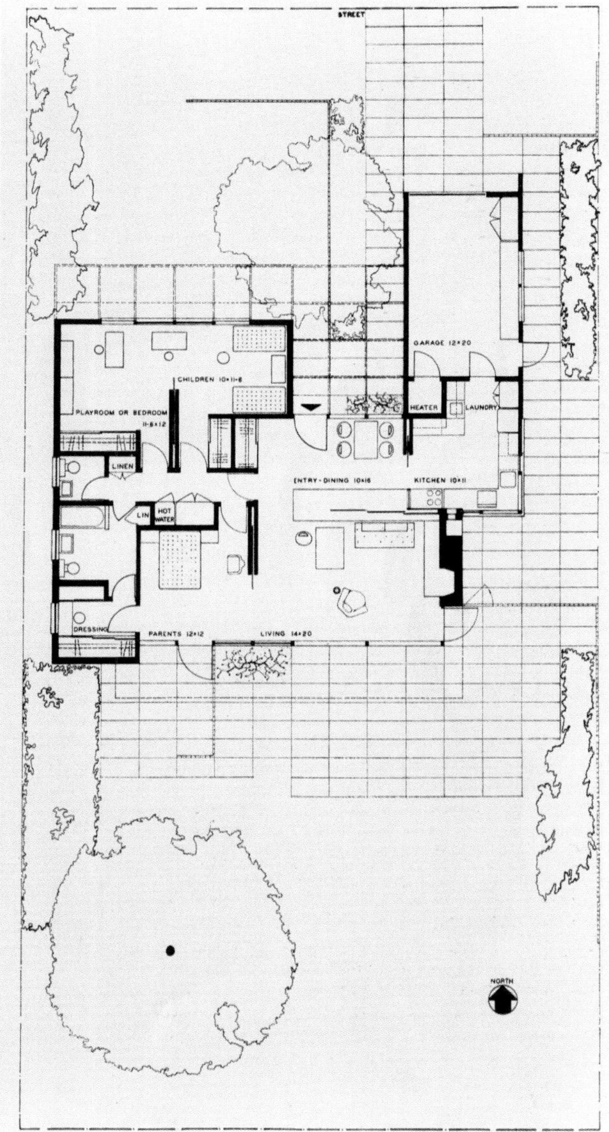

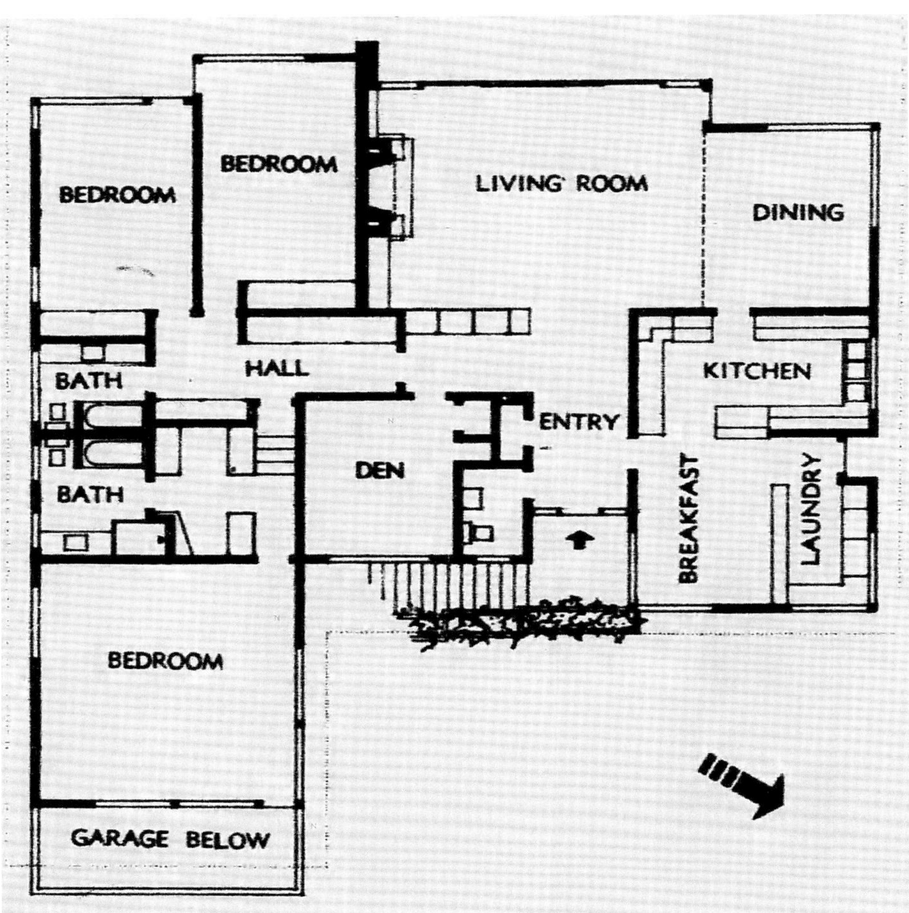

5.17. Ulrich Plaut (US American, 1910–71, b. German in Japan), possibly with Leopold Fischer (US American, 1901–75, b. Austria-Hungary).

Cannon house (1950–51), Westwood, Los Angeles, California.

Floor plan.

From Lee Howard, "Spaciousness a Servant," *Los Angeles Times,* 1 March 1953, H8.

if we may never know which, if either, of the two men implanted the basic idea of such a floor plan in the other. Certain, however, is that Fischer had developed the bare bones of his version of the plan in Dessau in the mid-1920s.

Other architects in Fischer's peer group of émigré architects also used the three-zoned plan, most notably Ulrich Plaut for the Cannon house (Los Angeles, 1950–51), completed just before Fischer began planning Verdugo Village (fig. 5.17). Placing some of the Cannon house's spaces and rooms like the garage, storage rooms, and the maid's quarters a little lower down the slope recalls comparable arrangements at the Kohlmeier house; the Cannon house's floor plan anticipates those of Verdugo Village, especially the clearly visible three zones. The bedroom zone of the Cannon house reaches from the front to the rear of the home, as does the central zone with the entrance, the living-cum-dining room, and a den adjacent to the main door. The service zone (kitchen, breakfast nook, and laundry room) reaches only up to the dining area, which occupies a shared volume of space with the living room. In addition to their similar internal organizations, the Cannon house and Fischer's Verdugo Village houses share details: for example, the wooden trellis on the street facade of at least some Verdugo Village homes, and, in both, the rear of the living room fireplace visible as an exposed brick wall in an adjacent room. These similarities suggest Fischer's possible involvement with the Cannon house; indeed, I suspect that Fischer worked on the project for Plaut. Yet, the lack of archival sources for Plaut and Fischer precludes further research.[82]

• • •

Variations of the functionally organized three-zoned floor plan were relied upon by many architects and builders for designs of contemporary houses of any style, construction method, and size, whether for individual owners or anonymous occupiers. The plan transcends the (assumed) juxtaposition between traditional revival styles in California and emerging architectural modernism, such as Neutra's domestic designs and, later, the Case Study Houses. Stepping *outside* this rigid framework that prioritizes juxtaposition allows one to assess Fischer's pursuit of the best possible floor plan for his ideal modern, middle- to upper-middle-class detached house. Three aspects of the plan stand out in particular: an easy-to-comprehend, legible arrangement of the functional zones; the entrance into the house and, related to this, which room or rooms are adjacent to the entry; and finally, the adaptability of the plan to changing ideas of what rooms a single-family home should offer.

Considering the arrangements of the three zones within a single home, the floor plan of the Homewood house from 1938 is a problematic example (see fig. 5.16a). The entrance hall permanently separates the dining room from the living room; a dressing room and a bathroom are placed on opposite ends of a bedroom; and the passage from the garage into the home suggests that the owner or inhabitant employ a chauffeur to drop him or her off at the main door, for otherwise, he or she is made to leave the garage through a side door onto a short, covered walk, and from there through the service porch, kitchen, and dining room to the entrance hall proper. By contrast, the S shape of Spaulding's design suggests spatial and functional clarity, except that the simple form means the bedroom zone is accessible only through the living room (see fig. 5.16c). No such issues affect Fischer's floor plans (see figs. 5.9, 5.10), which assign to the bedroom zone a dedicated small corridor and place the garage next to the main door. Fischer also offers a rear exit that allows a person to enter the service zone via the laundry room—whose position and usage recall the rear porch between the garage and kitchen of the Kohlmeier house (see fig. 4.6)—or to access stairs at the far end of the home to the outdoor deck.

Comparably clearly arranged is the entrance situation into the Fischer houses that begins with the already noted external recess. Internally, a short corridor follows as a buffer between the living room ahead and the den and the private bedroom zone on either side. There is no need to search for the entrance in the depth of the building as in Harris's Lowe house (see fig. 5.15d); to enter a home by stepping right away into the living room as in Neutra's example (which Arthur Drexler once described as Neutra's perfunctory entrance; see fig. 5.15b);[83] or to sneak inside behind the backs of people seated at the dinner table as in Ain's model home (see fig. 5.16d).

Moreover, Fischer turns the forecourt into another outdoor "room" by orienting the garage door perpendicular to the house and the street (see fig. 5.13). The size and topography of most lots determined the garage's position in the front of the house, and deliberately orienting the garage door toward the main entrance of the house ensures the shortest possible way into the home. It also avoids reducing the forecourt to a barely used welcome gesture. Arriving, driving into the garage, leaving, and closing it before entering one's home are visibly part of ordinary domestic activity. Even more, the possibility of parking one's car in front of one's property—rather than on the street—pleased the homeowners' sense of self, given that displaying a vehicle in front of a home was on the rise since the 1920s as a "new medium for statements of identity" and social standing.[84]

Lastly, there are the dens in Fischer's houses, which are adjacent to, even part of, the entrance areas, and which bring up the issue of the adaptability of the plans. The *New Oxford American Dictionary* defines a den as "a small, comfortable room in a house where a person can pursue an activity in private."[85] In the world of US American postwar suburbia, the den was sometimes considered to be "a room for casual living."[86] Austrian immigrant and émigré architects were fond of dens; for example, in 1929, Joseph Urban designed a "Man's Den" as part of an exhibition at New York's Metropolitan Museum of Art, with the den being an "opportunity to retire for smoking, conversation,reading, and cards... in a space so small that order is imperative."[87] Approximately twenty-five years later, the émigré architect Frederick Reichl envisioned a den as one of the distinguishing spaces of the standardized houses that the partnership Reichl and Starkman was designing for the new subdivision of Monterey Hills (Monterey Park, ca. 1956–60) (figs. 5.18a, 5.18b).[88] The three-zone floor plan is reminiscent of Fischer's plans for Verdugo Village, though not as well zoned, as bedrooms are adjacent to different zones. The interior design of the den revolves around a military theme suitable to the veterans who were among the targeted buyers.[89] The sketch shows a man, presumably the homeowner, posing with a rifle in front of a built-in wardrobe in which a second rifle is visible. Behind him is a tin-soldier collection on a built-in shelf in the background, with images of parades and military personnel on the wall to the right. Another man sits on the couch facing him, holding an image of a soldier while smoking a pipe. In front of the couch, a drum that is decorated with an image of an eagle doubles up as a couch table on which another pipe, a tobacco tin, and a box of matches are

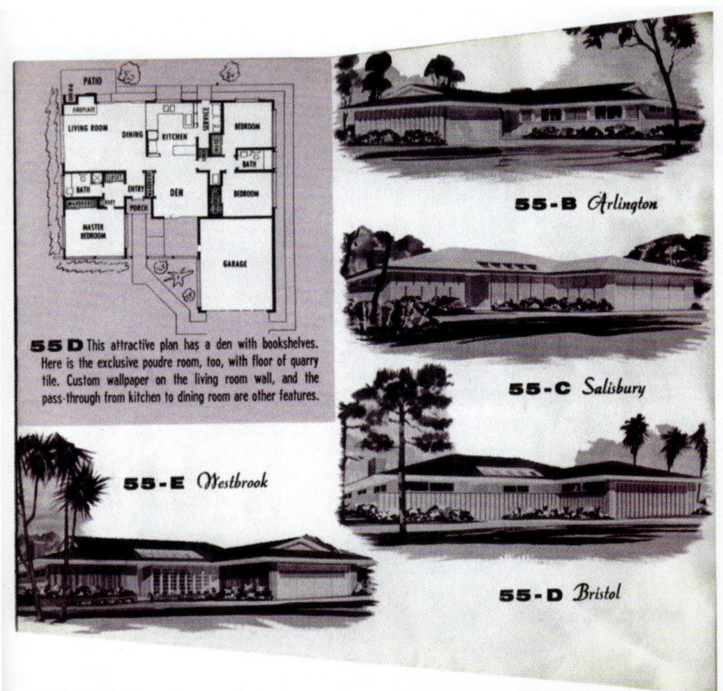

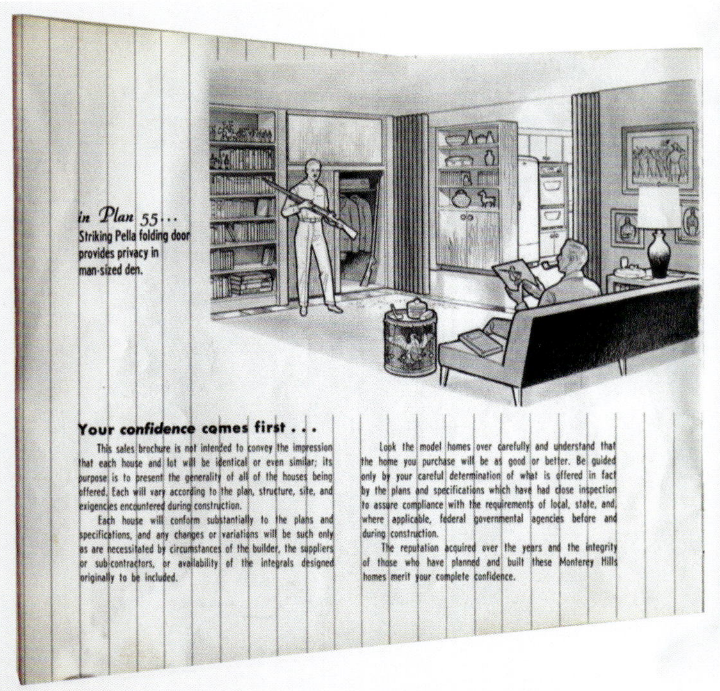

placed. Putting an antler or a stuffed boar's head on the walls would turn this den into a game room or trophy room (*Jagdzimmer*). Yet, whatever feelings of male coziness (*Gemütlichkeit*) may thus arise, they would not last long, considering that only a retractable, hygienic plastic divider prevents domestic chores from invading this male realm from the adjacent kitchen.

In Fischer's standardized houses for Verdugo Village, living rooms are accessible from two sides, allowing family members to use the spaces in multiple ways. In contrast, private bedrooms and bathrooms can be entered only through one door (unless there is an additional door into an adjacent garden). The den belongs to the former set of rooms, which strongly implies that Fischer—in opposition to the real estate display ads cited earlier—did not intend it to be a permanent third bedroom.[90] Moreover, access to the den from the entrance corridor is through a double door whose two leaves, when shut, do not interlock to ensure privacy. The den's second doorway to the laundry room and, from there, into the kitchen suggests its possible use as a room for household duties such as sewing, ironing, and folding linen and as a room where children could play within hearing distance even if not visible from the kitchen. Such activities would also make the den an early version of the family room that became popular in the later 1950s and introduced "two areas for living"[91] into postwar houses. The family room was intended for more informal family activities, with the living room proper reserved for more formal activities involving guests or for a private, quiet area to retreat, a division of tasks between family and living rooms that Fischer's floor plan illustrates perfectly.

A third possible use for the den would be as a parlor. The double door into the den indicates an important space comparable to a reception room or parlor in traditional domestic architecture in Europe and the United States. This impression is supported by an unusual interior design element immediately behind the double door. There, a shallow niche makes visible the rear of the brick fireplace in the living room on the other side of the wall (figs. 5.19a, 5.19b). Above the brickwork, shelves offer space for knickknacks. On a practical level, the exposed brickwork transmits warmth into the den from any fire lit in the fireplace that heats up the thermal mass of the bricks, a feature that, on a much larger scale, also exists in the Cannon house. In the den of the Verdugo Village houses, this feature evokes faint remembrances of the interior of houses and apartments that Adolf Loos had designed in Vienna and Central Europe, where often a hall with a brick

5.18a. Frederick Reichl (Austrian, 1890–1959) and Maxwell Starkman (Canadian, 1921–2003).

House type 55-D Bristol (ca. 1956–60), Monterey Hills subdivision, Monterey Park, California.

Floor plan.

From [Key Land Company], *Monterey Hills: "Island in the Sky"* (Los Angeles: John D. Roche, n.d. [ca. 1955]), [12].

5.18b. Frederick Reichl (Austrian, 1890–1959) and Maxwell Starkman (Canadian, 1921–2003).

House type 55 (ca. 1956–60), Monterey Hills subdivision, Monterey Park, California.

Interior of den.

From [Key Land Company], *Monterey Hills: "Island in the Sky"* (Los Angeles: John D. Roche, n.d. [ca. 1955]), [12].

5.19a. Leopold Fischer (US American, 1901–75, b. Austria-Hungary).

House Type A-2, Verdugo Village (1953–55), Los Angeles, California, April 2022.

Living room with exposed brick fireplace.

5.19b. Leopold Fischer (US American, 1901–75, b. Austria-Hungary).

House Type A-2, Verdugo Village (1953–55), Los Angeles, California, April 2022.

Den with the exposed brick rear wall of the fireplace.

fireplace underneath a mantelpiece welcomed visitors. Somebody as familiar with Loosian and Central European domestic architecture as Fischer will have experienced in such a way the glimpse of the red-brown exposed brickwork (today often painted over) with shelving above that was visible when entering a Verdugo Village home, especially at moments when the double door into the den was swung wide open.

The den, when taken as Fischer's California rendering of a traditional domestic parlor or reception room, also sheds light on the corner window—a modernist detail if Fischer had let the two sheets of glass meet with a miter joint rather than a corner post—that appears to overlook the forecourt and street but in actuality grants visitors glimpses into a parlor-like space. In the late 1940s, the architect John N. Douglas designed the Jeffries house (Rancho Santa Anita) with a floor plan that, while larger in size, is similar to Fischer's homes for Verdugo Village.[92] In the Jeffries house, a corner window overlooking the main entrance accommodates a coffee corner, which is part of the service wing that includes the kitchen, laundry room, and maid's quarters. Whoever worked in the kitchen could observe anyone approaching the house and vice versa. By comparison, looking out through the corner window of the den in Verdugo Village is less relevant, as the view does not visually connect to a more regularly used interior space such as the kitchen. However, no such practical considerations restrain the gaze into the den when entering, for example, a Verdugo Village home; indeed, social historians of space have pointed out that traditionally, a parlor was located adjacent to the entrance and often featured a window in the direction of the entry as well, which allowed views from the outside into the inside.[93]

Whichever way the den was used then and is used today, the room highlights the qualities of Fischer's Central European–influenced floor plans for these detached houses. They are tightly organized, give proper shape to each room, do not waste floor space, allow flexible usage of some rooms, offer representative spaces for social occasions, and provide privacy where and when needed. The houses of Verdugo Village that Fischer planned for anonymous middle-class and upper-middle-class occupants are a fascinating California version of bourgeois homes, to use the term that would have been applied in Central Europe.

Table 5.2. First adult occupants of Fischer-designed houses on Palmero Drive, Verdugo Village

House no.	First owners or occupants, 1954–58	Occupations as per US Census, 1950
4360	Arthur M. and Lillian M. Stiles (VR 1956, 1958)	Mr. Stiles: Sports columnist for Los Angeles newspapers
4354	David Busby K. Rice Sr., David Busby King Rice Jr. (VR 1956, 1958)	Mr. Rice Sr.: Building contractor
4351	1954: Ethel E. Mendenhall (VR 1954) 1956 onward: Jack and Arline Beckett, Ms. Mabelle Beckett (VR 1956, 1958)	Mr. Mendenhall: Owner/manufacture of electric motors Mr. Beckett: Supervising clerk, Dept. of Water & Power, Los Angeles
4342	Richard W. and Ruth S. Tullar (VR 1956, 1958)	Mr. Tullar: [In] charge of merchandising newspaper
4337	1955: Mr. and Ms. Rupert L. Randall (*Eagle Rock Sentinel*, 12 September 1957, 17) 1958 onward: Cecil A. and Lyda J. Roley (VR 1958)	Mr. Randall: Mechanic Mr. Roley: Lawyer, law practice (in Portland, OR)
4331	Mildred L. Brown (VR 1956, 1958)	Unknown
4319	1956 onward: Hipolito L. Barron (*L.A. City Directory* 1956, 1960) 1958: Dorothy R. Barron (VR 1958)	Mr. Barron: Veteran of the US military
4306	Wolfgang C. Jochheim (VR 1956, 1958)	Building contractor for tract condos
4300	Kalmar W. and Betty L. Gadd (VR 1956, 1958)	Mr. Gadd: Office manager, carbon paper distribution company
4259	George E. and Rachel L. Brooks (VR 1958)	Mr. Brooks: Investor and contractor; initiated Verdugo Village
4219	Norma Jean and Salvatore Fazzi (VR 1958)	Unknown
4207	1956: Pratt, H. Clayton (*LA City Directory* 1956) 1958 onward: Stanley M. and Opal K. Cundiff (VR 1958)	Mr. Cundiff: Teacher (*The Southwest Wave*, 19 May 1960, 1)

VR: *Voter Rolls Los Angeles County*, Precinct 3568: 1954 (roll 098, sheet 582); 1956 (roll 114, sheets 33–34); and 1958 (roll 132, sheets 30–31 [ancestry.com, subscription required]).

Verdugo Village, the "Heartbreak Hills of Southern California"?

The sale of new houses in Verdugo Village continued until 1957, after which display ads and real estate articles advertising the development disappeared from local newspapers.[94] Fischer's involvement with Verdugo Village had ended with the twelve homes listed in table 5.2, of which the last two were certified as suitable for occupation in April 1955, with the majority approved in June and September 1954.

When heavy rain in the early months of 1958 revealed the unstable ground on which parts of Verdugo Village were built, no Fischer-designed houses were directly damaged. The slopes behind some homes on Alegre Place started sliding downhill once the rain had soaked the land, which began moving toward the houses on the lower part of Palmero Drive.[95] The possibility that the hilly terrain would become an issue for Verdugo Village homes had been known earlier: for example, in July 1957, a real estate ad referenced a "new retaining wall" carving out a patio from a rising slope behind the property for sale.[96] In 1958, Verdugo Hills turned into another instance of the "Heartbreak Hills of Southern California," as Richard H. Jahns, a professor of geology at Stanford University, christened the same year those hillsides all over the region of Los Angeles where soil conditions, topography, the grading of building lots, and weather events regularly resulted in damage to residential buildings, if not their total loss.[97]

Presumably, much earlier than 1958, Verdugo Village broke the heart of Leopold Fischer, as can be concluded from Fischer suddenly registering copyright with the Library of Congress for all of his architectural designs from approximately when his work in Verdugo Village ended.[98] Perhaps the subdivision developer was not enticed to build more of Fischer's designs because the initial twelve Fischer-designed homes had not sold fast enough. The general similarities of the L-shaped forms of many homes in the part of the development where Fischer built his types of houses may also suggest that Fischer's designs inspired similar dwellings on lots that were sold without one of his houses being commissioned. This leads to an almost philosophical question: can one copy (or even plagiarize) a plan inspired as much by Fischer's work in Weimar Germany as by a widely used contemporary California plan for smaller (and larger) detached houses? Still, that his architectural plans might give rise to knock-off designs apparently occupied Fischer's mind after Verdugo Village. Those copyright entries are a happy coincidence for the historian, as they add projects to Fischer's exile oeuvre. Considering the loss of Fischer's personal and professional papers, it is not astonishing to learn that the illustrations (or photographs) Fischer was obliged to submit with the copyright applications can no longer be located.[99]

Notes

1 Classified ad, *Los Angeles Times,* 2 January 1954, B13, column 3; see also, for example, real estate ad, *El Sereno Star,* 18 February 1954, 8, column 2, where it reads "Exclusively Designed" instead of "Exquisitely Designed." These classified ads appeared in both newspapers throughout the first half of 1954.

2 See "New Subdivision Slated for First Display Today," *Los Angeles Times,* 10 January 1954, F10; "Verdugo Home Offers Quiet, Seclusion," *The Mirror* (Los Angeles), 21 May 1954, part 3, p. 8; "Brisk Activity Paces Sales of Verdugo Village," *The Mirror* (Los Angeles), 29 January 1954, 29; "Verdugo Homes Feature View," *Pasadena Independent,* 23 May 1954, 18; "Verdugo Village Homes Offer Impressive Luxury Appointments," *Los Angeles Daily News,* 4 June 1954, 28; and "Wide Panoramic View Cited as One of Village Features," *Los Angeles Times,* 13 June 1954, E13.

3 It was not the first subdivision of that name. Already in 1947, the square mile east of Warner Brothers Ranch Movie Studio in Burbank was supposed to be developed as "Verdugo Village"; later that same year, another subdivision of the same name was envisioned for twenty-one acres in the Mount Washington area of Highland Park. More recently, the name has been resurrected for a commercial strip in Glassell Park. See "New Valley Community Projected in Burbank," *Valley Times* (North Hollywood), 21 February 1947, 2; "Planners OK Junior High School Site," *Valley Times* (North Hollywood), 8 November 1947, 1; and "Where Is Verdugo Village? Just Look for the New Signs," *The Eastsider,* 29 January 2011, https://www.theeastsiderla.com/real_estate/where-is-verdugo-village-just-look-for-the-new-signs/article_1dd4c5af-573b-5ea9-ae22-2891081411da.html.

4 On suburbia as a bourgeois utopia and its critique, see, for example, Robert Fishman, *Bourgeois Utopias: The Rise and Fall of Suburbia* (New York: Basic, 1987); and Kenneth T. Jackson, *Crabgrass Frontier: The Suburbanization of the United States* (Oxford: Oxford University Press, 1985). On suburbs as housing for the masses, see Gwendolyn Wright, *Building the Dream: A Social History of Housing in America* (New York: Pantheon, 1981); and for the environmental consequences of suburbanization, see Dolores Hayden, *Building Suburbia: Green Fields and Urban Growth, 1820–2000* (New York: Pantheon, 2003). Greg Hise, *Magnetic Los Angeles: Planning the Twentieth-Century Metropolis* (Baltimore: Johns Hopkins University Press, 1997), discusses the post–World War II suburbanization of the Los Angeles metropolitan area as a form of regional urbanism; Dianne Harris, *Little White Houses: How the Postwar Home*

Constructed Race in America (Minneapolis: University of Minnesota Press, 2013), analyzes racism and suburbia; and Barbara Miller Lane, *Houses for a New World: Builders and Buyers in American Suburbs, 1945–1965* (Princeton: Princeton University Press, 2015), focuses on merchant builders and their clients.

5 Kate Ellen Rogers, *The Modern House U.S.A.: Its Design and Decoration* (New York: Harper & Brothers, 1962), 38.

6 Rogers, *The Modern House U.S.A.,* 38.

7 Paul Goldberger, "Foreword," in *The City Observed: Los Angeles; A Guide to Its Architecture and Landscapes,* ed. Charles Moore, Peter Becker, and Regula Campbell (1984; Santa Monica: Hennessey & Ingalls, 1998), xi.

8 David Gebhard and Robert Winter, *A Guide to Architecture in Los Angeles & Southern California* (Salt Lake City: Peregrine Smith, 1982), 27.

9 Moore, Becker, and Campbell, *The City Observed,* 282.

10 On the wartime housing projects in the Los Angeles area, see, for example, "Supplement—Los Angeles Housing Authority," *California Arts & Architecture* (May 1943): 47–66.

11 "Park Planned Homes, 1947, Altadena, CA" and "Mar Vista Housing, 1948, Mar Vista, Los Angeles," in *Notes from Another Los Angeles: Gregory Ain and the Construction of a Social Landscape,* ed. Anthony Fontenot (Cambridge, MA: MIT Press, 2022), 258, 259.

12 Friedrich Ratzel, *Städte und Culturbilder aus Nordamerika,* vol. 1 (Leipzig: Brockhaus, 1876), 7, 3, respectively.

13 Gustav Diercks, *Kulturbilder aus den Vereinigten Staaten* (Berlin: Allgemeiner Verein für deutsche Litteratur, 1893), 332.

14 Alice Salomon, *Kultur im Werden: Amerikanische Reiseeindrücke* (Berlin: Ullstein, 1924), 41.

15 Max Reinhardt, quoted in Edda Fuhrich-Leisler and Gisela Prossnitz, *Max Reinhardt in Amerika* (Salzburg: Otto Müller, 1976), 247–48 (my emphasis). See also Volker M. Welter, "Salzburg in Los Angeles: Max Reinhardt and Paul Lászlό's Vision of a *Festpielstadt* in the Hollywood Hills," in *Wie sich Salzburg inszeniert: Vom Werden einer Musiktheaterstadt,* ed. Sigrid Brandt and Thomas Wozonig (Vienna: Hollitzer, 2023), 242–56.

16 Theodor W. Adorno, *Letters to His Parents 1939–1951,* ed. Christoph Gödde and Henri Lonitz, trans. Wieland Hoban (Cambridge: Polity, 2006), letter 44, 30 November 1941, 70 (translation slightly amended by the author).

17 Adolf Rading, "Die Typenbildung und ihre städtebaulichen Folgerungen," in *Probleme des Bauens: Der Wohnbau,* ed. Fritz Block (Potsdam: Müller & Kiepenheuer, 1928), 76 (translation by Iain Boyd Whyte).

18 "Heinz (Henry) Blanke (1901–1980)," *Wilhelm Blanke Archiv,* http://www.wilhelm-blanke-archiv.de/0000019b6a0b14d0e/index.html.

19 "Residence of Mr. & Mrs. Phil Freeman—Los Angeles, California," *Architectural Digest* 14, no. 1 (1953): 56–61.

20 Mary Ann Thayer, "Spaciousness Is a State of Mind," *Los Angeles Times Home Magazine,* 19 April 1953, H14–H15. The home is at 3572 Park Side Drive in San Bernardino.

21 For example, 812 East Val Mar Street (today Drive), San Bernardino; see "City Hall Roofing Project Shows on List of New Building Permits," *San Bernardino Sun-Telegram,* 26 October 1953, 48.

22 See, for example, display ads, *San Bernardino Sun-Telegram,* 20 April 1953, 47, and 8 October 1953, 47, for homes at 812 and 813 East Marshall Boulevard, San Bernardino. Attempts to contact the current owners of the Zimbler-designed homes have remained without replies.

23 See Matthias Boeckl, "Villen in Los Angeles—Siedlungen in Puerto Rico: Über die Wirkungen des Neuen Wiener Wohnens im Exil," in *Visionäre & Vertriebene: Österreichische Spuren in der modernen amerikanischen Architektur,* ed. Matthias Boeckl (Berlin: Ernst & Sohn, 1995), 311–25, esp. 315.

24 Conversations and correspondence of the author with S. Sklarek, Rolf Sklarek's daughter, and D. Fairweather, a stepson of Sklarek's, June–August 2022. On Gruen, see Victor Gruen and Larry Smith, *Shopping Towns USA: The Planning of Shopping Centers* (New York: Van Nostrand Reinhold, 1960); and M. Jeffrey Hardwick, *Mall Maker: Victor Gruen, Architect of an American Dream* (Philadelphia: University of Pennsylvania Press, 2004).

25 Layne Karafantis and Stuart W. Leslie, "'Suburban Warriors': The Blue-Collar and Blue-Sky Communities of Southern California's Aerospace Industry," *Journal of Planning History* 18, no. 1 (2019): 13.

26 D. Frankel, correspondence with the author, August 2021; the American Institute of Architects Archives, membership file "Fredric Rachmiel Frankel," https://content.aia.org/sites/default/files/2021-07/Frankel_FredericR.pdf; and John F. Gane and George S. Koyl, eds., *American Architects Directory,* 3rd ed. (New York: R. R. Bowker, 1970), 297.

27 R. Plaut, correspondence with the author, July–August 2021; the American Institute of Architects Archives, membership file "Ulrich Hermann Plaut," https://content.aia.org/sites/default/files/2021-07/Plaut_UlrichHermann.pdf; George S. Koyl, ed., *American Architects Directory* (New York: R. R. Bowker, 1955), 437; and George S. Koyl, ed., *American Architects Directory,* 2nd ed. (New York: R. R. Bowker, 1962), 555.

28 For example, see Betty M. Nicolaides, *The New Suburbia: How Diversity Remade Suburban Life in Los Angeles after 1945* (New York: Oxford University Press, 2024), which became available only after this study was completed.

29 "Verdugo Home Offers Quiet, Seclusion," part 3, p. 8.

30 "Verdugo Homes Feature View," 18.

31 "View Homes Verdugo Village" (display ad), *Pasadena Independent,* 23 May 1954, 18.

32 See also Dominique Rouillard, *Building the Slope: Hillside Houses, 1920–1960,* trans. Ronald A. Masi (Santa Monica: Arts & Architecture Press, 1987); and *Survey LA, Los Angeles Historic Resources Survey, Los Angeles Citywide Historic*

Context Statement, Context: Architecture and Engineering, 1850–1985, Sub-Context: Engineering, Theme: Technological Developments in Construction, Subtheme: Hill Houses, 1920–1985 (Los Angeles: City of Los Angeles Department of City Planning Office of Historic Resources, 2017), https://planning.lacity.org/odocument/c6f7f7ba-efc3-4ff-8cc4-691ea56ba171/Hill%20Houses_1920-1985.pdf.

33 Carey McWilliams, *Southern California: An Island on the Land* (Salt Lake City: Peregrine Smith, 2010), 234.

34 "Verdugo Village Close to Downtown," *Mirror and Daily News* (Los Angeles), 25 February 1955, part 4, p. 5.

35 "Last Close-In Development," *Valley Times* (North Hollywood), 22 June 1956, 7.

36 Max Stiles, "High in Green Verdugo Hills—Max Stiles and Family Find a New Frontier," *Mirror and Daily News* (Los Angeles), 25 February 1955, part 4, p. 5.

37 Frederick J. Turner, "The Significance of the Frontier in American History," *Annual Report of the American Historical Association* (1 January 1893): 197–227, www.historians.org/resource/the-significance-of-the-frontier-in-american-history.

38 Laura R. Barraclough, *Making the San Fernando Valley: Rural Landscapes, Urban Development, and White Privilege* (Athens: University of Georgia Press, 2011), 13.

39 Flight C-300, frame K-201, 1928, University of California Santa Barbara (UCSB) Library Geospatial Collection.

40 Flight C-6630, frame 61, 1940, UCSB Library Geospatial Collection.

41 Flight AXJ-1952, frame 7k-27, 1952, UCSB Library Geospatial Collection.

42 Public Works Los Angeles County, land records information, map book 0494, tract map TR0494–019, sheets 494–19 to 494–22 (https://pw.lacounty.gov/sur/nas/landrecords/tract/MB0494/TR0494-019.pdf) and map book 0498, tract map TR0498–021, sheets 498–21 to 498–22 (https://pw.lacounty.gov/sur/nas/landrecords/tract/MB0498/TR0498-021.pdf).

43 "George E. Brooks, Fontana," obituary, *San Bernardino County Sun,* 30 December 1979, 21.

44 For the numbers of units in Weimar Germany, see Wolfgang Paul and Juliane Vierich, "Lage der Bauten im heutigen Sachsen-Anhalt," in *Leopold Fischer: Architekt der Moderne,* ed. Bauhaus Dessau e.V. (Dessau-Roßlau: Funk Verlag Bernhard Hein e.K., n.d. [2007]), 104–13.

45 Nomenclature according to Andreas Schwarting, *Die Siedlung Dessau-Törten 1926–1931* (Leipzig: Spector, 2012).

46 Ned Eichler, *The Merchant Builders* (Cambridge, MA: MIT Press, 1982), 55, 68.

47 Paul Adamson and Marty Arbunich, *Eichler: Modernism Rebuilds the American Dream* (Salt Lake City: Gibbs Smith, 2002).

48 Irene Below and Babette Scurrell, eds., *es gab nicht nur das bauhaus: wohnen und haushalten in dessauer siedlungen der 20er jahre* (Dessau: Stiftung Bauhaus Dessau, 1994). The publication reproduces an exhibition on social housing that Below organized with students from the Oberstufenkolleg in Bielefeld. It consists of a printed brochure and photomechanical reproductions of the display boards of the exhibition.

49 Rading, "Die Typenbildung und ihre städtebaulichen Folgerungen," 81, figs. 59, 60.

50 Below and Scurrell, *es gab nicht nur das bauhaus,* "dessau-ziebigk die siedlung am knarrberg," plate d 6.2 [*sic;* should be d 6.1].

51 James A. Jacobs, "Social and Spatial Change in the Postwar Family Room," *Perspectives in Vernacular Architecture* 13, no. 1 (2006): 72, 74.

52 Avi Friedman, "The Evolution of Design Characteristics during the Post-Second World War Housing Boom: The US Experience," *Journal of Design History* 8, no. 2 (1995): 137.

53 "New Subdivision Slated for First Display Today," F10 (homes: $17,600, lot sites: $3,500); "Verdugo Village Close to Downtown" and the adjacent ad, part 4, p. 5 (homes: $15,000, lot sites: $4,000 and up); and "Wide Panoramic View Cited as One of Village Features," E13 (homes: $19,000, lot sites: $4,000 and up).

54 The original square footages for houses on Palmero Drive are estimates. The figures given by Los Angeles County Office of the Assessor, *Property Assessment Information System* (https://maps.assessor.lacounty.gov/m/) were cross-checked with the overall dimensions per building as noted on the original permit applications for the houses (City of Los Angeles, Department of Building and Safety, Building Division, https://www.ladbs.org/services/check-status/online-building-records). In case of larger deviations, I searched for possible later applications to extend the original buildings. Building permits for the Kohlmeier and Slechta houses could not be viewed; the square footages come from the Los Angeles County Office of the Assessor, *Property Assessment Information System.*

55 Jacobs, "Social and Spatial Change," 74.

56 James A. Jacobs, *Detached America: Building Houses in Postwar Suburbia* (Charlottesville: University of Virginia Press, 2015), 101. See also the discussion of the checkered history and diverse, even contradictory, concepts of the terms *minimum* and *small houses* in chapter 2 of that book.

57 Federal Housing Administration, *Minimum Property Requirements for Properties of One or Two Living Units Located in the Southern California District* (Long Beach, Los Angeles, San Diego: Federal Housing Administration, 1952).

58 For the insurance to cover the maximum loan amount for an owner-occupant required a loan-value ratio of 95 percent for the first $9,000 and 75 percent for the remaining value. Federal Housing Administration, *Twenty-First Annual Report Federal Housing Administration for the Year Ending December 31, 1954* (Washington, DC: US Government Printing Office, 1956), 2. At an assessment of $15,000, this would amount to $8,550 of the first $ 9,000 value and $4,500 of the remaining $6,000, for a maximum loan amount of $13,050. Other qualifying conditions were, for example, whether insurance was requested by a builder

or an owner-occupier; if approval was before construction began; the length of the mortgage; the interest rates; the size of the (required) down payment, and so on.

59 Federal Housing Administration, *Twenty-First Annual Report,* 133, table 64.

60 The 33.5 percent of the rubric 1,200–1,399 square feet together with the 42.4 percent of homes between 1,000–1,099 and 1,100–1,199 square feet constituted the vast majority of all insured houses. Federal Housing Administration, *Twenty-First Annual Report,* 130, table 72.

61 The number six for the total rooms is taken from the building permits (City of Los Angeles, Department of Building and Safety, Building Division, https://www.ladbs.org/services/check-status/online-building-records), and, more generally, I adopted the principles of the Federal Housing Administration that counted rooms excluding "bathrooms, toilet compartments, closets, halls, storage and similar spaces" (Edith Porter Lapish, "The Trend toward Larger Houses," *Insured Mortgage Portfolio* 17, no. 2 [1952–53]: 8). At 17.6 percent of the total, six-room houses were the second largest group of all mortgage-insured, detached homes; a significant number but still way behind five-room homes that came in at 70.9 percent. Federal Housing Administration, *Twenty-First Annual Report,* 133, table 73.

62 Federal Housing Administration, *Twenty-First Annual Report,* 135, table 75.

63 Edward Dimendberg, "Introduction," in Anton Wagner, *Los Angeles: The Development, Life, and Structure of the City of Two Million in Southern California,* ed. Edward Dimendberg, trans. Timothy Grundy (Los Angeles: Getty Research Institute, 2022), 25. See chapter 4, note 11.

64 The dimensions of the lots are taken from the building permits and have not been double-checked on-site. City of Los Angeles, Department of Building and Safety, Building Division, https://ladbsdoc.lacity.org (search "By Address": [house number] Palmero Dr).

65 James Steele, *How House: RM Schindler* (London: Academy, 1996).

66 Fritz Becker, "Wohnen in der Knarrbergsiedlung," in Bauhaus Dessau e.V., *Leopold Fischer,* 44.

67 The published literature on the Knarrberg estate does not specify whether both types were built and how many of each. See the bibliography in this volume for literature.

68 Leopold Fischer in *Siedlungswirtschaft,* no. 9/10, 1926, cited from Below and Scurrell, *es gab nicht nur das bauhaus,* "raumaufteilung und nutzung," plate d6.10 (Below and Scurrell do not note the page numbers of Fischer's original text). For those buyers of a house in the estate who preferred a more conventional floor plan, houses of Type 2 added to the scullery the cooking niche with a conventional door into the adjacent living room. The latter, the contemporary critic Hans Josef Zechlin wrote, had accordingly more the character of a hall (*Diele*) as the stair to the upper level rose from this room in Type 2 houses rather than from the scullery as in Type 1 houses. Hans Josef Zechlin, "Siedlungen von Adolf Loos und Leopold Fischer," *Wasmuths Monatshefte für Baukunst,* no. 2 (1929): 70.

69 Jacobs, "Social and Spatial Change," 74.

70 Friedman, "The Evolution of Design Characteristics," 132.

71 See Lane, *Houses for a New World,* 63–74, for a concise history of the development of the ranch house in the United States.

72 Friedman, "The Evolution of Design Characteristics," 131.

73 Harris, *Little White Houses,* 47.

74 See, for example, the articles by Jacobs, "Social and Spatial Change," esp. 75–81; and Friedman, "The Evolution of Design Characteristics," esp. 141–44.

75 The history of this floor plan is outside of the scope of this study. The plan was not confined to small and modest middle-class houses; for earlier examples of large single-story, upper-middle-class and upper-class residences, see Alfred Hopkins, *American Country Houses of To-Day, 1927* (New York: Architectural Publishing Co., 1926 [*sic*]), 29, 133, and 155. My use of the term *three-zoned plan* should not be confused with the "zoned house" Jacobs denotes with floor plans of postwar houses that accommodated in different spatial zones varying activities in a house throughout the day and nighttime; see Jacobs, *Detached America,* chap. 5.

76 The floor plan by H. H. Harris was subsequently plagiarized by a Chicago firm; see Thomas S. Hines, *Architecture of the Sun: Los Angeles Modernism 1900–1970* (New York: Rizzoli, 2010), 487–88.

77 "Dwelling Charm Demonstrated," *Los Angeles Times,* 11 December 1938, E2. For the name of the architect, see City of Los Angeles, Department of Building and Safety, Building Division, "Application for the Erection of a Building," #27265, 24 August 1938, https://ladbsdoc.lacity.org (search "By Address": 109 Homewood).

78 New York World's Fair, *The Town of Tomorrow: House No. 1—No. 1: The Dual Duty House* (New York: Burland, [1939]).

79 "'House in the Sun' Opened," *Los Angeles Times,* 14 January 1940, E4.

80 *The Museum of Modern Art—Woman's Home Companion Exhibition House,* exh. cat. (New York: Museum of Modern Art, 1950), https://assets.moma.org/documents/moma_catalogue_2746_300062079.pdf. The house was commissioned by MoMA and a publication called *The Woman's Home Companion* produced; see "Three-Bedroom House Being Built by the Museum of Modern Art and the Woman's Home Companion," press release, https://assets.moma.org/documents/moma_press-release_325732.pdf.

81 *The Museum of Modern Art—Woman's Home Companion Exhibition House,* 3.

82 It is possible that blueprints for the Cannon house that may offer proof of Fischer's involvement still exist in the private papers of the second owner of the house. It was unfortunately not possible to view these papers, which are today stored in Texas.

83 Arthur Drexler and Thomas S. Hines, *The Architecture of Richard Neutra: From International Style to California Modern,* exh. cat. (New York: Museum of Modern Art, 1982), 54.

84 Katherine C. Grier, "The Decline of the Memory Palace: The Parlor after 1890," in *American Home Life, 1880–1930: A Social History of Spaces and Services,* ed Jessica H. Foy and Thomas J. Schlereth (Knoxville: University of Tennessee Press, 1992), 69.

85 *New Oxford American Dictionary,* 2nd ed. (Oxford: Oxford University Press, 2005), 452 (under "den").

86 Jacobs, *Detached America,* 148.

87 Metropolitan Museum of Art, *The Architect and the Industrial Arts: An Exhibition of Contemporary American Design,* exh. cat. (New York: Metropolitan Museum of Art, 1929), 49.

88 The subdivision Monterey Hills is part of the city of Monterey Park; see Key Land Company, *Monterey Hills: "Island in the Sky"* (Los Angeles: John D. Roche, n.d. [ca. 1955]). On Reichl, see Boeckl, *Visionäre & Vertriebene,* under "Fritz Reichl" in the section "Biographien" (340) and "Bibliographie" (361); and Petra Schumann, "Fritz Reichl," *Architektenlexikon Wien 1770–1945,* http://www.architektenlexikon.at/de/491.htm.

89 For example, see display ads in the *Los Angeles Times,* 30 December 1956, E6, and 11 May 1958, F8, which specifically mention preferred conditions for veterans wishing to purchase a home.

90 Another indicator that speaks against the den as a long-term bedroom is the built-in storage cupboard. The cupboard is deeper than those in the two bedrooms, indicating that it was intended for the storage of items other than personal clothing.

91 Jacobs, "Social and Spatial Change," 73–74.

92 "Redwood House on a Flat Plot," in *America's Best Small Houses,* ed. William J. Hennessey (New York: Viking, 1949), 111–14. The architects are identified as John N. Douglas and, as associates, Boyd Georgi and Jules Brady. Julius Shulman photographed the house in 1949; in his archive, the house is identified as the Jeffries house. See Job 025: Boyd Georgi, Jeffries house, 1946, Julius Shulman Photography Archive, 1935–2009, acc. no. 2004.R.10, Getty Research Institute, Los Angeles. The location of the house is unknown.

93 Grier, "The Decline of the Memory Palace," 52.

94 See, for example, the display ad "New Home," *Highland Park News-Herald and Journal,* 18 July 1957, classified page 2.

95 See, for example, "Two Families Flee Homes as Hill Slips," *Los Angeles Times,* 25 March 1958, 1–2; "Families Watch Slide Creeping Up on Homes," *Los Angeles Times,* 26 March 1958, 2; and "Disaster Aid Sought for HP Families in Land Slide Area," *Highland Park News-Herald and Journal,* 10 April 1958, 1.

96 "New Home," classified page 2.

97 Richard H. Jahns, "Residential Ills in the Heartbreak Hills of Southern California," *Engineering and Science* 22 (December 1958): 13–20. I wish to thank Alexander Luckmann for bringing the article to my attention.

98 See this volume, "List of Selected Architectural Works," for details on the copyrighted projects by Fischer.

99 Email correspondence of the author with Mari Nakahara, curator of architecture, design, and engineering, and Jonathan Eaker, reference librarian, Prints & Photographs Division, Library of Congress, Washington, DC, November to December 2020 and June 2021.

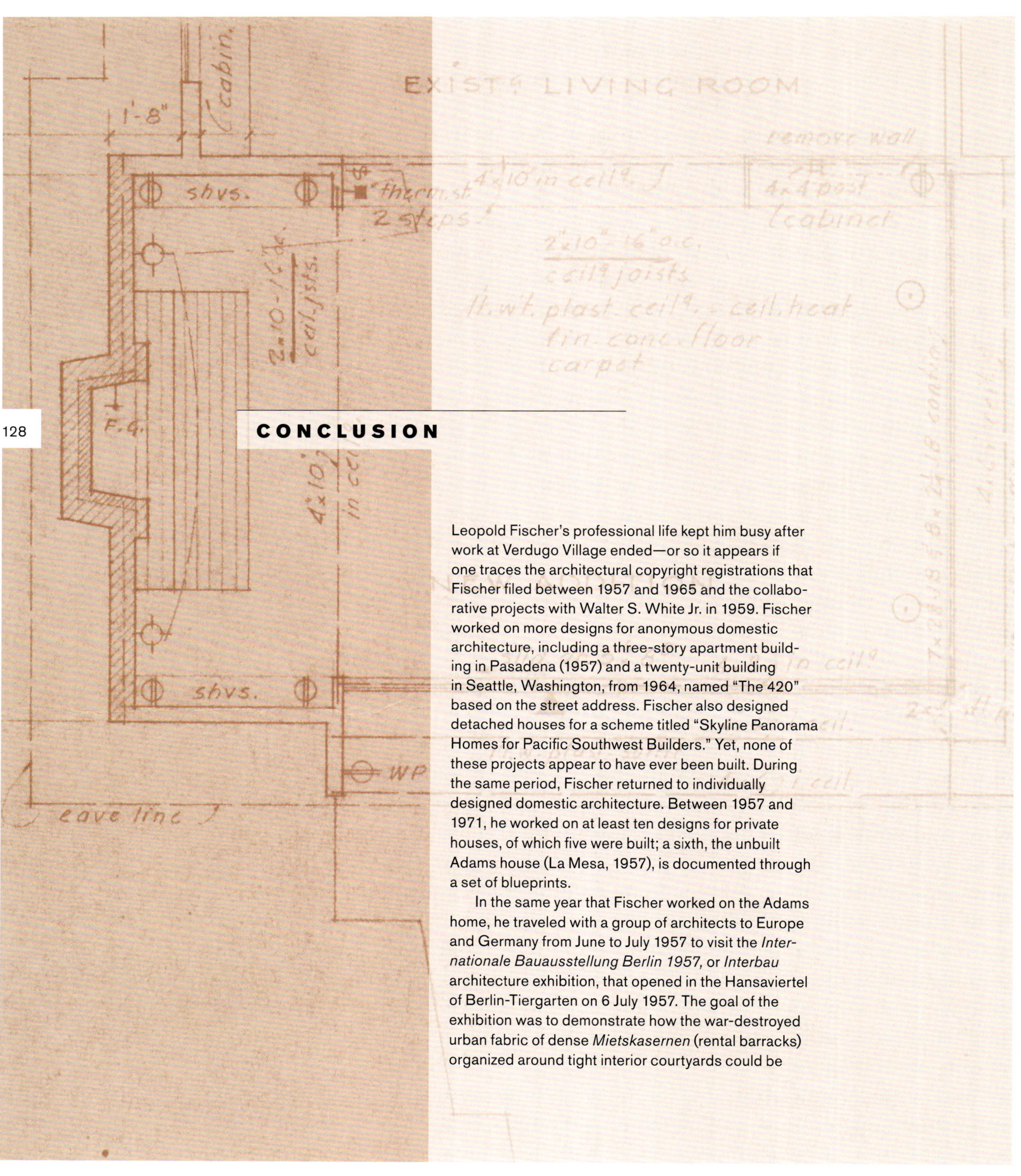

CONCLUSION

Leopold Fischer's professional life kept him busy after work at Verdugo Village ended—or so it appears if one traces the architectural copyright registrations that Fischer filed between 1957 and 1965 and the collaborative projects with Walter S. White Jr. in 1959. Fischer worked on more designs for anonymous domestic architecture, including a three-story apartment building in Pasadena (1957) and a twenty-unit building in Seattle, Washington, from 1964, named "The 420" based on the street address. Fischer also designed detached houses for a scheme titled "Skyline Panorama Homes for Pacific Southwest Builders." Yet, none of these projects appear to have ever been built. During the same period, Fischer returned to individually designed domestic architecture. Between 1957 and 1971, he worked on at least ten designs for private houses, of which five were built; a sixth, the unbuilt Adams house (La Mesa, 1957), is documented through a set of blueprints.

In the same year that Fischer worked on the Adams home, he traveled with a group of architects to Europe and Germany from June to July 1957 to visit the *Internationale Bauausstellung Berlin 1957,* or *Interbau* architecture exhibition, that opened in the Hansaviertel of Berlin-Tiergarten on 6 July 1957. The goal of the exhibition was to demonstrate how the war-destroyed urban fabric of dense *Mietskasernen* (rental barracks) organized around tight interior courtyards could be

6.1. Leopold Fischer at the northeast corner of Shirley Place and West Olympic Boulevard, Beverly Hills, California, photographed by his ex-fiancée, Gerda Vogt, during her visit to Los Angeles in ca. 1957.

replaced with contemporary urban architecture, dispersing within a park-like setting high-rise towers, slabs with apartments, and one- or two-story dwellings and townhouses in various forms ranging from terraced houses to detached bungalows. Among the architects rebuilding the Hansaviertel were pre–World War II modernists such as Walter Gropius as well as a generation of younger, international modern architects.

According to Gerda Vogt, her once-fiancé also visited "selected of his former clients and houses" from his pre-exile life. In the fall of the same year, Vogt, in turn, traveled to the United States and spent a week in California to see Fischer. By then, Fischer "lived in a large apartment in the elegant city of Beverly Hills and drove a stylish white Cadillac. His office was on a different street. He drove me around town for quite a while and showed me numerous houses he had designed" (fig. 6.1).[1] Vogt's retrospective recollections reinforce the impression that by the later 1950s, Fischer made a decent living as an architect: he had a large

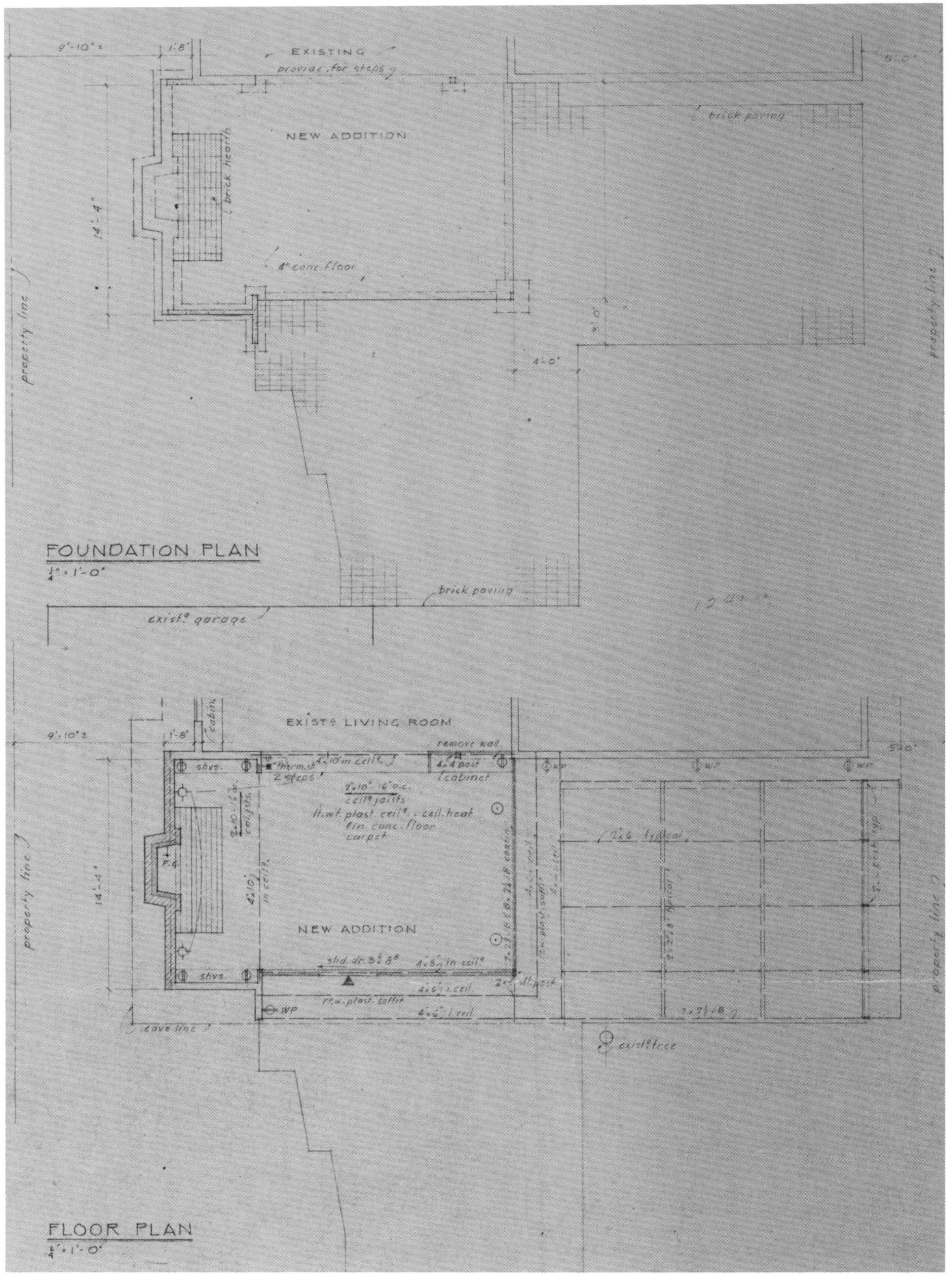

6.2. Leopold Fischer (US American, 1901–75, b. Austria-Hungary).

Dr. Ward & Mrs. Marguerite Youry house (1965), Long Beach, California.

Floor plan from *Addition to Residence of Mr. & Mrs. Ward Youry,* sheet 1, 1965.

The floor plan shows the extension containing a glass room with a fireplace niche, an outdoor seating area with brick paving, and an indication of a privacy fence toward the existing garage.

enough number of buildings to his name to warrant an extended tour to see them all, and he could afford to live in an appropriate apartment and own a decent car. It remains arguable whether and how much Vogt's impression was determined by the fact that she visited California from a Germany that was still rebuilding its cities after the war it had started, not to mention personal sentimentalities and memories of two people who had been in love with each other at a time when the Nuremberg Laws made their affections illegal.

It was a momentary impression anyway, for by the end of the decade, Fischer had closed down his office, left Beverly Hills, and collaborated for about a year or so with Walter S. White Jr. on projects in the desert east of Los Angeles before finally moving to the small coastal town of Seal Beach, just south of Long Beach. Local city directories have listed Fischer as an architect in Seal Beach from 1965 onward. Indeed, in the 1973 edition of the local telephone directory, his entry refers to "arch[itec]ts" as if he had taken on a partner.[2] Retirement turned out to be part-time, given that Fischer kept designing architectural projects, of which only a few progressed to being built. Among these is the extension of the Youry house (Long Beach, 1965), a small project that allowed Fischer one final opportunity to express most beautifully his ideas about domestic architecture.

• • •

The Youry house is a tract home from 1952 in a suburban area on the edges of Long Beach, close to the local college where Dr. Ward Youry was a founding ceramics and art department faculty member. Fischer took the extension of a nondescript detached house as an opportunity to design a glass room that once more fused his knowledge about contemporary California and American domestic architecture with his architectural origins in Central European domestic architecture. That the room is the smallest of Fischer's designs—unless the not-yet-located Kohlmeier mountain cabin turns out to be smaller—does not diminish the achievement; that it is Fischer's last built project coincidentally transforms the glass room into the architect's third and final manifesto of his architectural oeuvre in exile.

The task was to expand the house by adding space at the garden side of the existing building, which included creating an outdoor seating area, a privacy fence, a new carport adjacent to the house, and a ceramics studio at the existing garage at the far end of the garden to the rear of the home. The project was tackled in three stages.[3] In 1965, Fischer designed the glass room that extended the living room overlooking the garden to the east of the home and placed a patio with a wooden trellis as an outdoor room adjacent to the extension (fig. 6.2).[4] In 1967, Fischer drew plans for a ceramics studio as an add-on to the existing garage. (This studio was never built; only two years after Fischer's death, today's studio was erected in 1977, to plans by a different architect.) Finally, in 1969, Fischer worked on a porte cochere that could also function as a carport and covered the driveway adjacent to the house.

The heart of the remodel is the living room extension at the southwestern corner of the building. Fischer removed the eastern wall facing the garden from the existing living room and extended the new space by a little over fourteen feet, to which a generous roof overhang added approximately three more feet. On the south side of the home, which looks out to the driveway, the new space projects nearly two feet beyond the main house. Accordingly, the projecting extension is perceivable as a stand-alone addition when seen from the outside. Yet, the hipped roof covering it appears merely a perpendicular extension of the existing hipped roof on the main house (fig. 6.3). More such architectural juxtapositions can be observed elsewhere in the glass room; indeed, they are an architectural theme woven into the design and physical fabric of the small extension.

For example, the ceiling of the extension continues the ceiling plane of the adjacent existing room, visually uniting new and old space into a single volume quite similar to the living-cum-dining rooms of the Kohlmeier and Slechta houses. Yet, the floor level of the extension lies below that of the older building. Where once the demolished exterior wall rose, now two low steps lead down to the extension; the slight height difference subtly recalls the *Raumplan* of Adolf Loos (fig. 6.4). Or, take the room-wide opening that in lieu of the removed exterior wall merges old and new spaces. In contrast, the all-glass wall opposite this opening establishes visual continuity but maintains a physical separation between inside and outside. The opening also gives access to the extension across almost its entire width; opposite it, Fischer placed again a single door, this time a sliding one, that grants access to the outside in the most controlled manner.

Similarly, across the new room's other horizontal dimension, a floor-to-ceiling fixed glass wall on the north side faces a windowless niche on the south side. The niche is as wide and high as the entire room, creating a juxtaposition between enclosing space with massive walls and enclosing it with transparent

6.3. Leopold Fischer (US American, 1901–75, b. Austria-Hungary).

Dr. Ward & Mrs. Marguerite Youry house (1965), Long Beach, California, April 2022.

Extension with a glass room and adjacent patio with trellis.

The privacy fence to the left stands approximately where Fischer's extension plan suggested such a fence. It is not known whether this fence was a design by Fischer. The folly in front of the glass room was created by a different designer, at a later stage, to accommodate a wind chime by Paolo Soleri.

6.4. Leopold Fischer (US American, 1901–75, b. Austria-Hungary).

Dr. Ward & Mrs. Marguerite Youry house (1965), Long Beach, California, April 2022.

Interior of the glass room with the new patio and trellis.

The privacy fence to the left is not a design by Fischer. The studio building in the background to the right was not built to Fischer's design.

6.5. Leopold Fischer (US American, 1901–75, b. Austria-Hungary).

Dr. Ward & Mrs. Marguerite Youry house (1965), Long Beach, California, April 2022.

Fireplace niche with display shelves at south end of glass room extension.

The built-in cabinets in the dining area to the right were designed by Fischer as well.

materials such as glass. Inside the niche, Fischer arranged a fireplace with an eight-foot-wide and three-foot-deep hearth extension in front and a floor-to-ceiling fireplace surround covering the entire south wall (fig. 6.5). At either end, the massive wall wraps around the corner, forming the rear of shelves rising from floor to ceiling on either side. In the floor plan, Fischer identified the shelving as bookshelves; as finished, each shelf's surfaces (including back and sides) are glazed with mirrors to allow all-around views of handmade ceramic vessels and objects that Ward Youry displayed there. The fireplace, hearth slab, and surround are made from exposed Roman brick laid in a stack bond whose thick horizontal and vertical mortar joints create a rigid grid pattern. In short, the fireplace niche and shelves juxtapose mass-produced bricks with artistically formed clay, the *prima materia* of ceramists.

This juxtaposition can equally be described as one between industrially produced materials and forms on the one hand and hand-crafted, perhaps even rare or unique, objects on the other. The effect, however, is an impression not of strict opposites but of a union—indeed, a *re*union between the arts and crafts and industry. In argument with each other, these two modes of production gave birth to modernism in art and architecture around 1900, and their relationship was an ongoing subject matter of debate in the Bauhaus, especially during its early years in Weimar. That the spirit of the art school influenced the design of the extension, if not the ceramist's choice of architect, is suggested by a biographical-professional link between Ward Youry and the Weimar Republic art school: in 1952, Youry studied for one summer at Pond Farm in Northern California with Marguerite Friedlaender-Wildenhain (1896–1985),[5] a Bauhaus-trained Jewish ceramist who fled Germany in 1933 and came to the United States in 1940.[6]

Of course, all of this did not re-create the Bauhaus in a small glass room in Long Beach. Still, the design for the extension illustrates in an exemplary manner how Fischer orchestrated in his California projects manifold points of architectural references that mostly touch on three areas of concern. First, the references address the circumstances, wishes, and ideas of the clients. Second, the designs comment on contemporary California domestic architecture, the Kohlmeier house on Frank Lloyd Wright's Usonian homes, and the Slechta house on some of Richard Neutra's post–World War II houses. Moreover, these houses and the Youry glass room critique midcentury modernist architectural ideas, such as the notion that sliding glass doors moved out of sight will allow the inside and the outside to merge. Third, and in stark contrast to such reductionist approaches to contemporary California domestic architecture, Fischer drew on his Central European architectural background to design more complex domestic environments.

Sometimes, Fischer's designs recall Adolf Loos's architecture—for example, in the ways the Kohlmeier house is organized in the vertical dimension, taking advantage of its location on the promontory, or in how fireplaces are integral to the interiors of homes. Fireplaces in Fischer-designed houses physically warm a room, provide visual interest whether or not a fire is burning, and gather the occupants socially. However, similar to many Loos-designed homes, the fireplaces are not the center of the space but one among other architectural elements that order space to make it usable and comfortable for the inhabitants.

At other times, Fischer refers back to a typology of houses and to his work as the designer of social housing estates, as in his plans for Verdugo Village. He also repeatedly inserts similar features into most of his domestic designs in California. Take, most notably, his use of outdoor rooms as intermediate spaces (as defined by Leberecht Migge) in conjunction with generously fenestrated living spaces.

In short—and harking back to the analogy drawn in the introduction to Alexander Humboldt's reflections on how to come to terms with life in a distant country—Fischer's exile oeuvre continuously oscillates between the new or unfamiliar and the old (or past) or familiar. According to Humboldt, the unfamiliar eventually would grow stronger, though the familiar would never entirely disappear. In the case of Fischer, the relation between both is permanently more balanced. The old (be this his pre-exile work and experience or his earlier works in exile) never overwhelms newer projects (the "unfamiliar" of Humboldt). And vice versa, his newer projects are never purely innovative, meaning there are still references to, if not roots in, his architectural works and experiences up to that moment. Strictly architecturally speaking, Fischer was entirely at home in exile, as can be concluded from studying select existing buildings and documented designs from his California oeuvre. Whether, in turn, the history of architecture in California can accommodate an oeuvre like Fischer's depends on overcoming the notions that modern domestic architecture in the state is, by default or definition, innovative and required to continuously reinvent itself to find the attention of clients, the public, critics, and, eventually, historians. By pushing, even if not entirely setting aside, such ideas for this study, Fischer's exile oeuvre and selected works of some of his fellow émigré architects become visible as they stand all over Los Angeles, beloved by their owners, more or less ignored by architectural history.

Fischer's oeuvre also points to interesting and potentially rewarding future inquiries—for example, the realization that for many émigré architects, midcentury suburbia amounted to an important part of their post–World War II exile careers in California. In *Little White Houses,* Dianne Harris discusses suburbia as a place where Jewish émigrés from Germany chose to settle in exile.[7] Other émigrés, such as Fischer and some of his peers, contributed to building that suburbia. This insight adds an important angle to architectural-historical studies of exile and suburbia, even if it may not absolve suburban life from the alleged racist foundations and ecological misgivings that more recent criticism focuses on.

Other intriguing avenues of study are the various biographical and professional adjacencies, if not overlaps, between Fischer and Gregory Ain, serving to map alternative routes along which knowledge about Central European modernism may have reached and shaped Los Angeles. The adjacencies begin with Ain and his office partner, James H. Garrott, moving into the Granada Buildings just around when Fischer moved out, making it possible to speculate whether Ain and Garrott took over Fischer's unit.

Before moving offices, Ain designed the Dunsmuir Apartments (Los Angeles, 1937). The zigzagging staggering of the apartments is usually compared to the similarly staggered modernist Bruchfeldstraße estate (1926–28) in Frankfurt that the German architect and socialist Ernst May had designed.[8] May ordered the seesawing units in Frankfurt on either side of a traditional view axis leading to one narrow end of the larger rectangular footprint of the estate. Yet, with Fischer being in Los Angeles from early 1937 onward, there may have potentially been a different source of inspiration for Ain. Fischer had designed a pre-exile social housing scheme that made far more radical use of a seesawing pattern when he arranged the zigzagging houses of the Friedrichshöhe estate (1928–30) in Bernburg in repetitive rows, one row behind the other. Ultimately, only 90 homes were built, yet, looking at figure 1.8, one can easily imagine the heroic impression the estate would have made had all 2,800 units been erected.

6.6. **Gregory Ain (US American, 1908–88).**

One Family Defense Housing (1939–40), unbuilt.

Site plan, n.d.

University of California, Santa Barbara, Architecture and Design Collection.

Similarly, Ain's One Family Defense Housing scheme (1939–40, unbuilt) and Park Planned Homes (Altadena, 1946–47) have been linked to Walter Gropius's Törten estate (1926–31) in Dessau, not least because of the "mirrored units" and the shared walkways leading up to adjacent units' main doors, characteristics that Ain subsequently used to great effect in the layout of other neighborhoods he designed.[9] However, the basic arrangement of the Törten estate in rows or terraces of houses was rooted in Fischer's familiarity with Adolf Loos's patented scheme for "houses with only one wall." Accordingly, Fischer's presence in Los Angeles raises again the possibility that Ain may have learned firsthand about the Törten estate from the very architect who worked out the essentials of the scheme when he was employed in Gropius's office. This genealogy of Dessau-Törten sheds potentially new light not only on Ain's housing neighborhoods but also on broader issues, such as the type of affordable housing these neighborhoods represent.

Adolf Loos and Fischer's take on mass housing for workers was grounded in ideas of individual ownership of pieces of land on which to erect houses combined with use gardens (*Nutzgärten*) for small husbandry, vegetables, and fruits, enabling the owners of such units to support themselves. Fischer's scheme for the Knarrberg estate in Dessau is probably one of the clearest applications of these ideas (see figs. 1.5–1.7). Comparing the Knarrberg estate with Ain's One Family Defense Housing emphasizes noticeable differences, such as two-story, semidetached houses in Dessau versus single-family houses in Los Angeles, and use gardens versus pleasure gardens (fig. 6.6). More striking, however, are the similarities between the schemes. Both arrange buildings in a strictly

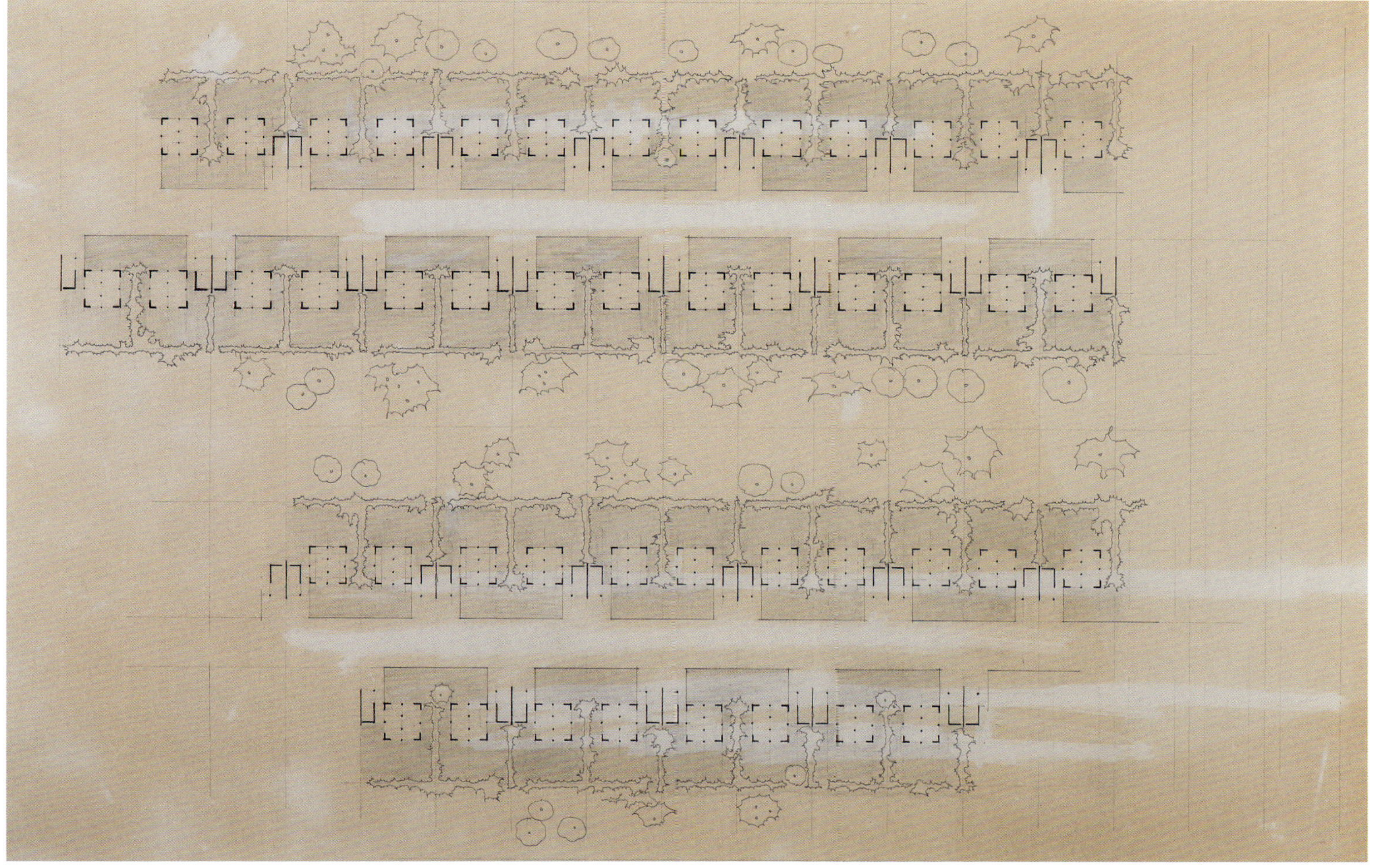

linear fashion on either side of a street, place gardens behind each home that back onto gardens from the next row of houses over on the next street, and use smaller buildings located between the main ones as storage sheds or possible garages in Dessau and as car garages in Los Angeles.[10]

Whether the specter of socialism, to paraphrase the threat Karl Marx and Friedrich Engels uttered in the *Communist Manifesto,* haunts the scheme by Ain (who was a member of the local Communist Party)[11] and other middle-class neighborhoods of detached single-family houses in midcentury Los Angeles may be fascinating to speculate about. More immediately apparent are the echoes of Fischer's Knarrberg estate and, consequently, ideas about housing based on individual land ownership as favored by Adolf Loos and Leberecht Migge that reverberate through schemes like Ain's. These concepts aimed at the working classes but became favored by the middle classes who could afford to acquire such property, whether this was in Weimar Germany or Los Angeles, illustrating once more the conflation between middle-class homes and affordable housing that, according to Nicholas Olsberg, mars housing debates in Los Angeles.[12]

The point is not to claim that Ain's achievements are Fischer's or vice versa—to each his success and failures—but to emphasize that learning from history never stops, not even in Los Angeles and California. Instead, it can move in unexpected directions if and when the history of domestic architecture in California turns its gaze away from architectural modernism's twin lodestars of prominence and innovation and toward architects like Fischer and his émigré architect peers. Their works have fallen by the wayside because they do not easily entice a Hollywood-like fascination with famous architecture, and they have remained invisible to an architectural history that often occupies itself with fashionable but fleeting topics of the current moment.

• • •

In light of the possibility that Fischer's firsthand contributions to and knowledge about Central European modernism in architecture reverberated among fellow Southern California architects, was the émigré architect then to a comparable degree at home with contemporary California and American architecture as his California designs indicate that he was "at home in exile"? This question can be answered on firmer ground than others thanks to two surviving letters that Fischer wrote in 1956 and 1967 to Lewis Mumford. The two men had known each other since 1956, when Fischer traveled to New York "with the hope of seeing you," as he put it in a short note sent to the critic from the Plaza Hotel on Fifth Avenue. The first paragraph of this note addresses why Fischer wished to meet Mumford at that time:

> Having myself been close to the development of the architecture of our generation[,] your writings for years have been a ray of hope and a sense of encouragement for me.[13]

Fischer firmly locates himself within modern and contemporary architecture in just one sentence, as concise with words as his designs and buildings are with architectural details. He is part of the modern movement in architecture, an ongoing commitment of his generation that involves efforts for which Fischer finds support in Mumford's writings. Fischer wrote this at the height of his career in exile; he had just completed his share of buildings in Verdugo Village and projected an impression of an architect doing well to visitors such as Gerda Vogt.

A decade later, a second letter to Mumford speaks very differently about contemporary architecture. After repeating his admiration for Mumford's writing and recalling their earlier meeting, Fischer turns to his contemporary fellow architects:

> [T]hose sinister proponents of nothingness, playing with meaningless, inhuman forms have been roaming the field, and "historians" and trade magazines have supported and propagandized the shamelessly and insidiously spurious instigators of the hoax, which has completely taken over and cornered the established media of publications and activities.[14]

Fischer's acute disappointment with contemporary architecture affected his usually concise and elegant writing style: here, he is rambling and embittered. More importantly, Fischer feels severed from his architectural origin, describing himself now as merely "[b]y destiny involved in being the witness of some of the earlier significant developments" of the modern movement, of which "some of the most 'illustrious' names even have paid me the supreme compliment." To the initiated, this is a barely veiled reference to the lifelong animosity between Fischer and Gropius that harked back to Fischer's work on the Törten estate. Closer to the time of Fischer's second letter to Mumford, Gropius—then one of the most prominent German modernist architects in the United States—had completed the

New York Pan Am Building (1959–63, with Pietro Belluschi), a building that symbolized, already then, the shattering of the modernist dream, as Meredith Clausen memorably phrased it more recently.[15]

Whether Fischer's feeling of having no place in contemporary architecture was rooted in disappointment that a fellow member of the early modernist movement betrayed the ideas and ideals of that movement or whether it can be attributed to any embitterment over the fact that vast swaths of the American architectural scene fell for that kind of contemporary architecture remains arguable, and it will remain so due to the unknown whereabouts of Fischer's papers. A manuscript, which Fischer was working on at the time of the 1967 letter, went missing with them. As Fischer told Mumford in the letter, that manuscript discussed the history of the modern movement and contemporary architecture.

• • •

A few years after completing the Youry glass room—which developed into his final manifesto (indeed his legacy) of what modern domestic architecture could be, especially in California—Fischer was admitted to a hospital in Hawaiian Gardens, Los Angeles County, where he passed away on 2 August 1975.[16] His remains were embalmed and later cremated; his ashes were scattered in the desert, presumably somewhere in the Coachella Valley. The single man who had walked as an émigré architect across the border between Mexicali and Calexico in 1937 passed away thirty-eight years later in his adopted home country shrouded in much the same anonymity with which he had arrived. Indeed, the protective claim to be a man without relatives and thus history that Fischer uttered when facing the border agent echoes today even stronger than during the architect's exile in California. For reasons of privacy, the mortuary cannot share whether any name or names are on file for those who arranged the cremation of the remains and the scattering of the ashes, much less what those names might be, making the silence around Fischer's private life complete.[17] At least Fischer's still existing architectural oeuvre in exile holds what Johann Wolfgang von Goethe's *Faust* proclaimed centuries ago: "The trace of my days on earth cannot perish in eons,"[18] not even in metropolitan Los Angeles, on the surface fast-paced and without memories, but full of history underneath. One just has to look around by deliberately overlooking prominent and innovative architectural sights.

Notes

1 Gerda Vogt to Irene Below and students, n.d., cited from Irene Below and Babette Scurrell, eds., *es gab nicht nur das bauhaus: wohnen und haushalten in dessauer siedlungen der 20er jahre* (Dessau: Stiftung Bauhaus Dessau, 1994), "verschollen—der siedlungsarchitekt leopold fischer," plate d 7.1. See also Irene Below, "Das Leben von Leopold Fischer," in *Leopold Fischer: Architekt der Moderne,* ed. Bauhaus Dessau e.V. (Dessau-Roßlau: Funk Verlag Bernhard Hein e.K., n.d. [2007]), 22–23.

2 For example, "Fischer, Leopold archt. 125 2nd Street Seal Beach 430-2565," *Long Beach Southern Section Telephone Directory October 1965* (n.p.: General Telephone Company of California, 1965), 343; and "Fischer, Leopold archts. 125 2nd Street Seal Beach 430-2565," *Long Beach Southern Section Telephone Directory September 1973* (n.p.: General Telephone Company of California, 1973), 110. The abbreviation "archts." remains part of Fischer's entry until 1975, the year of his death.

3 Department of Building & Safety, City of Long Beach, Calif., Application for Building Permit, no. B2513, 26 June 1952; "Add to existing Living Room to Rear," 30 June 1965; "Add Port Cochere," 28 October 1969; "Addition to existing Garage," 20 June 1977 (City of Long Beach Document Center, City of Long Beach Document Repository, item ID 003838321.

4 The plan also indicates a privacy fence between the glass room and the adjacent driveway to the garage; today's fence approximately follows the direction Fischer had specified, but it could not be ascertained that it is a Fischer design.

5 Vera Williams, "Local Colleges Do Artists Smocks," *Independent Press-Telegram* (Long Beach), 13 October 1953, W-4. Ward Youry studied at Pond Farm in 1952; see Dean Schwarz and Geraldine Schwarz, eds., *Marguerite Wildenhain and the Bauhaus: An Eyewitness Anthology* (Decorah, IA: South Bear, 2007), 444 (3rd column).

6 On Friedlaender-Wildenhain, see Jenni Sorkin, *Live Form: Women, Ceramics, and Community* (Chicago: University of Chicago Press, 2016), chap. 2. No records have been found indicating that Friedlaender-Wildenhain, her non-Jewish husband, Frans Wildenhain, who had also studied ceramics at the Bauhaus, and Fischer may have known one another from their time in Germany. The fact remains that with Fischer, Youry commissioned the one architect in Southern California who biographically had been the closest to the Bauhaus in pre–World War II Germany other than Fischer's colleague from times in Dessau, Rolf Sklarek, who by the time of the glass room was commissioned worked already for Victor Gruen and was unavailable for private commissions.

7 Dianne Harris, *Little White Houses: How the Postwar Home Constructed Race in America* (Minneapolis: University of Minnesota Press, 2013), ix.

8 Anthony Fontenot, "Social Housing: Shared Space and the Urban Pattern," in *Notes from Another Los Angeles: Gregory Ain and the Construction of a Social Landscape,* ed. Anthony Fontenot (Cambridge, MA: MIT Press, 2022), 141.

9 Fontenot, "Social Housing," 139.

10 On the One Family Defense Housing scheme, see also Brooke Ashton Devenney, “The Evolution of Gregory Ain’s Interwar and Postwar Planned Housing Communities, 1939–1948” (master’s thesis, University of California, Riverside, 2014), 14–50.

11 Anthony Denzer, “Gregory Ain: Under Surveillance,” in Fontenot, *Notes from Another Los Angeles,* 181–91, esp. 184–85. A request filed under the Freedom of Information/Privacy Acts (FOIPA) for possible records of the FBI on Leopold Fischer did not yield any results. US Department of Justice, Federal Bureau of Investigation, correspondence with the author, 2 December 2022.

12 Nicholas Olsberg, “Common Ground,” in Fontenot, *Notes from Another Los Angeles,* 88.

13 Leopold Fischer to Lewis Mumford, 22 May 1956, folder 1573, Lewis Mumford Papers (Ms. Coll. 2), Kislak Center for Special Collections, Rare Books and Manuscripts, University of Pennsylvania.

14 Leopold Fischer to Lewis Mumford, 9 April 1967, folder 1573, Lewis Mumford Papers (Ms. Coll. 2), Kislak Center for Special Collections. All subsequent quotes by Fischer in this paragraph are from this letter.

15 Meredith Clausen, *The Pan Am Building and the Shattering of the Modernist Dream* (Cambridge, MA: MIT Press, 2004).

16 County of Los Angeles, Registrar-Recorder/County Clerk, Certificate of Death 0190-048726, recorded 4 September 1975.

17 Email correspondence of the author with Huimin Lai, Advanced Service Arrangements Representative 1, CY Service Arrangements, Forest Lawn Memorial-Parks & Mortuaries, April 2023.

18 Johann Wolfgang von Goethe, *Faust,* part 2, act 5, scene 4, lines 11583–84, here cited from Walter Benjamin, “Experience and Poverty [1933],” trans. Rodney Livingstone, in *Walter Benjamin, Selected Writings, Volume 2 1927–1934,* ed. Michael W. Jennings, Howard Eiland, and Gary Smith, trans. Rodney Livingstone et al. (Cambridge, MA: Belknap, 1999), 736n8.

List of Selected Architectural Works

The section on Leopold Fischer's buildings in Austria and Germany is compiled from the German-language literature on Fischer, most notably the publications by Dr. Irene Below; see the bibliography in this volume for details. Wherever possible, dates and names are taken from Bauhaus Dessau e.V., ed., *Leopold Fischer: Architekt der Moderne* (Dessau-Roßlau: Funk Verlag Bernhard Hein e.K., n.d. [ca. 2007]). Occasionally, these dates differ from those listed in Ute Bednarz et al., eds., *Sachsen Anhalt II Regierungsbezirke Dessau und Halle* (Munich: Deutscher Kunstverlag, 1999); in those cases, the diverging dates are noted in parentheses after the names of the projects. The sections on Fischer's buildings and projects in Poland and the United States are based on my research.

Austria

1923–24

- Spanner country house, with Adolf Loos, Gumpoldskirchen

Germany

SOCIAL HOUSING ESTATES

CA. 1925–27

- Ratskiefer estate, Coswig, with Bruno Taut, unknown number of buildings with semidetached homes

1926–29

- Törten estate, Dessau-Törten, thirty buildings with sixty semidetached homes after W. Gropius had left Dessau

1926–28

- Kleinkühnau estate, Dessau-Kleinkühnau, nineteen buildings with thirty-eight semidetached homes plus one semidetached home in another building

- Knarrberg estate (1927–29), Dessau-Ziebigk, with Leberecht Migge (see figs. 1.5–1.7, 5.14)

The available literature refers to between 182 and 184 buildings comprising four or five types. Most buildings contain two semidetached homes, and there are some terraced homes and detached single-family homes; the latter are listed separately in the section "Detached Houses and Villas," below.

1927–28

- Obstmustergarten estate, Zerbst, with Bruno Taut, nineteen buildings with thirty-eight semidetached homes (out of 130 buildings that were planned), plus three buildings with six semidetached homes to plans by Taut

1927–30

- Geuz estate, Köthen-Geuz, ten terraced homes and thirteen buildings with twenty-six semidetached homes and buildings

1928–30

- Friedrichshöhe estate (1927–33), also called "Zickzackhausen," Bernburg, ninety terraced homes (of 2,800 planned homes) arranged in several parallel rows, a general store (*Konsum*), and an apartment building (see fig. 1.8)

DETACHED HOUSES AND VILLAS

1924–25

- Leberecht and Andrea Migge house (Sonnenhof), Worpswede, extension and remodel

1925

- Settler houses and gardens for the *Heim und Scholle* exhibition, with Leberecht Migge, Braunschweig, 7 June to 8 July 1925 (see fig. 1.4)

1926–28

- Four detached houses (at street corners within the Knarrberg estate), Dessau-Ziebigk

1927–28

- Liebig villa, Dessau (see figs. 1.10, 3.7)

1929

- Theis house (within the Knarrberg estate), Dessau-Ziebigk

CA. 1929–30

- Krause house, Oranienbaum, near Dessau

CA. 1930

- Dobert house, Dresden

1931

- Tittel house, Bielefeld (see fig. 1.11) (remodeled in ca. 1970s)

1933

- Steinborn house with office for medical doctor, Werther

- Hummel house, Stuttgart (remodeled in 1950–51 by Rolf Gutbrod)

1935

- Klara Vogt house, Berlin-Wannsee (demolished in ca. 2023)
- Franz and Clara Mutzenbecher house, Berlin-Wannsee

NOT DATED

- Kunkat house, Kronach

7.1. Leopold Fischer (US American, 1901–75, b. Austria-Hungary).

Apartment building for Stefanie Schmalzbach and Emil Zollmann (1936–37), Kapitana Aleksandra Kunickiego 8, Bielsko-Biała, Poland.

Street facade, n.d., photograph.

Poland

1936–37

- Stefanie (Stefanja) Schmalzbach and Emil Zollmann apartment building, Kapitana Aleksandra Kunickiego 8, Bielsko-Biała (fig. 7.1)

DRAWINGS

Archiwum Śląskiego Wojewódzkiego Konserwatora Zabytków w Katowicach—Delegatura w Bielsku-Białej (Archives of the Silesian Voivodeship Conservator of Monuments in Katowice—Branch Office in Bielsko-Biała)

United States

CALIFORNIA

CA. 1938–39

- Ralph and Phyllis Kohlmeier mountain cabin, location unknown

1940

- Robert Henry Ewing Jr. house, Studio City (see fig. 3.8)

1940–41

- Ralph and Phyllis Kohlmeier house, South Pasadena (see figs. 4.5–4.12)

1942–43

- Columbia Steel's production facility, Torrance, planning of an expansion of the steel mill, not known whether realized

1943–44

- Military designs and designs of flood controls in Southern California, as assistant engineer at the US Engineering Office, Los Angeles

1944[–1945?]

- Works while employed as chief of the engineering branch, San Bernardino Engineer Depot, US Army Engineers (details of works not known)

CA. 1945–46

- Leroy C. and Carol D. Floyd house, Santa Monica, demolished 2004

1950–51

- Harold Hunt and Agnes K. Johnson house, Bel Air, Los Angeles, with émigré interior designer Herbert Cordier (né Kugelmann, 1915–2002) (see fig. 3.9)

LITERATURE

"Residence of Mr. & Mrs. H. H. Johnson, Bel Air, California," *Architectural Digest* 13, no. 2 (1951): n.p.; Shan Stewart, "When the Rain Comes: To Hold a Hill," *Los Angeles Times*, 12 December 1954, L54

- Adolph and Mary Slechta house, View Park, Los Angeles (see figs. 4.21–4.27)

1952

- Four-unit apartment building, 349 South Linden Drive, Beverly Hills (see fig. 3.10)

1953–55

- Neighborhood of detached single-family houses, Verdugo Village, Los Angeles (see figs. 5.1, 5.3–5.13, 5.19a, 5.19b)

Houses are named after the first known occupant or owner

- Pratt house, Type C-1, 4207 Palmero Drive
- Fazzi house, Type C-2, 4219 Palmero Drive
- Brooks house, Type [D]-2, 4259 Palmero Drive
- Gadd house, Type A-2, 4300 Palmero Drive
- Jochheim house, Type B-2R, 4306 Palmero Drive
- Barron house, Type B-1, 4319 Palmero Drive
- Brown house, Type B-2R, 4331 Palmero Drive
- Randall house, Type A-2R, 4337 Palmero Drive
- Tullar house, Type B-1R, 4342 Palmero Drive
- Mendenhall house, Type A-1, 4351 Palmero Drive
- Busby house, Type A-2, 4354 Palmero Drive
- Stiles house, Type B-1R, 4360 Palmero Drive

1957

- Mr. & Mrs. Richard C. Adams house, La Mesa, project, unbuilt (fig. 7.2)

DRAWINGS

Leopold Fischer Papers, Architecture and Design Collection, Art, Design & Architecture Museum, University of California, Santa Barbara

LITERATURE

Copyright Office, *Catalog of Copyright Entries,* 3rd series, vol. 11, parts 7-11A, no. 1, January–June 1957 (Washington, DC: Library of Congress, 1958), "Works of Art Current Registrations," 180, IP 4218

- Clark estate apartment building (for Edward M. Wickman), Pasadena, location unknown, not known if built

LITERATURE

Copyright Office, *Catalog of Copyright Entries,* 3rd series, vol. 11, parts 7-11A, no. 1, January–June 1957 (Washington, DC: Library of Congress, 1958), "Works of Art Current Registrations," 180, IP 4270

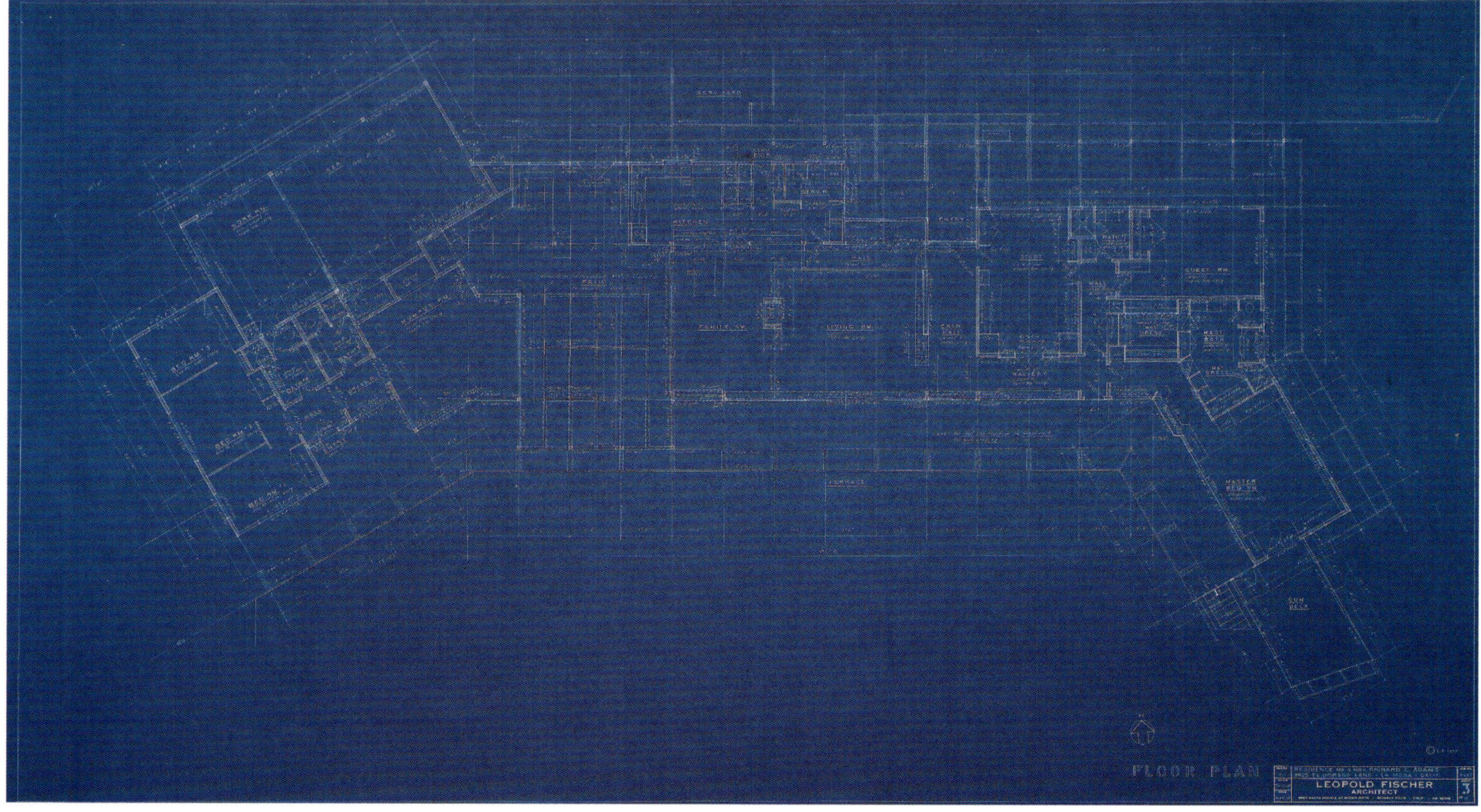

1959

- Mr. & Mrs. Joseph Benitz house, Indio, with Walter S. White Jr., not known if built
- Cecil Head, Rambler Jeep commercial building, Indio, Highway 111 at corner of Grace Street, with Walter S. White Jr., current state of building unknown
- Pearson, Scott & Company and Pearson Mortgage Company, Indio, Highway 111, exact location unknown, with Walter S. White Jr., current state of building unknown (see figs. 3.11, 3.12)
- Mr. & Mrs. Guy Eldridge office addition and dwelling, Palm Desert, exact location unknown, not known if built
- Thomas N. Campbell, restaurant and store building, Thermal, exact location unknown, not known if built

DRAWINGS AND RELATED MATERIALS FOR ALL 1959 PROJECTS

Walter S. White Papers, Architecture and Design Collection, Art, Design & Architecture Museum, University of California, Santa Barbara

1960

- Mr. & Mrs. John N. Mercer house (former Johnson house, 1950–51), Bel Air, Los Angeles, addition of second-story bedroom and bath

1960–62

- Lorene Hubbard house, Seal Beach, two-unit building (Leopold Fischer lived in one unit from the early 1960s onward)

LITERATURE

Copyright Office, *Catalog of Copyright Entries,* 3rd series, vol. 15, parts 7-11A, no. 1, January–June 1961 (Washington, DC: Library of Congress, 1962), "Works of Art Current Registrations," 42, IP 5377

1961

- Carl Grover house, Palm Desert, based on a design by or with Walter S. White Jr.

DRAWINGS AND RELATED MATERIALS

Walter S. White Papers, Architecture and Design Collection, Art, Design & Architecture Museum, University of California, Santa Barbara

- Portable Donut Kitchen for Mercury Enterprises, South San Gabriel

7.2. Leopold Fischer (US American, 1901–75, b. Austria-Hungary).

Mr. & Mrs. Richard C. Adams house, La Mesa, California, unbuilt.

Floor plan, March 1957.

University of California, Santa Barbara, Architecture and Design Collection.

LITERATURE

Copyright Office, *Catalog of Copyright Entries,* 3rd series, vol. 16, parts 7-11A, no. 1, January–June 1962 (Washington, DC: Library of Congress, 1963), "Works of Art Current Registrations," 181, IP 6140

- Ready-built sectional structures, general plan

LITERATURE

Copyright Office, *Catalog of Copyright Entries,* 3rd series, vol. 16, parts 7-11A, no. 1, January–June 1962 (Washington, DC: Library of Congress, 1963), "Works of Art Current Registrations," 38, IP 5963

- E. S. Richardson house, 806 Fourth Street, Encinitas, additions, not known if built

LITERATURE

Copyright Office, *Catalog of Copyright Entries,* 3rd series, vol. 16, parts 7-11A, no. 1, January–June 1962 (Washington, DC: Library of Congress, 1963), "Works of Art Current Registrations," 181, IP 6119

- Remodel of an unidentified house in an unknown location (possibly the Richardson house), landscape design by John Catlin, current state of building unknown (fig. 7.3)

1965

- Dr. Ward & Mrs. Marguerite Youry house, Long Beach, addition of a glass room, an outdoor room with trellis, and a privacy fence (see figs. 6.2–6.5)

1967

- Dr. Ward Youry ceramics studio, Long Beach, project, unbuilt (fig. 7.4)

1969

- Dr. Ward & Mrs. Marguerite Youry house, Long Beach, addition of a porte cochere

7.3. Leopold Fischer (US American, 1901–75, b. Austria-Hungary).

Remodel of unidentified house in unknown location, 1961 or earlier.

From "Screen Out the Defects," *Los Angeles Times,* 21 January 1962, 22.

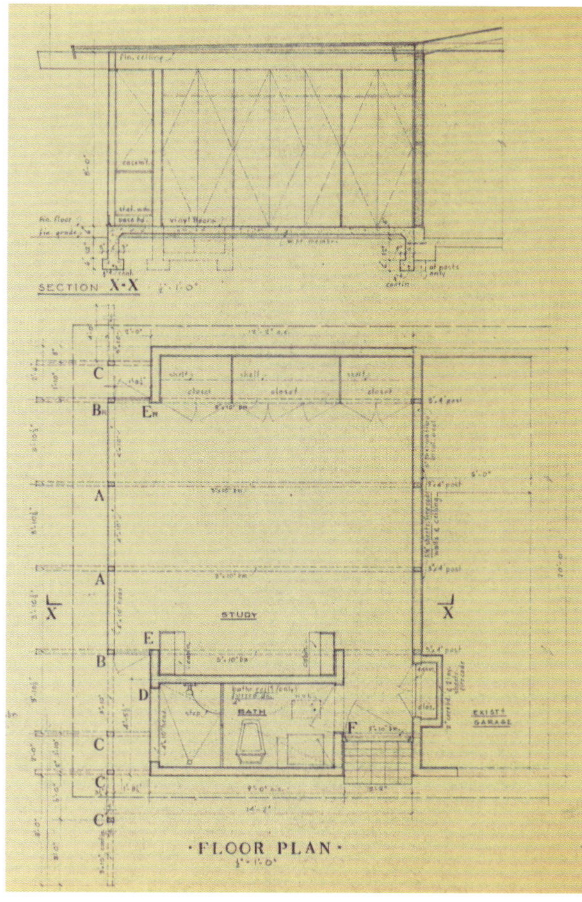

7.4. Leopold Fischer (US American, 1901–75, b. Austria-Hungary).

Dr. Ward Youry ceramics studio, Long Beach, California, unbuilt.

Floor plan and section from *Addition to Residence of Mr. & Mrs. Ward Youry,* sheet 1, 1967.

FLORIDA

1969

- Mr. & Mrs. Ward Theisen house, Bay Hill, not known if built

LITERATURE

Copyright Office, *Catalog of Copyright Entries,* 3rd series, vol. 25, parts 7-11A, no. 1, January–June 1971 (Washington, DC: Library of Congress, 1972), "Works of Art Current Registrations," 64, IP 9896

WASHINGTON, DC

1967

- Franklin Delano Roosevelt Memorial

Fischer mailed sketches and a description of his ideas for the memorial to Lewis Mumford. The whereabouts of the sketches and the description are not known.

LITERATURE

Leopold Fischer to Lewis Mumford, 9 April 1967, Lewis Mumford Papers (Ms. Coll. 2), Kislak Center for Special Collections, Rare Books and Manuscripts, University of Pennsylvania

7.5. Leopold Fischer (US American, 1901–75, b. Austria-Hungary).

Fireplace Study, Ainscough Residence, unknown location, n.d.

Interior perspective.

University of California, Santa Barbara, Architecture and Design Collection.

WASHINGTON STATE

1964

- The 420, twenty-unit apartment building, 420 Thirty-Fourth Avenue, Seattle, with or for Harvey R. Dodd, engineer, project unbuilt

LITERATURE

Copyright Office, *Catalog of Copyright Entries,* 3rd series, vol. 18, parts 7-11A, no. 1, January–June 1964 (Washington, DC: Library of Congress, 1966), "Works of Art Current Registrations," 45, IP 6655

Other Projects and Designs

UNIDENTIFIED LOCATION

1963

- Skyline Panorama Homes for Pacific Southwest Builders, location unknown, including plot plan dated 13 August 1961, prepared by William A. Ayer, project, not known if built

LITERATURE

Copyright Office, *Catalog of Copyright Entries,* 3rd series, vol. 19, parts 7-11A, no. 1, January–June 1965 (Washington, DC: Library of Congress, 1966), "Works of Art Current Registrations," 35, IP 7478

UNDATED

- Ainscough residence, (outdoor) fireplace, location unknown, not dated, project, not known if built (fig. 7.5)

DRAWING

Leopold Fischer Papers, Architecture and Design Collection, Art, Design & Architecture Museum, University of California, Santa Barbara

POSSIBLY BY LEOPOLD FISCHER WITH OR FOR OTHER ARCHITECTS

1950–51

- Cannon house, Westwood, Los Angeles, with or for émigré architect Ulrich Plaut (see figs. 4.15a, 4.15b, 5.17)

PROJECTS THAT ARE KNOWN ONLY BY HEARSAY

- Building or buildings for a ranch or farm in Santa Barbara or Santa Barbara County
- A modernist-appearing detached house in or near the historical downtown area of Long Beach

Selected Bibliography

Archival Collections and Archives Consulted

Archieven van de Holland Amerika Lijn (HAL), Stadsarchief Rotterdam
Architecture and Design Collection, Art, Design & Architecture Museum, University of California, Santa Barbara
Arnold Schönberg Center, Vienna
California Architects Board
Deutsches Architekturmuseum, Hannes Meyer Nachlaß
Geospatial Collection, UC Santa Barbara Library, University of California, Santa Barbara
Historical Museum Bielsko-Biala (Muzeum Historyczne w Bielsku-Białej)
Julius Shulman Photography Archive, Getty Research Institute, Los Angeles
Legat der Peter-August-Böckstiegel-Stiftung, Kreisarchiv Gütersloh, Germany
Lewis Mumford Papers (Ms. Coll. 2), Kislak Center for Special Collections, Rare Books and Manuscripts, University of Pennsylvania, Philadelphia
Malibu Historical Collection, Special Collections and University Archives, University Libraries, Pepperdine University, Malibu
The National Archives in St. Louis, Missouri
Technische Universität Wien Archiv (TUWA)
UCLA Library Special Collections, Charles E. Young Research Library, University of California, Los Angeles

Selected Publications about or in Reference to Leopold Fischer and His Oeuvre

Alofsin, Anthony, ed. *Frank Lloyd Wright: An Index to the Taliesin Correspondence.* 5 vols. New York: Garland, 1988.
Bauhaus Dessau e.V., ed. *Leopold Fischer: Architekt der Moderne.* Dessau-Roßlau: Funk Verlag Bernhard Hein e.K., n.d. [ca. 2007].
Bednarz, Ute, et al., eds. *Sachsen Anhalt II Regierungsbezirke Dessau und Halle.* Munich: Deutscher Kunstverlag, 1999.
Below, Irene, and Babette Scurrell, eds. *es gab nicht nur das bauhaus: wohnen und haushalten in dessauer siedlungen der 20er jahre.* Dessau: Stiftung Bauhaus Dessau, 1994.
Below, Irene. “Das Leben von Leopold Fischer.” In *Leopold Fischer: Architekt der Moderne,* edited by Bauhaus Dessau e.V., 12–23. Dessau-Roßlau: Funk Verlag Bernhard Hein e.K., n.d. [ca. 2007].

Below, Irene. "Leopold Fischer—der Architekt von 'Zickzack-hausen.'" In *Bernburger Heimatblätter 2001,* edited by Kulturbund Bernburg e.V., 12–18. Bernburg: Salzland Druck, 2001.

———. "Der unbekannte Architekt und die andere Moderne: Leopold Fischer in Dessau." In *Mythos Bauhaus,* edited by Anja Baumhoff and Magdalene Droste, 244–71. Berlin: Reimer, 2009.

Böse-Vetter, Helmut, and Hinge Meta-Hülbusch, eds. *Worpswede und Umzu: Haus und Hof—Land und Leute.* Marburg: Völker & Ritter, 1998. Originally published in 1991 by Kassel University Press.

Gropp, David. "Das Haus des Dr. Steinborn in Werther und sein Architekt Leopold Fischer." *Denkmalpflege in Westfalen-Lippe,* no. 2 (2021): 42–50.

Hartley, John. "Screen Out the Defects." *Los Angeles Times,* 21 January 1962, 22.

Hausdörfer, Tina. "Dessau-Ziebigk—Selbstversorgersiedlung am Knarrberg 1926." In *Das "Land in der Mitte" Architektur, Denkmals—und Wohnungsbauprojekte der Moderne,* edited by Christiane Wolf, 103–20. Weimar: Bauhaus-Universität Universitätsverlag, 2004.

Hlawatsch, Robert. "Erinnerungen an Adolf Loos und an die Loos-Schule." *Bauwelt* 72, no. 42 (1981): 1893.

Kuschnerus, Katina Anne Marie. "Die Knarrbergsiedlung in Dessau-Ziebigk von Leopold Fischer 1926–1928." Master's thesis, Philosophische Fakultät der Christian-Albrechts-Universität zu Kiel, 2021.

Lückmann, Rudolf. "Walter Gropius ./. Leopold Fischer—Ungleiche Rivalen um die Gartenstädte der Moderne." In *Zukunftsfähige Perspektiven in der Landschaftsarchitektur für Gartenstädte,* edited by Nicole Uhrig, 85–112. Wiesbaden: Springer Fachmedien, 2020.

Plaisier, Peter. *De leerlingen van Adolf Loos.* Delft: Delftse Universitaire Pers, 1987.

Polster, Bernd. *Walter Gropius: Der Architekt seines Ruhms.* Munich: Carl Hanser, 2019.

Rading, Adolf. "Die Typenbildung und ihre städtebaulichen Folgerungen." In *Probleme des Bauens: Der Wohnbau,* edited by Fritz Block, 55–86. Potsdam: Müller & Kiepenheuer, 1928.

"Residence of Mr. & Mrs. H. H. Johnson, Bel Air, California," *Architectural Digest* 13, no. 2 (1951): n.p.

Riedel, David. *Dunkle Jahre, voller Farben: Der Künstler Peter August Böckstiegel 1933–1945.* Exh. cat. Werther: Museum Peter August Böckstiegel, 2020.

———. *Peter August Böckstiegel: The Expression of His Roots.* Munich: Klinkhardt & Biermann, 2021.

"Rising in Beverly Hills." *Los Angeles Times,* 15 June 1952, E2.

Rukschcio, Burkhardt, and Roland Schachel. *Adolf Loos: Leben und Werk.* Salzburg: Residenz, 1982.

Scheiffele, Walter. *Bauhaus Junkers Sozialdemokratie: Ein Kraftfeld der Moderne.* Berlin: Form+ Zweck, 2003.

Schwarting, Andreas. *Die Siedlung Dessau-Törten 1926–1931.* Leipzig: Spector, 2012.

Slechta, Mary. *My Recollections.* Santa Ana, CA: Friis-Pioneer, 1987.

Vierich, Juliane. *Die Villa Liebig: Denkmalpflege der Moderne.* Diploma thesis. Köthen: Edition der Hochschule Anhalt, 2006.

Welter, Volker M. *Walter S. White: Inventions in Mid-Century Architecture.* Santa Barbara: University of California, Santa Barbara, 2015.

Zechlin, Hans Josef. "Siedlungen von Adolf Loos und Leopold Fischer." *Wasmuths Monatshefte für Baukunst* 13, no. 2 (1929): 70–78.

Selected Other Publications

Abrahamson, Eric John. *Building Home: Howard F. Ahmanson and the Politics of the American Dream.* Berkeley: University of California Press, 2013.

Adamson, Paul, and Marty Arbunich. *Eichler: Modernism Rebuilds the American Dream.* Salt Lake City: Gibbs Smith, 2002.

Adorno, Theodor W. *Letters to His Parents 1939–1951.* Edited by Christoph Gödde and Henri Lonitz. Translated by Wieland Hoban. Cambridge, UK: Polity, 2006.

Altmann-Loos, Elsie. *Adolf Loos, der Mensch.* Vienna: Herold, 1968.

———. *Mein Leben mit Adolf Loos.* Vienna: Amalthea, 1984.

Amtliches Fernsprechbuch für Berlin und Umgegend April 1936. Berlin: Reichspostdirektion, 1936.

Architekturzentrum Wien, ed. *Architektenlexikon Wien 1770–1945.* http://www.architektenlexikon.at.

Armsby, Henry H. "ESMWT." *Journal of Higher Education* 15, no. 2 (February 1944): 86–94.

"Art: Rich Man's Architect." *Time Magazine,* 18 August 1952. https://time.com/archive/6619052/art-rich-mans-architect.

Ascher, Wolf Dieter. *My Three Stories: Shanghai U.S. Air Force City Planner* [2000]. N.p.: n.p., [2006?].

Ash, Mitchell G., and Alfons Söllner, eds. *Forced Migration and Scientific Change: Émigré German-Speaking Scientists and Scholars after 1933.* Cambridge: Cambridge University Press, 1996.

Augenfeld, Felix. "Erinnerungen an Adolf Loos." *Bauwelt* 72, no. 42 (6 November 1981): 1907.

Bahr, Erhard. *Weimar on the Pacific: German Exile Culture in Los Angeles and the Crisis of Modernism.* Berkeley: University of California Press, 2007.

Banham, Reyner. *Los Angeles: The Architecture of Four Ecologies.* London: Allen Lane, 1971.

Barraclough, Laura R. *Making the San Fernando Valley: Rural Landscapes, Urban Development, and White Privilege.* Athens: University of Georgia Press, 2011.

Benton, Charlotte. *A Different World: Émigré Architects in Britain 1928–1958.* London: RIBA Heinz Gallery, 1995.

Berliner Adreßbuch 1932: Unter Benutzung amtlicher Quellen. Vol. 1. Berlin: Scherl, n.d. [1932].

Berliner Adreßbuch 1936: Unter Benutzung amtlicher Quellen. Vol. 1. Berlin: Scherl, n.d. [1936].

Berliner Handels-Register. Vol. 67. Berlin: Ullstein, 1931.

Beverly Hills City Directory, 1960–61. Beverly Hills: Chamber of Commerce and Civic Association, 1960.

Blau, Eve. *The Architecture of Red Vienna, 1919–1934.* Cambridge, MA: MIT Press, 1999.

Boeckl, Matthias, ed. *Visionäre & Vertriebene: Österreichische Spuren in der modernen amerikanischen Architektur.* Berlin: Ernst & Sohn, 1995.

Borries-Knopp, Mechthild, ed. *Building Paradise: Exile Architecture in California; Villa Aurora Architecture Symposium 2003* (Berlin: Kreis der Freunde und Förderer der Villa Aurora e.V., 2004).

Brandstetter, Jutta. "Alexander Neumann." *Architektenlexikon Wien 1770–1945.* Edited by Architekturzentrum Wien. http://www.architektenlexikon.at/de/425.htm.

———. "Hans Mayr." *Architektenlexikon Wien 1770–1945.* Edited by Architekturzentrum Wien. http://www.architektenlexikon.at/de/390.htm.

Brierly, Cornelia. *Tales of Taliesin: A Memoir of Fellowship.* San Francisco: Pomegranate, 2000.

Cohen, Jean-Louis. *Scenes of the World to Come: European Architecture and the American Challenge, 1893–1960.* Exh. cat. Montreal: Canadian Centre for Architecture, 1995.

Cronan, Todd. *Nothing Permanent: Modern Architecture in California.* Minneapolis: University of Minnesota Press, 2023

Culver, Lawrence. *The Frontier of Leisure: Southern California and the Shaping of Modern America.* Oxford: Oxford University Press, 2012.

Davie, Maurice R. *Refugees in America: Report of the Committee for the Study of Recent Immigration from Europe.* New York: Harper & Brothers, 1947.

Denzer, Anthony. *Gregory Ain: The Modern Home as Social Commentary.* New York: Rizzoli, 2008.

"Desert House Richard Neutra Architect." *Arts & Architecture* 66, no. 7 (June 1949): 30–33.

Dogramaci, Burcu, and Birgit Mersmann, eds. *Handbook of Art and Global Migration: Theories, Practices, and Challenges.* Berlin: Walter de Gruyter, 2019.

Dogramaci, Burcu, and Andreas Schätzke, eds. *A Home of One s Own: Émigré Architects and Their Houses, 1920–1960.* Stuttgart: Axel Menges, 2019.

Drexler, Arthur, and Thomas S. Hines. *The Architecture of Richard Neutra: From International Style to California Modern.* Exh. cat. New York: Museum of Modern Art, 1982.

"Egon Riss." *Dictionary of Scottish Architects 1660–1980.* https://www.scottisharchitects.org.uk/apex/r/dsa/dsa/architects?session=16661606147152.

Eichler, Ned. *The Merchant Builders.* Cambridge, MA: MIT Press, 1982.

Federal Housing Administration. *Minimum Property Requirements for Properties of One or Two Living Units Located in the Southern California District.* Long Beach, Los Angeles, San Diego: Federal Housing Administration, 1952.

———. *Twenty-First Annual Report Federal Housing Administration for the Year Ending December 31, 1954.* Washington, DC: US Government Printing Office, 1956.

Fields, Harold. *The Refugee in the United States.* New York: Oxford University Press, 1938.

Fishman, Robert. *Bourgeois Utopias: The Rise and Fall of Suburbia.* New York: Basic, 1987.

Fontenot, Anthony, ed. *Notes from Another Los Angeles: Gregory Ain and the Construction of a Social Landscape.* Cambridge, MA: MIT Press, 2022.

Friedland, Roger, and Harold Zellman. *The Fellowship: The Untold Story of Frank Lloyd Wright and the Taliesin Fellowship.* New York: Regan, 2006.

Friedman, Avi. "The Evolution of Design Characteristics during the Post-Second World War Housing Boom: The US Experience." *Journal of Design History* 8, no. 2 (1995): 131–46.

Gane, John F., and George S. Koyl, eds. *American Architects Directory,* 3rd ed. New York: R. R. Bowker, 1970.

Gebhard, David. *Schindler.* San Francisco: William Stout, 1997

Gebhard, David, and Robert Winter. *A Guide to Architecture in Los Angeles & Southern California.* Salt Lake City: Peregrine Smith, 1982.

Göckede, Regina. *Adolf Rading (1888–1957): Exodus des Neuen Bauens und Überschreitungen des Exils.* Berlin: Gebr. Mann, 2005.

Granach, Alexander. *Du mein liebes Stück Heimat: Briefe an Lotte Lieven aus dem Exil.* Edited by Angelika Wittlich and Hilde Recher. Augsburg: Ölbaum, 2008.

Grebler, Leo. *German-Jewish Immigrants to the United States during the Hitler Period: Personal Reminiscences and General Observations.* Los Angeles: n.p., 1976.

Grier, Katherine C. "The Decline of the Memory Palace: The Parlor after 1890." In *American Home Life, 1880–1930: A Social History of Spaces and Services,* edited by Jessica H. Foy and Thomas J. Schlereth, 49–74. Knoxville: University of Tennessee Press, 1992.

Gruen, Victor, and Larry Smith. *Shopping Towns USA: The Planning of Shopping Centers.* New York: Van Nostrand Reinhold, 1960.

Hahn, Peter. "Bauhaus and Exile: Bauhaus Architects and Designers between the Old World and the New." In *Exiles + Émigrés: The Flight of European Artists from Hitler,* edited by Stephanie Barron with Sabine Eckmann, 211–23. Exh. cat. Los Angeles: Los Angeles County Museum of Art, 1997.

Hall, W. Ham. *Irrigation Development: History, Customs, Laws, and Administrative Systems Relating to Irrigation, Water-Courses, and Waters in France, Italy, and Spain; The Introductory Part of the Report of the State-Engineer of California on Irrigation and the Irrigation Question.* Sacramento: State Office James J. Ayers, Supt. State Printing, 1886.

Haney, David H. *When Modern Was Green: Life and Work of Landscape Architect Leberecht Migge.* London: Routledge, 2010.

Hanslick, Erwin. *Biala, eine deutsche Stadt in Galizien: Geographische Untersuchung des Stadtproblems.* Vienna: K. Prochaska, 1909.

Hardwick, M. Jeffrey. *Mall Maker: Victor Gruen, Architect of an American Dream.* Philadelphia: University of Pennsylvania Press, 2004.

Harris, Dianne. *Little White Houses: How the Postwar Home Constructed Race in America.* Minneapolis: University of Minnesota Press, 2013.

Hayden, Dolores. *Building Suburbia: Green Fields and Urban Growth, 1820–2000.* New York: Pantheon, 2003.

Heilbut, Anton. *Exiled in Paradise: German Refugee Artists and Intellectuals in America, from the 1930s to the Present.* New York: Viking, 1983.

Heinze-Greenberg, Ita. "'I Often Fear the Envy of the Gods': Success, House, and Home." In *Eric Mendelsohn: Architect, 1887–1953,* edited by Regina Stephan, 170–81. New York: Monacelli, 1999.

Henderson, Wesley Howard. "Two Case Studies of African-American Architects' Careers in Los Angeles, 1890–1945: Paul R. Williams, FAIA and James H. Garrott, AIA." PhD diss., University of California, Los Angeles, 1992.

Henken, Priscilla J. *Taliesin Diary: A Year with Frank Lloyd Wright.* New York: W. W. Norton, 2021.

Hennessey, William J., ed. *America's Best Small Houses.* New York: Viking, 1949.

Henning, Randolph C., ed. *"At Taliesin": Newspaper Columns by Frank Lloyd Wright and the Taliesin Fellowship, 1934–1937.* Carbondale: Southern Illinois University Press, 1992.

Hess, Alan. *Frank Lloyd Wright: The Houses.* New York: Rizzoli, 2005.

Hines, Thomas S. *Architecture of the Sun: Los Angeles Modernism 1900–1970.* New York: Rizzoli, 2010.

———. *Irving Gill and the Architecture of Reform: A Study in Modernist Architectural Culture.* New York: Monacelli, 2000.

———. *Richard Neutra and the Search for Modern Architecture.* New York: Oxford University Press, 1982.

Hirsch, Lily E. *Anneliese Landau's Life in Music: Nazi Germany to Émigré California.* Rochester, NY: University of Rochester Press, 2019.

Hirschfeld, Max. "Ein Wiener Architekt bei Kaiser," *Der Aufbau–Reconstruction* 9, no. 40 (18 October 1943), Die Westküste section, no. 3, 20, p. 18.

Hise, Greg. *Magnetic Los Angeles: Planning the Twentieth-Century Metropolis.* Baltimore: Johns Hopkins University Press, 1997.

Hitchcock, Henry-Russell, and Arthur Drexler, eds. *Built in USA: Post-War Architecture.* Exh. cat. New York: Museum of Modern Art, 1952.

Hitchcock, Henry-Russell, and Philip Johnson. *The International Style: Architecture since 1922.* New York: W. W. Norton, 1932.

Hopkins, Alfred. *American Country Houses of To-Day, 1927.* New York: Architectural Publishing Co., 1926 [*sic*].

Hughes, Edan Milton. *Artists in California, 1786–1940.* San Francisco: Hughes, 1989.

Ingersoll, Richard. *Munio Gitai Weinraub: Bauhaus Architect in Eretz Israel.* Milan: Electa, 1994.

Ingram, Susan, Markus Reisenleitner, and Cornelia Szabo-Knotik, eds. *Reverberations: Representations of Modernity, Traditional and Cultural Value in-between Central Europe and North America.* Frankfurt: Peter Lang, 2002.

Jackson, Kenneth T. *Crabgrass Frontier: The Suburbanization of the United States.* Oxford: Oxford University Press, 1985.

Jacobs, James A. *Detached America: Building Houses in Postwar Suburbia.* Charlottesville: University of Virginia Press, 2015.

———. "Social and Spatial Change in the Postwar Family Room." *Perspectives in Vernacular Architecture* 13, no. 1 (2006): 70–85.

Jaeger, Roland. *Block & Hochfeld: Die Architekten des Deutschland Hauses; Bauten und Projekte in Hamburg 1921–1938, Exil in Los Angeles.* Berlin: Gebr. Mann, 1996.

———. *Photo-Eye Fritz Block: New Photography, Modern Color Slides.* Zurich: Scheidegger & Spiess, 2018.

Jahns, Richard H. "Residential Ills in the Heartbreak Hills of Southern California." *Engineering and Science* 22 (December 1958): 13–20.

James, Kathleen. "Changing the Agenda: From German Bauhaus Modernism to U.S. Internationalism; Ludwig Miës van der Rohe, Walter Gropius, Marcel Breuer." In *Exiles + Émigrés: The Flight of European Artists from Hitler,* edited by Stephanie Barron with Sabine Eckmann, 235–52. Exh. cat. Los Angeles: Los Angeles County Museum of Art, 1997.

———. "Zwischen Expressionismus und Neuer Sachlichkeit: Das Seidenhaus Weichmann in Gleiwitz." *Oberschlesisches Jahrbuch* 10 (1994): 153–62.

Jordy, William H. "The Aftermath of the Bauhaus in America: Gropius, Miës, and Breuer." In *The Intellectual Migration: Europe and America, 1930–1960,* edited by Donald Fleming and Bernard Bailyn, 485–543. Cambridge, MA: Belknap Press of Harvard University Press, 1969.

Karafantis, Layne, and Stuart W. Leslie. "'Suburban Warriors': The Blue-Collar and Blue-Sky Communities of Southern California's Aerospace Industry." *Journal of Planning History* 18, no. 1 (2019): 3–26.

[Key Land Company]. *Monterey Hills: "Island in the Sky."* Los Angeles: John D. Roche, n.d. [ca. 1955].

Kirker, Harold. *California's Architectural Frontier: Style and Tradition in the Nineteenth Century.* Salt Lake City: Gibbs Smith, 1986.

Koyl, George S., ed. *American Architects Directory.* New York: R. R. Bowker, 1955.

———, ed. *American Architects Directory.* 2nd ed. New York: R. R. Bowker, 1962.

Kuhn, Walter. *Geschichte der deutschen Sprachinsel Bielitz (Schlesien).* Würzburg: Holzner, 1981.

Kulka, Heinrich, ed. *Adolf Loos: Das Werk des Architekten.* Vienna: Löcker, 1979. Originally published in 1931 by A. Schroll & Co.

Lamprecht, Barbara. *Richard Neutra, 1892–1970: Survival through Design.* Cologne: Taschen, 2009.

Landau, Anneliese. "Bilder und Menschen eines Lebens: Autobiografische Aufzeichnungen." In *Von Berlin nach Los Angeles: Die Musikwissenschaftlerin Anneliese Landau,* edited and translated by Daniela Reinhold, 17–217. Berlin: Hentrich & Hentrich, 2017.

Lane, Barbara Miller. *Houses for a New World: Builders and Buyers in American Suburbs, 1945–1965.* Princeton, NJ: Princeton University Press, 2015.

László, Paul. *Designing with Spirit: Paul László Interviewed by Marlene L. Laskey.* Los Angeles: Oral History Program, University of California, Los Angeles, 1986. https://archive.org/details/designingwithspi00lasz.

Lawrence, Anne. "Feminist Design Methodology: Considering the Case of Maria Kipp." Master of arts thesis, University of North Texas, December 2003.

Lewis, Arnold. "Hinkeldeyn, Vogel and American Architecture." *Journal of the Society of Architectural Historians* 31, no. 4 (1972): 276–90.

Long, Christopher. "An Alternative Path to Modernism: Carl König and the Architectural Education at the Vienna Technische Hochschule, 1890–1913." *Journal of Architectural Education* 55, no. 1 (September 2001): 21–30.

———. *Jock Peters, Architecture and Design: The Varieties of Modernism.* New York: Bauer and Dean, 2021.

———. *Kem Weber: Designer and Architect.* New Haven: Yale University Press, 2014.

———. *The New Space: Movement and Experience in Viennese Modern Architecture.* New Haven: Yale University Press, 2016.

———. *Paul T. Frankl and Modern American Design.* New Haven: Yale University Press, 2007.

Loos, Adolf. *Sämtliche Schriften in zwei Bänden.* Edited by F. Glück. Vienna: Herold, 1962.

Los Angeles City Directory 1939. Los Angeles: Los Angeles Directory Co., 1939.

Los Angeles City Directory 1940. Los Angeles: Los Angeles Directory Co., 1940.

Los Angeles City Directory 1941. Los Angeles: Los Angeles Directory Co., 1941.

Malharek, Joseph. *Free-Market Socialists: European Émigrés Who Made Capitalist Culture in America, 1918–1968.* Budapest: Central European University Press, 2022.

Mann, Thomas. *Tagebücher 1940–1943.* Edited by Peter de Mendelssohn. Frankfurt: S. Fischer, 1982.

Manning, Susan A. *Ecstasy and the Demon: Feminism and Nationalism in the Dances of Mary Wigman.* Berkeley: University of California Press, 1993.

McCoy, Esther. *Richard Neutra.* New York: Braziller, 1960.

———. *Vienna to Los Angeles: Two Journeys.* Santa Monica: Arts & Architecture Press, 1979.

McWilliams, Carey. *Southern California: An Island on the Land.* Salt Lake City: Peregrine Smith, 2010.

Meder, Iris. "Offene Welten: Die Wiener Schule im Einfamilienhausbau, 1910–1938." PhD diss., Institut für Kunstgeschichte der Universität Stuttgart, 2004.

Mendelsohn, Erich. *Amerika: Bilderbuch eines Architekten.* 6th edited and enlarged edition. Berlin: Rudolf Mosse Buchverlag, 1928. Originally published in 1926 by Rudolph Mosse Buchverlag.

Minner, Kelly. "AD Classics: S. C. Johnson and Son Administration Building / Frank Lloyd Wright." *ArchDaily,* 21 November 2010. www.archdaily.com/90519/ad-classics-s-c-johnson-and-son-administration-building-frank-lloyd-wright.

Mock, Elizabeth, ed. *Built in USA: 1932–1944.* Exh. cat. New York: Museum of Modern Art, 1944.

Moon, Kavior. "Strick House." In *SAH Archipedia,* edited by Gabrielle Esperdy and Karen Kingsley. Charlottesville: University of Virginia Press, 2012.

Moore, Charles, Peter Becker, and Regula Campbell. *The City Observed: Los Angeles; A Guide to Its Architecture and Landscapes.* Santa Monica: Hennessey & Ingalls, 1998. Originally published in 1984 by Vintage.

Morgenthaler, Hans R. "'It Will Be Hard for Us to Find a Home': Projects in the United States 1941–1953." In *Eric Mendelsohn: Architect 1887–1953,* edited by Regina Stephan, 242–61. New York: Monacelli, 1999.

Moya, Max. "Who Has Seen Adolf Loos? Images of Adolf Loos's Architecture in the Media 1899–1927." PhD diss., Akademie der bildenden Künste Wien, 2021.

The Museum of Modern Art—Woman's Home Companion Exhibition House. Gregory Ain in collaboration with Joseph Johnson and Alfred Day. Exh. cat. New York: Museum of Modern Art, 1950.

Musicant, Marlyn. "Maria Kipp: Autobiography of a Hand Weaver." *Studies in the Decorative Arts* 8, no. 1 (2000): 92–107.

Nenik, Francis, and Sebastian Stumpf. *Seven Palms: Das Thomas-Mann-Haus in Pacific Palisades, Los Angeles.* Leipzig: Spector, 2018.

Neutra, Dione. *To Tell the Truth: Dione Neutra Interviewed by Lawrence Weschler.* Los Angeles: Oral History Program, University of California, Los Angeles, 1983. https://archive.org/details/totelltruthoralh00neut.

Neutra, Richard Joseph. *Amerika. Die Stilbildung des neuen Bauens in den Vereinigten Staaten.* Vienna: Anton Schroll, 1930.

———. *Life and Shape* [1962]. Los Angeles: Atara, 2009.

———. *Richard Neutra on Building: Mystery and Realities of the Site.* Scarsdale, NY: Morgan & Morgan, 1951.

———. *Wie baut Amerika.* Prepared for publication by Dione Neutra. Stuttgart: Julius Hoffmann, 1927.

New York World's Fair. *The Town of Tomorrow: House No. 1—No. 1: The Dual Duty House.* New York: Burland, [1939].

Nicolai, Bernd, ed. *Architektur und Exil: Kulturtransfer und architektonische Emigration von 1930 bis 1950.* Trier: Porta Alba, 2003.

Olsberg, Nicholas. "Common Ground." In *Notes from Another Los Angeles: Gregory Ain and the Construction of a Social Landscape,* edited by Anthony Fontenot, 87–133. Cambridge, MA: MIT Press, 2022.

Penick, Monica. "Paul László and the Atomic Future." In *Émigré Cultures in Design and Architecture,* edited by Alison J. Clarke and Elana Shapira, 91–104. London: Bloomsbury Academic, 2017.

Pfaff, Lilian. *J. R. Davidson: A European Contribution to California Modernism.* Basel: Birkhäuser, 2019.

———. "J. R. Davidson." In *Thomas Mann's Los Angeles: Stories from Exile 1940–1952,* edited by Nikolai Blaumer and Benno Herz, 186–87. Los Angeles: Angel City Press, 2022.

Piesch, Gerd-Ulrich. "Zum Jugendstil in Bielitz: Zwei Bauten des Wiener Architekten Hans Mayr." *Oberschlesisches Jahrbuch* 12 (1996): 77–92.

Polyzoides, Stefanos, Roger Sherwood, and James Tice. *Courtyard Housing in Los Angeles.* New York: Princeton Architectural Press, 1992.

Porter Lapish, Edith. "The Trend toward Larger Houses." *Insured Mortgage Portfolio* 17, no. 2 (Winter 1952–53): 8.

Prokop, Ursula. "Ernst Lindner." *Architektenlexikon Wien 1770–1945.* Edited by Architekturzentrum Wien. http://www.architektenlexikon.at/de/1343.htm.

———. "Jacques Groag." *Architektenlexikon Wien 1770–1945.* Edited by Architekturzentrum Wien. http://www.architektenlexikon.at/de/182.htm.

———. *Zum jüdischen Erbe in der Wiener Architektur: Der Beitrag jüdischer ArchitektInnen* [sic] *am Wiener Baugeschehen 1868–1938.* Vienna: Böhlau, 2016.

"Refugees and the Professions." *Harvard Law Review* 53, no. 1 (1939): 112–22.

"Residence of Mr. & Mrs. Phil Freeman—Los Angeles, California." *Architectural Digest* 14, no. 1 (1953): 56–61.

Reuß, Jürgen von. "Leberecht Migge—Spartakus in Grün." In *Leberecht Migge 1881–1935: Gartenkultur des 20. Jahrhundert,* edited by Fachbereich Stadt- and Landschaftsplanung der Gesamthochschule Kassel, 10–13. Worpswede: Worpsweder Verlag, 1981.

Rifkind, Donna. *The Sun and Her Stars: Salka Viertel and Hitler's Exiles in the Golden Age of Hollywood.* New York: Other, 2020.

Riley, Terence, and Barry Bergdoll, eds. *Mies in Berlin.* Exh. cat. New York: Museum of Modern Art, 2001.

Rochlin, Harriet. "A Distinguished Generation of Women Architects in California." *AIA Journal* 66, no. 9 (1977): 38–41.

Rogers, Kate Ellen. *The Modern House U.S.A.: Its Design and Decoration.* New York: Harper & Brothers, 1962.

Rouillard, Dominique. *Building the Slope: Hillside Houses, 1920–1960.* Translated by Ronald A. Masi. Santa Monica: Arts & Architecture Press, 1987.

Salomon, Alice. *Kultur im Werden: Amerikanische Reiseeindrücke.* Berlin: Ullstein, 1924.
Sandul, Paul J. P. *California Dreaming: Boosterism, Memory, and Rural Suburbs in the Golden State.* Morgantown: West Virginia University Press, 2014.
Sarnitz, August E. "Proportion and Beauty—the Lovell Beach House by Rudolph Michael Schindler, Newport Beach, 1922–1926." *Journal of the Society of Architectural Historians* 45, no. 4 (1986): 374–88.
Scheidl, Inge. "Paul Engelmann." *Architektenlexikon Wien 1770–1945.* Edited by Architekturzentrum Wien. http://www.architektenlexikon.at/de/108.htm.
Schmitz, Franz. *Landhäuser in Berlin 1933–1945.* Berlin: Gebr. Mann, 2007.
Schumann, Petra. "Egon Riss." *Architektenlexikon Wien 1770–1945.* Edited by Architekturzentrum Wien. http://www.architektenlexikon.at/de/510.htm.
———. "Fritz Reichl." *Architektenlexikon Wien 1770–1945.* Edited by Architekturzentrum Wien. http://www.architektenlexikon.at/de/491.htm.
Schwarz, Dean, and Geraldine Schwarz, eds. *Marguerite Wildenhain and the Bauhaus: An Eyewitness Anthology.* Decorah, IA: South Bear, 2007.
Sheine, Judith. *R. M. Schindler: Works and Projects.* Barcelona: GG, 1998.
Smith, Elizabeth A. T., ed. *Blueprints for Modern Living: History and Legacy of the Case Study Houses.* Exh. cat. Los Angeles: Museum of Contemporary Art, 1989.
Sorkin, Jenni. *Live Form: Women, Ceramics, and Community.* Chicago: University of Chicago Press, 2016.
Spalek, John M., and Joseph Strelka. *Kalifornien.* Vol. 1 of *Deutsche Exilliteratur seit 1933.* Bern: Francke, 1976.
Stadtarchiv Bad Kissingen. "Herbert Kugelmann." *Biografisches Gedenkbuch der Bad Kissinger Juden während der NS Zeit,* n.d. https://www.biografisches-gedenkbuch-bk.de/kurzbiographien/datenbank/38566.Kurzbiografien.html (search: Kugelmann).
Starr, Kevin. *Inventing the Dream: California through the Progressive Era.* New York: Oxford University Press, 1985.
Steele, James. *How House: RM Schindler.* London: Academy, 1996.
Stewart, Shan. "When the Rain Comes: To Hold a Hill." *Los Angeles Times,* 12 December 1954, L54.
Stiles, Max. "High in Green Verdugo Hills—Max Stiles and Family Find a New Frontier." *Mirror and Daily News* (Los Angeles), 25 February 1955, part 4, p. 5.
Strzygowski, Josef. *Die bildende Kunst der Gegenwart: Ein Büchlein für Jedermann.* Leipzig: Quelle und Meyer, 1907.
Stuckenschmidt, Hans Heinz. *Schoenberg: His Life, World and Work.* Translated by Humphrey Searle. New York: Schirmer, 1977.
Stülpnagel, Rupert von. *Ein Haus ist mehr als die Summe seiner Steine: Aus der Geschichte des Landhauses Ahornallee 33 in Berlin-Westend.* Berlin-Lichterfelde: Mediaray-graphics, 2018.
"Supplement—Los Angeles Housing Authority," *California Arts & Architecture* (May 1943): 47–66.

Survey LA, Los Angeles Historic Resources Survey, Los Angeles Citywide Historic Context Statement, Context: Architecture and Engineering, 1850–1985, Sub-Context: Engineering, Theme: Technological Developments in Construction, Subtheme: Hill Houses, 1920–1985. Los Angeles: City of Los Angeles Department of City Planning Office of Historic Resources, 2017. https://planning.lacity.org/odocument/c6f7f7ba-efc3-4ffd-8cc4-691ea56ba171/Hill%20Houses_1920-1985.pdf.
Tafel, Edgar. *About Wright: An Album of Recollections by Those Who Knew Frank Lloyd Wright.* New York: John Wiley & Sons, 1993.
Taylor, John Russell. *Strangers in Paradise: The Hollywood Émigrés 1933–1950.* New York: Holt, Rinehart and Winston, 1983.
Thayer, Mary Ann. "Spaciousness Is a State of Mind." *Los Angeles Times Home Magazine,* 19 April 1953, H14–H15.
Vennemann, Kevin. *Sunset Boulevard: Vom Filmen, Bauen und Sterben in Los Angeles.* Berlin: Suhrkamp, 2012.
Viertel, Salka. *The Kindness of Strangers.* New York: New York Review of Books, 2019. Originally published by Holt, Rinehart, and Winston, 1969.
Voigt, Wolfgang. *Hans und Oskar Gerson: Hanseatische Moderne; Bauten in Hamburg und im kalifornischen Exil 1907 bis 1957.* Hamburg: Dölling und Galitz, 2000.
Vorspan, Max, and Lloyd P. Gartner. *History of the Jews of Los Angeles.* San Marino, CA: Huntington Library, 1970.
Wagner, Anton. *Los Angeles: The Development, Life, and Structure of the City of Two Million in Southern California.* Edited by Edward Dimendberg. Translated by Timothy Grundy, with a foreword by Anthony Vidler. Los Angeles: Getty Research Institute, 2022.
———. *Los Angeles: Werden, Leben und Gestalt der Zweimillionenstadt in Südkalifornien.* Leipzig: Bibliographisches Institut, 1935.
Wall, Alex. *Victor Gruen: From Urban Shop to New City.* Barcelona: Actar-D, 2005.
Walter, Karen, ed. *Julius Frank: Eine jüdische Fotografenfamilie zwischen Deutschland und Amerika.* Munich: Dölling und Galitz, 2022.
Warhaftig, Myra. *Deutsche jüdische Architekten vor und nach 1933—das Lexikon.* Berlin: Reimer, 2005.
———. *Sie legten den Grundstein: Leben und Wirken deutschsprachiger jüdischer Architekten in Palästina 1918–1948.* Tübingen: Ernst Wasmuth, 1996.
Wedhorn, Katja. *Licht und Schatten: Neue Gestaltungsweisen der Fotografie von 1920 bis 1960 und der Beitrag Edmund Kestings.* Marburg: Tectum, 2021.
Wefing, Heinrich. "'We Are at Home Where the Desk Stands': Thomas Mann's Residence in Pacific Palisades." In *Building Paradise: Exile Architecture in California; Villa Aurora Architecture Symposium 2003,* edited by Mechthild Borries-Knopp, 48–101. Berlin: Kreis der Freunde und Förderer der Villa Aurora e.V., 2004.
Welter, Volker M. "Berlin in London, Hiddensee in Walberswick: On Ernst L. Freud's Exile Architecture in England." In *Sites of Interchange: Modernism, Politics and Culture between Britain and Germany,* edited by Lucy Wasensteiner, 195–214. Oxford: Peter Lang, 2022.
———. *Ernst L. Freud, Architect: The Case of the Modern Bourgeois Home.* Oxford: Berghahn, 2012.

——. "Ernst L. Freud: Domestic Architect: *Zuhause* in Berlin, At Home in London." In *Freud and the Émigré—Austrian Émigrés and the Legacy of Psychoanalysis in Britain, 1930–1970s,* edited by Elana Shapira and Daniela Finzi, 61–76. Cham: Palgrave Macmillan, 2020.

——. "From the *Landscape of War* to the Open Order of the Kaufmann House: Richard Neutra and the Experience of the Great War." In *The Good Gardener? Nature, Humanity, and the Garden,* edited by Annette Giesecke and Naomi Jacobs, 216–33. London: Artifice Books on Architecture, 2014.

——. "Lutah Maria Riggs: A Portrait of a Modern Revival-Style Architect." In *The Routledge Companion to Women in Architecture,* edited by Anna Sokolina, 129–41. New York: Routledge, 2021.

——. "Salzburg in Los Angeles: Max Reinhardt and Paul László's Vision of a *Festpielstadt* in the Hollywood Hills." In *Wie sich Salzburg inszeniert: Vom Werden einer Musiktheaterstadt,* edited by Sigrid Brandt and Thomas Wozonig, 242–56. Vienna: Hollitzer, 2023.

——. *Tremaine Houses: One Family's Patronage of Domestic Architecture in Midcentury America.* Los Angeles: Getty Research Institute, 2019.

Wertheim, Ernest, with Linda Hamilton. *Chasing Spring.* N.p.: Lulu, 2014.

Whyte, Iain Boyd. "Nikolaus Pevsner: Art History, Nation, and Exile." *RIHA Journal* 0075 (23 October 2013). https://journals.ub.uni-heidelberg.de/index.php/rihajournal/article/view/69832/67262.

Wijdeveld, Paul. *Ludwig Wittgenstein: Architect.* Amsterdam: Pepin, 2000. Originally published by Löcker, 1993.

Winkler, Klaus Jürgen. *Der Architekt Hannes Meyer: Anschauungen und Werk.* Berlin (DDR): VEB Verlag für das Bauwesen, 1989.

Wodziński, Marcin, and Janusz Spyra, eds. *Jews in Silesia.* Krakow: Księrgania Academicka, 2001.

Wolf, Christa. *City of Angels; or, The Overcoat of Dr. Freud* [2010]. Translated by Damion Searls. New York: Farrar, Straus and Giroux, 2013. Originally published in German (Berlin: Suhrkamp, 2010).

Wolman, Ruth E. *Crossing Over: An Oral History of Refugees from Hitler's Reich.* New York: Twayne, 1996.

Wolsdorff, Christian. "Deutsche Architekten im Exil Erwartungen—Hoffnungen—Reaktionen." In *Kunst im Exil in Großbritannien 1933–1945,* edited by Neue Gesellschaft für bildende Kunst Berlin, 105–10. Berlin: Frölich & Kaufmann, 1986.

Worbs, Dietrich. "Die Loos-Schule." *Bauforum* 16, no. 98 (1983): 27–32.

Wörmann, Heinrich-Wilhelm. *Widerstand in Charlottenburg.* Berlin: Gedenkstätte Deutscher Widerstand, 1991.

Wright, Gwendolyn. *Building the Dream: A Social History of Housing in America.* New York: Pantheon, 1981.

About the Author

Volker M. Welter is a professor in the Department of the History of Art and Architecture at the University of California, Santa Barbara. He specializes in the history and historiography of modern California architecture. Currently, Welter's research focuses primarily on émigré, female, gay, and lesbian architects and their clients, and on how their contributions to the built environment broaden the historiography of California architecture. He is the author of *Biopolis: Patrick Geddes and the City of Life* (2002), *Ernst L. Freud, Architect: The Case of the Modern Bourgeois Home* (2012), *Walter S. White: Invention in Mid-Century Architecture* (2015), and *Tremaine Houses: One Family's Patronage of Domestic Architecture in Midcentury America* (2019).

Acknowledgments

I wish to express gratitude for the support of my research into Leopold Fischer and his California architecture by the current owners of homes designed by Fischer and German-speaking émigré architects; descendants of Fischer's clients and of émigré architects; and fellow historians, academic colleagues, and friends in the United States, Germany, Austria, the United Kingdom, France, and Israel. Special thanks go to Maoz Azaryahu and Renate Schein-Azaryahu, Irene Below, Esther Cohen and Yael Cohen Weitz, the late Jean-Louis Cohen, Marta Dąbrowska, Ed Dimendberg, Simon Elliott, Thomas Hines, Annemarie Jaeggi, Otto Kapfinger, Piotr Kenig, Steven Keylon, Markus Kristan, Katina Kuschnerus and Martin Kunze, Barbara Lamprecht, Raymond Neutra, Arnat Ornstein, Steffen Panzner and Gudrun Weigelt, Silvia Perea, Steven Price, Vernon Price, Ursula Prokop, Marccus Reinhardt, Elana Shapira, Willem Swârt, Iain Boyd Whyte, Sian Winship, and the late Dietrich Worbs.I also would like to thank all individuals, archives, and libraries who kindly granted permission to quote from and reproduce documents in their possession.

Illustration Credits

Photographs of items in the holdings of the Getty Research Institute are courtesy the Research Institute. The following sources have granted additional permission to reproduce illustrations in this volume.

Figs. 1.1, 1.2, 7.1. Courtesy of Esther Zollmann Cohen.
Fig. 1.3. Courtesy of Wienbibliothek im Rathaus. WBR, H.I.N. 235440.
Figs. 1.9, 1.12, 6.1. Courtesy Dr. Irene Below, Germany.
Fig. 1.11. Adam / Springmann.
Figs. 3.1, 3.6. Arnold Schönberg Center, Vienna.
Fig. 3.2. Security Pacific National Bank Photo Collection / Los Angeles Public Library.
Fig. 3.3. USC Digital Library. Los Angeles Examiner Photographs Collection.
Fig. 3.8. Courtesy of Robert Ewing.
Figs. 3.10–3.12, 4.3c, 5.15c, 6.6, 7.2, 7.5. Architecture and Design Collection. Art, Design & Architecture Museum, University of California, Santa Barbara.
Fig. 4.1. California Historical Society.
Figs. 4.3a, 4.4a. Courtesy of Richard Berlner.
Figs. 4.3b, 4.4c. Special Collections and University Archives, University Libraries, Virginia Polytechnic Institute and State University.
Figs. 4.5, 4.6, 4.8, 4.11. Courtesy of Dan Bishop.
Figs. 4.7, 4.10, 4.12, 4.23–4.25, 4.27, 5.11–5.13, 5.19a, 5.19b, 6.3–6.5. Content Production.
Figs. 4.9, 4.15a, 4.15b, 4.20. Author collection.
Fig. 4.14. Leonard Nadel / Housing Authority Collection / Los Angeles Public Library.
Fig. 4.16. Courtesy of Mary Trunk.
Fig. 4.17. Courtesy of David Fairweather.
Fig. 4.21. Photo by Nate Williams of AARRCC Architectural Photography.
Figs. 4.22, 4.26. Courtesy of Eraka Bath.
Fig. 5.3. Flight c-22555, frame 12-31, 1956. Courtesy of UCSB Library Geospatial Collection.
Fig. 5.4. Public Works Los Angeles County.
Figs. 5.5, 5.9, 5.10. Courtesy of Willem Swârt.
Fig. 5.15d. Internet Archives.
Figs. 5.16a, 5.16c. Hathi Trust.
Figs. 6.2, 7.4. Courtesy of Erik Akin.

Index

Note: page numbers in italics refer to figures or tables. Those followed by n refer to notes, with note number.

Published by the Getty Research Institute, Los Angeles
Getty Publications
1200 Getty Center Drive, Suite 500
Los Angeles, California 90049-1682
getty.edu/publications

Laura Santiago, *Editor*
Ariel Waitkuweit, *Editorial Assistant*
Jeffrey Cohen, *Designer*
Victoria Gallina, *Production*
Karen Ehrmann, *Image and Rights Acquisition*

Distributed in the United States and Canada by the University of Chicago Press
Distributed outside the United States and Canada by Yale University Press, London

Authorized Product Safety Representative in the European Union:
Easy Access System Europe, Mustamäe tee 50, 10621 Tallinn, Estonia,
gpsr.requests@easproject.com

Type composed in Akzidenz-Grotesk and Vista Slab

Printed in China

Library of Congress Cataloging-in-Publication Data
Names: Welter, Volker, author.
Title: Exiled in L.A. : the untold story of Leopold Fischer's domestic architecture / Volker M. Welter.
Description: Los Angeles : Getty Research Institute, [2025] | Includes bibliographical references and index. | Summary: "The first English-language volume to explore the work of architect Leopold Fischer, and the inaugural study of his California legacy"—Provided by publisher.
Identifiers: LCCN 2025003975 (print) | LCCN 2025003976 (ebook) | ISBN 9781606069868 (hardback) | ISBN 9781606069875 (pdf) | ISBN 9781606069882 (epub)
Subjects: LCSH: Fischer, Leopold, 1901–1975—Criticism and interpretation. | Architecture, Domestic—California—Los Angeles—History—20th century. | Los Angeles (Calif.)—Buildings, structures, etc.
Classification: LCC NA737.F487 W45 2025 (print) | LCC NA737.F487 (ebook) | DDC 728.092—dc23/eng/20250521
LC record available at https://lccn.loc.gov/2025003975
LC ebook record available at https://lccn.loc.gov/2025003976

Every effort has been made to contact the owners and photographers of illustrations reproduced here whose names do not appear in the captions or in the illustration credits at the back of this book. Anyone having further information concerning copyright holders is asked to contact Getty Publications so this information can be included in future printings.

Front cover. Leopold Fischer, Adolph and Mary Slechta house (1950–51), View Park, Los Angeles, California. Partial view of the garden facade, after the installation of wall-to-wall sliding glass windows on the lower level. Photo by Nate Williams of AARRCC Architectural Photography.

Back cover. Inset: Passport-sized photograph and signature of Leopold Fischer from 1938. See fig. 2.1. Background: Leopold Fischer, Adolph and Mary Slechta house (1950–51), View Park, Los Angeles, California. Floor plan for first floor (detail). See fig. 4.22.

Endpapers. Leopold Fischer, Mr. & Mrs. Richard C. Adams house, La Mesa, California, unbuilt. Floor plan (detail). See fig. 7.2.

p. ii. Dr. Ward & Mrs. Marguerite Youry house (1965), Long Beach, California. Exterior view of the glass room and adjacent patio with trellis (detail). See fig. 6.3.

p. iii. Leopold Fischer, Dr. Ward & Mrs. Marguerite Youry house (1965), Long Beach, California. Interior of the glass room with the new patio and trellis (detail). See fig. 6.4.

pp. 1, 8. Leopold Fischer, Ralph and Phyllis Kohlmeier house (1940–41), South Pasadena, California. Floor plan for main level (detail). See fig. 4.6.

pp. 26, 39. Leopold Fischer, Adolph and Mary Slechta house (1950–51), View Park, Los Angeles, California. Floor plan for first floor (detail). See fig. 4.22.

pp. 58, 94. Leopold Fischer, Adolph and Mary Slechta house (1950–51), View Park, Los Angeles, California. Floor plan for second floor (detail). See fig. 4.26.

p. 128. Leopold Fischer, Dr. Ward & Mrs. Marguerite Youry house (1965), Long Beach, California. Floor plan from *Addition to Residence of Mr. & Mrs. Ward Youry,* sheet 1 (detail). See fig. 6.2.

This publication was peer reviewed through a single-masked process in which the reviewers remained anonymous.

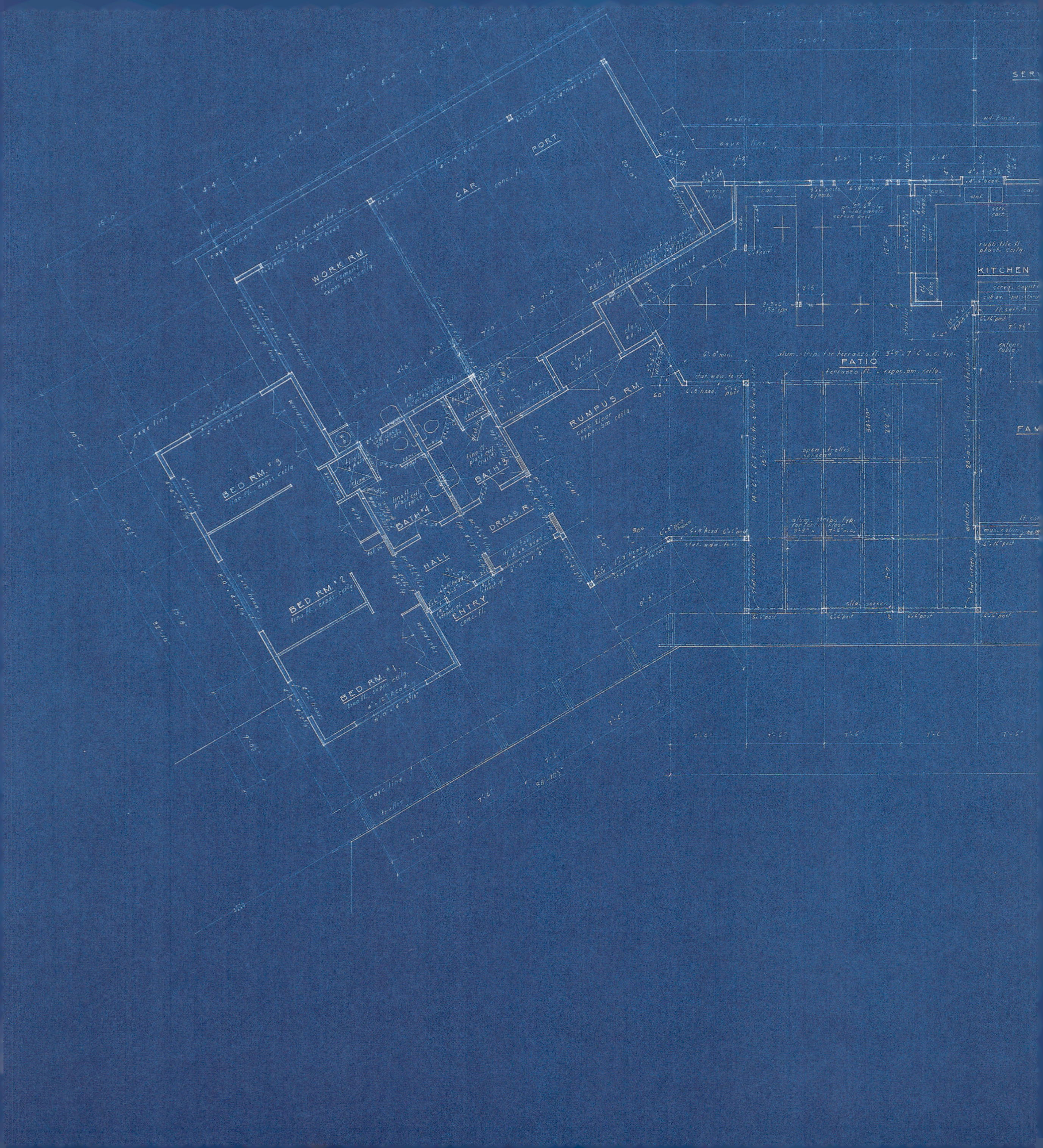

CAR PORT
WORK RM.
BED RM. #3
BED RM. #2
BED RM. #1
BATH #4
BATH #3
HALL
DRESS. R.
ENTRY
RUMPUS RM.
PATIO
KITCHEN